Essentials of Computing

Second Edition

A note about the Instructor's Edition with Annotations

The **Instructor's Edition with Annotations** is an invaluable teaching tool that forms the cornerstone of the extensive supplements package for *Essentials of Computing, Second Edition*. In the **Instructor's Edition** you get the complete student text with a variety of carefully prepared annotations that put lecture and course organization at your fingertips.

The **Instructor's Edition** provides Learning Objectives at the beginning of each chapter to streamline your lecture preparation. It also includes page references to the test bank and transparencies to help you coordinate the supplements with your lectures. In addition, the **Instructor's Edition** includes Lecture Activities, Lecture Hints, Discussion Questions, Class Projects, and Key Terms to give you flexibility and support as you teach. As you look through this text, you will notice, in total, eight different types of annotations in the margin in an easy-to-read distinctive blue typeface.

- Learning Objectives
- Lecture Activities
- Discussion Questions
- Lecture Hints
- Class Projects
- Test Bank references
- References to the Transparency Acetates
- Key Terms in alphabetical order at the Chapter Review

For further information about *Essentials of Computing, Second Edition* and its outstanding instructional package, please contact your local Benjamin/Cummings sales representative or call 800/854-2665. We look forward to hearing from you and helping you meet your teaching needs.

Essentials

H. L. Capron

**Instructor's Edition
with Annotations,**

Second Edition

**Annotations by S. Langman
with H. L. Capron**

The Benjamin/Cummings

Publishing Company, Inc.

Redwood City, California

Menlo Park, California

Reading, Massachusetts

New York

Don Mills, Ontario

Wokingham, U.K.

Amsterdam

Bonn

Singapore

Tokyo

Madrid

San Juan

of

Computing

SECOND EDITION

Sponsoring Editor	Maureen A. Allaire
Developmental Editor	Sue Ewing
Editorial Assistant	MaryLynne Wrye
Senior Production Editor	Jean Lake
Photo Editor	Kelli d'Angona-West
Photo Researcher	Sarah Evertson
Design Manager	Michele Carter
Marketing Manager	Melissa Baumwald
Text Designer	Mark Ong
Cover Designer	Yvo Riezebos
Illustrations	Illustrious, Inc.
Copy Editor	Barbara Conway
Senior Promotions Specialist	James Fisher
Film	York Graphic Services
Manufacturing Coordinator	Janet Weaver
Printing and Binding	R. R. Donnelley and Sons

Library of Congress Cataloging-in-Publication Data

Capron, H.L.
　　Essentials of Computing/H.L. Capron, —2nd ed.
　　　　p.　　cm.
　　Includes index.
　　ISBN 0-8053-1380-X, —ISBN 0-8053-1381-8
　　1. Electronic data processing.　I. Title.
QA76.C359　1994
004—dc20　　　　　　　　　　　　　　　　　　　94-23445
　　　　　　　　　　　　　　　　　　　　　　　CIP

SE	ISBN 0-8053-1380-X	
AIE	ISBN 0-8053-1381-8	
MC	IBSN 0-8053-0812-1	

2 3 4 5 6 7 8 9 10　　　　　　DO　　　　　99 98 97 96 95

The Benjamin/Cummings Publishing Company, Inc.
390 Bridge Parkway
Redwood City, CA 94065

Dedicated to

▼ *Nancy*

▼ *Bill*

▼ *Wendy*

▼ *Robin*

The Capron

Supplements to the Text

- **Interactive multimedia packages.** Through two completely interactive tutorial packages, your students can explore the inner workings of computer components, chart the history of computers, and examine related topics such as artificial intelligence, virtual reality, and programming. Benjamin/Cummings offers CD-ROMs for the Macintosh and PC. The PC version is also available on disk. Contact your Benjamin/Cummings sales representative for more information.

- **Instructor newsletter: *BC Link*.** Benjamin/Cummings is now offering an instructor-oriented newsletter for teaching introductory computing. This useful resource includes articles on the use of computer technology in education, teaching strategies, and a section designed for use with students in the classroom.

- **Instructor's Edition with Annotations for *Essentials of Computing, Second Edition*** by S. Langman with H. L. Capron. This special edition contains annotations for lecture preparation and includes supplementary material not found in the Instructor's Guide. The annotations include Learning Objectives, Lecture Activities, Discussion Questions, Lecture Hints, Class Projects, test bank references, transparency references, and Key Terms.

- **Test bank for *Essentials of Computing, Second Edition*** by H. L. Capron. The test bank contains multiple choice, true/false, matching, and completion. Each question is referenced to the text by page number, and the answers are provided. The test bank is available both in printed form and in a computerized format for the IBM PC and compatibles, and Macintosh computers.

- **Color transparency acetates.** The 100 full-color transparency acetates include artwork and diagrams taken directly from the text.

- **Instructor's Guide for *Essentials of Computing, Second Edition*** by H. L. Capron. For each chapter there are Learning Objectives; a Chapter Overview; a detailed Lecture Outline; and a list of Key Words. The Instructor's Guide also includes a reference guide to the CD-Rom offerings, the lecture support software screens, and to the videotape offerings.

- **Videotapes.** Benjamin/Cummings makes available to qualified adopters free videotapes from our library of commercially produced tapes. Use this valuable resource to enhance your lectures on concepts presented in the text. Your Benjamin/Cummings sales representative has details about this offer.

Collection
A Complete Supplements Package

- **Lecture support software** by J. Huhtala. This seven-disk package for the IBM PC and compatibles or the IBM PS/2, provides 280 color screens containing animation and text that summarize key concepts for each section of the book. The accompanying student workbook (300 pages) supports the software with additional text, learning objectives, key terms, review questions, and completion questions. The software and workbook can be used in lecture or lab. The Instructor's Guide contains a reference guide to help you incorporate these materials.
- **University Gradebook.** This class record-keeping software is available for the IBM PC and compatible computers.

Of Related Interest

The Student Edition of Lotus 1-2-3, Second Edition (509 pages); *The Student Edition of dBASE IV* (704 pages).

Brief Table of

Part 1
A First Look at Computers 2

Part 2
Exploring Hardware 46

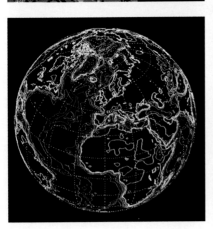

Contents

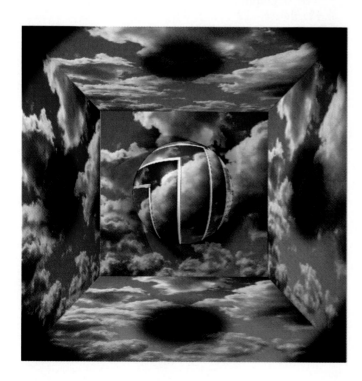

Detailed Table of

Contents

Part 3
Exploring Software 132

Interview: Computers at the Bottom of the Ocean

Part 4
Computers and Business   176

Chapter 10
Security, Privacy, and Ethics: Protecting Hardware, Software, and Data   194

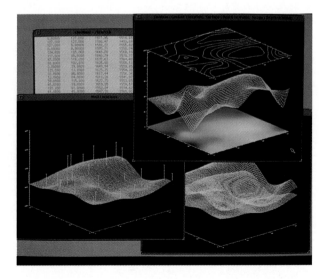

Part 5
Applications   232

Interview: Computers Creating Building Designs

Chapter 12
**Word Processing and Desktop
Publishing: Preparing Printed
Communications   234**

Chapter 13
**Spreadsheets and Business Graphics:
Facts and Figures   262**

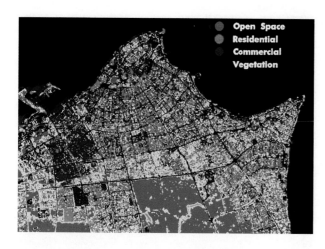

Open Space
Residential
Commercial
Vegetation

Chapter 14
Database Management Systems: Getting Data Together   286

The Buyer's Guide and Galleries

How to Buy Your Own Personal Computer

This special eight-page section presents an overview of points to consider before buying a personal computer and software. If you are thinking about buying a personal computer now or in the future, read this section carefully.

Multimedia

The New Sight and Sound

This section describes the hardware/software combination that supports multimedia, and presents a sample of popular multimedia programs. Such programs offer text, photos, art, sound, and—best of all—the opportunity to participate interactively.

Color Graphics

Computers at their Best

The computer is an artistic virtuoso. In this colorful montage, the computer's talents are shown in a spectrum from art to whimsy to photo manipulation.

Preface

Most introductory computer books are comprehensive in scope. *Essentials of Computing, Second Edition* is too, but we want to offer more than just the basics of computing. We want to engage you and draw you into the text without detracting from the seriousness of the material. We want to present a book that sounds and feels like everyday living. To do that we offer part opening interviews with real people who use computers in a wide variety of businesses. Each chapter opener is a life-with-computers vignette that correlates chapter content with a story about computing. Real examples are sprinkled throughout the text to show how computers actually affect the lives of people who use them.

The everyday living theme also shows up in our extensive photo collection. Rather than standard shots of people in front of computers, we have chosen photos showing computers being used in a variety of settings. In fact, photos are a prime way of drawing readers into the text.

The second edition retains all of the elements that made the first edition a best-seller. We have updated material and added new features. Our hope is that this book and its related learning materials offers students everything they need to make computers a part of their own everyday living.

New and Updated in the Second Edition

The entire manuscript has been updated to reflect current technology. New topics, such as the Internet and the PENTIUM chip, have been added. A significant addition to this edition is the Multimedia Gallery. Although the technology of multimedia is described in Chapter 5, "Storage Devices," the flavor of the multimedia phenomenon is presented in a gallery of eight glorious color pages.

For those of you who used the first edition of this book, you can note these changes. The CPU is now in its own chapter. There is expanded coverage of networking, systems analysis and design, and Windows. The Buyer's Guide has been upgraded to indicate current offerings and buying trends. All part-opening interviews and the Macintosh boxes have been rewritten. Computing Highlights boxes have been replaced with the more significant Computing Trends boxes.

If you are not in a lab environment, note that the three personal computer software chapters (Chapters 12, 13, and 14 on word processing, spreadsheets, and database management, respectively) have been rewritten generically to present the core ideas on these topics. And, finally, a small matter that loomed large to current users, the answers to the built-in study guide are now included in the book.

Organization of the Text

The text is divided into five parts:

- Part 1 offers an overview of computer systems and their uses in our society, and an introduction to the personal computer.
- Part 2 explores computer hardware, including coverage of the central processing unit, input/output, storage, and communications.
- Part 3 looks at software, including programming, programming languages, and operating systems.
- Part 4 examines personal computers in the workplace: management of information systems; security, privacy, and ethics; and artificial intelligence, expert systems, robotics, and virtual reality.
- Part 5 includes three chapters on applications: word processing and desktop publishing, spreadsheets and business graphics, and database management systems. These applications are presented in a generic manner to introduce students to the concepts of these applications without teaching commands specific to software packages.
- Appendices include a discussion of the history of computing and information on number systems.

Key Themes

- **Extensive personal computer coverage.** We place a strong emphasis on personal computers, reflecting their continuing prominence in business and in people's personal lives. Each chapter features a Personal Computers in Action box and Chapter 9, "Computers on the Job: Action and Power," focuses specifically on business issues related to the personal computer. In addition, we have incorporated a wide variety of personal computer examples throughout the text.
- **Focus on computers in business settings.** We provide several features that focus on the uses of computers in the business environment. Each of the five parts of the text begins with a personal interview, in which individuals from a variety of situations discuss how they use computers on the job. Part 4, "Computers and Business," is devoted to issues of current interest in business computing. Topics include the use of personal computers; the role of the information systems manager; security, privacy, and ethics; and artificial intelligence, expert systems, robotics, and virtual reality.

Special Features

- **Appealing style.** When students enjoy what they read, they remember it. The text's friendly style encourages the reader to continue and increases students' comprehension. For example, each chapter begins with an engaging story that leads the student into the material. The real-world applications included throughout the text pique student interest as well as illustrate key points from the chapter.

- **Buyer's Guide.** Students and their families are making important economic decisions about the purchase of a computer for their educational, personal, and business needs. This concise eight-page guide offers students information to aid hardware and software purchases.
- **Multimedia gallery.** This color photo essay provides an in-depth look at multimedia and what it has to offer.
- **Graphics gallery.** This color photo layout vividly shows the sophistication of computer graphics.
- **Computing Trends.** To give students a glimpse of the new directions computer technology is taking, each chapter provides a brief essay that focuses on issues and trends in the world of computing. Examples include electronic résumés, courtroom computers, "wearable" computers, and the issue of privacy in office electronic mail.
- **Personal Computers in Action.** Each chapter includes a feature article on personal computers that demonstrates the range of tasks personal computers perform. The articles include a broad range of topics, from saving the whales to handling diskettes to making online connections.
- **Built-in Study Guide.** To allow students to review concepts and to confirm their comprehension of the material, each chapter concludes with a study guide. The Chapter Review provides an end-of-chapter summary of core concepts and key terms, followed by a Student Personal Study Guide that includes true/false, multiple-choice, and completion questions. In response to suggestions from current users, the answers to all questions now are provided for the student at the end of the study guide.
- **Margin notes.** To further engage the student, margin notes are carefully placed throughout the text. The margin notes extend the text material by providing additional information and highlighting interesting applications of computers.
- **The Macintosh computer** is highlighted in six chapters through brief discussions of Macintosh applications and procedures. Topics covered include the wise use of disk space, America Online, GUI interface, desktop publishing software, graphics, and HyperCard.

In-Text Learning Aids

Each chapter includes the following pedagogical support.

- A chapter **preview** outlines key concepts.
- **Key terms** are boldfaced throughout the text.
- A **Chapter Review** offers summaries of core concepts and boldfaced key terms. The **Student Personal Study Guide** gives students three types of questions (true/false, multiple choice, and completion) that they can answer to check their comprehension of essential concepts. All answers are provided for the student at the end of the Chapter Review.
- An extensive **glossary** and comprehensive **index** are included.

Special Note to the Student

We welcome your reactions to this book. It is written to open up the world of computing for you. Your comments and questions are important to us. Write to the author in care of Computer Information Systems Editor, Benjamin/Cummings Publishing Company, 390 Bridge Parkway, Redwood City, California 94065. All letters with a return address will be answered by the author.

Acknowledgments

Many people contributed to the success of this project. Although a single sentence hardly suffices, we would like to thank some of the key people: Developmental Editor Sue Ewing executed a multi-faceted role with enthusiasm and ingenuity. Jean Lake, as production editor, skillfully coordinated the efforts of many people, keeping the book on the accelerated schedule that contributes to its currency. Michele Carter, as art and design manager, patiently refereed endless discussions relating to the needs and desires of artists and nonartists. Kelli d'Angona-West showed early enthusiasm for the photo research task and was persistent in tracking down outstanding pictures. Editorial Assistant MaryLynne Wrye provided able assistance, on matters large and small, on a daily basis. Sponsoring Editor Maureen Allaire's vision placed the project on the right track, and her steadying hand kept it there.

Reviewers and consultants have provided valuable contributions that improved the quality of the book. Their names are listed in the following section, and we wish to express our sincere gratitude to them.

Reviewers

Tom Affholter
Spokane Community College
Spokane, Washington

Ann Ban
Skyline College
San Bruno, California

Roger R. Bossert
State University of New York
College at Brockport
Brockport, New York

Patricia L. Clark
North Seattle Community College
Seattle, Washington

Jill L. Davis
State University of New York at
Stony Brook
Stony Brook, New York

Fredia F. Dillard
Samford University
Birmingham, Alabama

Laura I. Doig
Embry-Riddle Aeronautical University
Daytona Beach, Florida

William J. Dorin
Indiana University Northwest
Gary, Indiana

Joyce M. Farrell
McHenry County College
Crystal Lake, Illinois

Darrell Z. Gobel
Catonsville Community College
Pasadena, Maryland

Ananda Gunawardena
University of Houston, Downtown
Houston, Texas

Margaret Jamison
Ferrum College
Ferrum, Virginia

John W. Krogman
Albuquerque Vocational Technical Institute
Albuquerque, New Mexico

Della Y. Lee-Lien
Quinnipiac College
Hamden, Connecticut

Jean L. Lutt
Wayne State College
Wayne, Nebraska

Linda Lynam
Central Missouri State University
Warrensburg, Missouri

Barbara J. Maccarone
North Shore Community College
Danvers, Massachusetts

J. Michael McGrew
Ball State University
Muncie, Indiana

Walter Merrick
Johnson County Community College
Overland Park, Kansas

Vincent J. Motto
Asnuntuck Community-Technical College
Enfield, Connecticut

Lucy Parakhovnik
California State University-Northridge
Northridge, California

E. Raydean Richmond
Tarrant County Junior College,
South Campus
Fort Worth, Texas

Ingrid Russell
University of Hartford
West Hartford, Connecticut

Patricia A. Stans
University of New Mexico
Albuquerque, New Mexico

Larry Stroud
Edgecombe Community College
Tarboro, North Carolina

Matthew Tucker
University of Iowa
Iowa City, Iowa

Lloyd C. Vaught
Modesto Junior College
Modesto, California

P. Lynn Wermers
North Shore Community College
Lynn, Massachusetts

Deborah Wheeler
University of Arkansas at Little Rock
Little Rock, Arkansas

The SELECT

The Benjamin/Cummings Publishing Company is pleased to offer the SELECT System, an innovative approach to custom publishing. The SELECT System is our response to your request for textbooks tailored to your course. We believe it is an unprecedented opportunity for educators to evaluate flexible text components and build them into a customized teaching support system suitable for individual course configurations.

A Text with Concepts and Customized Application Coverage

With the SELECT System you can combine the concepts coverage in *Essentials of Computing, Second Edition* with your choice of hands-on instructional modules. The modules you select along with *Essentials of Computing, Second Edition* are bound into one convenient, durable text. We offer a selection of modules as shown in the table on the next page.

Application Modules

Each of the modules, written by an experienced author and instructor, follows a consistent, pedagogically sound format. The modules begin with an introduction to basic concepts for each software application—concepts such as using the program, getting help, and an explanation of the conventions the modules use. Students then learn problem-solving techniques by completing seven or more increasingly challenging projects. This approach both enhances and reinforces comprehension of each specific software application package.

The projects are the core of the student's learning process. They are designed to motivate students by offering both general-interest and business-related examples. Each project title identifies the functional context within which specific commands are mastered. Students gains an appreciation of both the conceptual and keystroke levels of a software application. Projects include student learning objectives, case studies, numbered step instructions, key terms, screen captures, margin figures, tips, reminders, and exit points. Student Study Questions (multiple choice, short answer, and discussion), Review Exercises, and Assignments follow the list. Each module concludes with a comprehensive Operations Reference, an extensive Glossary, and an Index. SELECT modules are intended for the first-time computer user, but they contain selected advanced topics for more experienced students.

System

	Windows	DOS
Word Processing	WordPerfect 6 Projects for Windows	WordPerfect 6.0 Projects for DOS
	WordPerfect 5.2 Projects for Windows	Projects for WordPerfect 5.1
	Word 6 Projects for Windows	
Spreadsheets	Lotus 1-2-3 Rel. 4 Projects for Windows	Projects for Lotus 1-2-3, Rel. 2.3/2.4
	Excel 5 Projects for Windows	Projects for Lotus 1-2-3, Rel. 2.2
	Excel 4.0 Projects for Windows	Projects for Quattro Pro 4.0/5.0
	Projects for Excel 3.0	
	Quattro Pro 1.0/5.0 Projects for Windows	
Database	Access 2 Projects for Windows	Projects for dBASE IV
	Paradox Projects for Windows	Projects for dBASE III PLUS
		Projects for Paradox 3.5
Integrated Packages		Microsoft Works 3.0 Projects for Windows
		Projects for Microsoft Works 3.0 for PCs
		Projects for Microsoft Works 2.0 for PCs
DOS/Windows	Projects for DOS 6.0 and Windows 3.1	
	Projects for DOS 5.0 and Windows 3.1	
	Projects for DOS 2.0/3.3 and Windows 3.0	
Programming	Structured Basic for Beginners	
	QBasic for Beginners	

We introduce new modules regularly, so call the SELECT Hotline at 800-854-2595 or contact your sales representative for the most current information.

The Advantages of SELECT Publishing

The SELECT System brings you and your students many advantages.

■ **Flexibility.** Now you can adapt your textbook to your curriculum instead of the other way around. You can choose any combination of the modules you prefer. And if your course should change next term, you can choose a new selection of modules to meet your new course needs. Each semester, Benjamin/Cummings introduces new modules that contain the most current releases of new software or programming applications. If we don't currently publish modules for the specific software packages you need, contact your Benjamin/Cummings sales representative or call 800-854-2595. We will do our best to address your textbook requirements.

- **Convenience.** The SELECT System gives you computer concepts plus the exact lab coverage you want all in one text and from one publisher. And with our low minimum-order policy, we can offer the SELECT Publishing concept to almost every educator. Also, your students will like the ease of carrying only one text for both lecture and lab.

- **Affordability.** Each module is individually priced. Because you select just those modules you plan to teach, your students pay for only what they need. And because we offer the text and modules bound into one volume, students are not paying for additional costly binders and packaging.

- **Improved Instructional Package.** With computers so much a part of our daily lives, your students deserve the best preparation possible. The SELECT System and *Essentials of Computing, Second Edition* give you up-to-date coverage of computer concepts by the best-known author in computer information systems; pedagogically consistent, customized lab instruction; and the most complete instructional support available.

In addition to the complete instructional support package for the *Essentials of Computing, Second Edition* textbook, we will make available to qualified adopters an instructor's manual for each of the modules with transparency masters, and a test bank. Qualified adopters will also receive an instructor's data disk that contains student data files, answers to selected end of project questions, and the test files from the instructor's manual in ASCII format.

Complimentary Review Copies

We have prepared the following materials for review and adoption consideration.

The Instructor's Edition with Annotations for *Essentials of Computing, Second Edition*

This edition contains the complete contents of the student text plus eight types of margin annotations to support instruction.

Custom complimentary copies of *Essentials of Computing, Second Edition*, bound with your choice of SELECT modules, can be ordered upon request. Contact your Benjamin/Cummings sales representative if you wish to order a complimentary review copy.

Ordering and Pricing Information

Your Benjamin/Cummings representative will be happy to work with you and your bookstore manager to outline the ordering process and provide pricing and delivery information. To take advantage of the SELECT System, you may call Benjamin/Cummings Publishing Company at 800-854-2595. This special Hotline number is attended by service representatives ready to answer your inquiries and provide you with additional complimentary or desk copies.

SELECT Reviewers

We would like to thank the following reviewers who provided valuable input into various stages of our SELECT Publishing Process.

Joseph Aieta, Babson College

Tom Ashby, Oklahoma City Community College

Bob Barber, Lane Community College

Robert Caruso, Santa Rosa Junior College

Robert Chi, California State University, Long Beach

Jill Davis, State University of New York at Stony Brook

Fredia Dillard, Samford University

Peter Drexel, Plymouth State College

Ralph Duffy, North Seattle Community College

David Egle, University of Texas, Pan American

Jonathan Frank, Suffolk University

Patrick Gilbert, University of Hawaii

Maureen Greenbaum, Union County College

Sally Ann Hanson, Mercer County Community College

Sunil Hazari, East Carolina University

Bruce Herniter, University of Hartford

Lisa Jackson, Henderson Community College

Cynthia Kachik, Santa Fe Community College

Bennett Kramer, Massasoit Community College

Charles Lake, Faulkner State Junior College

Ron Leake, Johnson County Community College

Randy Marak, Hill College

Charles Mattox, Jr., St. Mary's University

Jim McCullough, Porter and Chester Institute

Gail Miles, Lenoir-Rhyne College

Steve Moore, University of South Florida

Anthony Nowakowski, Buffalo State College

Gloria Oman, Portland State University

John Passafiume, Clemson University

Leonard Presby, William Paterson College

Louis Pryor, Garland County Community College
Michael Reilly, University of Denver
Dick Ricketts, Lane Community College
Dennis Santomauro, Kean College of New Jersey
Pamela Schmidt, Oakton Community College
Gary Schubert, Alderson-Broaddus College
T. Michael Smith, Austin Community College
Cynthia Thompson, Carl Sandburg College
Marion Tucker, Northern Oklahoma College
JoAnn Weatherwax, Saddleback College
David Whitney, San Francisco State University
James Wood, Tri-County Technical College
Minnie Yen, University of Alaska, Anchorage
Allen Zilbert, Long Island University

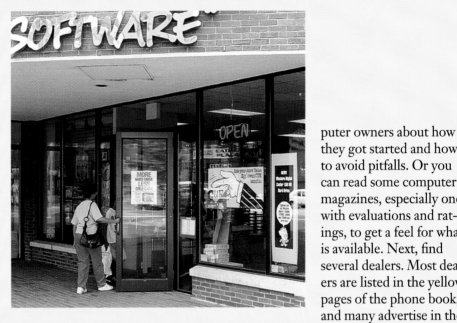

We cannot choose your new computer system for you any more than we might select a new car for you. But we can tell you about various features to look for or avoid. We do not mean that we can lead you to a particular brand and model—so many new products are introduced every month that doing so would be impossible. If you are just starting out, however, we can help you define your needs and ask the right questions.

puter owners about how they got started and how to avoid pitfalls. Or you can read some computer magazines, especially ones with evaluations and ratings, to get a feel for what is available. Next, find several dealers. Most dealers are listed in the yellow pages of the phone book, and many advertise in the business section of the local newspaper. Visit several dealers. Don't be afraid to ask questions. You are considering a major purchase, so plan to shop around.

Finally, you may consider buying a computer system by direct mail. You can find advertisements in any computer magazine. Call a company's listed 800 number and ask them to send you a free brochure. Some reputable companies that sell heavily by direct mail are Dell Computer, Gateway 2000, Compaq, and even IBM.

Where Do You Start?

Maybe you have already done some thinking and have decided that owning your own personal computer offers advantages. Now what? You can start by talking to other personal com-

Questions to Ask the Salesperson at the Store

- ❏ Can I expand the capabilities of the computer later?
- ❏ Whom do I call if I have problems configuring the machine at home?
- ❏ Does the store offer or recommend classes on how to use this computer and software?
- ❏ What kind of warranty comes with the computer?
- ❏ Does the store or manufacturer offer a maintenance contract with the computer?

Analyze Your Needs and Budget

Begin with a wants-needs analysis. Why do you want a computer? Be realistic: Will you use it mostly for games or for business applications? People use personal computers for a variety of reasons. At some point you will have to establish

1

What to Look for in Hardware

The basic personal computer system consists of a central processing unit (CPU) and memory, a monitor (screen), a keyboard and a mouse, a storage device—probably a 3½-inch diskette drive and a hard disk drive—and a printer. Unless you know someone who can help you out with technical expertise, the best advice is to look for a packaged system—that is, one in which the hardware components (with the exceptions of the mouse and the printer) are assembled and packaged by the same manufacturer. This gives you some assurance that the various components will work together.

Central Processing Unit

If you plan to purchase an IBM or compatible machine, many software packages run most efficiently on computers using at least an 80486—also called a "486"—microprocessor. Many 486 processors are upgradable to the more powerful Pentium chip. If you want the most powerful machine, Pentium computers are available and are becoming more affordable.

a budget ceiling. After you have examined your needs, you can relay them to the sellers who will help you select the best hardware-software combination for your budget.

An Early Consideration

Although many brands of computers are available, the business standard is an IBM or IBM-compatible machine. If you will be using your computer for business applications and, in particular, if you need to exchange files with others in a business environment, consider sticking with the standard. However, the Apple Macintosh is an attractive alternative. The Macintosh is noted for ease of use, especially for beginners.

Memory

Memory, or RAM, is measured in bytes, with each byte representing a character of data. The amount of memory you need in your computer is determined by the amount of memory required by the applications programs (like word processing or spreadsheets) that you want to use. The minimum memory threshold keeps rising, as software makers produce sophisticated products that run efficiently only with ever larger amounts of memory. Some people buy 2 or 4 megabytes with their first personal computer, but we recommend 8 megabytes (8MB) or even more. However, most machines have expandable memory, so you can add more later if you need it.

Monitor

Sometimes called a video display screen, the monitor is a very important part of your computer system—you will spend all your computer time looking at it.

Color or Monochrome

Monochrome (usually green or white on a black background) monitors are a possibility when a computer will be used almost exclusively for simple word processing applications. However, a color monitor is strongly suggested. Most software, even for business use, makes impressive use of color. You will certainly want color if you want to create graphics on your screen or if you plan to run entertainment programs on your computer.

Screen Size

Monitors usually have a screen display of between 12 and 15 inches, measured diagonally. Generally, a larger screen provides a display that is easier to read, so most monitors sold today have at least 14-inch screens.

Screen Readability

Be sure to compare the readability of different monitors. First, make certain that the screen is bright and has minimum flicker. Glare is another major consideration. Harsh lighting nearby can cause glare to bounce off the screen, and some screens seem more susceptible to glare than others.

A key factor affecting screen quality is resolution—a measure of the number of dots, or pixels, that can appear on the screen. The higher the resolution—that is, the more dots—the more solid the text characters appear. For graphics, more pixels means sharper images. Color monitors most commonly available are—in ascending order of good res-

olution—enhanced graphics adapter (EGA), video graphics adapter (VGA), and super VGA (SVGA).

Ergonomic Considerations

Can the monitor swivel and tilt? If so, this will reduce your need to sit in one position for a long period. The ability to adjust the position of the monitor becomes an important consideration when several users share the same computer, particularly people of different sizes, such as parents and children. Another possibility is the purchase of add-on equipment that allows you to reposition the monitor. Furthermore, if you expect to type for long periods of time, you would be wise to buy a wrist pad to support your hands and wrists.

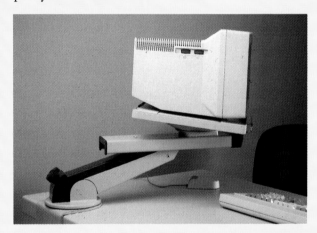

Input Devices

There are many input devices. We will mention only the two critical ones here: a keyboard and a mouse.

Keyboard

Keyboards vary in quality. To find what suits you best, sit down in the store and type. Consider how the keys feel. You may be surprised by the real differences in the feel of keyboards. Make sure the keys are not cramped together; you will find that your typing is error-prone if your fingers are constantly overlapping more than one key.

A detachable keyboard—one that can be held on your lap, for example—is the norm. You can move a detachable keyboard around to suit your comfort. This feature becomes indispensable when a computer is used by people of different sizes.

Most keyboards follow the standard QWERTY layout of typewriter keyboards. Many have a separate numeric keypad. In addition, most keyboards have separate function keys that simplify applications software commands.

Assess the color and layout of the keyboard. Ideally, keys should be gray with a matte finish. The dull finish reduces glare.

Mouse

A mouse is a device that you roll on a tabletop to move the cursor on the screen to make selections. A mouse was, until recently, considered a convenient option. However, since many applications software packages and even operating systems are designed to be used with a mouse, a mouse has become a necessity.

Secondary Storage

You will need disk drives to read programs into your computer and to store programs and data that you wish to keep.

Diskette Drive

Most personal computer software today comes on diskettes, so you need a diskette drive to accept the software. Further, many users keep backup copies of their software and data files on diskette. Most com-

puter systems today come with a 3½-inch diskette drive, with a 5¼-inch diskette drive as an option. If you have no need to be compatible with 5¼-inch diskettes, either from your old computer system or from someone else's computer, you probably do not need a 5¼-inch diskette drive.

Hard Disk Drive

Although more expensive than a diskette drive, a hard disk drive is fast and reliable and holds more data. Once merely an attractive option, a hard disk drive is now considered a necessity. Modern software comes on a set of several diskettes; it would be unacceptably unwieldy to load all of them each time the software is used. Instead, the software on the diskettes is stored on the hard drive, where it is conveniently accessed from that point forward.

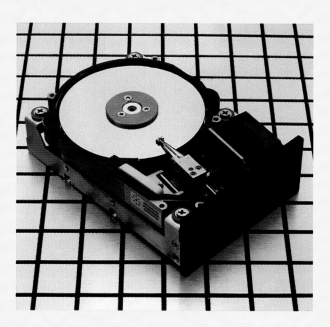

Most computer systems offer a built-in hard disk drive, with variable storage capacity—the more storage, the higher the price. Storage capacity is measured in terms of millions of bytes—characters—of data. Keep in mind that software, as well as your data files, will be stored on the hard disk. Since even a simple word processing program can fill up ten million bytes or more, you can understand why most users elect a minimum of 100 million bytes on a hard disk. Some users buy many times that capacity.

Printers

A printer is probably the most expensive peripheral equipment you will buy. Although some inexpensive models are available, you will find that those costing $400 and up are the most useful. When choosing a printer, consider speed, quality, and cost.

Until recently the **dot-matrix printer** was the standard for everyday printing. A dot-matrix printer forms each character with a series of closely spaced dots. But dot-matrix printers are being phased out in favor of affordable ink-jet and laser printers; each type produces high-quality output and is much quieter than a dot-matrix printer.

Ink-jet printers, in which ink is propelled onto the paper by a battery of tiny nozzles, can produce text and graphics that surpass that of dot-matrix printers. In fact, the quality of ink-jet printers approaches that of laser printers. The further attractions of low cost and quiet operation has made the ink-jet printer a current favorite among buyers.

Laser printers, which use technology similar to copying machines, are the top-of-the-line printers for quality and speed. The price of a low-end laser printer is

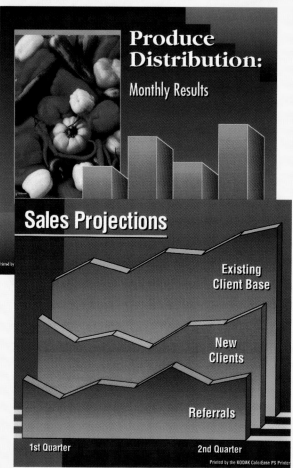

now within the budget of most users. Laser printers are particularly favored by desktop publishers to produce text and graphics on the same page. For years, standard laser printers have printed text and graphics at 300 dots per inch, a resolution that produced crisp, professional documents. Now, powerful—and expensive—laser printers produce output at 600 dots per inch, giving graphic images a sharpness that rivals photographs. However, this rich resolution may be of little value to a buyer who plans to produce mostly text.

Although a few **color printers** are available for less than $500, most are priced at well over $5000. Even at this price, color printers are not perfect. The color seen on the computer screen is not necessarily the color that will appear on the printed output. Furthermore, color printers often have high operating costs for staples such as special coated paper and color ink cartridges. Still, color printers, once prohibitively expensive and slow, are approaching affordable prices and speeds.

Portability

Do you plan to use your computer in one place, or will you be moving it around? Portable computers have found a significant niche in the market, mainly because they are packaged to travel easily. A laptop computer is lightweight (often under 8 pounds) and small enough to fit in a briefcase.

Generally, you should look for the same hardware components in a portable computer as you would consider in a desktop computer: a fast microprocessor, plenty of memory, clear screen, and a diskette drive and hard drive. You will have to make some compromises on input devices. The keyboard will probably be attached and the keys more cramped than a standard keyboard. Also, traveling users often do not have a handy surface for rolling a mouse, so you may want to consider an attached trackball to move the cursor on the screen.

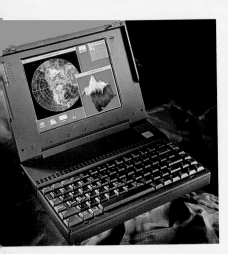

Other Hardware Options

There are a great many hardware variations; we will mention a few here.

Communications Connections

If you wish to connect your computer via telephone lines to electronic bulletin boards, mainframe computers, or information utilities such as America Online or Prodigy, or if you wish to send and receive electronic mail, you need a modem. This device converts computer data into signals that can be transmitted over telephone lines. The Hayes family of products has become the industry standard; most new modems claim some degree of Hayes compatibility.

You may choose an external modem that can be used on different computers. But most buyers prefer an out-of-sight internal modem that fits inside the computer.

Other Input Devices

If you are interested in games, you may wish to acquire a **joystick**, which looks like the stick shift on a car. A joystick allows you to manipulate a cursor on the screen. A **scanner** is useful if you need to store pictures and typed documents in your computer. Scanners are frequently purchased by people who want to use their computers for desktop publishing.

Multimedia Access

A fast-growing area is multimedia: sophisticated software that offers text, sound, photos, graphics, and even movie clips. To take advantage of multimedia, which is presented on optical disks, you need a **CD-ROM disk drive**. Furthermore, you will probably want to invest in a sound card to be installed in your computer and a set of speakers.

Surge Protectors

These devices protect against the electrical ups and downs that can affect the operation of your computer. Some of the more expensive models provide up to 10 minutes of full power to your computer if the electric power in your home or office is knocked out. This gives you time to save your work on disk (so that the work won't be lost if the power fails) or to print out a report you need immediately.

Plotters

These output devices draw hard-copy graphics: maps, bar charts, engineering drawings, overhead transparencies, and even two- or three-dimensional illustrations. Plotters often come with a set of six pens in different colors.

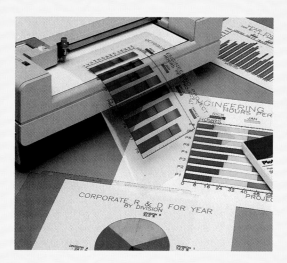

What to Look for in Software

The first software decision is made by the choice of an IBM-compatible or Macintosh computer: you will use the operating system that matches that machine. In the case of an IBM-compatible machine, the operating system called MS-DOS can be overlayed with a software shell called Microsoft Windows. Since so much software is being written for the Windows environment, we recommend that you make Windows part of your purchase.

Hardware Requirements for Software

Identify the type of hardware required before you buy software. Under the heading "system requirements" right on the software package, a list will typically include a particular kind of computer and operating system, and a certain amount of memory and hard disk space.

Brand Names

In general, publishers of well-known software offer better support than lesser-known companies. Support may be in the form of tutorials, classes by the vendor or others, and the all-important hot-line assistance. In addition, makers of brand-name software usually offer superior documentation and upgrades to new and better versions of the product.

Where to Buy Software

Not very long ago, computer users bought their software at small specialty stores where they hoped they could understand the esoteric language of the sales staff. In contrast, buyers now go to enormous stores and pile software packages into their shopping carts like so many cans of soup. The choices of software vendors have expanded considerably.

Computer Superstores

The superstores, such as CompUSA, sell a broad variety of computer hardware and software. Although their primary advantages are a vast inventory, they also offer on-site technical support.

Warehouse Stores

Often billed as clubs, such as Wal-Mart's SAM's, these giant stores sell all manner of merchandise, including computer software.

Mass Merchandisers

Stores such as Sears sell software along with their other various merchandise.

Software-only Stores

These stores, such as Egghead Software, offer a wide selection of software. Furthermore, in marked contrast to the larger stores, these stores are

System Requirements

Make sure your hardware is compatible with the requirements of the software you are buying. You can find the requirements by reading the fine print on the software package. Here is a typical blurb from a software package: Requires an IBM or compatible PC with one diskette drive, a hard drive, Windows 3.1 or higher, and a minimum of 4MB RAM.

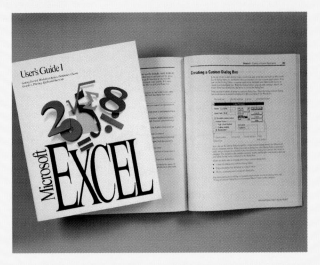

staffed with people who are familiar with the software.

Computer Dealers

These smaller retail stores, such as MicroAge or CompuAdd, sell hardware systems and the software that runs on them. Such a store usually has a well-informed staff, and may be your best bet for in-depth consulting.

Mail Order

Users who know what they want can get it conveniently and reasonably through the mail. Once an initial contact is made, probably from a magazine advertisement, the mail-order house will send catalogs of software regularly.

Now That You Have It, Will You Be Able to Use It?

Once the proud moment has come and your computer system is at home or in the office with you, what do you do with it?

Documentation

Computer systems today come with extensive documentation—the written manuals that accompany hardware. Installation procedures, however, is often largely (and conveniently) on a diskette. Usually, a simple brochure with detailed drawings will help you plug everything together and then help you invoke the software on the diskette. The computer configures itself, largely without any assistance from you.

Software documentation usually includes a user's guide—a reference manual for the various commands available with the software. Many software packages also include a workbook of some sort to help you train yourself. Software tutorials are also common, and useful for the novice and experienced user alike. Software tutorials usually come on a separate diskette, which guides you as you work through sample problems using the software.

Training

Can you teach yourself? In addition to the documentation supplied with your computer, numerous books and magazines offer help and answer readers' questions. Consult these sources. Other sources are classes offered by computer stores and local colleges. These hands-on sessions may be the most effective teaching method of all.

Maintenance Contract

Finally, when purchasing a computer, you may wish to consider a maintenance contract, which should cover labor and parts. Such contracts vary in comprehensiveness. Some cover on-site repairs; others require you to pack up the computer and mail it in. Another option is that the replacement part, say, a new monitor, is sent to you and then you return the old monitor in the same packaging.

Essentials of Computing

Second Edition

Joe Mondello (above) and Bruce Detrick (below), founders of the Tamarand Foundation, talk about how computers helped them get started.

Tell us about the foundation and why you started it.

Joe: In 1987, when my 6-month-old niece Tamara and her mother died of AIDS, I wanted to do something personal to help AIDS sufferers. Bruce saw a way that we could do something that would directly affect the quality of their lives—bringing nature and the arts to them. *Bruce*: Institutional money was just barely enough for the basics—medicine, care, and education. We found that we could make a difference by bringing joy and beauty and a *garden*—the things that really nurture human beings—into institutions. Since we were starting out with no money, we networked with landscape architects, organizations, volunteers who love to garden, and schools that had school children who wanted to do something for sick children. The response was wonderful.

Joe: We began with small things, like going into an AIDS ward with bulbs and gravel and water and little plastic trays, and having a January planting day. We helped create little minigardens with paper whites and narcissus bulbs that would bloom in a few weeks and create a wonderful fragrance. The patients get to nurture their own bedside garden and watch it grow.

I'm curious how the computer fit in your plans.

Joe: Right off the bat the computer gave us a look of legitimacy. We started without any money, even though we put *Foundation* after our name to make it sound like we were something. We could make a very nice-looking letter on the computer to send to organi-

Before. The Tamarand foundation coordinated landscape architects, New York landlords, and an army of volunteers to tackle this Manhattan wasteland.

zations such as the Parks Department and the World Health Organization.

The computer gave us the flexibility to create our own posters, flyers, leaflets. It is like having a graphic arts studio right there in the apartment. I knew if we had to do it on the outside, it could take weeks or months to get people to volunteer to do that stuff for us.

A First Look

The plan. The design firm Arca Terra used computer graphics software to generate this design, which includes a play area, cedar playhouse, lawn, wooden bridges, fountain, murals, and plenty of flowers.

After. The new garden is a safe haven for sick children at Variety House, a transitional home for sick toddlers. The garden is maintained by the Association to Benefit Children, which also created the home.

What else do you use the computer for?

Joe: We do our own mailings, and we keep track of all of our regular business stuff on the computer. You know, it even goes beyond that. We're just two guys with a phone and a Macintosh who decided to create a charity. Having the computer, I think, gave us the courage to try it.

What about the gardens?

Joe: Some of the gardens are designed on the computer by landscape architects. Bruce has an overall design concept, and the designers work under his guidance.

Bruce: We work with a team of landscape artists and horticulturists and volunteers to create gardens at health-related facilities throughout the New York area. Sites are selected to provide outdoor therapy for people living with AIDS. Horticultural therapy is the dream.

> *We're just two guys with a phone and a Macintosh who decided to create a charity. Having the computer, I think, gave us the courage to try it.*

at Computers

LEARNING OBJECTIVES

- Appreciating the breadth and drama of the Computer Revolution
- Appreciating why our society can no longer do without computers
- Understanding the meaning of and need for computer literacy
- Understanding the extent of the computer's impact on graphics, commerce, energy, transportation and travel, paperwork, money, communications, agriculture, government, robotics, health and medicine, education, the home, the sciences, training, and human beings

When Lashalla Richards began college, she was fairly sure that she wanted to be a journalist. Her college counselor advised her to get a little experience along the way, so Lashalla decided to seek a part-time job at the local newspaper. Although she envisioned herself pursuing hot stories, she was actually hired to key in the classified advertisements on the newspaper's computer.

The Ongoing

Lashalla knew her way around a computer keyboard and quickly picked up the procedures for entering the customer's name and billing address and the advertisement message. She also learned how to pick the correct code for the type of advertisement. But that was just the beginning. Lashalla also learned that the computer could sort the ads by code, so that advertisements of the same type, such as apartment rentals, would appear together. The customer data, of course, was used for computer-prepared bills and mailing labels.

Lashalla was surprised to learn that the newspaper used the customer data for a variety of purposes not related to the original advertisement. The newspaper staff extracted from the computer certain customer names and addresses and placed them on lists to be sold to other interested customers. For example, customers who advertised fishing gear or sports equipment might be placed on a list to be conveyed to sports magazines.

When she eventually did some reporting for the paper, Lashalla discovered that reporters have computer access to stored background information. For example, when she reported

that a city council member was going to run for mayor, she fleshed out her story with computer-collected material about the candidate, such as the candidate's past employment and current philanthropic activities.

Lashalla was impressed with her computer savvy but knew she had a lot to learn about how computers worked and what they had to offer. To broaden her knowledge, she included a computer literacy class in her college schedule. As it turned out, Lashalla ended up with a career in publishing, where her computer skills serve her very well.

Revolution
Computers in Your Life

The Computer Revolution

It is hard to remember a time, just a few years ago, when computers were not everywhere. They were not on desks or sales counters or bank walls. They also were not *in* everything, from watches to ovens to cars. The Computer Revolution has come upon us with amazing speed. You could compare this revolution to the Industrial Revolution.

The Industrial Revolution changed human society on a massive scale, introducing electricity, telephones, radios, automobiles, and airplanes. The Computer Revolution also is bringing dramatic shifts in the way we live, but it is happening a great deal more quickly than the Industrial Revolution.

The Computer Revolution is unfinished; it will probably roll on into the next century. Nevertheless, perhaps we can glimpse the future now. Let us see how far we have come, first in society and then on a more personal level.

The Information Age: Forming a New Society

Computers have gone beyond acceptance; they are shaping society in fundamental ways. Traditionally, economics courses taught that the cornerstones of an economy were land, labor, and capital. That tenet is now being challenged, and we speak of *four* key economic elements: land, labor, capital, and information. We have converted from an industrial society to an information society. We are moving from physical labor to mental labor, trading muscle power for brain power. Just as people moved from farms to factories when the Industrial Revolution began, so must we adjust to the information age. You have already taken that first step by taking a computer class and reading this book. But how will computers become a part of your life beyond the classroom? Let us look at some ways in which we're already adjusting to this information age.

How You Will Use a Computer

Personal computers have moved into many facets of our lives. In our homes we use them for a variety of purposes, including keeping track of bank accounts, writing term papers and letters, learning foreign languages, designing artwork, turning on lawn sprinklers or coffeemakers, monitoring temperature and humidity, presenting math and reading skills to children, and organizing mailing lists or directories.

Many people are also using computers on the job, whether they sit at a desk in an office or run a farm. Personal computers are now used for writing memos and reports; forecasting and updating budgets; creating and maintaining files; searching for information; and producing charts, graphs, and newsletters. Almost any job you hope to obtain in the future will involve a computer in some way. A relatively new wrinkle in the job arena is a concept called skill-based pay. Instead of the old idea of across-the-board raises, companies are rewarding employees who have more job skills. It should not come as a surprise that computer skills are among the most prized.

Clearly, the computer user no longer has to be a scientist or mathematician. We are all computer users (Figure 1-1).

▲
Figure 1-1 Personal computer users.
All these people—whether at home, at work, or at school—are making use of the
personal computer.

Computer Literacy for All

Why are you reading this book? Why are you studying computers? In
addition to fulfilling a course requirement or satisfying your curiosity,
you probably recognize that it will not be easy to get through the rest of
your life if you know nothing about computers.

We offer a three-part definition of computer literacy:

- **Awareness.** As you study computers and their uses, you will become
  aware of their importance, their versatility, their pervasiveness, and
  their potential for good and ill in our society.
- **Knowledge.** You will learn what computers are, how they work, and
  their functions. This requires learning some new terminology that
  will help you deal with computers and the people who work with
  them.
- **Interaction.** Computer literacy also means learning to use a computer for some basic tasks. Many courses include a hands-on component; after such training you should feel comfortable sitting down at a
  computer and using it for some suitable purpose.

Climb Aboard

Is it really that important to be computer literate? Yes. But people have not always thought so. In the early days of the Computer Revolution, the average person worried about the disadvantages of computers but failed to recognize the advantages. The situation was similar to that in the early 1900s, when cars were first introduced. Historians tell us that the reaction to that newfangled contraption was much the same as people's reactions to computers. Today's traffic crush, however, is a good indication that attitudes changed somewhere along the way.

The analogy between cars and computers is illuminating. In the very near future, people who refuse to have anything to do with computers may be as inconvenienced as people who refuse to learn to drive.

TEST BANK

T/F 6-19

DISCUSSION QUESTION

Why can someone be computer literate without knowing how to write instructions to tell computers what to do?

DISCUSSION QUESTION

Describe the six key reasons why computers have become an indispensable part of our lives.

LECTURE HINT

The speed of computers has been increasing exponentially. The ENIAC computer (completed in 1946) is considered the first large-scale electronic digital computer. It operated at 357 multiplications per second. The processing speed of the fastest computers today ranges from 10 to 1000 million instructions per second. Experts predict that by the turn of the century computers will contain a billion processors, enabling them to surpass the capabilities of humans.

Note that no part of this definition suggests that you must be able to write the instructions that tell a computer what to do. That would be akin to saying that everyone who plans to drive a car should become an auto mechanic. Someone else can write the instructions for the computer; the interaction part of the definition merely implies that you should be able to make use of those instructions. For example, a bank teller should be able to use a computer to see if an account really contains as much money as a customer wants to withdraw. Computers can also be used by an accountant to prepare a report, a farmer to check on market prices, a store manager to analyze sales trends, or a teenager to play a video game. We cannot guarantee that these people are computer literate, but they have at least grasped the hands-on component of the definition—they can interact with computers.

Since part of the definition of computer literacy is awareness, let us now look at what makes computers so useful. We will then turn to the various ways computers can be used.

Everywhere You Turn

It seems that everywhere you turn these days, you see computers—in stores, cars, homes, offices, hospitals, banks. What are some of the features of computers that make them so useful?

The Significance of Computers

The computer is a workhorse. It is generally capable of laboring 24 hours a day, does not ask for raises or coffee breaks, and will do the 10,000th task exactly the same way it did the first one—without complaining of boredom.

Computers have become an indispensable part of our lives for six key reasons. The first three are key reasons because they are inherent to computers; the last three are valuable by-products.

- **Speed.** We all appreciate fast service, whether we are waiting in line at the supermarket or waiting for grades to come in the mail. More often than not, the computer is a key element in providing fast service. So unless we are prepared to do a lot more waiting—for paychecks, grades, telephone calls, travel reservations, bank balances, and many other things—we need the split-second processing of the computer. The speed of the computer also makes the machine ideal for processing large amounts of data, as in accounting systems and scientific applications.
- **Reliability.** Computers are physically reliable and can thus be counted on to be accurate. Of course, you might not think this from hearing stories about "computer errors." Unfortunately, what these stories almost never bring out is that most mistakes are not the fault of the computers themselves. True, equipment sometimes fails. But most errors supposedly made by computers are really human errors, often caused by someone hitting a wrong key when giving data to the computer. Although the phrase *computer error* is quite common, the blame usually lies elsewhere.
- **Storage capability.** Computer systems are able to store tremendous amounts of data, which can then be retrieved quickly and efficiently. This storage capability is especially important in an information age.

Personal Computers In Action

Saving the Whales

Pieter Folken's "desk" is a craggy cliff along the coast of Alaska. A committed environmentalist, Pieter uses his perch to observe humpback whales and make immediate notations of sightings using his portable laptop computer. For environmentalists trying to save the whales, part of the dif-

ficulty is that too little is known about their behavior to take appropriate action. Pieter's hands-on research will help change all that. The on-site data collected on size, movement, and range of whale populations eventually will be used to help make global decisions on their conservation.

- **Productivity.** Unfortunately, computers sometimes eliminate jobs, most notably in factories, but computers also free human beings for other work. Although a learning curve can cause an initial slow-down, most users will notice increased productivity. In particular, office workers using computers do their jobs better and faster.
- **Decision making.** Because of expanding technology, communications, and the interdependency of people, we suffer from an information deluge. This overload is in part brought on by the computer, but the computer will also help solve it. To make essential business and governmental decisions, managers need to take into account a variety of financial, geographical, logistical, and other factors. Using problem-solving techniques originally developed by humans, the computer helps decision makers sort through and organize this vast amount of information and make better choices.
- **Reduction in costs.** Finally, because it enhances productivity and the decision-making process, the computer helps reduce duplication of effort and hold down costs for labor and energy. Thus, computers help reduce the costs of goods and services. Trend watchers who study the impact of computers on the overall economy have hedged their bets for years, noting the increased level of competition but the still-stagnant economy. Although they are usually reluctant to make robust predictions, some experts seem to agree on a mid-1990s productivity burst, due largely to the impact of computers.

With all these wonderful features to its credit, it is no wonder that computers have made their way into almost every facet of our lives. Let us look at some of the ways computers are being used to make our workdays more productive and our personal lives more rewarding.

Some Applications of Computers

The jobs that computers do are as varied as we can imagine, but the following are some of the principal uses:

Getting Older Via Computer

The Hollywood special-effects folks call it morphing—the gradual computerized transformation of one image to another. Here is a demonstration of the aging process.

LECTURE HINT

In the past people with complicated tax questions required the advice of tax professionals, which could be very expensive. Today tax software is available that not only provides expert tax advice but also prepares tax returns.

DISCUSSION QUESTION

Describe three examples of computer graphics.

- **Graphics.** There is no better place to get a sense of the computer's impact than in the area of computer graphics—computer-produced visual images. The computer as artist is evidenced in medicine, where brain scanners produce color-enhanced "maps" to help diagnose mental illness. Biochemists use computers to model, in three dimensions, the structure of molecules. Architects use computer-animated graphics to give clients visual walk-throughs of proposed buildings, to show possible exteriors, and to subject buildings to hypothetical earthquakes.

  Business executives play artist, making bar graphs and pie charts out of tedious figures and using color to convey information with far more impact than numbers alone can create. Finally, a new kind of artist has emerged who uses computers to create cartoon animation, landscapes, television logos, action sketches, print commercials, and still lifes (Figures 1-2 and 1-3).

- **Commerce.** Products from meats to magazines are now packaged with zebra-striped symbols that can be read by scanners at supermarket checkout stands to determine the prices of the products. These stripes, called the Universal Product Code (UPC), are part of one of the most highly visible uses of computers in commerce; however, there are numerous others. Modern warehousing and inventory management could not exist without computers. Take your copy of this book, for instance. From printer to warehouse to bookstore, its movement was tracked with the help of computers.

- **Energy.** Energy companies use computers and geological data to locate oil, coal, natural gas, and uranium. Meter readers use hand-held computers to record how much energy is used each month in homes and businesses. The utility companies also use computers to monitor and analyze their vast power networks. Building managers use computers to control lighting, heating, and cooling in skyscrapers and warehouses. In addition, computers can analyze the efficiency of the insulation in your home and the fuel consumption in your car.

- **Transportation and travel.** Computers are used to help run rapid transit systems, load cargo ships, keep track of what trucks and railroad cars have been sent where and with what cargo, fly and land air-

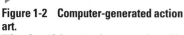

Figure 1-2 Computer-generated action art.
This fanciful art work was produced by a computer artist, using special graphics software.

(a)   (b)

▲
Figure 1-3   Computer-generated still life.
(a) This stunning artwork is called Glass Planets. (b) This dizzying rendition was prepared to convey the variety of offerings on multiple-channel cable television.

planes and keep them from colliding, schedule airline and hotel reservations, and monitor traffic.

■ **Paperwork.** There is no doubt that our society runs on paper. In some ways the computer contributes to this problem—as in adding to the amount of junk mail you find in your mailbox—but in many other ways it reduces paper handling. The techniques of word processing, for example, let you prepare documents in draft form and place them in computer storage. If the document needs to be changed, it can be retrieved, edited, and saved again or printed without retyping. Even Supreme Court justices use word processing, storing their opinions for future reference. Computerized bookkeeping, record keeping, and document sending have also made paperwork more efficient.

■ **Money.** Computers have revolutionized the way money is handled, and nowhere is this more obvious than in banking (Figure 1-4). Once upon a time it was possible to write a check for the rent on Tuesday and cover it with a deposit on Thursday, knowing it would take a few days for the bank to process the rent check and debit it against the account. With computers, however, the recording of deposits and withdrawals is done more quickly. Computers have also brought us the age of do-it-yourself banking, with automated teller machines (ATMs) available for simple transactions. Furthermore, in many grocery stores you can use your ATM card to transfer money from your account to pay for your groceries—with no cash changing hands. Computers have helped fuel the cashless economy, enabling the widespread use of credit cards and instant credit checks by banks, department stores, and other retailers. Some oil companies are now using credit-card-activated, self-service gasoline pumps.

■ **Communications.** Users have the potential to link up one computer with another through a communications system such as telephone lines. Most businesses use computer communications systems to send memos and reports and messages, transfer computer data files, and even have "meetings" among people in dispersed locations. In fact, computer networking is the fastest growing area in the industry.

DISCUSSION QUESTION

What is the meaning of the phrase "our society runs on paper," and how does the computer contribute to this problem?

LECTURE HINT

Beginning in the 1996–97 school year, students will be able to take the Graduate Record Examination (GRE) by computer. Instead of registering for one of five annual test dates, the test is offered at computer centers throughout the country on over 150 days a year. Instead of waiting for test, the students can obtain their test results on the same day.

DISCUSSION QUESTION

How have computers revolutionized the way money is handled? What is meant by the phrase "do-it-yourself banking?"

LECTURE HINT

Automatic teller machines are an example of electronic funds transfer (EFT). EFT uses computers to transfer money electronically between both individual accounts and banks. It has been estimated that on a typical work day financial institutions can transfer over $1 trillion using EFT.

DISCUSSION QUESTION

How do businesses use computer communication systems?

COMPUTING TRENDS

Your Resume: Untouched, Unseen

You send out dozens of copies of your resume, knowing that it will sit in stacks with hundreds of others or, even worse, be placed "on file" in a deep drawer. The waiting begins; you know that this is the tough part of a job search. But wait: a phone call, just two days later. You are interviewed and you are hired.

Has something changed in the hiring process? Yes. A computer is checking the resumes. Instead of human eyes, the computer reviews the current resume collection, looking for particular job qualifications. Resume preparers must make some adjustments for this latest trend in corporate hiring.

Many time-honored methods of getting attention no longer work. A flashy resume meant to catch a recruiter's eye may not be helpful. Skip all the flourishes—fancy typefaces, underlining, graphics, colored paper. Do use a good printer, with easily readable print. Send an original rather than a copy. Use standard-size paper, but do not fold the resume because the words on a crease may be hard for the computer to read. And, for once, technical jargon is a good idea; the computer may search for those words.

Of course, we must add a disclaimer: not *all* companies are scanning resumes by computer. Try to find out what would be appropriate for the companies to which you are applying.

RESUME

L. Banfield Harrison
5738 East Green Lake Way North
Redmond, WA 98052
(206) 634-9808

SYNOPSIS — College faculty and department head, Computer Information Systems department. Author of college textbooks. Consultant, reviewer, lecturer, systems analyst, attorney.

EDUCATION — JD, University of Washington School of Law (Honors)
MSE, Seattle University
BA, University of Notre Dame, Mathematics

COMPUTER EXPERIENCE
Machines — HP 3000, IBM and CDC mainframes, PRIME, IBM PS/2, Macintosh.

Software — Lotus 1-2-3, dBASE, Rbase, WordPerfect.
Languages — Pascal, FORTRAN, BASIC, others.

Applications Areas — Industrial relations, marketing, sales, food brokerage, cattle registration, accounts payable, aircraft design, terminal reservations, marketing, personnel, political organizations, mass mailing, customer surveys.

Positions — Instructor, department head, author, consultant, lecturer, project lead. Major responsibilities in feasibility, analysis, design, and development of large-scale computer systems.

Courses Taught — Database management, systems analysis and design, operating systems, data communications, logic, PC applications, computer literacy.

MANAGEMENT — Department manager, 30 employees, computer systems
Division head, 18 college professors

▶

Figure 1-4 Computers where you expect them: in banks.
The employees of Louisiana's Hibernia National Bank can concentrate their time and attention on their customers because the bank contracted with IBM for a service agreement to manage the bank's computing resources.

◄
Figure 1-5   A farmer's computer.
This farmer uses his laptop computer to enter crop data from the field.

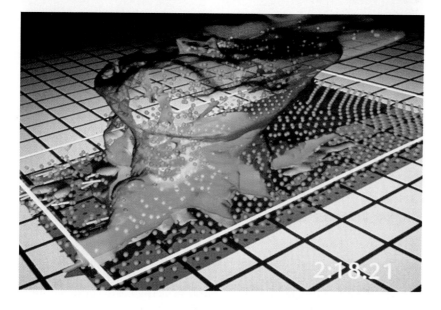

2:18.21

◄
Figure 1-6   When will the storm get here?
To improve the science of weather forecasting, researchers program various weather conditions into a computerized global weather model. In this graphic, different colors represent different water densities.

■ **Agriculture.** High tech down on the farm? Absolutely. Farming is big business, and computers can help with billing, crop information, cost per acre, feed combinations, and automatic irrigation. A Mississippi cotton grower, for example, boosted his annual profit 50 percent by using a computer to determine the best time to fertilize. Cattle breeders use computers to generate information about livestock breeding and performance. Some farmers even take along computers as they check their crops (Figure 1-5).

■ **Government.** The federal government is the largest single user of computers. The Social Security Administration, for example, produces millions of benefit checks each month, with the help of computers. Computers are also used for forecasting weather (Figure 1-6), for admitting vacationers to parks, for processing immigrants, for meting out justice, and yes, for collecting taxes. The FBI keeps track of suspected criminals by compiling separate bits of information into elabo-

LECTURE HINT

The National Park Service is spending $577,000 to create computerized images of the Lincoln Memorial, the Washington Monument, and the Jefferson Memorial. The images will both serve as historical records and be used as blueprints for future repairs. It is estimated that the cost for the Lincoln Memorial alone would be $2 million without computers compared with only $200,000 with the help of a computer.

▶

Figure 1-7   The Swift-Tuttle comet.
Space is filled with objects that threaten the earth, notably the so-called Swift-Tuttle comet, seen with powerful telescopes on October 22, 1992, and enhanced by computer. The comet is a six-mile-long frozen dirt ball, which astronomers give a 1-in-10,000 chance of colliding with the earth on August 14, 2126.

▶

Figure 1-8   The tactile robot.
Robot chores require delicate maneuvers such as those required of this robot "hand," which has the dexterity to use a screwdriver.

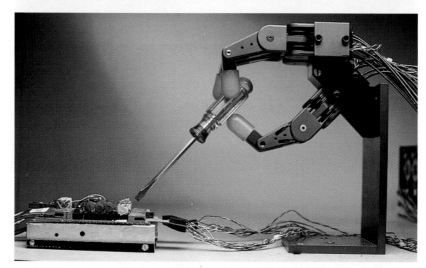

DISCUSSION QUESTION

What is a troublesome social problem caused by robots?

LECTURE HINT

Section 504 of the Rehabilitation Act of 1973 requires office buildings to be accessible to the handicapped. The act ensures that disabled workers will be allowed entry into offices, but once inside a building they can still be isolated from other workers. Now with the use of such devices as large-print screens, braille printers, and speech recognition systems, disabled workers can become an active part of the work force.

rate dossiers, including computer-produced mug shots, that have already helped put several organized crime lords behind bars. On a more positive note, computer technology is the basis of the technology that has provided information about space (Figure 1-7).

■ **Robotics.** With the age of the computer has arrived the age of the robot (Figure 1-8). Robots are information machines with the manual dexterity to perform some tasks too unpleasant, too dangerous, or too exacting to assign to human beings. Examples are robots used by the military for bomb removal; robots used in defense to perform underwater military missions; robots used by fruit growers to pick fruit; and even robots that patrol jail corridors at night and report any persons encountered. Especially controversial are the robots that do tedious jobs better than human beings do, jobs such as welding or paint spraying in factories. Clearly, these robots signal the end of those jobs for some factory workers—a troublesome social problem. However, improved technology has always meant some workers must be retrained, as blacksmiths did with the advent of the automobile.

■ **Health and medicine.** Computers have long been used on the business side of medicine for record keeping, but the most impressive

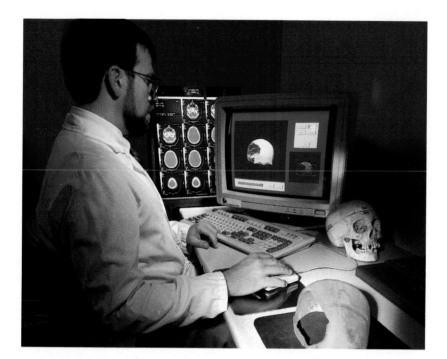

◀
Figure 1.9 Surgeon planning operation.
A patient with a gunshot wound to the head was given a computer-assisted tomography (CAT) scan of the internal damage. The pictures are then assembled into the three-dimensional view shown here on the screen, which the surgeon can use to plan the operation.

advances have been in the diagnostic and healing processes. A key application of computers is to produce cross-sectional views of the body that physicians can study before proceeding with treatment (Figure 1-9). It is estimated that computers make disease diagnoses with 85 percent accuracy. (Doctors, of course, make the final diagnoses.) Another application helps pharmacists test patients' medications for drug compatibility. If you are one of the thousands who suffer one miserable cold after another, you will welcome the news that computers have been able to map, in exquisite atomic detail, the structure of a human cold virus; this is a big step on the way to a cure for the common cold (Figure 1-10). Computers are also being used to monitor everything from weight loss to heart rates.

■ **Education.** Computers have been used behind the scenes for years in colleges and school districts for record-keeping and accounting purposes. Now, of course, they are rapidly coming into the classrooms— elementary, secondary, and college. At the college level, many students realize that they need at least a fundamental grounding in computers. Some colleges require that incoming students purchase computers because many of their class assignments will be done directly on the computer. At the high-school and elementary-school levels, many parents and teachers feel that computer education is a necessity. Parents want to be sure their children are not left behind in the computer age (Figure 1-11).

■ **The home.** Are you willing to welcome the computer into your home? Many people already have, often justifying it as an educational tool for their children. But that is only the beginning. Adults often keep records, write letters, prepare budgets, draw pictures, prepare newsletters for volunteer organizations, and communicate with other computer users—all with their own computers at home. The adventurous make their homes "smart" by using computers to control heating and air conditioning, water their yards, turn lights on and off, and even "watch" for burglars.

▲
Figure 1-10 Cold virus.
This computer-produced model of a cold virus raises hope that a cure for the common cold may be possible after all. With the aid of a computer, the final set of calculations for the model took one month to complete. Researchers estimate that, without the computer, the calculations would have required ten years of manual effort.

▶
Figure 1-11 Painting for kids.
Elementary schoolchildren love to learn how to make pictures on the computer. This splashy high-seas scene was made by a 6-year-old.

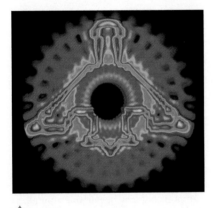

▲
Figure 1-12 Airplane design.
The precise design of this plane has yet to be determined, but this computer-generated image of a delta-wing craft suggests one possible shape.

■ **The sciences.** Computers are used extensively in the sciences. For example, the Food and Drug Administration uses a computer to replace live subjects, such as mice, in experiments. Computers are also used to generate models of DNA, the molecule that houses the genetic instructions that determine the specific characteristics of organisms. Aerospace engineers use computers to design and test airplane parts (Figure 1-12). In England researchers have used computers to invent a "bionic nose" that can distinguish subtle differences in fragrance—an invention that could have major benefits for the food, perfume, and distilling industries. Academicians can be graphically creative even as they study mathematical relationships (Figure 1-13).

■ **Training.** Computers are being used as training devices in industry and government. To teach aspiring sea captains to navigate, for instance, it is much cheaper (and, of course, safer) to use computerized training simulators rather than real ships. Likewise, novice engineers or pilots can get the experience of running a train or flying a plane with the help of a computerized device (Figure 1-14). Computer-based training simulators are also used in medical schools, environmental agencies, science labs, and business schools.

■ **The human connection.** Do computers seem cold and impersonal? Look again. The disabled don't think so. Neither do other people who use computers in very personal ways. Computers can be used to assist humans in areas in which we are most human. Can the disabled walk again? Some can with the help of computers. Can dancers and athletes improve their performance? Often they can by using computers to monitor and analyze their movements. Can we learn more about our ethnic backgrounds and our cultural history with the aid of computers? Indeed we can.

Try making an early assessment of your computer literacy at this point. You probably know more than you think you do. Even though you may not know a lot about computers yet, you have been exposed to computer hype, computer advertisements and discussions, and magazine articles and newspaper headlines about computers. You have interacted

Figure 1-13 Fractals.
Each point on a screen is assigned a color, depending on its behavior under a series of simple repeated mathematical operations.

◀
Figure 1-14 Pilot training.
Pilots practice airplane handling in a computer-controlled simulator. The computer alters instrument readings and the appearance of the runway as the pilot maneuvers from a ground-based cockpit.

with computers in the various activities of your life—at the grocery store, your school, the library, and more. The beginnings of your computer literacy are already apparent.

▼ ▼ ▼

Most careers involve computers in some way. This book will provide you with the foundation you need in computer literacy. If the computer is to help us rather than confuse or threaten us, we must assume some responsibility for understanding it.

Chapter **Review**

Summary

- Like the Industrial Revolution, the Computer Revolution is making massive changes in society. However, the Computer Revolution is happening more quickly than the Industrial Revolution did.
- Land, labor, capital, and information are the cornerstones of our economy. We are changing from an industrial society to an information society.
- Personal computers can be used in business and in the home for a variety of purposes.
- Computer literacy includes (1) an awareness of computers, (2) knowledge about computers and their functions, and (3) interaction with computers.
- Three key characteristics make computers an indispensable part of our lives: speed, reliability, and storage capacity. By-products of these characteristics include increased productivity, enhanced decision making, and reduced costs.
- Computers are used in many areas, including graphics, commerce, energy, transportation and travel, paperwork, money, agriculture, government, education, the home, health and medicine, robotics, the sciences, and training.

Student Personal Study Guide

Review Questions

1. In what ways are the Industrial Revolution and the Computer Revolution similar? In what ways are they different?
2. What are the four cornerstones of today's economy?
3. List four uses of personal computers in the home.
4. List four uses of personal computers in business.
5. What are the three components of computer literacy?
6. List three characteristics that make computers indispensable.
7. Name one use of computers in each of the following areas: graphics, commerce, energy, transportation, paperwork, money, agriculture, government, education, the home, health and medicine, robotics, the sciences, and training.

Discussion Questions

1. Do you believe that computers make life easier and better? Explain.
2. Why are you taking this class? What do you expect to learn from this class?
3. Some people are afraid of computers because they think they might somehow break something or, even worse, appear stupid. Can you think of other reasons that people might be afraid of computers?
4. How will you, individually, be part of the Computer Revolution?

True/False

T   F   1. The Computer Revolution will take about the same amount of time as the Industrial Revolution.

T   F   2. The Computer Revolution is almost complete.

T F 3. Jobs assigned to robots often are those that are too unpleasant, dangerous, or exacting for humans to do.

T F 4. Computers have had a significant impact on cutting down on junk mail.

T F 5. Computer literacy means being able to write instructions to tell the computer what to do.

T F 6. The federal government is the largest single user of computers.

T F 7. Three key reasons why computers have become indispensable are speed, reliability, and storage capability.

T F 8. A "computer error" is usually the result of a breakdown in the computer.

T F 9. Computers are generally used only in office settings.

T F 10. Computers can help reduce waste and hold down costs.

Fill-In

1. The four cornerstones of today's economy are _____, _____, _____, and _____.

2. The three components of computer literacy are _____, _____, and _____.

3. The Computer Revolution is happening more quickly than the _____.

4. Computers are used in the home to _____, _____, _____, and _____.

5. Three much-valued by-products of computers are _____, _____, and _____.

Answers

True/False: 1. F, 2. F, 3. T, 4. F, 5. F, 6. T, 7. T, 8. F, 9. F, 10. T
Fill-In: 1. land, labor, capital, information; 2. awareness, knowledge, interaction; 3. Industrial Revolution; 4. (any four of the following) keep records, write letters, prepare budgets, draw pictures, prepare newsletters, communicate with other computers, control heating and air conditioning, water yards, turn lights on or off, watch for burglars; 5. productivity, decision making, reduction in costs.

LEARNING OBJECTIVES:

- Becoming familiar with the basic components of a computer system: input, processing, output, and storage
- Getting acquainted with some common input, output, and storage media
- Knowing the various classifications of computers and to centralized versus decentralized computer systems
- Getting acquainted with software, including common applications software
- Knowing the equipment associated with personal computers

Curtis Burbank had been the division office manager for 21 years, and his knowledge of the company was encyclopedic. He knew everything from the broad company mission statement to the new product development plans and the routes of new sales employees. He even had a general understanding of the computer-produced reports that came from the headquarters office. However, when Curtis learned that the company was planning to bring personal computers to the division office, it caused him to pause. Computers might be a part of everyday life to his teenage children, but to Curtis they were still a mystery.

Overview of a

At Curtis's suggestion the company sent him to a three-day seminar on the role of computers in the office. He knew the seminar alone would not make him computer savvy, but it did increase his comfort level somewhat. The instruction was very basic, beginning with the difference between hardware and software: Hardware is the computer itself, and related equipment, while the software is a set of instructions to tell the computer how to do a task. Curtis was determined to learn more.

Back in the office Curtis gathered the staff together to explain the impact of the impending new equipment. He began with a homey example, describing the functions of the new computers in terms of already-familiar equipment. Each computer, he noted, took on the roles of several old systems. Word processing software let the computers and printers behave as sophisticated typewriters. Spreadsheet software turned the computer into a flexible accounting system. Database software let the computer's storage act as a super-convenient filing cabinet. Furthermore, the wires that linked all the computers let the staff exchange mail via computer, reducing the amount of paper memos and alleviating the company's problem with "telephone tag."

For the next two weeks, Curtis and a dozen other staffers spent their afternoons at a hands-on class provided by the computer vendor. Each of them acquired a passing acquaintance with the computers and how they could be used in the office.

The arrival of the computers at the company was quite an event. Typewriters were, for the most part, stowed away. New wiring was installed to link the computers together. Gleaming new computers were set up on each desk. Most work came to a halt. But gradually, with the temporary help of an on-site instructor sent by the vendor, Curtis and the staff began to pick up speed. Eventually, Curtis and four other staffers enrolled in an evening computer literacy class, paid for by the company, at a local college.

All this happened a year and a half ago. Now Curtis routinely uses the computer on his desk, just as he does other office equipment. He has joined the people who cannot imagine how they ever got along without computers.

Computer System
Hardware and Software

The Computer As a Tool

When most people think of tools, they think of hand tools such as hammers and saws, or perhaps lug wrenches and screwdrivers. But think of a tool in a broader sense, as anything used to do a job. This expands the horizon to include stethoscopes, baseball bats, kettles, shovels, and yes, computers.

The computer is a sophisticated tool, but a tool nonetheless. Who would use such a tool? Carrying our analogy further, would you buy a baseball bat if you had no intention of hitting a ball? Probably not. You probably would not purchase a computer either, or learn how to use it, unless you had some use in mind. Business people are not interested in buying useless tools. Instead, they have a plan in mind. Businesses purchase computers because they have problems to solve or tasks to perform.

TEST BANK

Mult. Choice 1, 16-17
T/F 37, 53
Matching I 65, 68
Fill In 81, 90

TEST BANK

Mult. Choice 2, 3, 6-13, 22-23, 25-26, 28, 29-30
T/F 32, 35-36, 39-40, 47-52, 54-56, 57-59
Matching I 60-63, 67
Matching II 70-75
Fill In 80, 82, 84-85, 88-89, 91-98

DISCUSSION QUESTION

How does hardware differ from software?

DISCUSSION QUESTION

How does a computer programmer differ from an end-user?

The Beginning: Some Basic Terminology

Knowing just a few basic concepts will prepare you for meeting a computer for the first time, whether at school, at home, or on the job. If you are a beginner, you may have heard of hardware and software but still have only a vague notion of what they are.

The computer and its associated equipment are called **hardware.** The instructions that tell a computer what you want it to do are called **software.** Software is also referred to as programs. To be more specific, a **program** is a set of step-by-step instructions, written in a language a computer understands, that directs the computer to do the tasks you want it to do and to produce the results you want. A **computer programmer** is a person who writes programs. But most of us do not write programs; we *use* programs written by someone else. This means we are **users**—people who use computer software. In business, users are sometimes called **end-users** because they are at the end of the "computer line," actually making use of the computer's capabilities.

As we continue the chapter, we will examine first hardware and then software. Along the way we will note how these components work together to turn raw data into useful information. Then we will return to look at the personal computer in more detail. As the title of this chapter indicates, what follows is an overview, a look at the "big picture" of a computer system. Thus, many of the terms introduced in this chapter are defined only briefly. In subsequent chapters we will discuss the various parts of a computer system in greater detail.

Hardware

What is a computer? A **computer** is a machine that can be programmed to accept raw data (input) and process it into useful information (output). For example, a computer in a company's payroll department could be programmed to accept input data about an employee's rate of pay and hours worked and process that data to create the employee's paycheck. The processing is directed by the software but performed by the hardware, which we will examine in this section.

To function, a computer system requires four main areas of data handling: input, processing, output, and storage (Figure 2-1). The hardware responsible for these four areas operates as follows:

■ *Input devices* accept data in a form that the computer can use and send the data to the computer's processing unit. These devices allow you to get data into the computer.
■ The *central processing unit (CPU)* has the electronic circuitry that manipulates input data into the information wanted. The central processing unit actually executes computer instructions. *Memory* is associated with the central processing unit. Memory consists of the electronic circuitry that temporarily stores the data and instructions (programs) needed by the central processing unit.

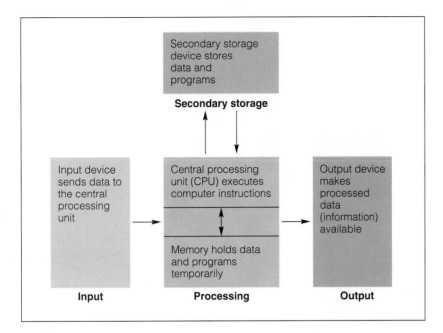

◀

Figure 2-1   The four primary components of a computer system.
To function, a computer system requires input, processing, output, and storage.

TRANSPARENCY ACETATE #1

Figure 2-1

■ *Output devices* show you the processed data, or information, in a form that is useful to you.

■ *Secondary storage devices*, such as disk drives, can store additional data and programs permanently. These devices, which may or may not be physically attached to the computer, supplement the computer's memory.

Now let us consider the equipment making up these four parts in terms of what you would find on a personal computer.

LECTURE ACTIVITY

Take apart an old computer and have the students identify the various hardware components.

From a Personal Computer Perspective

Suppose you want to do word processing on a personal computer, perhaps writing a letter or memo, using the hardware shown in Figure 2-2. Word processing software allows you to input data such as a letter, save it, revise and resave it, and print it whenever you wish. The *input device*, in this case, is a keyboard, which you use to type, or key in, the original letter and any changes you want to make to it. All computers, large and small, must have a *central processing unit* (on a personal computer it is within the personal computer housing). The central processing unit uses the word processing software to accept the data you input through the keyboard. Processed data from your personal computer is usually *output* in two forms, on a screen and on a printer. As you enter the letter on the keyboard, it appears on the screen in front of you. After you examine the letter on the screen, make changes, and determine that the new version is acceptable, you can print the letter on a printer. Your *secondary storage device* could be a disk drive, which accesses the diskette that stores the letter until it is needed again. The personal computer is a convenient vehicle for examining the overall hardware configuration. We will return to the personal computer in more detail later in the chapter.

Now we will take a general tour of the hardware needed for input, processing, output, and storage. All computer systems—whether small,

CLASS PROJECT

Divide the class into groups. Have each group identify one-time computer costs (at time of purchase) and on-going computer costs (such as disks, paper, and printer ribbons).

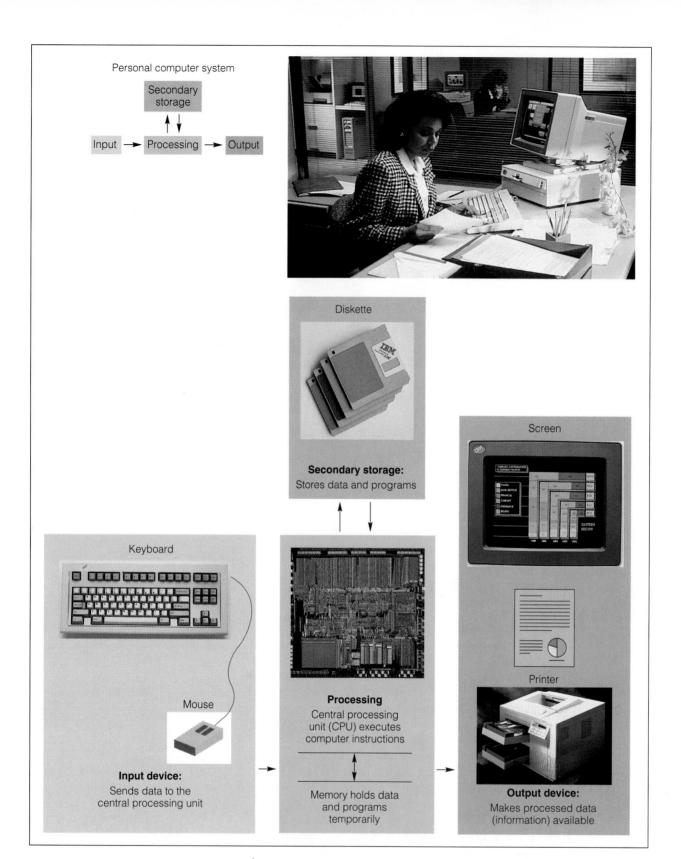

Figure 2-2 A personal computer system.
In this IBM PS/2 personal computer system, the input devices are both a keyboard and a mouse, which feed data to the central processing unit. The central processing unit is an array of electronic circuits on a piece of silicon in the computer housing. The two output devices in this example are the screen and the printer. Secondary storage is on both diskettes and hard disk. These four components of the system operate together to make the computer work for you.

medium, or large—are composed of these same components. These topics will be covered in more detail in subsequent chapters.

Input: Raw Data

Input is the data put into the computer system for processing. Some of the most common ways of feeding input data into the system are by

- Enterring on a **keyboard.** The layout of a computer keyboard is similar to that of an electric typewriter keyboard. The computer responds to what you enter; that is, it "talks back" to you by displaying on the screen what you type (Figure 2-3a).
- Moving a **mouse** over a flat surface. As the ball on its underside rotates, the mouse movement causes corresponding movement on the computer screen, so the user can use the mouse to point to commands on the screen. Buttons on the mouse let the user invoke commands (Figure 2-3a).
- Reading with a **wand reader,** which can be used to scan the special letters and numbers on price tags in retail stores (Figure 2-3b). Wand readers can read data directly from the source, such as a price tag, into the computer. Thus, they significantly reduce the cost and potential error associated with manually entering data on a keyboard.
- Moving a product over a **bar code reader,** which scans **bar codes,** the zebra-striped symbols now carried on nearly all products (Figure 2-3c). Like wand readers, bar code readers collect data at the source, reducing errors and costs.

An input device may be part of a **terminal** connected to a large computer. A terminal includes (1) an input device—a keyboard, wand reader,

DISCUSSION QUESTION

What are some of the most common ways of feeding input data into a computer system?

LECTURE HINT

The Internal Revenue Service uses a scanning system to convert tax returns and correspondence it receives into electronic images for faster processing. The system is designed to allow taxpayers to file as usual, while the IRS processes the forms electronically. Furthermore, some taxpayers can file their returns electronically.

LECTURE HINT

A new type of bar code is available that not only identifies a product, but also supplies additional shipping information. These codes store information in two dimensions and can contain several hundred characters in a square inch.

▼

Figure 2-3   Input.
(a) The most widely used input device is the keyboard. The mouse, under the user's right hand, is a common substitute for some keyboard functions. Movement of the mouse on a flat surface causes corresponding movement of a pointer on the screen. (b) To input data, this wand reader scans special letters and numbers on price tags. Wand readers are often found in department stores. (c) Bar code readers are used in supermarkets to input the bar codes found on product labels.

(a)

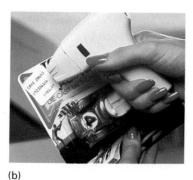
(b)

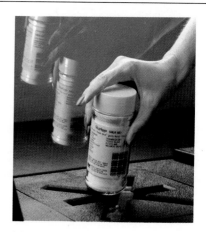
(c)

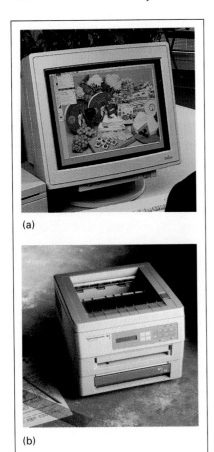

▲
Figure 2-4 Output.
Screens and printers are two types of output devices. (a) The graphics displayed on this screen are one form of output. (b) This laser printer produces output in the form of printed documents.

or bar code reader, for instance; (2) an output device—usually a television-like **screen;** and (3) a connection to the main computer. The screen displays the data that has been input. After the computer processes this data, the screen displays the results of the processing—the information you wanted. In a store, for instance, the terminal screen displays the individual prices (the data) and the total cost (the desired information).

The Central Processing Unit and Memory: Data Manipulation

The **central processing unit,** or **CPU,** is the computer's center of activity. The central processing unit consists of electronic circuits that interpret and execute program instructions as well as communicate with the input, output, and storage devices.

It is the central processing unit that, using software, actually transforms data into information. **Data** is the raw materials to be processed by a computer. Such materials can be letters, numbers, or facts—such as grades in a class, baseball batting averages, or light and dark areas in a photograph. Processed data becomes **information**—data that is organized, meaningful, and useful. Data that is very uninteresting to one person may become very interesting information to another. The raw facts—the *data*—of births, eating habits, and growth rates of calves, for instance, may mean nothing to most people. But the computer-produced relationships among feed, growth, and beef quality are critical pieces of *information* to a cattle breeder.

Computer **memory,** also known as **primary storage,** is closely associated with the central processing unit but not actually part of it. Memory holds the data after it is input to the system but before it is processed. It also holds the data after it has been processed but before it has been released to the output device. In addition, memory holds the programs (computer instructions) needed by the central processing unit. Memory consists of electronic circuits, just as the CPU does.

Output: Information

The results produced by the central processing unit are, of course, a computer's whole reason for being; **output** is usable information. That is, raw input data has been processed by the computer into relevant and useful information. Some ingenious forms of output have been devised, such as music and synthetic speech, but the most common forms are words, numbers, and graphics. Words, for example, may be the letters and memos prepared by office workers using word processing software. Other workers may be more interested in numbers, such as those found in formulas, schedules, and budgets. As we will see, numbers can often be understood more easily when they are output in the form of computer graphics.

Two common output devices are screens and printers. You already read about screens when you read the description of input. Screens can show lines of text, a numerical display, or color graphics (Figure 2-4a).

Printers are machines that produce printed documents at the instruction of a computer program (Figure 2-4b). Some printers form typed images on paper as typewriters do; they strike a character against a rib-

COMPUTING TRENDS

Wearable Computers

Can it really be true? Will we soon be *wearing* our personal computers around our waists or necks, or perhaps slung over our shoulders? According to industry spokespersons, the personal computer is about to become such an integral part of our daily lives that we will indeed add it to our wardrobes. For those who need a keyboard on hand at all times, a notebook personal computer with a shoulder strap is underway. As for all the rest of the computer wardrobe accessories, we will have to wait a bit longer.

bon, which makes an image on the paper. Other printers form characters or graphics by using lasers, photography, or sprays of ink.

Secondary Storage

Secondary storage is additional storage that can hold data and programs permanently (recall that primary storage can hold data only temporarily). Secondary storage has several advantages. For instance, it would be unwise for a college registrar to try to house student records in computer memory; if this were done, the computer probably would not have room to store anything else. Also, memory holds data and programs only temporarily—hence the need for permanent secondary storage.

The two most common secondary storage media are magnetic disk and magnetic tape. A **magnetic disk** is a flat, oxide-coated disk on which data is recorded as magnetic spots. A disk can be a diskette or a hard disk. A **diskette,** usually 3½ inches in diameter (or perhaps 5¼ inches), is used with a personal computer and looks something like a small stereo record, although it is housed in a square container (Figure 2-5a). A **hard disk** is inflexible and is often in a sealed shell. Used by both small and large computers, hard disks hold more data and can store and retrieve data faster than diskettes. Hard disks usually hold the programs users need to perform tasks. Users in a public setting, such as a school lab or business office, usually keep their own data on diskettes they can take with them. Disk data is read by **disk drives** (Figure 2-5b).

Magnetic tape, which comes on a reel or in a cassette-like cartridge, is similar to tape that is played on a tape recorder. Magnetic tape reels are

LECTURE HINT

New printers are available that include software that can identify printer problems and tell you steps to take to solve the problem. The software bases its diagnosis on past experience of typical problems and solutions.

DISCUSSION QUESTION

How does secondary storage differ from primary storage?

▶

Figure 2-5 Secondary storage.
(a) A 5¼-inch diskette is being inserted into a disk drive. (b) Hard disks are contained within the round disk pack shown on the top of the cabinets, which contain the disk drives. When it is to be used, a disk pack is lowered into the open compartment. (c) Magnetic tape, shown here being mounted on a tape drive, travels off one reel and onto another. (d) Optical disk technology uses a laser beam to store large volumes of data.

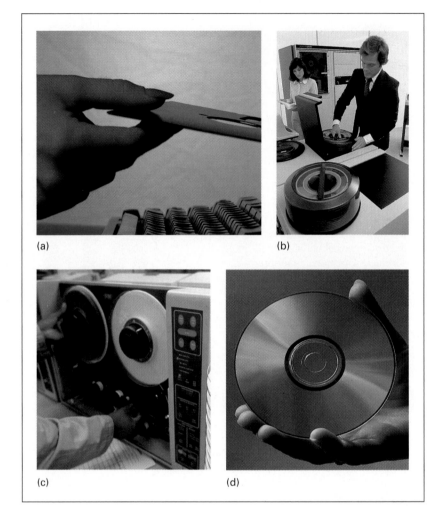

(a) (b)

(c) (d)

mounted on **tape drives** when the data on them must be read by the computer system or when new data is to be written on the tape (Figure 2-5c).

The most recent storage technology, however, is **optical disk,** which uses a laser beam to store large volumes of data at low cost (Figure 2-5d). This interesting medium, and its fascinating applications, will be explored in more detail in Chapter 5, which focuses on storage devices.

The Complete Hardware System

The hardware devices attached to the computer are called **peripheral equipment.** Peripheral equipment includes all input, output, and secondary storage devices. In the case of personal computers, some of the input, output, and storage devices are built into the same physical unit. In the personal computer we saw in Figure 2-2, for instance, the CPU and disk drive are contained in the same housing; the keyboard and screen are separate.

In larger computer systems, however, the input, processing, output, and storage functions may be in separate rooms, separate buildings, or even separate countries. For example, data may be input on terminals at a branch bank and then transmitted to the central processing unit at the bank's headquarters. The information produced by the central processing unit may then be transmitted to the bank's international offices, where it is printed out. Meanwhile, disks with stored data may be kept in the bank's headquarters, and duplicate data may be kept on disk or tape for safekeeping in a warehouse across town.

Although the equipment may vary widely, from the simplest computer to the most powerful, by and large the four elements of a computer system remain the same: input, processing, output, and storage. Now let us look at the various ways computers are classified.

Computer Classifications: Diminishing Differences

Computers come in sizes from tiny to monstrous, in both appearance and power. The size of a computer that a person or an organization needs depends on the computing requirements. The National Weather Service, keeping watch on the weather fronts of many continents, has different requirements from those of a car dealer's service department that is trying to keep track of its parts inventory. The requirements of both of them are different from the needs of a salesperson using a small hand-held computer to record client orders on a sales trip.

DISCUSSION QUESTION

How do the following differ: super-computer, mainframe, minicomputer, supermicro, microcomputer, laptop computer?

Supercomputers

The mightiest computers—and, of course, the most expensive—are known as **supercomputers** (Figure 2-6a). Supercomputers process *billions* of instructions per second. If you ever work for the federal government in an area such as worldwide weather forecasting, oil exploration, and weapons research, you might use a supercomputer. Supercomputers are now moving toward the mainstream for activities as varied as creating special effects for movies and analyzing muscle structures. Super-computers can also produce super graphics (Figure 2-7).

Mainframes

In the jargon of the computer trade, "ordinary" large computers are called **mainframes** (Figure 2-6b). Mainframes are capable of processing data at very fast speeds—several million program instructions per second, for example—and they have access to billions of characters of data. The price of a mainframe varies from several hundred thousand to many millions of dollars. With that kind of price tag, you will not buy a mainframe for just any purpose. The principal use of such a powerful computer is for processing vast amounts of data quickly. You will be most likely to use a mainframe if you work for a bank, an insurance company, a government agency, a utility company, or a manufacturer. This list is not all-inclusive; you might also use such a computer if you ever work for a large mail-order house, an airline with a sophisticated reservations system, an aerospace company doing complex aircraft design, or the like.

Minicomputers

The next step down from mainframe computers are **minicomputers** (Figure 2-6c). Minicomputers are generally slower than mainframes and are less costly. In fact, when minicomputers first appeared on the market,

(a)

(b)

(c)

(d)

▲

Figure 2-6 Computer classifications.
(a) The Cray-2 supercomputer has been nicknamed Bubbles because of its bubbling, shimmering coolant liquids. You can own it for a mere $17.6 million. (b) Shown here is the Control Data 7600 mainframe computer. Despite the sterile look of this staged photo, it does show that a mainframe computer has many components. (c) The VAX, a popular minicomputer made by Digital Equipment Corporation (DEC). (d) This personal computer is made by Macintosh.

their lower price fell within the range of many small businesses, greatly expanding the potential number of computer users.

Minicomputers were originally intended to be small and serve some special purpose. However, in a fairly short time they became more powerful and more versatile, and the line between minicomputer and mainframe has blurred. In fact, the appellation *mini* no longer seems to fit very well. The term **supermini** has been coined to describe minis at the top of the speed/price scale. If you ever work in a retail business, a small college, or a state or city agency, you may use a minicomputer. However, the market for minicomputers, and for mainframes, too, is diminishing as buyers choose computers that are less expensive and nearly as powerful: microcomputers.

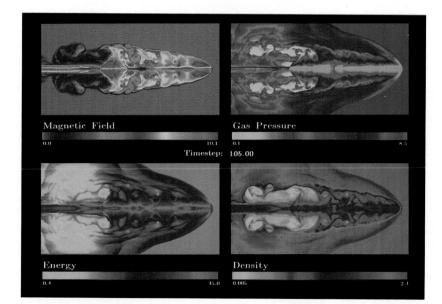

◄

Figure 2-7   Super supercomputers.
These graphics, prepared on a supercomputer, represent a magnetic field,
gas pressure, energy, and density.

Microcomputers

Computers that are the next step down in size are called **microcomputers** (Figure 2-6d). Microcomputers are often called by other names, such
as desktop, home, or personal computers; we will use the common name
personal computer (PC) in this book. For many years, the computer
industry was on a quest for the biggest computer; the search was always
for more power and greater capacity. Prognosticators who timidly suggested a niche for a smaller computer were subject to ridicule by people
who, as it turned out, could not have been more wrong. Now, for a few
hundred dollars, anyone can have a small computer. (Most people, however, are more likely to choose a computer that costs a few *thousand* dollars.) **Supermicros**, generally faster and more powerful than other personal computers, are found in offices that use the top of the line.
Supermicros have significantly increased memory and hard disk storage
capacity.

Laptop computers

A computer that fits in a briefcase? A computer that weighs less than a
newborn baby? A computer you do not have to plug in? A computer to
use on your lap on an airplane? Yes, to all these questions. **Laptop computers,** also called **notebook computers,** are wonderfully portable and
functional, and popular with travelers who need a computer that can go
with them (Figure 2-8). Most laptops accept diskettes, so it is easy to
move data from one computer to another. Laptops are not as inexpensive
as their size might suggest; many carry a price tag equivalent to a full-size
personal computer for business.

Getting smaller still

Using a pen-like stylus, **pen-based computers** accept handwritten
input directly on a screen (Figure 2-9). Users of the hand-held pen-based
computers, also called **personal digital assistants (PDAs)**, are mainly
people in companies who want to automate the work of their clipboard-
carrying workers, such as parcel delivery drivers and meter readers.

LECTURE HINT

The performance of the more powerful
personal computers of the early 1990s
is comparable to the minicomputers of
the early 1980s.

LECTURE HINT

An increasing number of software
packages are supplying their documentation online. You can use the help
commands to obtain general instructions about the software as well as
context-sensitive help, which provides
varying information depending on
what you are doing at the time.

(a)

(b)

(c)

Figure 2-8   Laptops
All these users, whether in the office or working outdoors, find it convenient to use laptop computers.

Other potential users are workers who cannot easily use a laptop computer because they are on their feet all day: nurses, sales reps, real estate agents, and insurance adjusters.

◥ Software

When you first interact with a computer system—whether at school, at home, or on the job—you will probably be captivated by the hardware.

▲
Figure 2-9   Pen-based computers.
Workers on the job sometimes prefer lightweight pen-based computers, which will
accept handwritten input.

But you will soon discover that it is really the software—the planned,
step-by-step instructions required to turn data into information—that
makes a computer useful.

Categories of Software

Generally speaking, software can be categorized as system software or
applications software. **System software,** also called **operating systems,**
is the underlying software found on all computers. **Applications software** is software that is *applied*, or put to use, to solve a particular problem or perform a particular task. Applications software may be either
custom or packaged. Many large organizations pay programmers to
write **custom software**—software that is specifically tailored to their
needs. The average person is most likely to deal with **packaged software,** also called commercial software—the software that is literally
packaged in a container of some sort, usually a box or folder, and sold in
stores or catalogs. Packaged software for personal computers often
comes in a box as colorful as a Monopoly game. Inside the box you will
find one or more diskettes holding the software and an instruction manual, also referred to as **documentation** (Figure 2-10). To use the software, you begin by inserting the diskette in the disk drive. Then,

DISCUSSION QUESTION

What is the difference between system software and applications software?

Personal Computers
In Action

But What Would I Use It For?

In addition to the general categories we have mentioned in the text, there are some very specific—and idiosyncratic—software packages that find their way into home computers. See if any of the offerings in this sampler appeal to you.

■ **Taxis.** If you are a frequent traveler to—or live in—a big city, you will appreciate what the New York Times calls "one of the hottest new guidebooks of the decade." The software provides a unique combination of mapping ability and ratings of hotels and restau-

rants. Cities currently available are New York, Chicago, Los Angeles, San Francisco, and Washington, D.C. (from Zagat-Axxis)

■ **Calendar Creator Plus.** Create your own customized calendar, a whole month at a time, to hang on the refrigerator. You can list single or recurring events and include graphics icons for drama. Try these icons: a gift box (birthday), football (the big game), or a tooth (dentist appointment). (from Power Up!)

■ **Auto Insight.** Learn how a car works with software that takes you on a journey through the inner workings of a car. Check out the braking system, cooling system, engine, steering, suspension, fuel injection system, transmission, emission control, and more.

■ **Design and Build Your Deck.** This software lets you lay out a simple deck just by manipulating an image on the screen, using a mouse. You can view your design from the top, the side, or in a real-

istic 3-D view. As you change the deck's size and shape, and add stairs and railings, the program automatically creates the necessary structural underpinnings and updates a list of materials needed and a cost estimate. (from Books That Work)

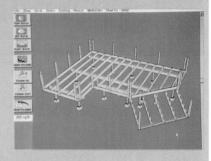

■ **Roots.** If you have studied your family's history, you know how much fun—and how confusing—it can be. Easy enough for amateurs but powerful enough for professionals, Roots provides an organizational framework to help you untangle the family data. Its

TRANSPARENCY ACETATE #3

Figure 2-PCA

depending on the hardware and software, you either type specified instructions on the keyboard or give a command with the click of a mouse to begin running the software on the computer.

There is a great assortment of software to help you with a variety of tasks—writing papers, preparing budgets, drawing graphs, playing games, and more. The wonderful array of software available is what makes computers so useful.

Most personal computer software is planned to be user friendly. The term **user friendly** has become a cliché, but it still conveys meaning. It usually means that the software is supposed to be easy—perhaps even intuitive—for a beginner to use or that the software can be used with a minimum of training. Even so, such software may seem overwhelming at

searching and sorting capabilities let you note relationships among newly discovered ancestors. You can look up family members by name, date, location, and more. (from Commsoft)

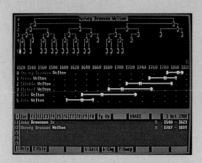

■ **Print Shop.** Design cards, posters, banners, or invitations that use a built-in art library of ready-made pictures and symbols and a dozen backgrounds and borders. Choose type style and size, all with optional outline and three-dimensional effects. You cannot produce cards that are as nice looking as those you buy in a store, but you can say, "Look Mom, I made it myself." (from Broderbund)

■ **Orbits: Voyage Through the Solar System.** Explore the mountains of the moon, the rings of Saturn, the coronas of the sun, and other worlds through full-color animation and 3-D graph-

ics. (from Software Marketing Corporation)

■ **The Running Program.** Take just a few minutes each day to input your running data so that the program can produce graphs of how you performed over different distances at different paces. It also has screens full of advice—from warm-up exercises (including graphic demonstrations) to remedies for knee pains to what you should wear. About the only thing it does not do is get you out of bed in the morning. (from MECA Software)

■ **World Atlas.** It's an atlas, an almanac, and a fact book all in one. The screen maps are especially useful with a mouse: just point and click on a country, state, or city and be supplied with facts such as population and an array of climatic information. (from Power Up!)

■ **Personal Physician.** Mindful of soaring medical costs, ordinary folks are using their personal computers as supplements to MDs. This software quizzes you on-screen about symptoms, suggests treatment, and (dubiously) comes with a real stethoscope. (from FamilyCare Software)

■ **Personal Law Firm.** Write your own will, leases, contracts, or prenuptial agreement. Just answer simple on-screen questions. The forms are valid in all states except Louisiana. (from BLOC Publishing)

■ **Flight Simulator.** Climb into the cockpit of a Cessna 182 and get ready for almost anything in a flight simulation so realistic that even licensed pilots have their hands full with it. More than a game, this approaches training and is a real challenge. (from Microsoft)

first. Although software is usually generalized enough to be marketed to a broad audience, it is possible to set up the features of the software to match a particular user's needs.

Some Task-Oriented Software

Most users, whether at home or in business, are drawn to task-oriented software, sometimes called productivity software, that can make their work faster and their lives easier. The collective set of business tasks is limited, and the number of general paths toward performing these tasks is limited, too. Thus, the tasks and the software solutions fall, for the most part, into just a few categories that can be found in most business environments. These major categories are word processing (including

▶

Figure 2-10   Packaged software.
Each of the software packages shown here includes one or more disks containing the software needed to run the program and an instruction manual, or documentation, describing how to use the software.

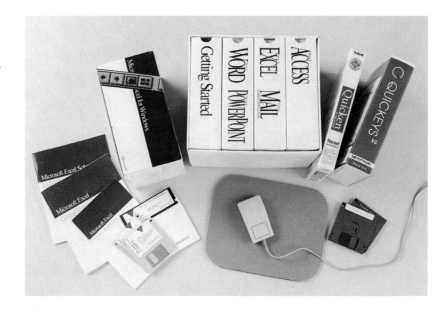

desktop publishing), spreadsheets, database management, graphics, and communications. We will present a description of each category here.

Word Processing

The most widely used software is for **word processing.** This software lets you create, edit, format, store, and print text. From this definition, it is the three words in the middle—*edit*, *format*, and *store*—that make word processing different from plain typing. Since you can store on disk the memo or document you type, you can retrieve it another time, change its content or appearance, save it again, and reprint it. The timesaving factor is that the unchanged parts of the saved document do not need to be retyped, and the whole document can be reprinted as if new. Businesses use word processing for every conceivable type of document—in fact, for everything that used to be typed.

In the task called **desktop publishing,** users employ software and a high-quality printer to produce printed materials that combine graphics with text. The resulting professional-looking newsletters, reports, and brochures can improve communication and help organizations make a better impression on the outside world (Figure 2-11). Although sophisticated users invoke software specifically designed for desktop publishing, many users produce similar results with the desktop publishing features inherent in their word processing software. Since publishing in one form or another typically consumes up to 10 percent of a company's gross revenues, desktop publishing has been given a warm welcome by business. Home users are becoming just as captivated by this technology, as evidenced by the improved look of club newsletters and other "homemade" publications you may find in your mailbox.

Spreadsheets

Used to organize and analyze business data, a **spreadsheet** is a worksheet divided into columns and rows. For example, the simple expense spreadsheet in Figure 2-12a shows time periods (months) as columns and

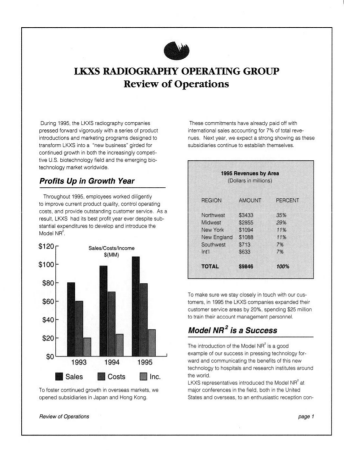

◀

Figure 2-11   Desktop publishing.
Desktop publishing software lets users produce attractive output that combines text and graphics.

various categories (rent, phone, and so forth) as rows. Notice the calculations: the figures in the rightmost column are the sums of the items in that row—the expense total—and the figures in the last row are the sum of the items in that column—the month total. Manual spreadsheets have been used as business tools for centuries. But a spreadsheet can be tedious to prepare by hand, and when there are changes a considerable amount of work may need to be redone. An **electronic spreadsheet** (Figure 2-12b) is still a spreadsheet, but the computer does much of the work. In particular, spreadsheet software automatically recalculates the results when a number used in calculations is changed. The ability to automatically recalculate lets businesses experiment with numbers based on different forecasts or predictions—a kind of experimentation called "What-if" analysis—and obtain the results quickly. Many spreadsheet programs will also convert the spreadsheet into a graph or chart (Figure 2-12c).

Database Management

Software used for **database management,** a variation on old-fashioned record keeping, is the management of a collection of interrelated facts. The software can store data, update it, manipulate it, and create reports in a variety of forms. A concert promoter, for example, can store and change data about upcoming concert dates, seating, ticket prices, and sales. The promoter can then use the software to retrieve information such as the number of tickets sold in each price range or the percentage of tickets sold the day before the concert. The promotor could list events

DISCUSSION QUESTION

How are spreadsheets used in "what-if" analysis?

EXPENSES	JANUARY	FEBRUARY	MARCH	APRIL	TOTAL
RENT	425.00	425.00	425.00	425.00	1700.00
PHONE	22.50	31.25	17.00	35.75	106.50
CLOTHES	110.00	135.00	156.00	91.00	492.00
FOOD	280.00	250.00	250.00	300.00	1080.00
HEAT	80.00	50.00	24.00	95.00	249.00
ELECTRICITY	35.75	40.50	45.00	36.50	157.75
WATER	10.00	11.00	11.00	10.50	42.50
CAR INSURANCE	75.00	75.00	75.00	75.00	300.00
ENTERTAINMENT	150.00	125.00	140.00	175.00	590.00
TOTAL	1188.25	1142.75	1143.00	1243.75	4717.75

(a)

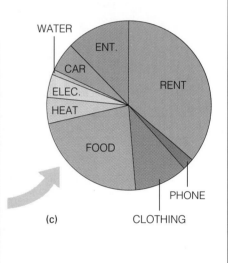

```
           A          B       C       D       E       F       G
 1    ▉▉▉▉▉▉▉▉▉
 2                    JAN     FEB     MAR     APR    TOTAL
 3
 4    EXPENSES
 5    RENT           425.00  425.00  425.00  425.00 1700.00
 6    PHONE           22.50   31.25   17.00   35.75  106.50
 7    CLOTHES        110.00  135.00  156.00   91.00  492.00
 8    FOOD           280.00  250.00  250.00  300.00 1080.00
 9    HEAT            80.00   50.00   24.00   95.00  249.00
10    ELECTRICITY     35.75   40.50   45.00   36.50  157.75
11    WATER           10.00   11.00   11.00   10.50   42.50
12    CAR INSURANCE   75.00   75.00   75.00   75.00  300.00
13    ENTERTAINMENT  150.00  125.00  140.00  175.00  590.00
14
15
16    TOTAL         1188.25 1142.75 1143.00 1243.75 4717.75
17
18
19
20
21
      02:39 PM
```

(c)

(b)

▲

Figure 2-12   A simple expense spreadsheet.
(a) This expense sheet is a typical spreadsheet of rows and columns. Note the calculations needed to generate the values in the rightmost column and the bottom row. (b) This spreadsheet summarizes the same information, but now the computer is doing the calculations. (c) Here the same information has been transformed into a simple computer-generated pie chart.

in order of data or ticket price. Database software can be useful to keep track of and extract subsets from large amounts of data.

Graphics

Maps, charts, and other **graphics** help people compare data, spot trends easily, and make decisions quickly (Figure 2-13). Six pages of numeric

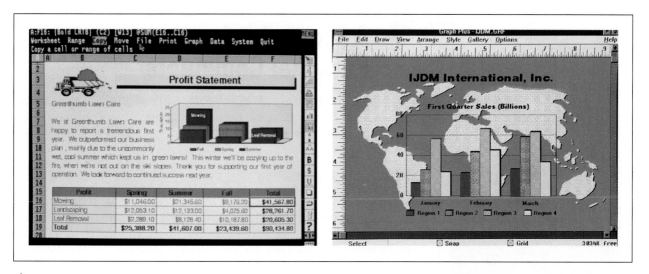

▲

Figure 2-13   Business graphics.
These colorful computer-generated graphics can help people compare data and
spot trends.

confusion can be made into a single chart that anyone can pick up and
understand.

Communications

From the viewpoint of a worker with a personal computer, data communications means—in simple terms—that he or she can link up the computer with the phone system or some other communications link and
send data to or receive data from a computer in another location. Business users send memos, exchange project data, leave messages, send data
to the headquarters office, access stock quotes, and on and on. Home
users send greetings to friends and family who have computers, transfer
bank funds, buy stocks, make airline reservations, access data banks such
as encyclopedias, and even order products.

 # People and Computers

We have talked about hardware, software, and data, but the most important element in a computer system is people. Anyone nervous about a
takeover by computers will be relieved to know that computers will
never amount to much without people—the people who help make the
system work and the people for whom the work is done.

As we noted earlier, computer users now are simply called users, a
nickname that has persisted for years. Whereas once computer users
were an elite breed—high-powered Ph.D.s, research-and-development
engineers, government planners—the population of users has broadened
considerably. This expansion is due partly to user-friendly software for
both work and personal use and partly to the availability of small, low-
cost computers.

So, I Don't Have to Be a Techie

To be computer literate, you do need to have some knowledge of the terminology. But, to put it in the vernacular, you do not have to become a professional "techie." Just what computer-related skills *are* desirable to take to the job world? Here is one person's list of the subjects you should know something about, no matter what career you pursue: word processing, desktop publishing, spreadsheets, graphics, databases, communications, interfacing with operating system software, getting on and off a computer network, using electronic mail, using fax software, buying a computer and peripherals, evaluating and buying software, and computer security and ethics.

It is too soon in your course of study to have even a passing acquaintance with all these concepts. But it is not too soon to set goals and begin meeting them.

A Closer Look at Personal Computers

We have taken a general tour of computer hardware, but for most people the computer of interest is the personal computer. Let us begin by considering what is inside a personal computer.

Basic Components

It is really pretty easy to have a look inside most personal computers; you may not even need a screwdriver. (Caution: Some manufacturers are *not* interested in having you peer under the hood, and doing so will void your warranty. Check your documentation—your instruction manual—first.) You will find an impressive array of electronic gear. If you look inside your personal computer, part of what you see before you is the central processing unit and memory.

A miniaturized central processing unit can be etched on a chip smaller than a thumbtack (Figure 2-14), hence the term *computer on a chip*. A central processing unit on a chip is called a **microprocessor.** The type of microprocessor in your personal computer depends on the computer you purchased. In addition to the microprocessor, a personal computer has two kinds of memory chips: random access memory (RAM) and read-only memory (ROM). **Random access memory (RAM)** chips hold the data and instructions currently being used. **Read-only memory (ROM)** stores programs that you cannot alter. We will explore microprocessors and memory components in some detail in Chapter 3.

External computer components vary. You need a keyboard, of course, so you can interact with the computer. Also, you need a video screen to display input and output. Most personal computers have a separate screen (or monitor) and a detached keyboard, so the positions of these components can be adjusted for individual comfort.

For secondary storage purposes, you need a disk drive to read and write on diskettes and, in particular, to load software into the computer. In addition, hard disks are available for most personal computers.

Basic personal computer hardware consists of memory, a central processing unit, a keyboard, a screen, and a storage device. In addition, most systems have a printer; paper is a communication medium that is hard to do without. The printers most often used with personal computers are dot-matrix and laser printers. Printers are described in more detail in Chapter 4 and in the "Buyer's Guide."

Additional Equipment

You have seen people buy every kind of gadget for their boat or car or camper. For computer users, the story is no different. In this discussion *add-ons* refers loosely to any device that attaches to the computer so that it can participate in the computer's work. An example is a mouse or an extra disk drive. *Accessories* are convenience items—such as dustcovers, lockup cables, and diskette trays—that are not directly related to the

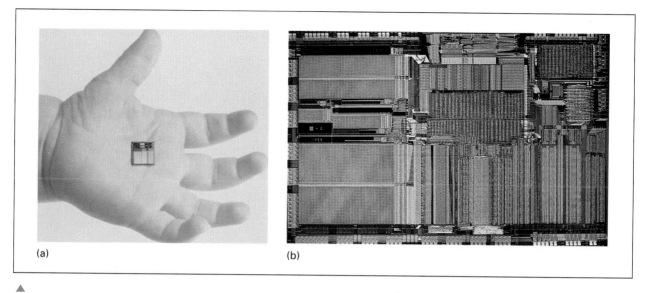

(a)   (b)

Figure 2-14   Computer on a chip.
(a) Microprocessors are small enough to fit on the palm of a baby's hand—with room to spare. (b) This is the Intel 80486 chip. Although the circuitry is complex, the entire chip is smaller than your thumbnail.

Figure 2-15   Extra circuitry.
This add-on circuit board is being inserted into an expansion slot of an IBM PS/2 computer.

computer's work. Finally, *supplies* are necessary consumable goods, such as printer paper and diskettes.

Is "the box" expandable or not? That is the heart of the personal computer add-on discussion. An expandable computer is designed so that users can buy additional circuit boards and insert them in **expansion slots** (slots inside the computer) to support add-ons (Figure 2-15). If the machine is not expandable, add-ons are limited to those that can be plugged into the back of the computer. If you have an expandable machine, there is a host of add-ons you might like to consider: more

DISCUSSION QUESTION

What is the purpose of expansion slots?

memory; a hard disk; a color monitor; a modem to access data communications systems; a video camera; and input devices, such as a joy stick, light pen, or mouse.

▼ ▼ ▼

In this chapter we have painted computer components with a broad brush, touching on hardware, software, data, and people. We will move on in the next chapter to examine hardware in more detail, beginning with the central processing unit.

Chapter **Review**

Summary and Key Terms

- The equipment in a computer system is called **hardware.** The **programs,** or step-by-step instructions that run the machines, are called **software. Computer programmers** write programs for **users,** or **end-users**—that is, people who use computer software.
- A **computer** is a machine that can be programmed to process data (input) into useful information (output). A computer system comprises four main categories of data handling—input, processing, output, and storage.
- **Input** is data put into the computer. Common **input devices** include a **keyboard;** a **mouse;** a **wand reader,** which scans special letters and numbers such as those on specially printed price tags in retail stores; and a **bar code reader,** which scans the zebra-striped **bar codes** on store products.
- A **terminal** includes an input device; an **output device,** usually a television-like **screen;** and a connection to the main computer. A screen displays both the input data and the processed information.
- The **central processing unit (CPU)** uses software to organize raw **data** into meaningful, useful **information.** It interprets and executes program instructions and communicates with the input, output, and storage devices. **Memory,** also called **primary storage,** is associated with the central processing unit but is separate from it. Memory holds the input data before and after processing, until the data is released to the output device.
- **Output,** raw data processed into usable information, is usually in the form of words, numbers, and graphics. Users can see output displayed on screens and use **printers** to display output on paper.
- Computer memory is limited and temporary. Therefore, **secondary storage** is needed, most commonly in the form of magnetic disks and magnetic tape. **Magnetic disks** can be diskettes or hard disks. **Diskettes** are usually 3½ inches (or perhaps 5¼ inches) in diameter. **Hard disks,** often contained in disk packs, hold more data than a diskette. Disk data is read by **disk drives. Magnetic tape** comes on reels that are mounted on **tape drives** when the data is to be read by the computer. **Optical disk** technology uses a laser beam to store large volumes of data relatively inexpensively.
- **Peripheral equipment** includes all the input, output, and secondary storage devices attached to a computer.
- Computers can be loosely categorized according to their capacity for processing data. The most powerful and expensive computers are called **supercomputers.** Large computers are called **mainframes. Minicomputers** were originally intended to be small but have become increasingly similar to mainframes in capacity. Therefore, the largest and most expensive minicomputers are now called **superminis.** The next step down in size are **microcomputers** or **personal computers (PCs). Supermicros,** generally faster and more powerful than other personal computers, have significantly increased memory and hard disk storage capacity. **Laptop computers,** also called **notebook computers,** are small portable computers. **Pen-based computers,** also called **personal digital assistants (PDAs),** accept handwritten input directly on a screen.
- **System software,** also called **operating systems,** is the underlying software found on all computers. **Applications software** solves a particular problem or performs a particular task. Applications software may be either custom or packaged. **Custom software** is

specifically tailored to user needs. **Packaged software,** also called commercial software, is packaged in a container and sold in stores or catalogs.

■ Software is accompanied by an instruction manual, also called **documentation.** Software that is easy to use is considered **user friendly.**

■ Task-oriented software falls, for the most part, into just a few categories: **word processing, desktop publishing, spreadsheet (or electronic spreadsheet), database management, graphics,** and **communications.**

■ The main components of a personal computer are the microprocessor, random access memory (RAM), and read-only memory (ROM). A keyboard is used for inputting data, and a video screen displays input and output. A disk drive is used for reading and writing diskettes.

■ A **microprocessor,** also called a computer on a chip, contains the computer's central processing unit. **Random access memory (RAM)** chips hold the data and instructions currently being used. **Read-only memory (ROM)** stores programs that cannot be altered by the user.

■ *Add-ons* refers to devices that attach to the computer so that they can participate in the computer's work. *Accessories* are convenience items that are not directly related to the computer's work. *Supplies* are necessary consumable goods, such as printer paper.

■ Expandable computers allow users to insert additional circuit boards into **expansion slots** inside the computers. Nonexpandable computers limit add-ons to those that can be plugged into the back of the computers.

Student Personal Study Guide

True/False

T F 1. The processor is also called the central processing unit, or CPU.

T F 2. Secondary storage units contain the instructions and data to be used immediately by the processor.

T F 3. Desktop publishing software is used primarily to store and retrieve information.

T F 4. Processed data that is organized, meaningful, and useful is called information.

T F 5. *User friendly* refers to a special kind of terminal.

T F 6. To use a computer, you need not know its internal functions.

T F 7. PDAs are also called mainframes.

T F 8. Mainframes are also called notebook computers.

T F 9. Computers can be classified, smallest to largest, as mainframes, microcomputers, or minicomputers.

T F 10. Custom software may be purchased off the shelf.

Multiple Choice

1. Holds instructions and data for processing:
   a. CPU   c. RAM
   b. slot   d. microprocessor
2. The storage technology that uses laser beams:
   a. optical tape   c. magnetic tape
   b. magnetic disk   d. optical disk
3. Another name for programs:
   a. software   c. data
   b. RAM   d. storage

4. Storage and retrieval of data is a key function of:
   a. desktop publishing   c. graphics
   b. database management   d. documentation
5. Software that prints high-quality combined text and graphics:
   a. spreadsheets   c. word processing
   b. desktop publishing   d. graphics
6. A "computer on a chip":
   a. RAM   c. optical disk
   b. microprocessor   d. primary storage
7. The zebra-striped identifier on a store product:
   a. key   c. bar code
   b. magnetic tape   d. wand
8. One type of secondary storage:
   a. RAM   c. wand reader
   b. mouse   d. optical disk
9. The computer converts raw data into:
   a. input   c. custom software
   b. processor   d. information
10. Another name for memory:
    a. primary storage   c. diskette
    b. hard disk   d. secondary storage

Fill-In

1. After it is input but just before it is processed, data is held in _____ .

2. The input, output, and secondary storage devices attached to a computer are called

   _____ .

3. Another name for laptop computers is _____ .

4. Another name for personal digital assistants is _____ .

5. Software to help people compare data and spot trends at a glance is called

   _____ .

6. Computers linked together are said to be part of a _____ .

7. Software that is easy to use is said to be _____ .

8. Software created for a specific user is called _____ .

9. The planned step-by-step instructions required to turn data into information are

   _____ .

10. The most powerful computers are called _____ .

Answers

True/False: 1. T, 2. F, 3. F, 4. T, 5. F, 6. T, 7. F, 8. F, 9. F, 10. F
Multiple choice: 1. c, 2. d , 3. a , 4. b, 5. b, 6. b, 7. c, 8. d, 9. d, 10. a
Fill-In: 1. memory, 2. peripheral equipment, 3. notebook, 4. pen-based computers, 5. graphics, 6. network, 7. user friendly, 8. custom , 9. software (or program), 10. supercomputers

Interview: The Information Superhighway

Randy Katz, who works for the Advanced Research Projects Agency (ARPA) of the Department of Defense, talks about the information superhighway.

Can you start with a little bit about your background?
I'm a professor of computer science at the University of California at Berkeley. After the 1992 election, I got excited about a bunch of young guys coming to Washington who seemed to have high technology as part of their agenda. I took a leave from the university to become a program manager at ARPA, which has a long tradition of being the federal government's lead agency in technology research and development.

Is it possible to give a simple explanation of the information superhighway?
OK. Everyone understands what a highway is. Before we had the interstate highway system, just about everything you purchased was grown or built locally. It would have been pretty unusual for someone in Florida to be eating apples that were grown in Washington state. But once the highway system was in place, in the 1950s, it opened up new markets. It really didn't matter where the stuff was produced; it could be sold anywhere in the country.

Now we'll do the same thing for information services. It doesn't matter where the information is located. The Library of Congress may have fabulous collections of ancient books and, if I am in Nebraska, I don't have to get on an airplane and fly to Washington, D.C., to gain access to those reference materials. The information is available by tapping into the information superhighway. Any information that is available anyplace can be accessed anywhere in the country if I'm on the information superhighway.

How does the information superhighway differ from the online services that we already have available, such as America Online or Internet?
Those services are early versions of the information superhighway. The problem is that they must be accessed through a computer, and computers are not in every home. But most homes in the United States do have a telephone and a television set, and almost

Exploring

everyone knows how to use them. These are the sort of components to consider for the information superhighway.

But what will the people connection to the information superhighway actually look like?
The truth is no one really knows. For one approach, industry is making major investments to incorporate the television system as part of the information superhighway. Your television will be like a computer screen, but it doesn't have a keyboard or anything like that. You would have some sort of remote

control device, sort of like the one you use with your television now, that you would use to make selections from menus of services and information. A good example is a movie-on-demand service. You turn on your television set, then use a remote control device to make your selection. The fact that there might be a computer embedded in that television set is pretty much immaterial to the person who is using the television set.

How does the federal government fit into the development of the information superhighway?

Consider this true story. In the mid-1800s, Samuel Morse, with government research funding, put in the first telegraph link between Washington, D.C., and Baltimore. So the idea came from an entrepreneur in the private sector, but the money came from the government. People thought it was incredible that you could send a message 50 miles. So

between the private sector and the federal government to demonstrate a concept, and then the private sector takes over. That's the model the government would like to have now for the information superhighway.

When will we have an information superhighway in place?
I firmly believe that the information superhighway is a

> **Any information that is available anyplace can be accessed anywhere in the country if I'm on the information superhighway.**

Morse said to the government, "Well, give me more money and we'll build this all around the country." But the government said, "No, if this is such a great idea, you should be able to provide your own backers to build a private sector system to do this," which is exactly what he did. And that's the basis of Western Union.

So the United States has a long tradition of a partnership in the early stages

ten-year, if not longer, development process. However, in the next few years, from the government's perspective, I think there will be a complete revolution in the regulatory environment for telecommunications. They will open things up so there will be much greater competition.

Hardware

Chapter Overview

LEARNING OBJECTIVES:

- Knowing the components of the central processing unit and how they work together
- Understanding how program instructions are executed by the computer
- Understanding how data is represented in the computer
- Knowing the chips available for personal computers
- Having an appreciation for computer processing speeds

Sue Ewing, an accounting major, worked with spreadsheets on a computer as part of her summer job. She decided that it would be helpful to have a personal computer of her own when she went back to college in the fall. But she felt unsure of how to make a purchase. In fact, she felt she did not even know what questions to ask. She discussed this with an office colleague, who casually noted that any computer setup comes with the "standard stuff"—processor, keyboard, screen, disk drives—and that all she had to do was go to a computer store and pick one that fit her price range. Sue was not satisfied with this approach, especially in light of the advertisements she had seen in the local newspaper and in computer magazines.

Most advertisements displayed photos of personal computers, accompanied by cryptic descriptions of the total hardware package. A typical ad was worded this way: *486DX, 50MHz, 8MB RAM, 128K cache, 1.44MB diskette drive, 320MB hard drive.* The price for this particular machine was pretty hefty—over $2000. Sue noticed in the ads that machines with lower numbers—for example, only 25MHz—also had lower price tags. Similarly, higher numbers meant higher price tags. Although she did recognize the term *disk drives*, she had no idea what the other items were or why the numbers mattered. Clearly, there was more to a

purchasing decision than selecting a system with the "standard stuff."

Sue tore out some of the ads and marched to a nearby computer store. After asking a lot of questions, she learned that *486* is a type of microprocessor, that *MHz* stands for megahertz and is a measurement of the microprocessor's speed, that *RAM* is the computer's memory, that *cache* is a kind of handy storage place for frequently used data and software instructions, and that *MB* is an abbreviation for megabytes, a measurement of the capacity of some parts of the computer. All this was somewhat understandable, but she remained confused about the

DX after the *486*—something about a *bus line*, a way for data to travel around. Most importantly, Sue learned that the number variations mattered because they were factors in determining the computer's capacity and speed.

Many buyers do select their personal computer systems merely on the basis of a sales pitch and price range. Those people could argue, with some success, that they do not need to know all the computer buzzwords any more than they need to know the technical details of their television sets or sound systems. They know that they do not have to understand a computer's innards to put it to work.

But there are rewards for those who want to dig a little deeper, learn a little more. Although this chapter is not designed to help you purchase a computer (see the "Buyer's Guide" for that), it does provide some background information and gives you the foundation on which future computer knowledge can be built.

Processing
What Goes On Inside the Computer

The Central Processing Unit

The human element in computing is involved with data input and information output, but the controlling activities of the computer lie in between. The **central processing unit (CPU)** is a highly complex, extensive set of electrical circuits. It executes the stored program instructions that accept the input, process the data, and produce the output. As Figure 3-1 shows, it consists of two parts:

■ The control unit
■ The arithmetic/logic unit

Let us consider each of these components of the central processing unit.

The Control Unit

The **control unit** contains circuitry that uses electrical signals to direct and coordinate the entire computer system in carrying out, or executing,

Figure 3-1   The central processing unit.
The two parts of the CPU are the control unit and the arithmetic/logic unit. Memory holds data and instructions temporarily at the time the program is being executed. The CPU interacts closely with memory, referring to it for both instructions and data.

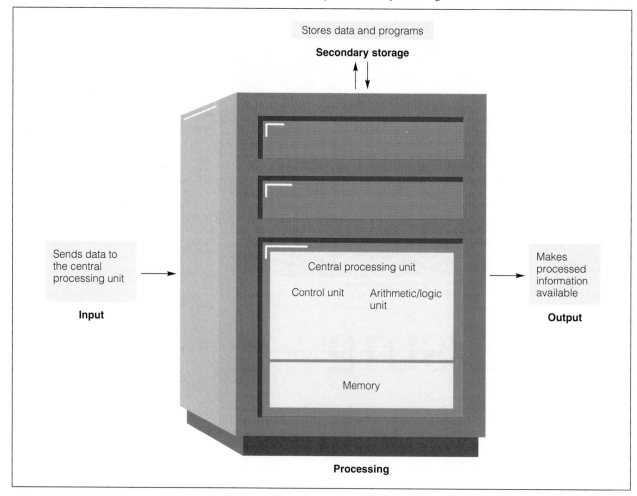

stored program instructions. Like an orchestra leader, the control unit does not execute the instructions itself; rather, it directs other parts of the system to do so. The control unit must communicate with both the arithmetic/logic unit and memory.

The Arithmetic/Logic Unit

The **arithmetic/logic unit (ALU)** contains the electronic circuitry that executes all **arithmetic operations,** such as addition and multiplication, and **logical operations,** which are usually comparing operations. The arithmetic/logic unit is able to compare numbers, letters, or special characters and take alternative courses of action. Comparing operations can determine whether one value is equal to, less than, or greater than another. This is a very important capability. It is by comparing that a computer is able to tell, for instance, whether an airplane has any unfilled seats, whether charge-card customers have exceeded their credit limits, or whether one candidate for Congress has more votes than another.

Registers: Temporary Storage Areas

As the control unit and the arithmetic/logic unit do their work, they use registers. **Registers** are temporary storage areas for instructions or data. Registers are associated with the CPU, not memory. They can operate very rapidly to accept, hold, and transfer instructions or data used in performing arithmetic or logical comparisons—all under the direction of the control unit of the CPU. In other words, they are temporary storage areas that assist transfers and arithmetic/logical operations.

Many machines assign special roles to certain types of registers, including

- An **accumulator,** which collects the results of computations.
- A **storage register,** which temporarily holds data taken from or about to be sent to memory.
- An **address register,** which tells where a given instruction or piece of data is stored in memory. Each storage location in memory is identified by an **address,** just as each apartment in an apartment building is identified by an address.
- A **general-purpose register,** which is used for several functions—for example, arithmetic and addressing purposes.

Consider registers in the context of the operation of the entire machine. Registers hold data *immediately* related to the operation being executed. Memory is used to store data that will be used in the *near future.* In contrast, secondary storage holds data that may be needed *later* in the same program execution or perhaps at some more remote time in the future. To compare the uses of registers, memory, and secondary storage, consider a payroll program as the computer calculates the salary of an employee. As the multiplication of hours worked by rate of pay of an employee is about to take place, these two figures are ready in their respective registers. Other data related to the salary calculation—overtime hours, bonuses, deductions, and so forth—is waiting nearby in memory. The data for other employees is available in secondary storage. As the computer continues executing the payroll program, the data for

DISCUSSION QUESTION

What are the functions of the ALU?

LECTURE HINT

The world's fastest computers are almost doubling in speed every three years. The current goal of supercomputer makers is to create computers that can perform 1 trillion calculations a second (called a teraflop), which is 1000 times faster than the most powerful supercomputers today.

DISCUSSION QUESTION

Describe the various types of registers available in computers.

Personal Computers In Action

A Computer in Your Pocket

When most people think of personal computers "in action," they picture someone sitting at a keyboard. What if your personal computer—or possibly one of your personal computers—were the size of your wallet? In fact, what if that tiny personal computer had everything in it that your wallet now carries, and also information that used to be maintained on your calendar or notebook?

Think about the contents of your wallet. Most of the items there are for some sort of identification: driver's license, credit cards, office entry

key cards, perhaps a membership card for a health organization. Your pocket personal computer could contain all your authentication credentials, which could be displayed on a small flat screen. Furthermore, the computer could store important

dates, meetings, and your daily schedule. It could even include pictures of the kids, whose smiling faces would beam from the screen on command.

This is part of the vision of the future put forth by Bill Gates, the energetic chairman of Microsoft Corporation, the world's largest software company. Noting that computers have made once-common items such as typewriters, ledger books, ticker tape, and adding machines pretty much obsolete, Gates thinks that the ordinary wallet will someday be added to that list.

the next employee is brought from secondary storage into memory and eventually into the registers as the calculations for that employee are ready to begin.

TEST BANK

T/F 23
Matching I 56
Fill In 91

LECTURE HINT

As microprocessors continue to increase in speed, they are often kept waiting due to slower memory chips. One approach is to create faster memory chips. Another approach is to create faster data pathways, which move the data between the microprocessors and memory.

DISCUSSION QUESTION

Why is it not feasible to keep your data in memory when your program is not running?

 ## Memory

Memory is also referred to as **primary storage, primary memory, main storage, internal storage,** and **main memory**—all these terms are used interchangeably. Memory (also called *random access memory*, or RAM, as noted in the previous chapter) is the part of the computer that holds data and instructions for processing. Although closely associated with the central processing unit, memory is technically separate from it. (However, specific items such as watches or microwave ovens may combine the CPU and memory on a single chip.) Memory is used only temporarily. That is, it holds your program and data only as long as your program is in operation. For this reason memory is often called the computer's scratch pad.

For the following reasons it is not feasible to keep your data in memory when your program is not running:

- Most types of memory store data only while the computer is turned on—the data disappears when the machine is turned off.
- If you share a computer (in a mainframe environment, for example), other people will be using the computer and need the memory space.

COMPUTING TRENDS

Don't Even Bother to Slow Down

Anyone who spends a few minutes of each day handing over change at a toll booth, or perhaps gingerly tossing coins out the car window into a toll container, will be pleased to learn about the trend toward automated toll collection. The concept is ingeniously simple and a solid example of how computers can help to iron out the wrinkles in everyday living.

Here's how it works. As a regular toll user, you buy a chip-imbedded tag and place it on your car's windshield. The tag has your identification and the amount of money in your prepaid toll account. As the car approaches the toll road, the tag exchanges radio signals with the

highway's computers, which charge a toll against the prepaid account. Surveillance cameras record the license numbers of cars without proper tags. Fare beaters may be nabbed by the police on the spot or fined by mail.

These systems are in the works in half a dozen states. In addition to saving time for motorists, other benefits include increased safety at toll plazas and possibly, due to lower expenses, reduced tolls in the future.

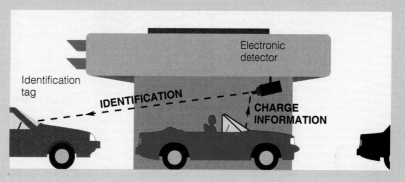

■ The computer may not have enough room in memory to hold your processed data.

Therefore, data and programs are kept in secondary storage, usually on disk, when not in use.

Data and instructions from an input device are put into memory by the control unit. Data is then sent from memory to the registers, where an arithmetic operation or logical operation is performed by the arithmetic/logic unit. After being processed the information is returned to memory, where it is held until it is ready to be incorporated into other calculations or released to an output unit.

How the CPU Executes Program Instructions

Let us examine the way the central processing unit, in association with memory, executes a computer program. We will be looking at how just one instruction in the program is executed. In fact, most computers today can execute only one instruction at a time.

Before an instruction can be executed, program instructions and data must be placed into memory from an input device or a secondary storage device. In the payroll example the program instructions tell the computer the formula for computing a salary. (Keep in mind that a user would not need to know anything about the program itself, only how to give it input.)

As Figure 3-2 shows, the central processing unit then performs the following four steps for each instruction:

▶ **Figure 3-2 The machine cycle.**
Program instructions and data are brought into memory from an external device, either an input device or secondary storage. The machine cycle executes instructions one at a time.

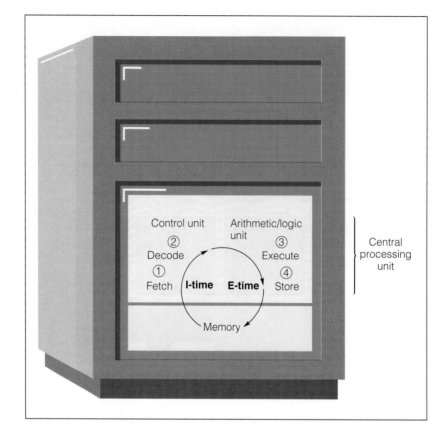

1. The control unit "fetches" (gets) the instruction from memory.
2. The control unit decodes the instruction (decides what it means) and gives instructions for necessary data to be moved from memory to the arithmetic/logic unit. These first two steps are called instruction time, or **I-time.**
3. The arithmetic/logic unit executes arithmetic and logic instructions. That is, the ALU is given control and performs the actual operation on the data.
4. The result of this operation is stored in memory or in a temporary location, a register. Steps 3 and 4 are called execution time, or **E-time.**

After the appropriate instructions are executed, the control unit directs memory to release the results to an output device or a secondary storage device. The combination of I-time and E-time is called the **machine cycle.**

 # Data Representation: On/Off

We think of computers as complex mechanisms, but the fact is that these machines basically know only two things: on and off. This on/off, yes/no, two-state system is called a **binary system.** Using the two states, which can be represented by electricity turned on or off, the computer can construct sophisticated ways of representing data.

Let us look at one way the two states can be used to represent data. Whereas the decimal number system has a base of 10 (with the digits 0, 1, 2, 3, 4, 5, 6, 7, 8, and 9), the binary system has a base of 2. This means it contains only two digits, 0 and 1, which correspond to the two states off and on. Physically, a 1 means an electrical circuit is on, whereas a 0 means the circuit is off.

Bits, Bytes, and Words

Each 0 or 1 in the binary system is called a **bit** (for *bi*nary digi*t*). The bit is the basic unit for representing data in computer memory. Since there are more numbers, letters, and special characters (such as $ and ?) than there are digits in the binary system, combinations of bits are used to represent them. Bits are put together in a group called a **byte.** Each byte, usually 8 bits, represents one character of data—a letter, a digit, or a special character. The process of coding groups of bits into bytes will be discussed shortly.

A computer **word,** typically the size of a register, is defined as the number of bits that constitute a common unit of data, as defined by the computer system. The length of a word varies by computer. Generally, the larger the word, the more powerful the computer. There was a time when word size alone could classify a computer. Common word lengths are 8 bits (for very early personal computers), 16 bits (for traditional minicomputers and some personal computers), 32 bits (for full-size mainframe computers, some minicomputers, and some personal computers), and 64 bits (traditionally for supercomputers). A recent microprocessor, Intel's Pentium, intended for both personal computers and larger machines, is a 64-bit chip. As you can see, the old stereotypes no longer fit very well. Note that an 8-bit machine can handle only one byte (character) at a time, whereas a 64-bit machine can handle 8 bytes at a time, making its processing speed eight times faster.

Computer manufacturers express the capacity of memory in terms of the number of bytes it can hold. The number of bytes is expressed as **kilobytes,** 2 to the 10th power (2^{10}), or 1024 bytes. *Kilobyte* is abbreviated **KB,** or simply **K.** Thus, the memory of a 640K computer can store 640×1024, or 655,360 bytes of data. Memory capacity is most often expressed in terms of a **megabyte** (1024×1024), abbreviated **MB.** One megabyte is roughly one million bytes. Some large computers express memory in terms of **gigabytes** (abbreviated **GB**)—billions of bytes.

Coding Schemes

As we said, a byte—a collection of bits—represents a character of data. But just what particular set of bits is equivalent to which character? In theory we could each make up our own definitions, declaring certain bit patterns to represent certain characters. Needless to say, this would be about as practical as each person speaking his or her own special language. Since we need to communicate with the computer and with each other, it is appropriate that we use a common scheme for data representation. That is, there must be agreement on which groups of bits represent which characters.

The code called **ASCII** (pronounced "AS-key"), which stands for American Standard Code for Information Interchange, uses 7 bits for

A Member of the Family: PENTIUM

The Intel Corporation has provided personal computer makers with several generations of microprocessor chips. The first was a standard-setter: the 8088 chip used by the first IBM PC (introduced in 1981) and its many imitators. The next member of the family, the 80186 chip, was merely a transitional chip, soon replaced by the 80286 chip, which powered the IBM PC AT and, again, a slew of clones.

Intel moved to increase power and flexibility with the introduction of the 80386 chip, first brought to the market in the Compaq 386. The 80386 chip let users run several programs at once, a capability formerly reserved for minicomputers and mainframes. Close on the heels of the 80386 chip was the 80486 (known as the 486), a chip whose speed and power made it popular through the early 1990s.

The next chip, trotted out in 1993, was expected to be christened the 80586. However, citing proprietary problems, Intel called it Pentium, based on the Latin root word meaning five. The amazing Pentium chip is twice as fast as the fastest 486 chip. But the most stunning news is its word size: 64 bits. Pentium's biggest contribution, however, may be that it can be used not only in personal computers but also in mid-size and mainframe computers, offering the possibility of using the same software on all these machines.

LECTURE HINT

An alternative coding system used for IBM mainframe computers is called EBCDIC (pronounced "EB-see-dik"), which stands for Extended Binary Coded Decimal Interchange Code. EBCDIC uses 8 bits and can represent up to 256 characters.

Character	ASCII–8
A	0100 0001
B	0100 0010
C	0100 0011
D	0100 0100
E	0100 0101
F	0100 0110
G	0100 0111
H	0100 1000
I	0100 1001
J	0100 1010
K	0100 1011
L	0100 1100
M	0100 1101
N	0100 1110
O	0100 1111
P	0101 0000
Q	0101 0001
R	0101 0010
S	0101 0011
T	0101 0100
U	0101 0101
V	0101 0110
W	0101 0111
X	0101 1000
Y	0101 1001
Z	0101 1010
0	0011 0000
1	0011 0001
2	0011 0010
3	0011 0011
4	0011 0100
5	0011 0101
6	0011 0110
7	0011 0111
8	0011 1000
9	0011 1001

(a)

Letter	ASCII–8
K	0100 1011
I	0100 1001
L	0100 1100
O	0100 1111
B	0100 0010
Y	0101 1001
T	0101 0100
E	0100 0101

(b)

▲

Figure 3-3 The ASCII code.
(a) Shown are the ASCII-8 binary representations for letters and digits. This is not the complete code; there are many characters missing, such as lowercase letters and punctuation marks. The binary representation is in two columns to improve readability. (b) ASCII-8 representation for the word *KILOBYTE*.

each character. Since there are exactly 128 unique combinations of 7 bits, this 7-bit code can represent only characters. A more common version is ASCII-8, also called extended ASCII, which uses 8 bits per character and can represent 256 different characters. For example, the letter *A* is represented by 01000001. The ASCII representation has been adopted as a standard by the U.S. government and is found in a variety of computers, particularly minicomputers and microcomputers. Figure 3-3 shows part of the ASCII-8 code.

Personal Computer Chips Revisited

TEST BANK

Mult. Choice 19
T/F 43-47
Matching I 59-60
Matching II 63-64
Fill In 71, 74

In Chapter 2 we gave you an overview of the microprocessor chip, and RAM and ROM memory chips. Here we will study them in more detail.

A Closer Look at Microprocessors

Over the years the architecture of microprocessors has become somewhat standardized. Microprocessors usually include these key components: a control unit and an arithmetic/logic unit (the CPU), registers, and a clock. (Clocks are often on a separate chip in personal computers.) Notably missing is memory, which usually comes on its own chips.

Three decades of extraordinary advances in technology have packed increasingly greater power onto increasingly smaller chips (Figure 3-4). Engineers can now imprint as much circuitry on a single chip as filled room-size computers in the early days of data processing.

Memory Components

Earlier in the chapter we talked about memory and how it interfaces with the central processing unit. Now we will examine the memory components. Historically, memory components have evolved from primitive vacuum tubes to today's modern semiconductors.

Semiconductor Storage

Most modern computers use **semiconductor storage,** which is made up of thousands of very small circuits—pathways for electric currents—on a silicon chip. Semiconductor storage has several advantages: reliability, compactness, low cost, and lower power usage. Since semiconductor memory can be mass-produced economically, the cost of memory has been considerably reduced. Chip prices have fallen and risen and fallen again, based on a variety of economic and political factors, but they remain a bargain. Semiconductor storage has one major disadvantage: It is **volatile.** That is, semiconductor storage requires continuous electric current to represent data. If the current is interrupted, the data is lost.

A chip is described as **monolithic** because the circuits on a single chip compose an inseparable unit of storage. Each circuit etched on a chip can be in one of two states: either conducting an electric current or not—on or off. The two states can be used to represent the binary digits 1 and 0. As we noted earlier, these digits can be combined to represent characters, thus making the memory chip a storage bin for data and instructions.

(a)   (b)

▲
Figure 3-4   Microprocessor chips.
(a) The tiny size of a microprocessor. (b) This is Intel's Pentium processor, which accommodates a 64-bit word. Although the circuitry is complex, the entire chip is smaller than your thumbnail.

RAM and ROM

RAM keeps the instructions and data for whatever programs you happen to be using at the moment. The data can be accessed in an easy and speedy manner. RAM is usually volatile; as previously noted, this means that its contents are lost once the power is shut off. RAM can be erased or written over at will by the computer software. ROM contains programs and data that are permanently recorded into this type of memory at the factory; they can be read and used, but they cannot be changed by the user. For example, a personal computer probably has a program for calculating square roots in ROM. ROM is nonvolatile—its contents do not disappear when the power is turned off.

The more RAM in your computer, the larger the programs you can run. In recent years the amount of RAM storage in a personal computer has increased dramatically. An early personal computer, for example, was advertised with "a full 4K RAM." Now an astonishing 8MB RAM is common. More memory has become a necessity because sophisticated personal computer software requires significant amounts of memory. You can augment your personal computer's RAM by buying extra memory chips to install in your memory board or by purchasing a **single in-line memory module (SIMM),** a board that contains memory chips. The SIMM board plugs into the computer's main circuit board, which is more convenient than attaching individual chips. In general, the more memory your computer has, the more (and bigger) tasks the computer can do.

Most personal computer memory is dynamic RAM, or **DRAM.** DRAM chips are periodically regenerated, allowing the chips to retain the stored data. Furthermore, DRAM chips offer size and cost advantages.

With specialized tools called **ROM burners,** the instructions within some ROM chips can be changed. These chips are known as **programmable read-only memory (PROM) chips.** There are other variations on ROM chips, depending on the methods used to alter them. The business of programming and altering ROM chips is the province of the computer engineer.

TEST BANK

Mult. Choice 5, 12-13, 20
T/F 48-50
Matching I 51-53, 58
Matching II 62, 69
Fill In 72-73, 75-81

DISCUSSION QUESTION

What factors contribute to the speed of a computer?

DISCUSSION QUESTION

Describe the function of a bus line.

 # Speed and Power

The characteristic of speed is universally associated with computers. Power is a derivative of speed, as well as other factors such as memory size. What makes a computer fast? Or, more to the point, what makes one computer faster than another? Several factors are involved, including microprocessor speed, bus line size, and the availability of cache. A user who is concerned about speed will want to address all of them.

Computer Processing Speeds

Although all computers are fast, there is a wide diversity of computer speeds. The execution of an instruction on a very slow computer may be measured in less than a **millisecond,** which is one-thousandth of a second. Most computers can execute an instruction measured in **microseconds,** one-millionth of a second. Some modern computers have reached the **nanosecond** range—one-billionth of a second. Still to be broken is the **picosecond** barrier—one-trillionth of a second.

Microprocessor speeds are usually expressed in **megahertz (MHz),** millions of machine cycles per second. Thus, a personal computer listed at 25MHz can handle 25 million machine cycles per second. A top-speed personal computer will be more than twice as fast.

Bus Lines

As is so often the case, the computer term *bus* is borrowed from its common meaning—a mode of transportation. A **bus line** is an electrical path that internally transports data from one place to another within the computer system. The amount of data that can be carried at one time is called the bus width. The greater the width, the more data can be carried at a time. Microprocessors are sometimes obscurely affixed with notations that indicate their bus size. For example, a 486DX chip has a bus width of 32 bits, whereas a 486SX chip uses a 32-bit bus within the processor, but only a 16-bit bus between the processor and memory. A buyer who cares about speed would prefer the DX chip, which carries exactly twice as much data, and therefore is twice as fast, as the SX chip.

Cache

A **cache** (pronounced "cash") is a relatively small amount of very fast memory designed for the specific purpose of speeding up the internal transfer of data and software instructions. Think of cache as a selective memory: The data and instructions stored in cache are those that are most recently and/or most frequently used. Data or instructions, when first requested by the microprocessor, must be retrieved from main memory, which delivers them at a relatively slow pace compared to the microprocessor's capabilities. As they are retrieved, those same data/instructions are stored in cache. The next time the microprocessor needs data or instructions, it looks first in cache; if the needed items can be found there, they can be transferred at a rate that far exceeds a trip from main memory. Of course, cache is not big enough to hold everything, so the wanted data or instructions may not be there. But there is a good chance that frequently used items will be in cache. That is, since the most frequently used data and instructions are kept in a handy place, the net result is an improvement in processing speed.

Just how much cache speeds performance depends on a number of factors, including the size of the cache, the speed of the memory chips in the cache, and the software being run. Caching has become such a vital technique that some of the newer microprocessors have cache built into the processor's design. Intel's 486 chip has an 8-kilobyte cache, and the new Pentium processor has dual 8-kilobyte caches, one for data and one for software.

Flash Memory

We have stated that memory is volatile—that it disappears when the power is turned off—hence the need for secondary storage to keep data on a more permanent basis. A long-standing speed problem has been the rate of accessing data from a secondary storage device such as the hard disk, a rate significantly slower than internal computer speeds. It seemed unimaginable that data might someday be stored on nonvolatile memory chips—actual nonvolatile RAM—close at hand. A breakthrough has emerged in the form of nonvolatile **flash memory.** Flash chips are currently being used in cellular phones and cockpit flight recorders, and they are replacing disks in some hand-held computers.

Flash memory is not without problems. The market for these chips has been held up partially because they wear out rather quickly compared to RAM chips. But the main delay is the prohibitive cost of building manufacturing facilities to make flash chips. Although flash memory is not yet commonplace, it seems likely that it will become a mainstream component. Since data and instructions will be ever-closer to the microprocessor, conversion to flash memory chips would have a pivotal impact on a computer's processing speed.

Parallel Processing

The ultimate speed solution is **parallel processing,** a method of using several processors at the same time. Consider the description of computer processing you have seen so far in this chapter: The processor gets an instruction from memory, acts on it, returns processed data to memory, and then repeats the process. This is conventional serial processing.

The problem with the conventional computer is that the single electronic pathway, the bus line, acts like a bottleneck. The computer has a one-track mind because it is restricted to handling one piece of data at a time. For many applications, such as simulating the air flow around an entire airplane in flight, this is an exceedingly inefficient procedure. A better solution? Many processors, each with its own memory unit, working at the same time: parallel processing.

A number of parallel processors are being built and sold commercially. However, do not look for parallel processing in personal computers just yet. Thus far, this technology is limited to larger computers.

▼ ▼ ▼

Doggie Chips

You are in Alaska, bundled up in your parka, monitoring a checkpoint on the annual 1000-mile Iditarod dog sled race. Here they come. But wait. Are those the same dogs that started the race? Let's check the computer.

The computer? Yes, the dogs are individually identifiable, even as they speed by, because each dog wears its own microchip. Organizers of the race use a hypodermic needle to (painlessly) inject a microchip the size of a grain of rice into the fatty folds just under each dog's skin. Then, at certain checkpoints, the dogs are computer scanned to make sure they are the same animals who started the race, thus preventing illegal substitutions. In the prior system, officials spray-painted markings on the dogs for identification. The microchip system has proved to be more effective and harmless to the dogs.

LECTURE HINT

Currently parallel systems account for approximately 10 percent of the world supercomputer market, with sales of about $270 million. This number is in contrast to the estimated $40 billion corporate and government data processing industry.

DISCUSSION QUESTION

How does parallel processing work?

LECTURE HINT

One key to the success of parallel processing is software that can take advantage of the technology. The new software needs to be designed so that several operations can be performed simultaneously.

The central processing unit, remaining unseen, continues to be an amazing workhorse, whether it labors inside a mammoth computer or within a tiny machine like a wristwatch. Users, however, invoke the power of the central processing unit by various computer input methods and reap the rewards from computer output. Input and output are the subjects of the next chapter.

Chapter **Review**

Summary and Key Terms

- The **central processing unit (CPU)** executes program instructions. It consists of a control unit and an arithmetic/logic unit.
- The **control unit** of the CPU coordinates the computer's execution of the program instructions by communicating with the arithmetic/logic unit—the part of the system that actually executes the program—and with memory.
- The **arithmetic/logic unit (ALU)** contains circuitry that executes **arithmetic operations** and **logical operations.** Logical operations are comparisons that determine if one value is equal to, less than, or greater than another.
- **Registers** are temporary storage areas associated with the CPU that quickly accept, hold, and transfer instructions or data. An **accumulator** is a register that collects the results of computations. A **storage register** temporarily holds data taken from memory or about to be sent to memory. An **address register** tells where instructions and data are stored in memory. Each storage location in memory is identified by an **address.** A **general-purpose register** can be used in several ways, such as for arithmetic operations or addressing.
- **Memory** is closely associated with the CPU but not part of it. Memory temporarily holds data and instructions before and after they are processed by the arithmetic/logic unit. Memory is also known as **primary storage, primary memory, main storage, internal storage,** and **main memory.**
- The central processing unit follows four main steps when executing an instruction: It (1) fetches (gets) the instruction from memory, (2) decodes the instruction and directs the transfer of data from memory to the arithmetic/logic unit, (3) directs the ALU to perform the actual operation on the data, and (4) sends the result of the operation to memory or a register. The first two steps are called **I-time** (instruction time), and the last two steps are called **E-time** (execution time). A **machine cycle** is the combination of I-time and E-time.
- Since a computer can only recognize whether electricity is on or off, data is represented by an off/on **binary system.** In a binary system two digits, 0 and 1, correspond to the two states off and on. Combinations of 0s and 1s can represent numbers, digits, or special characters.
- Each 0 or 1 in the binary system is called a **bit** (*bi*nary digi*t*). A group of bits is called a **byte.** Each byte can represent one character of data, such as a letter, digit, or special character. A computer **word** is defined as the number of bits that constitute a common unit of data, as defined by the computer system. Common word lengths are 8, 16, 32, and 64 bits. Memory capacity is expressed in **kilobytes (KB** or **K),** which are equal to 1024 bytes, and **megabytes (MB),** which are millions of bytes. A **gigabyte (GB)** is a billion bytes.
- A common coding scheme for representing characters is **ASCII** (American Standard Code for Information Interchange), which uses 7-bit characters. A variation of the code, called ASCII-8, uses 8 bits per character.
- **Semiconductor storage,** thousands of very small circuits on a silicon chip, is **volatile.** A chip is described as **monolithic** because the circuits on a single chip compose an inseparable unit of storage.

KEY TERMS

accumulator
address
address register
arithmetic/logic unit (ALU)
arithmetic operation
ASCII
binary system
bit
bus line
byte
cache
central processing unit (CPU)
control unit
DRAM
E-time
flash memory
general-purpose register
gigabyte (GB)
internal storage
I-time
kilobyte (KB or K)
logical operation
machine cycle
main memory
main storage
megabyte (MB)
megahertz (MHz)
memory
microsecond
millisecond
monolithic
nanosecond
parallel processing
picosecond
primary memory

primary storage

programmable read-only memory (PROM)

register

ROM burner

semiconductor storage

single in-line memory module (SIMM)

storage register

volatile

word

- RAM keeps the instructions and data for whatever programs you happen to be using at the moment. RAM is usually volatile. ROM contains programs and data that are permanently recorded into this type of memory at the factory; they can be read and used, but they cannot be changed by the user. ROM is nonvolatile.
- A **single in-line memory module (SIMM)** is a plug-in board that contains memory chips.
- Dynamic RAM (**DRAM**) chips are periodically regenerated, allowing the chips to retain the stored data.
- The instructions within some ROM chips can be changed using **ROM burners**; these chips are known as **programmable read-only memory (PROM) chips.**
- Computer instruction speeds fall in various ranges, from a **millisecond**, which is one-thousandth of a second; to a **microsecond**, one-millionth of a second; to a **nanosecond**, one-billionth of a second. Still to be achieved is the **picosecond** range—one-trillionth of a second.
- Microprocessor speeds are usually expressed in **megahertz (MHz)**, millions of machine cycles per second.
- A **bus line** is an electrical path that transports data from one place to another internally within the computer system. The amount of data that can be carried at one time is called the bus width.
- A **cache** is a relatively small amount of very fast memory that stores data and instructions that are used frequently, resulting in an improved processing speed.
- The emerging technology of **flash memory** will provide memory chips that are non-volatile.
- **Parallel processing** uses several processors in the same computer at the same time.

Student Personal Study Guide

True/False

T F 1. The control unit consists of the CPU and the ALU.
T F 2. Semiconductor storage is nonvolatile.
T F 3. A kilobyte (KB) is 1024 bytes.
T F 4. Primary storage is part of the central processing unit.
T F 5. A microsecond is briefer than a millisecond.
T F 6. Logical operations are comparing operations.
T F 7. A word represents one character of data.
T F 8. PROM chips are RAM chips.
T F 9. Parallel processing uses several processors at the same time.
T F 10. A SIMM is a type of register.

Multiple Choice

1. The electrical path that transports data:
   a. RAM   c. bus line
   b. megahertz   d. microprocessor
2. Fast memory that stores frequently used instructions and data:
   a. cache   c. PROM
   b. ALU   d. address register
3. Which is *not* another name for memory?
   a. register   c. primary storage
   b. main memory   d. internal storage

4. The combination of I-time and E-time:
   a. machine time
   b. machine cycle
   c. binary time
   d. megabyte

5. The American standard code for representing characters with bits:
   a. binary digits
   b. ASCII
   c. semiconductor storage
   d. cache

6. Which is *not* used to express memory capacity?
   a. DB
   b. MB
   c. GB
   d. KB

7. A plug-in board of memory chips:
   a. MB
   b. cache
   c. SIMM
   d. PROM

8. Fetch and decode instruction:
   a. CPU
   b. E-time
   c. accumulator register
   d. I-time

9. One-millionth of a second:
   a. millisecond
   b. picosecond
   c. nanosecond
   d. microsecond

10. Which is *not* a type of register?
   a. storage
   b. general purpose
   c. monolithic
   d. address

Fill-In

1. The combination of I-time and E-time: _____ .

2. The two binary digits are _____ .

3. Approximately a billion bytes: _____ .

4. Emerging nonvolatile RAM: _____ .

5. Combination of control unit and ALU: _____ .

6. SIMM stands for _____ .

7. Using several processors in the same computer at the same time: _____ .

8. A chip, whose circuits are on an inseparable unit, is said to be _____ .

9. Program instructions are executed by the _____ .

10. An internal electrical path: _____ .

Answers

True/False: 1. F, 2. F, 3. T, 4. F, 5. T, 6. T, 7. F, 8. F, 9. T, 10. F
Multiple choice: 1. c, 2. a , 3. a , 4. b, 5. b, 6. a, 7. c, 8. d, 9. d, 10.c
Fill-In: 1. machine cycle, 2. 0 and 1, 3. gigabyte, 4. flash memory, 5. central processing unit (CPU), 6. single in-line memory module, 7. parallel processing , 8. monolithic , 9. central processing unit (CPU), 10. bus line

LEARNING OBJECTIVES:

- Appreciating the various forms of input for computer systems.
- Understanding how data is input to a computer system, and appreciating the advantages and disadvantages of each method.
- Knowing the various forms of output for computer systems.
- Appreciating the variety of computer graphics output media and understanding how they work.

Just how are input and output related in a computer system? How do you "get into" a computer system? More formally, how do you provide your own input in a way that the computer can accept? If you can figure that much out, how do you get something back from the computer? Finally, what might the output from the computer be, considering what you gave it as input? There are many possible answers to these questions, but Paul Yen's experience is fairly typical.

Input and

Paul did not have computers in mind as he thumbed through the catalog for Lands' End, a mail-order firm in Wisconsin that offers quality classic dress and sports clothing. Paul wanted to order a turtleneck shirt. He decided on a shirt and a leather belt, and he wrote these items on the order form. Paul's action, whether he knew it or not, started the computer action rolling.

The items on the order form became the input data to the computer system. In this example, input is the data related to the customer order—customer name, address, and (possibly) charge-card number—and data about each item—catalog number, quantity, description, and price. If this input data is handwritten on an order form, it is keyed into the system as soon as it arrives in the mail; if the order is received on the company's toll- free phone line, the Lands' End operator keys the data as the customer speaks the order. This data is placed on customer and order files to be used with files containing inventory and other related data.

The computer can process this data into a variety of outputs, as shown in Box 4-1. Some outputs are for individual customers, and some show information combined from several orders: warehouse orders, shipping labels (to send the shirt and belt), back-order notices, inventory reports, supply reorder reports, charge-card reports, demographic reports (showing which merchandise sells best where), and so forth. To keep the whole process going, Lands' End also computer-prints Paul's name and address on the next catalog.

Output
The User Connection

TEST BANK

Mult. Choice 7

T/F 65-70

Matching I 75

Matching II 84

Fill In 91

DISCUSSION QUESTION

What are several common locations where input and output devices can be found? (grocery store, gas station, bank)

LECTURE HINT

The post office has joined the bar code act. For example, envelopes sent to potential magazine subscribers for use in returning their checks are bar-coded to represent the destination address. However, not every post office is equipped to process the bar codes.

TRANSPARENCY ACETATE #13

Box 4-1

How Users See Input and Output

The central processing unit is the unseen part of a computer system, and users are only dimly aware of its activity. But users are very much aware—and in control—of the input data given to the computer. They submit data to the computer to get processed data (information), which is the output. Output is what makes the computer useful to human beings.

Sometimes the output is an instant reaction to the input. For example:

■ Zebra-striped bar codes on supermarket items provide input that permits instant retrieval of output, price, and item name, right at the checkout counter.

■ You use a joystick—a kind of hand-controlled lever—to input data to guide the little airplane, rabbit, or whatever on the screen. The output is the movement of the on-screen object according to your wishes.

■ A bank teller queries the computer through the small terminal at the teller window by inputting a customer's account number; the teller immediately receives output in the form of the customer's account balance on that same screen.

■ A forklift operator speaks to a computer directly through a microphone. Words like *left*, *right*, and *lift* are the actual input data. The

▼

Box 4-1   Lands' End.
At this mail-order house, customer order data is input, processed, and used to produce a variety of outputs.

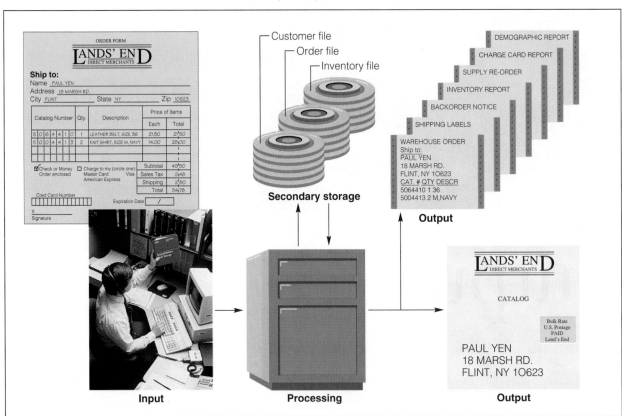

output is the computer's instant response, which causes the forklift to operate as requested.

- In an innovative restaurant, input is your finger touching the listing of the item of your choice on a computer screen. The output is the order that appears immediately on the kitchen screen, where employees get to work on your Chili Hamburger Deluxe.

Input and output are sometimes separated by time, distance, or both. Some examples are:

- Factory workers input data by using their plastic employee cards to punch in on a time clock as they go from task to task. The outputs, produced biweekly, are their paychecks and management reports that summarize hours per project and other information.
- Data from the checks we write is used as input to the bank's computer and eventually is processed to prepare a monthly bank statement.
- Charge-card transactions in a retail store provide input data that is processed at month's end to produce customer bills.
- Water-sample data is determined at lake and river sites, keyed in at the environmental agency office, and used to produce reports that show patterns of water quality.

The examples in this section have shown the diversity of computer applications, but in all cases the litany is the same: input–processing–output.

Everyday Input and Output

One way or another, delivering input to a computer is a common activity in our daily lives. Input activities in which you may have engaged could include items on the following list.

- Inserting your credit card (with data encoded on the magnetic strip) into a bank's automated teller machine (ATM)
- Buying an item whose price tag was scanned with a wand reader
- Filling out an application for a magazine subscription
- Purchasing groceries whose bar codes were scanned
- Filling out registration forms
- Recording test answers by using a pencil on an optical-mark recognition sheet

Many other activities require us to provide input to a computer. Over time, we may supply input in these circumstances: seeking credit, paying taxes, applying for a job, entering a contest, paying bills, entering the armed services, signing a petition, going to the doctor, joining an organization, applying for a scholarship, seeking government assistance, giving charitable donations, ordering products through the mail, and on and on.

This data is supplied willingly, and most people give little thought to the route it will travel. Almost all the data will end up in computer files, to reside there indefinitely.

 # Input: How You Get Data Into The Computer

Some input data can go directly to the computer for processing, such as reading bar codes, touching a computer screen, or even speaking to the computer. On the other hand, some input data must go through a great deal of intermediate handling, such as when it is handwritten on a **source document** (jargon for the original written data) and then translated to a medium that a machine can read, such as magnetic disk. In either case the task is to gather facts to be processed by the computer—sometimes called *raw data*—and convert them into some form the computer can understand.

Various input devices are used to gather data for processing by the computer. Generally, the trend in input devices is toward equipment that is easy to use, fast, and accurate.

Keyboard Entry

The most common input device is the keyboard. A computer keyboard is usually similar to a typewriter, with the traditional QWERTY layout of letter and digit keys, and additional numerical pad and function keys (Figure 4-1a). The keyboard may be part of a personal computer or part of a terminal connected to a computer somewhere else. Not all keyboards are traditional. A fast-food franchise like McDonald's, for example, uses keyboards with keys that represent items, such as large fries or a Big Mac (Figure 4-1b).

▶
Figure 4-1 Keyboards.
(a) A traditional computer keyboard. (b) Workers at McDonald's press a key for each item ordered. The amount of the order is totaled by the computer system, then displayed on a small screen so the customer can see the amount owed. (c) Chinese characters are significantly more complicated than the letters and digits found on a standard keyboard. To enter Chinese characters into the computer system, a person uses a stylus on this special keyboard to select the character wanted. A graphics interpretation of the character can be displayed on the computer screen.

TRANSPARENCY ACETATE #14

Figure 4-1

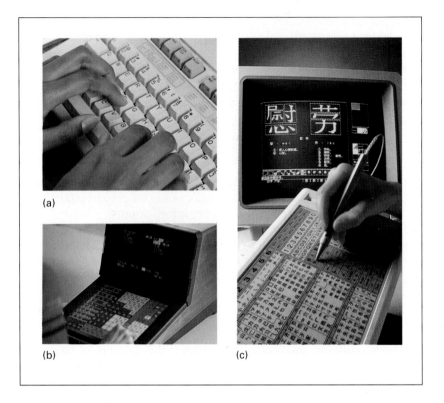

(a)

(b)

(c)

Mouse

A **mouse,** popularized by the Macintosh computer, is a computer input device that actually looks a little bit like a mouse (Figure 4-2). The mouse, which has a ball on its underside, is rolled on a flat surface, usually the desk on which your computer sits. The rolling movement that results when you push the mouse causes the related output, which is the corresponding movement on the screen. Moving the mouse allows you to reposition the **pointer,** or **cursor**—an indicator on the screen that shows where the next interaction with the computer will take place. The cursor is often flashing or blinking on and off, so it is easy to see. The cursor can also be moved by pressing various keyboard keys. In addition, you can communicate with the computer by pressing the button on top of the mouse. Many users turn to the mouse as a quick substitute for some functions of the keyboard.

Trackball

The mouse works fine until you find yourself without a flat surface on which to roll it. That is often the case for travelers using laptop computers. If you try to roll a mouse on a tiny airline tray, you will probably be digging an elbow into your neighbor. And, of course, an airport concourse or car offers no flat surface at all. The **trackball** is sort of an upside-down mouse. That is, the ball that usually rolls along a flat surface is facing up and is manipulated by hand. As with a mouse, movement of the ball causes a corresponding movement of the cursor on the screen. Trackballs are often built into laptop computers (Figure 4-3).

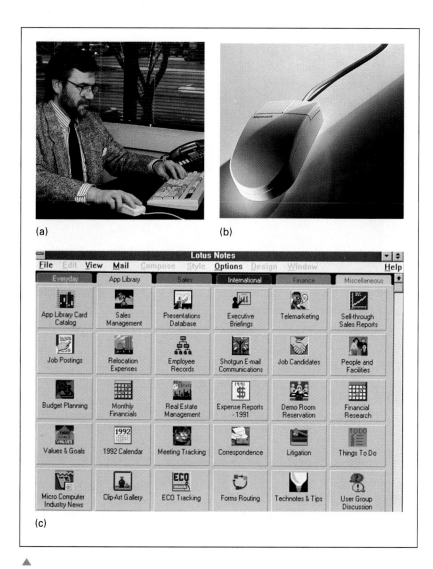

(a) (b)

(c)

▲

Figure 4-2 Mouse.
(a) As the ball on the underside of the mouse moves over a smooth surface such as a desktop, the pointer on the screen makes a corresponding movement. (b) The mouse is designed to fit smoothly under the hand. (c) Once the pointer is in position, a user can select an option from a list of choices, such as those shown here, by pressing the button on the mouse.

LECTURE HINT

A new cordless mouse is available, that works using remote control to send infrared signals to a receiver and charging stand. In order to work, the mouse requires an unobstructed line of sight between the mouse and the stand.

LECTURE HINT

A trackball does not require as much eye-hand coordination as a mouse and so is a good choice for children, older people, and people with disabilities.

DISCUSSION QUESTION

Why is source data automation an enticing alternative to keyboarding?

TRANSPARENCY ACETATE #15

Figure 4-2

Source Data Automation: Collecting Data Where It Starts

The key to productive data entry is clear: Cut down the number of intermediate steps required between the data input and data processing. The best way to do this is by **source data automation**—by using special equipment to collect data at the source and send it directly to the computer. Source data automation is an enticing alternative to keyboarding input, because it eliminates the intermediate keying function; therefore, source data automation reduces both costs and opportunities for human-introduced mistakes. Since data about a transaction is collected when

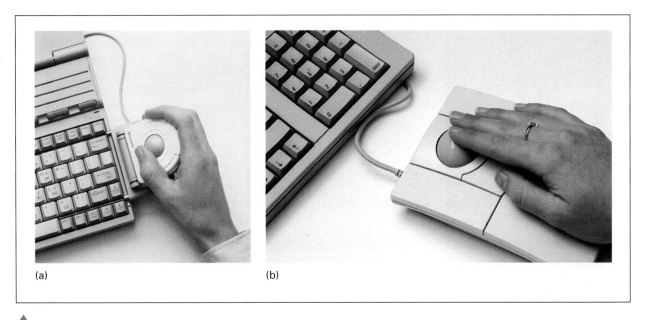

(a)   (b)

▲

Figure 4-3 Trackball.
The rotation of the ball causes a corresponding movement of the cursor on the screen. (a) Trackballs are often used with laptop computers because there may be no handy surface on which to roll a mouse. (b) Some users prefer trackballs even with their desktop computers.

DISCUSSION QUESTION

Describe the various types of optical-recognition devices.

DISCUSSION QUESTION

How do MICR and OCR differ?

and where the transaction takes place, source data automation also improves the speed of the input operation.

For convenience we will divide the discussion of source data automation into four areas: magnetic-ink character recognition, optical recognition, data collection devices, and voice input. Let us consider each of these in turn.

Magnetic-Ink Character Recognition

Magnetic-ink character recognition (MICR) is a method of machine-reading characters made of magnetized particles. The most familiar example of magnetic characters is the array of numbers on the bottom of your personal check. Figure 4-4 shows what these numbers represent.

The MICR process is, in fact, used mainly by banks for processing checks. Checks are read by a machine called a **MICR reader/sorter,** which sorts them into different compartments and sends electronic signals—read from the magnetic ink on the check—to the computer.

Optical Recognition

Optical recognition systems read numbers, letters, special characters, and marks. An electronic scanning device converts the data into electrical signals and sends the signals to the computer for processing. Various optical recognition devices can read these types of input:

- Optical marks
- Optical characters
- Handwritten characters
- Bar codes

The first type of system, **optical-mark recognition (OMR),** is sometimes called mark sensing because a machine senses marks on a piece of paper. As a student, you may immediately recognize this approach as a technique used to score certain tests. Using a pencil, you make a mark in a specified box or space that corresponds to your answer. The answer sheet is then graded by a device that uses a light beam to detect the marks

and convert them to electrical signals, which are sent to the computer for
processing.

Optical-character recognition (OCR) devices also use a light
source to read special characters and convert them into electrical signals
to be sent to the computer. The characters—letters, numbers, and symbols—can be read by both humans and machines. They are often found
on sales tags in department stores or imprinted on credit-card slips in gas
stations after the sale has been written up. A standard typeface for optical
characters, called **OCR-A,** has been established by the American
National Standards Institute (Figure 4-5).

The hand-held **wand reader** is a popular input device for reading
OCR-A. In retail stores the wand reader is connected to a **point-of-sale
(POS) terminal.** This terminal is like a cash register in many ways, but it
performs many more functions. When a clerk passes the wand reader
over the price tag, both the price and the merchandise number are
entered into the computer system. Given the merchandise number, the
computer can retrieve a description of the item from a file. This description is displayed on the screen of the POS terminal along with the price.
(Some systems, by the way, input only the merchandise number and
retrieve both price and description.) A small printer produces a customer
receipt that also shows both the item description and the price. The
computer calculates the subtotal, the sales tax, and the total. This information is displayed on the screen and printed on the receipt.

The raw purchase data becomes valuable information when summa-
rized by the computer system. This information can be used by a business's accounting department to keep track of how much money is taken
in each day, by buyers to determine what merchandise should be
reordered and by the marketing department to analyze the effectiveness
of its ad campaigns. Thus, capturing data at the time of the sale provides
many benefits beyond giving the customer a computerized receipt along
with the purchase.

Machines that can read **handwritten characters** are yet another
means of reducing the number of intermediate steps between capturing

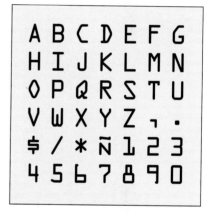

Figure 4-5 OCR-A typeface.
This is a standard font for optical-character recognition systems.

DISCUSSION QUESTION

Where have you seen point-of-sale
terminals?

CLASS PROJECT

Divide the class into groups and have
each group visit a different retail store
to see how they use OCR.

data and processing it. In many instances it is preferable to write the data and immediately have it available for processing rather than having it keyed in later by data entry operators. However, not just any kind of handwritten scrawl will do; appropriate size, completeness, and legibility of the handwriting contribute to readability (Figure 4-6). The post office makes extensive use of these machines to sort mail by zip code.

Each product on your store shelf has its own unique number, which is part of the **Universal Product Code (UPC).** This code number, representing the manufacturer and the individual product, is depicted on the product's label by a pattern of vertical marks, or bars, called **bar codes.** These zebra stripes can be sensed and read by a **bar code reader,** a photoelectric scanner that reads the code by means of reflected light (lasers). As with the wand reader in retail stores, the bar code reader in grocery stores is part of a point-of-sale (POS) terminal. For example, when you buy an item in a supermarket, the checker moves it past the scanner that reads the bar code (Figure 4-7a). The bar code merely identifies the product to the store's computer; the code does not contain the price, which may vary. The price is stored in a file that is accessed by a computer. (Obviously, it is easier to change the price once it is in the computer than to restamp the price repeatedly on each item.) The computer automatically tells the POS terminal what the price is, and a printer prints the item description and price on a paper tape for the customer.

Although bar codes were once found primarily in the supermarket, they have a variety of other interesting applications. Bar coding has been described as an inexpensive and remarkably reliable way to get data into a computer. It is no wonder that virtually every industry has found a niche for bar codes. In Brisbane, Australia, as well as in other countries, bar codes help the Red Cross manage its blood bank inventory (Figure 4-7b). Also, Federal Express attributes a large part of the corporation's success to the bar-coding system they use to track thousands of packages every day. As each package wends its way through the transportation system, its unique bar code is read at each point, and the bar code number is fed to a central computer. An employee can use a computer terminal to check the location of a given shipment at any time; the sender can request a status report on a package and receive a response within 30 minutes.

Data Collection Devices

Another direct source of data entry is a **data collection device,** which may be in a warehouse or factory or wherever an activity generates data. Using such a device eliminates intermediate steps that endanger accu-

DISCUSSION QUESTION

What are the advantages for stores that use the UPC system?

DISCUSSION QUESTION

What are some typical characteristics of data collection devices?

▶

Figure 4-6 Handwritten characters.
Legibility is important in making handwritten characters readable by optical recognition.

TRANSPARENCY ACETATE #19

Figure 4-6

	Good	Bad
1. Make your letters big	TAPLEY	TAPLEY
2. Use simple shapes	25370	25370
3. Use block printing	STAN	STAN
4. Connect lines	B5T	135T
5. Close loops	9068	9068
6. Do not link characters	LOOP	LOOP

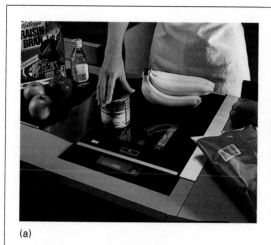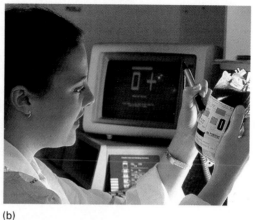

(a)   (b)

▲

Figure 4-7   Bar codes.
(a) This photoelectric bar code scanner, often seen at supermarket checkout counters, reads the product's zebra-striped bar code. The bar code identifies the product to the store's computer, which retrieves price information. The price is then automatically rung up on the POS terminal. (b) The Australian Red Cross combines personal computers and hand-held bar code readers to verify blood type labels.

racy. A factory employee who uses a plastic card to punch job data directly into a time clock is using a data collection device.

Data collection devices must be sturdy, trouble-free, and easy to use, because they are often in dusty, humid, or hot or cold locations. They are used by people such as warehouse workers, packers, forklift operators, and other nonclerical employees. Examples of remote data collection devices are machines for taking inventory, reading shipping labels, and recording job costs.

Voice Input

Have you talked to your computer recently? Has it talked to you? Both feats are possible with current technology, even though there are still some limitations. We will examine both "speakers"—you and the computer. Since we are discussing input here, we will begin with you, as you talk to your computer. What method of input could be more direct than speaking?

Voice input is the process of presenting input data to the computer through the spoken word. Voice input can be about twice as fast as keyed input entered by a skilled typist. A **speech recognition device** accepts the spoken word through a microphone and converts it into digital code that can be understood by the computer. This process has a great many uses, quite apart from its being an aid to those who hate to type. In fact, voice input has created new uses for computers (Figure 4-8). Typical users are those with "busy hands," hands that are too dirty for the keyboard, or hands that must remain cleaner than using a keyboard would permit. Among current uses are

- Controlling inventory in an auto junkyard
- Reporting analyses of pathology slides that are under a microscope

▶

Figure 4-8. Voice input.
This hospital patient is giving voice commands to her computerized bed, which responds to a list of commands. Since not all patients need to use voice commands, the voice capability modules can be moved from one bed to another.

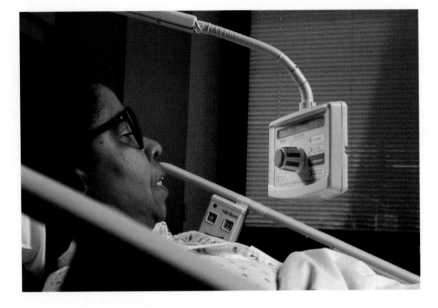

- Making phone calls from a car
- Calculating a correct anesthetic dosage for a patient in surgery
- Performing nonflight control jobs such as changing radio frequencies in airplane cockpits
- Asking for stock quotations over the phone
- Sorting packages
- Inspecting items moving along a factory assembly line
- Acting on commands from physically challenged users
- Commanding a car to start the motor, lock the doors, or turn on the windshield wipers

In a **speaker-dependent** system, the speech recognition device "learns" the voice of the user, who speaks isolated words repeatedly. The voiced words the system "knows" are then recognizable in the future. The worker sorting packages, for instance, can speak digits representing zip codes. The factory inspector can voice the simple words good or bad, yes or no. A biologist can tell a microscope to scan up, down, right, and left.

Speaker-independent systems, which can recognize commands from any speaker, are much more challenging to the computer industry. Experts have tagged speech recognition as one of the most difficult things for a computer to do, partly because human speech varies so much in accent, tone, and clarity. Someday machines that recognize speech will be commonplace. People will routinely talk to their computers, toys, TV sets, refrigerators, ovens, automobiles, and door locks. And no one will stare at them when they do.

DISCUSSION QUESTION

Describe the difference between a speaker-dependent and a speaker-independent speech recognition system.

LECTURE HINT

ATMs have sometimes been easy targets for crooks. Banks are considering switching to voice identification systems.

 Output: How Information Comes Back To You

As we have already seen, output can take many forms, such as screen output, paper printouts, and voice. Other forms of output include overhead transparencies, 35mm slides, and microfilm. Even within the same orga-

COMPUTING TRENDS

Computers in the Courtroom

Computers are not strangers to the courtroom. They have long been used by judges and their clerks for a variety of purposes, including monitoring dockets and checking defendant records. Now, in a giant leap forward, computers have gone beyond clerical functions.

In fact, attorneys are now using computers to re-create the crime scene, based on the recollection of eyewitnesses and crime scene data. It is conservatively estimated that such simulations save many hours of testimony, thus sparing the jury and help-

ing to unclog the overcrowded courts. However, some experts worry that such high-tech representations of evidence may sway jurors by lending an aura of factuality.

nization, there can be different kinds of output. You can see this the next time you go to a travel agency that uses a computer system. If you ask for airline flights to, for example, Toronto, Calgary, and Vancouver, the travel agent will probably make a few queries to the system and receive output on a screen: information about the availability of various flights. After the reservations have been confirmed, the agent can ask for printed output in three forms: the tickets, the traveler's itinerary, and the invoice. In addition, for management purposes the agency may periodically receive printed reports and charts, such as monthly summaries of sales figures or pie charts of regional costs.

Computer Screen Technology

A user's first interaction with a computer screen may be the screen response to the user's input. When data is entered, it appears on the screen. Furthermore, the computer response to that data—the output— also appears on the screen. Computer screens come in many varieties, but the most common kind is the **cathode ray tube (CRT).** Most CRT screens use a technology called **raster-scan technology.** The backing of the screen display has a phosphorous coating that will glow whenever it is hit by a beam of electrons. As the user, you tell the computer what image you want on the screen by typing, say, the letter *M*, and the computer sends the appropriate image to be beamed on the screen. This is essentially the same process used to produce television images.

A computer display screen that can be used for graphics is divided into dots that are called addressable because they can be *addressed* individually by the graphics software. Each dot can be illuminated individually on the screen. Each dot is potentially a *pic*ture *el*ement, or **pixel**. The **resolution** of the screen— its clarity—is directly related to the number of pixels on the screen: The more pixels, the higher the resolution.

There have been several color screen standards, relating paricularly to resolution. The first color display was **CGA** (color graphics adaptor), which had low resolution by today's standards: 320 by 200 pixels. This was followed by the sharper **EGA** (enhanced graphics adaptor), featuring

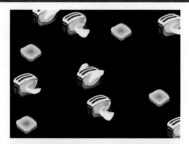

Flying Toasters

The computer industry has come up with an entertaining solution to a pesky problem. The problem is the possibility of screen burnout. Users often leave their computers unattended for periods of time to answer the phone, attend a meeting, or for any number of other reasons. While they are gone the static image that remains on the screen can "burn" into the screen, leaving a permanent faint shadow in the background whenever the monitor is turned on.

An early solution was screen saver software that caused the screen to go blank after a given period of non-use, perhaps a few minutes. When the user returned, the screen was easily revived to its prior display by the touch of any key.

Recent screen saver software is more fanciful, sending a variety of images coursing across the screen. The best-selling After Dark software allows you to choose from moving images of flying toasters, cityscapes, geometric shapes, aquariums, rain storms, spotlights, stained glass windows, and much more. Many people enjoy the novelty of bright images on their home or office computer screens.

640 by 350 pixels. Today, **VGA** (video graphics array), with 640 by 480 pixels, is a common standard. **SVGA** (super VGA) offers 800 by 600 pixels or 1024 by 768 pixels, the ultimate in clarity.

Types of Screens

Color monitors that display text and graphics in color are in common use today (Figure 4-9a). Some screens are **monochrome,** meaning only one color appears on a dark background. A common monochrome screen display is green text on a dark background, but amber characters are also available and are thought to be easier on the eyes (Figure 4-9b). Another type of screen is the **liquid crystal display (LCD),** a flat display often seen on watches and calculators. LCD screens are used on laptop computers (Figure 4-9c). These screens are usually smaller and lighter than CRTs, and the quality—both color and contrast—suffers somewhat. Screen size can vary from large screens that can show two facing pages to small screens on some point-of-sale terminals, which are just large enough to display the item name and price.

Terminals

A screen may be the monitor of a self-contained personal computer, or it may be part of a terminal that is one of many terminals attached to a large computer. A **terminal** consists of an input device, an output device, and a communications link to the main computer. Most commonly, a terminal has a keyboard for an input device and a screen for an output device, although there are many variations on this theme.

Printers

A **printer** is a device that produces printed paper output—known in the trade as **hard copy** because it is tangible and permanent (unlike **soft copy,** which is displayed on a screen). Some printers produce only letters and numbers, but most can also produce graphics.

Letters and numbers are formed by a printer either as solid characters or as dot-matrix characters. **Dot-matrix printers** create characters in the same way that individual lights in a pattern spell out words on a basketball scoreboard. A dot-matrix printer constructs a character by activating a matrix of pins that produce the shape of the character. Figure 4-10 shows how this works. A traditional matrix is 5×7—that is, five dots wide and seven dots high. These printers are sometimes called nine-pin printers, because they have two extra vertical dots for descenders on the lowercase letters *g, j, p,* and *y.* The 24-pin dot-matrix printer, which uses a series of overlapping dots, dominates the dot-matrix market. The more dots, the better the quality of the character produced. Some dot-matrix printers can produce color images.

There are two ways of printing an image on paper: the impact method and the nonimpact method. Let us take a closer look at the difference.

Impact Printers

The term *impact* refers to the fact that an **impact printer** uses some sort of physical contact with the paper to produce an image, physically striking paper, ribbon, and print hammer together. The impact may be produced by a print hammer character, like that of a typewriter key striking

▲
Figure 4-9   A variety of screens.
(a) This high-resolution brilliance is available only on a color graphics display. (b) An amber screen. (c) Laptop computers use liquid crystal display (LCD) technology for their small, lightweight screens.

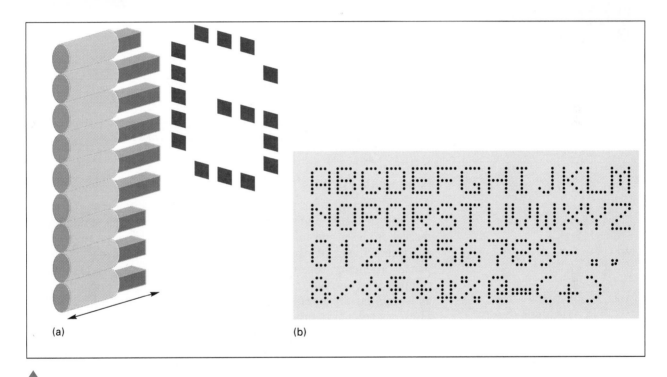

▲
Figure 4-10   Forming dot-matrix characters.
(a) This art shows the letter *G* being printed as a 5×7 dot-matrix character. The moving matrix head has nine vertical pins, which move in and out as necessary to form each letter. (b) Letters, numbers, and special characters formed as 5×7 dot-matrix characters. Although not shown in this figure, dot-matrix printers can print lowercase letters too. The two lowest pins are used for the parts of the lowercase letters *g, j, p,* and *y* that go below the line.

TRANSPARENCY ACETATE #21

Figure 4-10

a ribbon against the paper, or by a print hammer hitting paper and ribbon against a character. A dot-matrix printer is one example of an impact printer. High-quality impact printers print only one character at a time. However, users who are more concerned about high volume than high quality usually use line printers, impact printers that print an entire line at a time.

▲
Figure 4-11 Printers.
(a) The high-quality print of the Hewlett-Packard LaserJet printers make them best-sellers. (b) Ink-jet printers are noted for high-quality graphics output.

Nonimpact Printers

A **nonimpact printer** places an image on a page without physically touching the page. The major technologies competing in the nonimpact market are laser and ink-jet. Both use the dot-matrix concept to form characters. **Laser printers** use a light beam to help transfer images to paper, producing extremely high-quality results (Figure 4-11a). Laser printers print one page at a time. Initially very expensive, low-end black-and-white laser printers can now be purchased for well under $1000. However, color laser printers remain very expensive.

There are many advantages to nonimpact printers, but there are two major reasons for their growing popularity: They are faster and quieter. Other advantages of nonimpact printers over conventional mechanical printers are their ability to change typefaces automatically and their ability to produce high-quality graphics.

The rush to laser printers has been influenced by the trend toward desktop publishing—using a personal computer, a laser printer, and special software to make professional-looking publications, such as newsletters. We will examine desktop publishing in Chapter 12.

Ink-jet printers, by spraying ink from multiple jet nozzles, can print in several different colors of ink to produce excellent graphics (Figure 4-11b). As good as they are, color printers are not perfect. The color you see on your computer screen is not necessarily the color you will see on the printed output. Nor is it likely to be the color you would see on a four-color offset printing press. Nevertheless, with low-end printers now

Personal Computers In Action

Computer As Cadaver

Many of us have heard the stories of medical students and their laboratory cadavers, often given affectionate nicknames. We have an appreciation for what medical students must do to learn about human anatomy; some people go even further and will their bodies to science. But this is one science tradition that may be coming to a close. In just a few years, it is predicted, medical students will be using software on their personal computers for most of their training, using cadavers only occasionally.

The screens shown here, illustrating hip replacement, are generated by a software package called ADAM, which lets students use a mouse to

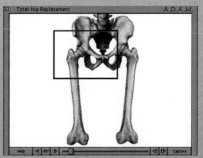

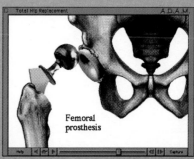

click away layers from skin to bone. A student can zoom in on specific tendons, muscles, and tissues, rotating the images to obtain different perspectives.

Medical personnel can look forward to having software that can be updated with the latest medical technology and can focus on a particular

specialty such as cardiology or pediatrics. The direction of the future seems clear: Just as architects and engineers use computers to simulate the real world, so will medical students—and even doctors—take voyages through the body.

---

under $1000, they may be a bargain for users who want their own color output capability.

Printers are discussed further in the "Buyer's Guide."

Voice Output

We have already examined voice input, a technology that still challenges the industry. **Speech synthesis**—the process of enabling machines to talk to people—is much easier than speech recognition.

"The door is ajar," your car says to you in a human-like voice. But this is not a real human voice; it is the product of a **voice synthesizer** (also called a **voice-output device** or **audio-response unit**), which produces sounds understandable as speech to humans.

Voice output has become common in such places as airline and bus terminals, banks, and brokerage houses. It is typically used when an inquiry is followed by a short reply (such as a bank balance or flight time). Many businesses have found other creative uses for voice output as it applies to the telephone. Automatic telephone voices ("Hello, this is a computer speaking . . . ") take surveys, inform customers that catalog orders are ready to pick up, and remind consumers that they have not paid their bills. Voice output is also used extensively in school administration to call families of students to remind them of such things as PTA meetings, Open Houses, and children's absences.

Music Output

Personal computer users have occasionally sent primitive musical messages, feeble tones that wheezed from the tiny internal speaker. Many users remain at this level, but a significant change is in progress.

Professional musicians lead the way, using special sound chips that simulate different instruments. A sound card, installed internally in the computer, and attached speakers complete the output environment. Now the computer can produce the sound of an orchestra or a rock band. Those of us who simply enjoy music can have a full sight/sound

▼

Figure 4-12 Computer graphics.
The world can look just a bit different when computer graphics enter the picture. (a,b, and d) These images were generated entirely on the computer by graphics artists. (c) This image is a wily combination of computer graphics and digitized photographs.

(a)

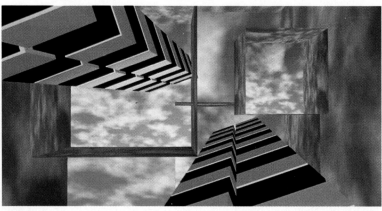
(b)

(c)

(d)

experience using multimedia, which we will explore in more detail in the next chapter, and also in a separate multimedia gallery.

 # Computer Graphics

Computer output in the form of graphics has come into its own in a major—and sometimes spectacular—way. Many readers of this book have seen the application of graphics to video games. Just about everyone has seen TV commercials or movies that use computer-produced animated graphics. Computer graphics can also be found in education, computer art, science, sports, and more (Figure 4-12). But perhaps their most prevalent use today is in business.

Business Graphics

It might seem wasteful to display in color graphics what could more inexpensively be shown to managers as numbers in standard computer printouts. However, colorful graphics, maps, and charts can help managers compare data more easily, spot trends, and make decisions more quickly. Also, the use of color helps people get the picture, literally. Finally, although color graphs and charts have been used in business for years—usually to make presentations to higher management or outside clients—the computer allows them to be rendered quickly, before information becomes outdated. One user refers to business graphics as "computer-assisted insight."

Video Graphics

Unfettered by reality, **video graphics** can be as creative as an animated cartoon (Figure 4-13). Although they operate on the same principle as a moving picture or cartoon—one frame at a time in quick succession—**video graphics** are produced by computers. Video graphics have made their biggest splash on television, but many people do not realize they are watching computers at work. The next time you watch television, skip the trip to the kitchen and pay special attention to the commercials. Unless there is a live human in the advertisement, there is a good chance that the moving objects you see, such as floating cars and bobbing electric razors, are computer output. Another fertile ground for video graphics is each television network's logo and theme. Accompanied by music and swooshing sounds, the network symbol spins and cavorts and turns itself inside out, all with the finesse that only a computer could supply.

Video graphics do not have to be commercial in nature. Some video artists produce beauty for its own sake. In science, video graphics have helped produce moving models, such as a model of DNA molecules whose atoms, represented by gleaming spheres, twist and fold.

Computer-Aided Design/Computer-Aided Manufacturing

For more than a decade, computer graphics have also been part and parcel of a field known by the abbreviation **CAD/CAM**—short for **computer-aided design/computer-aided manufacturing**. In this area computers are used to create two- and three-dimensional pictures of

(a)

(b)

(c)

(d)

▲
Figure 4-13 Video graphics.
These screens are from a computer-animated series featuring a walking clock—time marches on.

TEST BANK

Mult. Choice 1, 4, 12, 16-17
T/F 23, 27, 31, 62-64
Matching I 78-79
Matching II 83, 90
Fill In 111-116

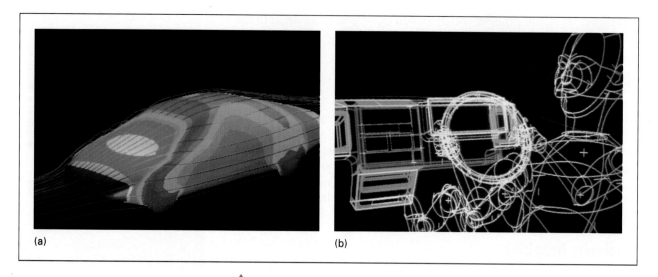

(a)   (b)

▲

Figure 4-14 CAD/CAM.
With computer-aided design/computer-aided manufacturing (CAD/CAM), the
computer can keep track of all details, maintain designs of parts in memory, and
combine parts electronically as required. (a) A computer-aided design wireframe
used to study design possibilities. (b) Engineers also use graphics to test designs relative to the customer who will use the car.

everything from hand tools to tractors. CAD/CAM provides a bridge
between design (planning what a product will be) and manufacturing
(actually making the planned product). As a manager at Chrysler said,
"Many companies have design data and manufacturing data and the two
are never the same. At Chrysler we have only one set of data that everyone dips into." For an example of their efforts, see Figure 4-14.

Graphics Input Devices

There are many ways to produce and interact with screen graphics. We
have already described the mouse; the following are some other common
devices that allow the user to interact with screen graphics.

Digitizer

An image, whether a drawing or a photo, can be scanned by a device
called a digitizer, which converts the image into digital data that the
computer can accept and represent on the screen. However, a digitizing
tablet lets you create your own images (Figure 4-15). This device has a
special stylus that can be used to draw or trace images, which are then
converted to digital data that can be processed by the computer.

Light Pen

For direct interaction with your computer screen, the light pen is ideal.
It is versatile enough to modify screen graphics or make a menu selection—that is, to choose from a list of activity choices on the screen. A
light pen has a light-sensitive cell at one end. When the light pen is
placed against the screen, it closes a photoelectric circuit that pinpoints
the spot the pen is touching. This tells the computer where to enter or
modify pictures or data on the screen.

▲

Figure 4- 15   Digitizer.
This engineer is using a digitizing tablet
to input his drawing to the computer.

Joystick

Another well-known graphics input device is the **joystick,** dear to the hearts of video game fans. This device allows fingertip control of figures on a CRT screen.

Touch Screen

If you disdain pens and sticks and mice, perhaps you would prefer the direct human touch, your finger. **Touch screens** accept input data by letting you point at the screen to select your choice (Figure 4-16). Sensors on the edges of the screen pinpoint the touch location and cause a corresponding response on the screen. Touch screens are widely used in public places, such as hospitals and airports to give directions, and tourist attractions such as Epcot Center to involve the user in demonstrations. Touch screens are even used for bridal registries in large department stores.

Scanner

"You are about to witness something amazing." This sentence is part of a demonstration of a hand-held **scanner.** The demonstration *is* rather amazing. As you watch the scanner being moved over written text and pictures, the same text and pictures appear on the screen of the attached computer and are stored in a disk file. Scanners come in both hand-held and desktop models (Figure 4-17). Although all scanners can scan images, they vary in their ability to scan text. Some files created by scanning can be used like any other file; that is, they can be edited, printed, and so forth.

Who would use such a device? Anyone who prefers scanning to typing. For example, teachers can scan text in books or magazines for use in class-

▲

Figure 4-16 Touch screen.
A pointing finger interrupts light beams emitted from the edges of the screen. The computer translates the interruption into a point on the screen.

▼

Figure 4- 17 Scanners.
(a) With a desktop scanner, the picture is laid face down on the scanner, which looks somewhat like a small copy machine. Once an image is scanned into the computer, it can be altered and combined with text to produce documents complete with illustrations. (b) As this hand-held scanner is moved over a picture, the image appears on the computer screen.

(a)

(b)

▶
Figure 4-18 Plotter.
Designers of circuit boards, street maps, schematic diagrams, and similar applications can work in fine detail on a computer screen, and then print the results on a plotter.

room exercises. Lawyers can scan contracts. In addition, a variety of users may wish to scan art or photographs to be manipulated by the computer.

Graphics Output Devices

Just as there are many different ways to input graphics to the computer, there also are many different ways to output graphics. Graphics are most commonly output on a screen or printed paper, as previously discussed. Another popular graphics output device is the **plotter,** which can draw hard-copy graphics output in the form of maps, bar charts, engineering drawings, and even two- or three-dimensional illustrations (Figure 4-18). A plotter often comes with a set of four pens in four different colors. Most plotters also offer shading features.

New forms of computer input and output are developed regularly, with an array of benefits for human use. The effectiveness of the new forms, however, depends on two components that we have not yet discussed: storage and software. We will study the first of these in the next chapter.

Chapter **Review**

Summary and Key Terms

- The keyboard is a common input device for personal computer users, as well as for those who use computer terminals to enter data from **source documents.**
- A **cursor** is an indicator on a screen that shows where the next interaction with the computer will take place.
- A **mouse** is an input device whose movement on a flat surface causes corresponding movement of the **pointer,** or **cursor,** on the screen.
- The **trackball** is sort of an upside-down mouse, in that the ball that usually rolls along a flat surface is facing up and is manipulated by hand, causing corresponding movement of the cursor on the screen.
- **Source data automation,** the use of special equipment to collect data and send it directly to the computer, is a more efficient method of data entry than keyboarding. Four means of source data automation are magnetic-ink character recognition, optical recognition, data collection devices, and voice input.
- **Magnetic-ink character recognition (MICR)** readers read characters made of magnetized particles, such as the preprinted characters on a personal check.
- **Optical recognition** systems convert optical marks, optical characters, handwritten characters, and bar codes into electrical signals sent to the computer. **Optical-mark recognition (OMR)** devices use a light beam to recognize marks on paper. **Optical-character recognition (OCR)** devices use a light beam to read special characters, such as those on price tags. These characters are often in a standard typeface called **OCR-A.** A commonly used OCR device is the hand-held **wand reader,** which is often connected to a **point-of-sale (POS) terminal** in a retail store. Some optical scanners can read precise **handwritten characters.** A **bar code reader** is a stationary photoelectric scanner used to input a **bar code,** the pattern of vertical marks representing the **Universal Product Code (UPC)** that identifies a product.
- **Data collection devices** allow direct, accurate data entry. **Voice input** processes data to the computer through the spoken word. **Speech recognition devices** convert spoken words into a digital code for the computer. In a **speaker-dependent** system, the speech recognition device "learns" the voice of the user; **speaker-independent** systems can recognize commands from any speaker.
- Some computer screens are **monochrome**—the characters appear in one color on a black background. Color screens display color text and graphics. The most common type of screen is the **cathode ray tube (CRT).** Using **raster-scan technology,** a screen image is formed by beaming electrons on a phosphorous-backed screen, causing it to glow.
- Each screen dot is potentially a *pic*ture *el*ement, or **pixel.** The more pixels, the higher the screen's **resolution,** or clarity.
- Color screen standards include **CGA** (color graphics adaptor) with 320 by 200 pixels, **EGA** (enhanced graphics adaptor) with 640 by 350 pixels, the common **VGA** (video graphics array) with 640 by 480 pixels, and **SVGA** (super VGA) with 800 by 600 pixels or 1024 by 768 pixels.
- Some screens are **monochrome,** meaning that only one color appears on a dark background. Another type is the **liquid crystal display (LCD),** a flat screen found on portable computers.

KEY TERMS

audio-response unit

bar code

bar code reader

cathode ray tube (CRT)

CGA

computer-aided design/computer-aided manufacturing (CAD/CAM)

cursor

data collection device

digitizer

digitizing tablet

dot-matrix printer

handwritten character

hard copy

impact printer

ink-jet printer

joy stick

laser printer

light pen

liquid crystal display (LCD)

magnetic-ink character recognition (MICR)

monochrome

mouse

nonimpact printer

OCR-A

optical-character recognition (OCR)

optical-mark recognition (OMR)

optical recognition

pixel

plotter

pointer

point-of-sale (POS)
terminal

printer

raster-scan
technology

resolution

scanner

soft copy

source data
automation

source document

speaker-dependent

speaker-independent

speech recognition
device

speech synthesis

SVGA

terminal

touch screen

trackball

Universal Product
Code (UPC)

VGA

video graphics

voice input

voice-output device

voice synthesizer

wand reader

- A screen may be the monitor of a self-contained personal computer, or it may be part of a **terminal,** an input-output device linked to a main computer.
- **Printers** produce **hard copy,** or printed paper output. (**Soft copy** is displayed on a screen.) Some printers produce solid characters; **dot-matrix printers,** however, construct characters by producing closely spaced dots.
- Printers can be classified as being either **impact printers,** which form characters by physically striking the paper, or **nonimpact printers,** which use a noncontact printing method. Nonimpact printers, which include **laser** and **ink-jet printers,** are faster and quieter than impact printers.
- Computer **speech synthesis** has been accomplished through **voice synthesizers** (also called **voice-output devices** or **audio-response units**).
- **Video graphics** are computer-produced pictures.
- In **computer-aided design/computer-aided manufacturing (CAD/CAM),** computers are used to create two- and three-dimensional pictures of manufactured products such as hand tools and vehicles.
- Common graphics input devices include the mouse, **light pen, digitizer, digitizing tablet, joystick, touch screen, and scanner.**
- Graphics output devices include screens, printers, and **plotters.**

Student Personal Study Guide

True/False

T F 1. A trackball is particularly appropriate for a laptop computer.
T F 2. Screen output is called soft copy.
T F 3. The 24-pin is the most popular dot-matrix printer.
T F 4. An ink-jet printer prints color output that exactly matches the screen colors.
T F 5. A pointer and cursor are the same thing.
T F 6. LCD stands for liquid crystal display.
T F 7. Bar code scanning is an optical recognition system.
T F 8. The cursor shows where the next computer interaction will take place.
T F 9. Laser printers use a light beam to transfer images to paper.
T F 10. Speaker-dependent systems can recognize the voice of any speaker.

Multiple Choice

1. A screen with one color on a black background:
   a. OCR-A   c. UPC
   b. dot matrix   d. monochrome
2. A printer that forms characters by physically striking the paper:
   a. laser   c. ink-jet
   b. nonimpact   d. impact
3. Which is *not* a graphics input device?
   a. plotter   c. light pen
   b. scanner   d. digitizer
4. The most common type of monitor:
   a. CRT   c. OMR
   b. UPC   d. LCD
5. Which is *not* a type of optical recognition?
   a. OMR   c. OCR
   b. CAD/CAM   d. UPC

6. MICR is used primarily in:
    a. retail   c. hospitals
    b. banking   d. testing

7. A "cash register" terminal in retail store:
    a. POS   c. bar code
    b. UPC   d. wand

8. The flat screen usually found on laptop computers:
    a. UPC   c. POS
    b. LCD   d. CRT

9. A voice synthesizer is also called:
    a. CAD/CAM   c. audio-response unit
    b. raster-scan unit   d. video unit

10. A graphics output device:
    a. plotter   c. light pen
    b. trackball   d. digitizer

Fill-In

1. A one-color screen is called : _____ .

2. The technology to create a screen image: _____ .

3. The use of special equipment to collect data at the source: _____ .

4. The method used mainly by banks for processing checks: _____ .

5. Screen output is called: _____ .

6. Printed computer output is called: _____ .

7. This device converts a graphic image to digital data: _____ .

8. UPC stands for: _____ .

9. CAD/CAM stands for: _____ .

10. Computer-produced animated pictures: _____ .

Answers

True/False: 1. T, 2. T, 3. T, 4. F, 5. T, 6. T, 7. T, 8. T, 9. T, 10. F
Multiple choice: 1. d, 2. d, 3. a, 4. a, 5. b, 6. b, 7. a, 8. b, 9. c, 10. a
Fill-In: 1. monochrome, 2. raster-scan technology, 3. source data automation, 4. MICR, 5. soft copy, 6. hard copy, 7. scanner, 8. Universal Product Code, 9. computer-aided design/computer-aided manufacturing, 10. video graphics

Chapter Overview

LEARNING OBJECTIVES

- Understanding the need for secondary storage
- Understanding how data is organized and processed
- Understanding the principal types of secondary storage—magnetic tape and magnetic disk
- Understanding the storage media available for personal computers
- Appreciating new approaches to storage, particularly optical technology
- Gaining knowledge of multimedia systems

Barbara McCormick, CEO for a sporting goods manufacturer, bought a personal computer for her office. She had seen what several of her colleagues were able to do with their computers and was intrigued. She knew that if computing was good for everyone else in the company, it would probably be good for her, too. Barbara was, of course, a little concerned about starting out and making all the right equipment choices.

Barbara took time to investigate personal computers. She wanted a machine that had growth potential. Working with a professional from the information systems department, Barbara decided on a midpriced model with ample speed and memory, a color monitor, and a laser printer.

Storage

Barbara hesitated about the storage, however. The information systems consultant convinced her that having both a diskette drive and a hard drive was a necessity. (As we will see, this arrangement is timesaving and convenient.) But Barbara had some misgivings about the capacity of the hard disk. Could she ever really use the 250-megabyte disk the consultant recommended? How could she possibly come up with 250 *million* characters of data? The consultant pointed out that Barbara would be storing software as well as data on her hard disk. Barbara finally chose a 100-megabyte disk, which seemed more than adequate to her at the time.

Barbara's hard disk *was* adequate for its original purposes—storing a few software packages plus her own data—notes, letters, outlines, documents, speeches, and position papers. However, Barbara soon began branching out in other directions, using various types of software. She tracked names and phone numbers, analyzed financial data, and produced business graphics. She began using her computer to file ideas that could be accessed instantaneously. All her new software and data used disk space, and Barbara eventually found that her hard disk was getting crowded.

To prevent a possible dilemma, computer professionals usually advise computer buyers to estimate disk needs generously and then double the estimate. However, estimating future needs is rarely easy. In particular, people tend to think only in terms of what data they might generate, not realizing that ever-emerging and attractive software packages will take up considerable disk space. Many users, therefore, make later adjustments. In this chapter we will examine several storage options, including the type of hard disk Barbara originally chose.

Devices
Electronic Filing Cabinets

TEST BANK

Mult. Choice 2
T/F 33, 41-45
Fill In 101

DISCUSSION QUESTION

What are the two reasons computers require secondary storage?

TEST BANK

Mult. Choice 1, 3-4, 7, 9-10
T/F 32, 38-39, 46-49
Matching I 81
Matching II 91, 97
Fill In 102-104, 123

 # Why Secondary Storage?

Whether considering your own personal computer storage or the broader needs of a corporation or government agency, the choices can be complicated. Picture, if you can, how many filing-cabinet drawers would be required to hold the millions of files of, say, criminal records kept by the U.S. Justice Department or employee records kept by General Motors. The rooms to hold the filing cabinets would have to be enormous. Computer storage, which allows the storage of many records in extremely compressed form and provides quick access to them, is unquestionably one of the computer's most valuable assets.

Secondary storage is needed for two reasons. First, primary storage—memory—is limited in size, whereas secondary storage media can store as much information as necessary. Also, memory can be used only temporarily; data disappears from memory when you turn most computers off. You need secondary storage to store indefinitely the data you have used or the information you have derived from processing.

Suppose, for example, you spend a long afternoon at the computer as part of your assignment as a management trainee. You have created and reworked a special report for the vice president of marketing to take on an upcoming sales trip. The report needs only another couple of hours of polishing, which you can do the next morning. It would be out of the question to begin again from scratch. Thus you need secondary storage, or **auxiliary storage,** to save your work so that you can retrieve it at a later time and carry on where you left off.

Personal computer users know that they need secondary storage as a place to keep the files they create. Files can include letters, memos, reports, and even complex output such as financial calculations or graphics. Writing files onto a personal computer output medium, usually a disk, is a relatively simple matter. A user needs only to learn the output commands associated with the software being used; the software package takes care of the details.

Working with business systems, whether on large or small computers, is often more complex. To begin with, business systems are usually concerned with records—possibly data about products, customers, or employees. A user who needs to plan computer output must understand how data is organized and processed and know the type of storage medium that will hold the data.

We begin by considering how data is organized and how it is processed. From there we will move on to different types of storage media, first for large computers and then for personal computers.

 # Data: Getting Organized

We have already described data representation in terms of bits and bytes in Chapter 3. Recall that a byte represents a character of data and that a series of bits represents a byte in the computer. We now consider how to organize data in convenient groupings. To be processed by the computer, data—represented by characters—is often organized into fields, records, files, and sometimes databases (Figure 5-1). Here is a brief description of each of these elements:

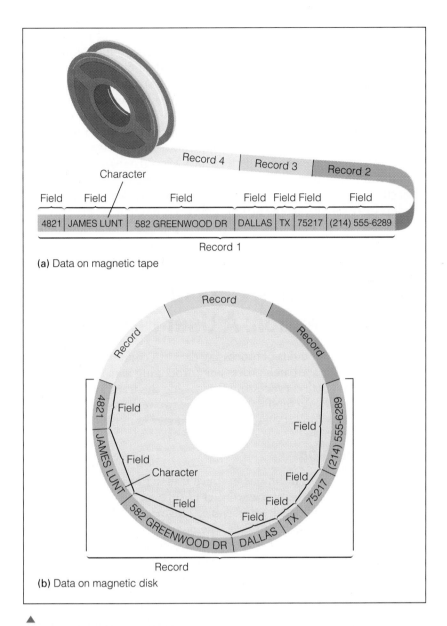

(a) Data on magnetic tape

(b) Data on magnetic disk

▲
Figure 5-1   How data is organized.
Data, represented by characters, is organized into fields, records, and files. A file is a
collection of related records.

- A **character** is a letter, digit, or special character (such as $, ?, or *).
  One or more related characters constitute a field.
- A **field** contains a set of related characters. For example, suppose a
  health club is making address labels for a mailing. For each person it
  has fields for membership number, name, street address, city, state, zip
  code, and phone number.
- A **record** is a collection of related fields. Thus, on the health club list,
  one person's membership number, name, address, city, state, zip code,
  and phone number constitute a record. (The fields are considered
  related because they are for the same person.)

- One kind of **file** is a collection of related records. All the member records for the health club compose a membership file. Note, however, that not all files are collections of records; a file can also contain, for example, a letter, an essay, a graphic, or a spreadsheet. But in the following section regarding processing, the files being discussed are collections of records.

- A **database** may be a collection of records or a collection of interrelated files stored together. (However, a file is not necessarily part of a database; many files exist independently.) In a database, specific data items can be retrieved for various applications. For instance, if the health club is opening a new outlet, it can extract the names and addresses of all the people with specific zip codes that are near the new club. The club can then send a special announcement about opening day to those people.

Processing Data Into Information: A User Perspective

There are several methods of processing data in a computer system. The two main methods are batch processing (processing data transactions in groups) and transaction processing (processing the transactions one at a time as they occur). A combination of these two techniques may also be used. We will now look at these methods and give examples of their use.

Batch Processing

Batch processing is a technique in which transactions are collected into groups, or batches, to be processed. Let us suppose that we are going to update the health club's address label file. The **master file,** a semipermanent set of records, is, in this case, the records of all members of the health club, including their names, addresses, and so forth.

To use an ordinary comparison, imagine a record for each member on a separate sheet of paper, and the file of collected records—the sheets of paper—in a file drawer. If we wanted to make simple changes manually, we could simply add a new sheet for a new member, scratch out an old phone number and pencil in the new number on the sheet for an existing member, or perhaps remove a sheet altogether for a member who is resigning from the health club. This method of updating a file drawer is cumbersome and time-consuming for a large file. Computerized batch processing takes a different approach to accomplish the same task more efficiently. All changes to be made to the master file are compiled on a separate **transaction file.** Such changes can be of the following types:

- *Additions* are transactions to create new master records for new members. If Beth Andrews is joining the club, a transaction containing the fields for Ms. Andrews—including her membership number, name, address, and so forth—will be prepared to add the new membership record to the file.

- *Revisions* are transactions to change fields, such as street addresses or phone numbers, on the master records. For example, if Jim Lawler changes his address and phone number, a transaction is prepared to reflect these changes on his record in the master file.

■ *Deletions* are transactions with instructions to remove master records of people who have resigned from the health club. For example, if Thuy Tran resigns from the club, a transaction is prepared to remove her record from the file.

At regular intervals, perhaps monthly, the master file is **updated** with the changes called for on the separate transaction file, which has been sorted in order by a key field such as a social security number. The result is a new, up-to-date master file. The new file in this example has a new record for Beth Andrews, has a changed record for Jim Lawler, and no longer has a record for Thuy Tran.

An advantage of batch processing is that it is usually less expensive than other types of processing because it is more efficient: A group of records is processed at the same time. A disadvantage of batch processing is that it is not immediate. Anyone who wants to know the exact status—customers or business users—has to wait. It does not matter that you want to know what the gasoline bill for your car is now; you have to wait until the end of the month, when all your credit-card gas purchases are processed together with those of other customers. Batch processing cannot give you a quick response to your question.

Transaction Processing

DISCUSSION QUESTION

Why is it necessary for real-time processing to be online?

Transaction processing is a technique of processing transactions one at a time in random order—that is, in any order they occur. Since transactions are processed at the time the transaction occurs, the files are always up-to-date. Transaction processing is handy for anyone who needs an immediate update or feedback from the computer, such as a contractor who needs to check a supplier's rates, an airline clerk making a reservation, or a retailer who wants to confirm product inventory. Transaction processing has become a staple in all kinds of service industries in which speedy service is a must.

Transaction processing is real-time processing. **Real-time processing** can obtain data from the computer system in time to affect the activity at hand. In other words, a transaction is processed fast enough for the results to come back and be acted upon immediately. For example, a teller at a bank (or you at an automatic teller machine) can find out immediately what your bank balance is. You can then decide how much money you can afford to withdraw. For processing to be real-time, it must also be **online**—that is, the user's terminal must be directly connected to the computer to which the data files are available.

The great leap forward that transaction processing represents was made possible by the development of magnetic disk as a means of storing data. With magnetic tape it is not efficient to go directly to the particular record you are looking for; the tape might have to be advanced several feet first. However, with disk you can go directly to one particular record. The development of magnetic disk meant that data processing is more likely to be **interactive,** as is possible with the personal computer. The user can communicate directly with the computer, maintaining a dialogue back and forth. The direct access to data on disk dramatically increased the use of interactive computing.

There are several advantages to transaction processing. The first is that you do not need to wait. For instance, a department store salesclerk using a POS terminal can key in a customer's charge-card number and a code that asks the computer "Is this charge card acceptable?" and get an immediate reply. Immediacy is a distinct benefit, since everyone expects fast service these days. Second, the process permits continual updating of a customer's record. Thus the salesclerk not only can verify your credit but also can record the sale in the computer, and you will eventually be billed through the computerized billing process.

Figure 5-2 provides an example of transaction processing, in which a patient submits a prescription.

Batch and Transaction Processing: Complementary

Numerous computer systems combine the best features of both of these methods of processing. A bank, for instance, may record your withdrawal transaction during the day at the teller window whenever you demand your cash. However, the deposit that you leave in an envelope in an

▼

Figure 5-2   How transaction processing works.
The purposes of this hospital-clinic pharmacy system are to verify that a patient's prescription is safe, produce a prescription label for the medication bottle, and update the patient's medical records. Since there is a possibility of patients having the same name, the file is organized by unique patient numbers rather than by names. Here Ryan Johnson, patient number 32689, brings his prescription to the pharmacist. (1) Through a terminal the pharmacist queries the computer system whether the ampicillin prescribed is apt to conflict with any other medication the patient is taking. (2) The computer screen verifies that 32689 is Ryan Johnson and displays the message "No conflict." The computer then updates Johnson's file so other physicians can see later that ampicillin was prescribed for him. (3) A printer attached to the computer system prints a prescription label that the pharmacist can place on the ampicillin bottle. All this is done while the patient is waiting.

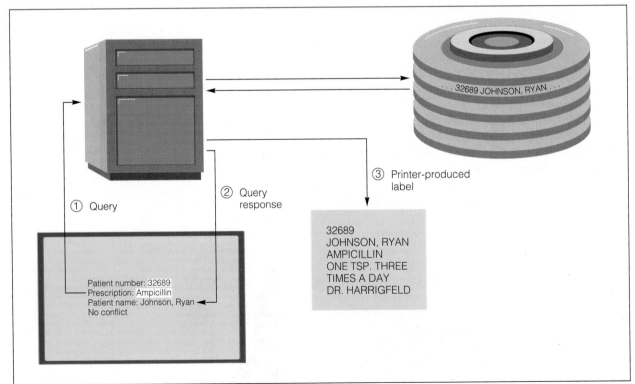

"instant" deposit drop may be recorded during the night by means of batch processing.

Another common example of both batch and transaction processing is in retail sales. Using POS terminals, inventory data is captured as sales are made; this data is processed later in batches to produce inventory reports.

Storage Media

As we have mentioned, two primary media for storing data are magnetic tape and magnetic disk. Since these media have been the staples of the computer industry for three decades, we will begin with them.

Magnetic Tape Storage

Magnetic tape looks like the plastic Mylar tape used in home tape recorders. Large computer systems typically use tape that is ½ inch wide and wound on a 10½-inch-diameter reel (Figure 5-3). Personal computers use tape only to back up disk files, that is, for emergency use if any harm comes to the disk files. Tape has an iron-oxide coating that can be magnetized. Data is stored as extremely small magnetized spots, which can then be read by a tape unit into the computer's main storage.

Figure 5-4a shows a **magnetic tape unit** that is part of a large computer system. The purpose of the unit is to write and to read—that is, to record data on and retrieve data from—magnetic tape. This is done by a

▲
Figure 5-3   Magnetic tape.
Magnetic tape on 10½-inch-diameter reels has been the workhorse of data processing for years. However, a smaller tape cartridge has been introduced that can hold 20 percent more data in 75 percent less space.

LECTURE HINT

The density of data on magnetic tapes is measured in bytes per inch (bpi); 800, 1600, and 6250 bpi are common densities. The tapes are typically 2400 feet long; but 300-, 600-, and 1200-foot tapes are also available. Current tapes have nine channels, one for each bit of a byte, plus parity (some old tapes have only seven channels).

▼
Figure 5-4   Magnetic tape units.
Tapes are always covered—in this case, by glass doors—to protect them from outside dust and dirt. (a) Magnetic tape on reels runs on these tape drives. (b) This diagram highlights the read/write head and the erase head found in magnetic tape units.

(a)

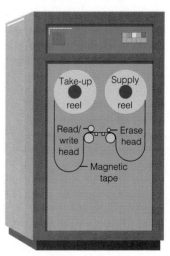

(b)

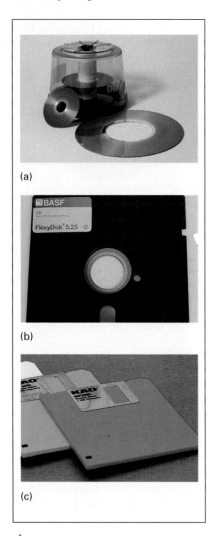

(a)

(b)

(c)

▲

Figure 5-5 Magnetic disks.
(a) Hard magnetic disks come in a variety of sizes, as shown by these three individual disks. Disk packs can vary in the number of disks they contain. (b) This 5¼-inch diskette is in a square protective thin plastic jacket. (c) This 3½-inch diskette is protected by a firm plastic exterior cover.

LECTURE HINT

Unlike audio tapes, magnetic tapes are not read and written to continuously. The tape drive must wait until the computer is ready to transfer data. Letting the tape move continuously while recording no data would waste tape. So the tape remains stationary between data transfers. Interrecord or interblock gaps are used on tapes so that the tape can reach the speed needed to transfer data.

read/write head (Figure 5-4b). Reading is done by an electromagnet that senses the magnetized areas on the tape and converts them into electrical impulses, which are sent to the processor. The reverse process is called writing. Before the machine writes on the tape, the **erase head** erases any previously recorded data, permitting the write head to write over the top of the erased data.

Records are stored on tape sequentially—in order by some identifier such as a social security number.

Magnetic Disk Storage

Magnetic disk storage is another common form of secondary storage. A **hard magnetic disk,** or **hard disk,** is a metal platter coated with magnetic oxide that looks something like a large brown compact disk. Hard disks come in a variety of sizes: 14, 5¼, and 3½ inches are typical diameters. Several disks of the same size can be assembled together to form a **disk pack** (Figure 5-5a). A disk pack looks like a stack of stereo records, except that daylight can be seen between the disks. There are different types of disk packs, with the number of platters varying by model. Each disk has a top and bottom surface on which to record data.

Another form of magnetic disk storage is the **diskette,** which is a round piece of plastic coated with magnetic oxide (Figure 5-5b, c). Both diskettes and hard disks are used with personal computers. We will discuss secondary storage for personal computers later in this chapter, but keep in mind that the principles of disk storage discussed here also apply to disk storage for personal computers.

How Data Is Stored on a Magnetic Disk

As Figure 5-6 shows, the surface of each disk has tracks on it. Data is recorded as magnetic spots on the tracks. The number of tracks per surface varies with the particular type of disk. A track on a disk is a closed circle, so any point on a particular track is always the same distance from the center. All tracks on one disk are concentric; that is, they are circles with the same center.

A magnetic disk drive is a **direct access storage device (DASD).** With such a random access device, you can go directly to the record you want. With tape storage, on the other hand, you must read all preceding records in the file until you come to the desired record. Records can be stored either sequentially or randomly (in whatever order the records occur) on a direct access storage device.

The Disk Drive

A **disk drive** is a device that allows data to be read from a disk or written on a disk. A diskette is inserted into a disk drive that is part of a personal computer. A disk pack, on the other hand, is mounted on a disk drive that is a separate unit connected to a large, shared computer. Some disks are permanently mounted inside a disk drive. Generally, these are used in personal computers or in cases where several users are sharing data. A typical example is a disk with files containing flight information that is used by several airline reservations agents.

The mechanism for reading or writing data on a disk is an **access arm** (Figure 5-7a). The access arm acts somewhat like the arm on a record

The screen photo that opens this gallery is taken from a multimedia offering called *From Alice to Ocean,* which beautifully chronicles a young woman's journey, with her camels, across the Australian outback.

Multimedia
The New Sight and Sound

The Multimedia Story

Multimedia is different. For example, have you ever thought that you could see a film clip from *Gone with the Wind* on your computer screen? One could argue that such treats are already available on videocassette, but the computer version provides an added dimension for this and other movies: reviews by critics, photographs of movie stars, lists of Academy Awards, and much more.

Although an "ordinary" personal computer is certainly adequate for most personal and business uses, a computer equipped for multimedia offers a greater variety of information. Multimedia software typically presents information with text, illustrations, photos, narration, music, animation, and film clips.

How Is This Possible?

The key to multimedia is the high-volume capacity of optical disks. One CD-ROM disk can hold approximately 500 times as much data as an ordinary data diskette. This capacity accommodates the kinds of data that take up huge amounts of storage space, such as photographs, film clips, and music.

From a hardware standpoint, a multimedia computer must be equipped with a CD-ROM drive to read the disks. Also needed are a sound card (installed internally) and speakers, which normally rest on either side of the computer. Special software

A multimedia computer looks much like an ordinary personal computer on the surface. The main difference that can be seen is the speakers on either side.

accompanies the drive and sound card.

To Buy or Not To Buy

Should your next computer be a multimedia personal computer? Absolutely. There is no doubt that multimedia applications will be the standard very shortly. Furthermore, if you get multimedia components pre-installed, it is the computer maker's job to see that everything works together properly.

But suppose you already own a personal computer and do not plan to get a new one any time soon. Should you upgrade your current computer with a multimedia kit? This is a tougher question. A multimedia kit usually includes a CD-ROM drive, a sound card, speakers, required

software, and several application diskettes. Installing the required hardware and software is not usually an easy task. Unless you are fairly skilled, you should make sure you have support from a vendor or some other source before you begin this task. Once a multimedia system is set up, you can take advantage of the growing list of multimedia software packages.

The Coming Deluge

If you take a moment to peruse the racks of multimedia software in your local store, you can see that most of the current offerings come under the categories of entertainment or education — or possibly both. You can study *and hear* works by Stravinsky or Schubert. You can explore the planets or the ocean bottom through film clips and narrations by experts. You can be "elected" to Congress, after which you tour the Capitol, decorate your office, hire staff, and vote on issues. You can study the Japanese language, seeing the symbols and hearing the intonation. You can buy reference books, magazines, children's books, and entire novels.

But this is just the beginning. Businesses are already moving to this high-capacity environment for street atlases, national phone directories, and sales catalogs. Coming offerings will include every kind of standard business application — all tricked out with fancy animation, photos, and sound. Educators will be able to draw upon the new sight and sound for everything from human anatomy to time travel. And just imagine the library of the future, consisting of not only the printed word but also photos, film, animation, and sound recordings — all flowing from the computer.

These scenes are from a multimedia package that provides a narrated tour of the London Gallery of Art. The scene above, by Titian, depicts the ancient myth of *Bacchus and Ariadne*. The scene below, by Renoir, is called *Boating on the Seine*.

People who wish to upgrade their existing computers can buy a multimedia kit, which typically contains a CD-ROM drive, a sound card, speakers, and several diskettes.

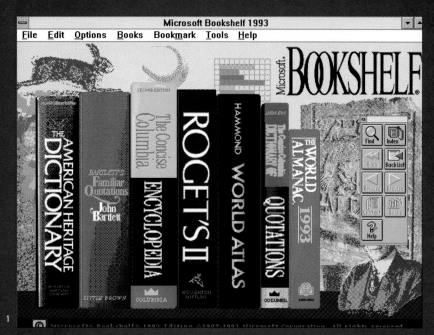

A2

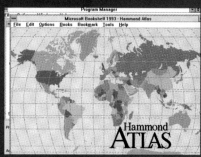

1

3

The pictures on the following pages are taken from screens presented by various multimedia packages. The photos must be shown in limited sizes to retain their clarity. However, this means that there is room for more screen shots.

1. The Microsoft Bookshelf software opens with this screen shot of actual volumes. Click on any book to access the information within. **2.** In the Bookshelf version of *Bartlett's Familiar Quotations,* a user can, by clicking a microphone icon, hear the words from John F. Kennedy's inaugural speech actually spoken by Kennedy. **3.** This world map is one of many in the Hammond Atlas that is part of Bookshelf.

The software called *Beyond Planet Earth* provides a complete tour of all the planets. Shown here are **4,** Jupiter's atmosphere and **5,** the phenomenon known as Jupiter's great red spot.

6. *Just Grandma and Me* is one of the Living Books series, in which youngsters of all ages can interact with and even change the story. **7.** In this deceptively simple scene, a click of the mouse on any object provokes action. A click on the tree, for example, prompts a chipmunk to poke its head out of a hole in the tree and chatter.

The Gas Giants

Jupiter

You gaze in wonder at a failed star.

Jupiter has more mass than all of the other planets put together. Its diameter is more than 11 times the size of Earth's. It radiates one-and-a-half times more heat than it receives from the Sun.

Jupiter is a ball of dense gas, each layer compressed by the layer above it. The core is so compressed that it has liquified into a ball more than 20 times the mass of Earth. Jupiter is the heaviest object in our solar system except for the Sun.

Jupiter's Atmosphere

1 of 8

Main Menu   Related Topics   Search

4

Jupiter's Great Red Spot

5 of 6

Menu   Topics   Search

5

Japanese   English   Spanish

JUST GRANDMA AND ME

READ TO ME

OPTIONS

6

We went to the beach, just Grandma and me.

7

athers at Asnières

EURAT
884

ll title *"Bathers at Asnières (Une
ignade, Asnières)"* Signed: Seurat.
nvas, 201 x 300 cm
. 3908, Purchased by the
urtauld Fund, 1924; returned
m the Tate Gallery, 1961.

nières is an industrial
burb west of Paris. A
lway bridge and smoking
tories form the background
this image of working
n at leisure.

is was the first of Seurat's
ge-scale compositions.
was made before he fully
olved pointillism and it
ploys a variety of techniques.

It was rejected by the official
*Salon in 1884 and displayed at
the Salon des Indépendants where
it receive...

*NEXT PAGES... Painting
Technique; Colour Theory;
Composition; Painting at
...Look*

Options... | Go Back | 1 of 6

Van Gogh's Chair

Van GOGH
1888

*Signed: Vincent
Canvas, 91.8 x 73 cm, No. 3862;
Purchased by the Trustees of the
Courtauld Fund, 1924; returned from
the Tate Gallery, 1961.*

Painted in November 1888, while Gauguin
was staying with van Gogh at Arles,
and retouched early in 1889. Van Gogh
also painted a companion picture of
Gauguin's armchair (Rijksmuseum
Vincent van Gogh, Amsterdam)
Although van Gogh gave no explanation
of his imagery, the paintings were
probably intended to represent the
contrasting temperaments and interests
of the two artists.

Help | Options... | Go Back | 1 of 4 paintings by van GOGH | Next Page | See Also | Contents

11

Art Gallery — PAINTINGS

Help | Options... | Go Back | 1 of 2 paintings by PICASSO | Next Page | See Also | Contents

12

---

rouville

Art Gallery — PAINTINGS

Monet's mistress, Camille, whom
he had recently married, and that
on the right may well be the wife

of ▶ **Boudin**, whose own beach
scenes were influential on the
young Monet.

NEXT PAGE... Technique.

Help | Options... | Go Back | 1 of 2 pages on The Beach at Trouville / 2 of 11 paintings by MONET | Next Page | See Also | Contents

13

A multimedia
package that tours
the London
Gallery of Art
offers commen-
tary on hundreds
of paintings.
Shown here are
8. Seurat's *Bathers
at Asnières;* **9,** a
vase of flowers by
Gauguin; **10,**
Degas' *Ballet
Dancers;* **11,** Van
Gogh's painting of a chair; **12,** Picasso's
Child with a Dove; and **13,** *The Beach at
Trouville,* by Monet.

The wonderful Dinosaurs offering shows
dinosaurs of every size and shape, complete with ominous dinosaur snorting.
Shown here are **14,** a Jurassic era scene,
15, a stegosaurus eating, and **16,** a bary-
onyx fishing.

Microsoft Dinosaurs — PICTURE GALLERY

Contents | Atlas | Timeline | Families | Index | Back | Options | Help

14

Microsoft Dinosaurs — PICTURE GALLERY

Contents | Atlas | Timeline | Families | Index | Back | Options | Help

15

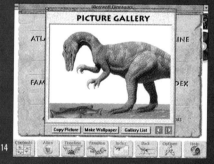

9

10

16

In the Company of Whales

The Discovery Channel

At a Glance	Whales in Motion
The World of Whales	Ask the Experts

EXIT

All multimedia packages offer several methods of exploring the information offered, including a menu of some sort. Here, **17** shows a menu that greets users of a package called *In the Company of Whales*. To the accompaniment of whale singing and much splashing, a user is presented with a variety of shots, including **18**, whales in shallow water and **19**, a killer whale breaching the water.

17

18

19

20

21

Notes On Louis Armstrong

LOUIS ARMSTRONG

Louis Armstrong was a legend in his own time. Very often musicians call him "Pops", because he is often referred to as the "Father of Jazz." Without argument, he was the greatest jazz figure in history.

6

Several comprehensive musical packages are offered through multimedia, including Franz Schubert's *Trout Quintet*. Although the emphasis is on listening, the package incudes many offerings, including **20**, a portrait of Schubert, **21**, a picture of a manuscript with his glasses, and **22**, a "trout game," an audio matching game.

23. In this unusual multimedia package, the first track contains exhaustive information on the life and music of jazz great Louis Armstrong, including film clips of contemporaries, such as Dave Brubeck, narrating portions of that history. The remaining tracks, to be played on an audio CD system, contain performances by Armstrong.

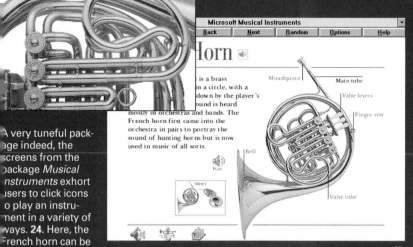

...orn

...is a brass
...n a circle, with a
...down by the player's
...ound is heard
...mostly in orchestras and bands. The
French horn first came into the
orchestra in pairs to portray the
sound of hunting horns but is now
used in music of all sorts.

Mouthpiece   Main tube
Valve levers
Finger rest
Bell
PLAY
VIEWS
Valve tube

A very tuneful pack-
age indeed, the
screens from the
package *Musical
Instruments* exhort
users to click icons
to play an instru-
ment in a variety of
ways. **24.** Here, the
French horn can be
...ipped (played rapidly) or hand stopped
...moving hand to change pitch). Clicking
...n any word gives a closeup, **25,** such as
...his valve tube.

25

27

The comprehen-
sive *Twain's
World* package
includes Mark
Twain's novels,
speeches, and
personal letters.
The media used
are narration, period music, illustrations,
photos, animation, and even a film clip of
Twain himself in 1909. **26.** Mark Twain,
shown in his later years. These illustrations accompany two of Twain's novels,
27, *The Adventures of Huckleberry Finn*
and **28,** *The Prince and the Pauper*.

28

31

30

33

Sleepless in Seattle (1993)
Skye, Ione
Slater, Christian
Slater, Helen
Sleeper (1973)
Sleeping Beauty (1959)
Sleepless in Seattle (1993)

...dezvous on the observation deck of the
...g Ryan) finds true love with Sam
...king son Jonah (Ross Mallinger),

34

When Belle (voice of Paige O'Hara) falls in love with the Beast (voice of
Robby Benson), their passion revives the magical rose that will restore
the Beast to his princely form, in BEAUTY AND THE BEAST.

32

Few Good Men, A (1992)
Ferrer, Mel
Ferris Bueller's Day Off (1986)
Fetchit, Stepin
Few Good Men, A (1992)
Field of Dreams (1989)
Field, Betty

Show Media
Go To Subject
All Media   Portraits
Movie Stills   Dialogue
Film Clip   Music
Exit Gallery

U.S. Marine Colonel Nathan Jessup (Jack Nicholson) engages in a courtroom
battle of wills against Navy attorney Lt. Daniel Kaffe (Tom Cruise) in the
climactic scene of A FEW GOOD MEN.

The package called *Cinemania* provides
users with everything they want to know about movies and
movie stars. This package specializes in film clips of action
scenes from movies as diverse as *Amadeus* and *Star Wars,* and
even has Gene Kelly performing *"Singing in the Rain."* Photos
are available of any star, including **29,** Denzel Washington, **30,**
Julia Roberts, and **31,** James Dean. **32.** This screen, for *A Few
Good Men,* shows a photo scene and, to the left, a menu of
choices. Similar screens are shown here for **33,** *Sleepless in
Seattle* and **34,** *Beauty and the Beast*.

35. This browse screen is one of several menu presentations for *Microsoft Encarta*, a multimedia encyclopedia that features photos, illustrations, narration, and animation. **36.** Screens typically present a photo accompanied by text, as shown here for the image orthicon tube. Other screen photos of interest, clockwise from the top, are **37**, integral calculus; **38**, a dry cell battery; **39**, a marmoset; **40**, altocumulus clouds; **41**, the *Mississippi Queen* paddleboat; **42**, Mount Rushmore; **43**, The University of Virginia; **44**, the international flag alphabet; and **45**, pilot Amelia Earhart.

37

38

$y = f(x)$

$a\ x_1\ x_1\quad x_2\ x_2\qquad x_3\ x_3\qquad x_{i-1}\ x_i\quad x$

35

Category Browser

Select an area of interest, then select a category

Area of Interest

Physical Science and Technology

Life Science

Geography

History

Social S...

Religion Philosop...

Art, Lang... and Liter...

Perform...

Sports, Hobbies

☐ Sociology
☐ Anthropology
☐ Archaeology
☐ Economics
☐ Political Science
☐ Education
☐ Psychology

Television

ICONOSCOPE

As a camera tube, the iconoscope has several disadvantages. One of the most important is that it requires extremely strong illumination of the subject produce a usable signal. When television cameras are used in the studio under controlled light conditions, this disadvantage is not serious, but the iconoscope is unsuitable for use in the televising of news events under adverse light conditions.

IMAGE ORTHICON

→ Figure 2: Image Orthicon Tube

A number of other camera tubes have been invented overcome this difficulty. The most sensitive of these the image orthicon, as shown in Fig. 2. The sensitivity of this tube is such that it will produce a camera sign under any lighting conditions that are suitable for the naked eye; in demonstrations, the image orthicon has the image orthico... l screen and can

Communications

Show List | Change Category | < | >

Figure 2: Image Orthicon Tube

Copy | Print | < | >

Print

36

45

44

43

42

40

41

39

COMPUTING TRENDS

Bride, Groom, Computer

A wedding really needs only a few essential ingredients: a bride, a groom, someone to marry them, and witnesses. So, how is it that wedding plans take weeks or months of frantic activity, with everyone desperately hoping that everything will go as planned? Those who have participated know about the complications, from invitations to caterers to photographers.

A new software offering called The Wedding Planner takes on all these activities and smooths the way. The software guides you in compiling and maintaining lists of invitations, RSVPs, gifts, and thank you notes—all on your own computer's storage. Furthermore, the software helps manage your budget, keeping a running tally of expenditures.

The calendar feature guides you prior to the wedding, giving detailed planning instructions sometimes months in advance. When it comes to the wedding day, specific times are listed, as well as a list of reminders and such homey tips as "allow more time than you would expect for taking a posed photograph." It is almost like having a wedding consultant at your service, day or night. Interested? The phone number is 1-800-265-5555.

player, although its read/write heads do not actually touch the surface of the disk (Figure 5-7b). A disk pack has a series of access arms that slip in between the disks in the pack (Figure 5-7c). Two read/write heads are on each arm, one facing up for the surface above it, one facing down for the surface below it. However, only one read/write head can operate at any one time.

Winchester Disks

In some disk drives the access arms can be retracted, and then the disk pack can be removed from the drive. In other cases the disks, access arms, and read/write heads are combined in a **sealed module** called a **Winchester disk.** Winchester disk assemblies are put together in clean rooms so even microscopic dust particles do not get on disk surfaces. Many Winchester disks are built in, but some are removable in the sense that the entire module can be lifted from the drive. The removed module remains sealed and contains the disks and access arms.

Winchester disks were originally 14 inches in diameter, but now smaller versions are available. Hard disks on personal computers—5¼ and 3½-inch disks—always employ Winchester technology. Until 1980 the most common type of high-speed storage consisted of removable disk packs. Since then that technology has been supplanted by Winchester disks; today around 85 percent of all disk storage units sold are of the fixed Winchester variety. The principal reason is that, compared to removable disk packs, Winchester disks cost about half as much and go twice as long between failures. This increased reliability results because operators do not handle the Winchester disk at all and because the sealed module keeps the disks free from contamination.

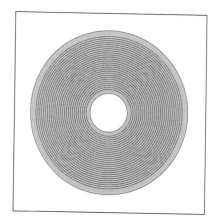

▲

Figure 5-6 Surface of a disk.
Note that each track is a closed circle, unlike the tracks on a stereo record. This drawing is only to illustrate the location of the tracks; you cannot actually see tracks on the disk surface.

TRANSPARENCY ACETATE #26

Figure 5-6

LECTURE HINT

Alan Shugart of IBM is the inventor of magnetic disk storage. He built the first hard disk drive in 1957 and the floppy disk drive in 1961.

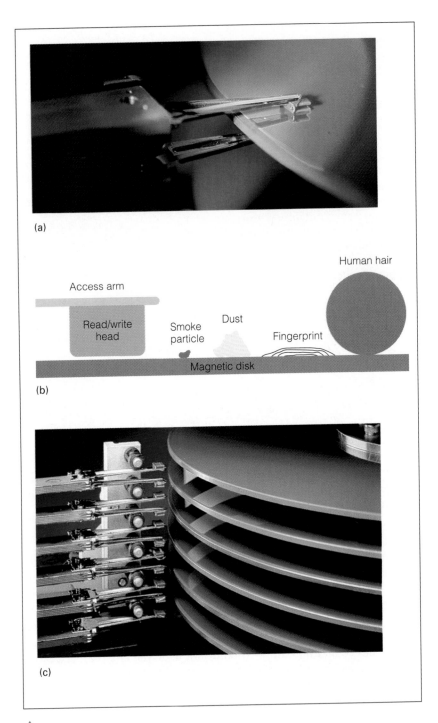

(a)

(b)

(c)

Figure 5-7 Read/write heads and access arms.
(a) This photo shows a read/write head on the end of an access arm poised over a hard disk. (b) When in operation the read/write head comes very close to the disk surface. In fact, particles as small as smoke, dust, fingerprints, and a hair loom large when they are on a disk. If the read/write head crashes into a particle like one of these, data is destroyed and the disk damaged. You can see why it is important to keep disks and disk drives clean. (c) Note that there are two read/write heads on each access arm. Each arm slips between two disks in the pack. The access arms move simultaneously, but only one read/write head operates at any one time.

MACINTOSH

Making Your Disk Space Count

Sooner or later it happens to almost everyone. No matter how inexhaustible we imagined our hard disks to be, the day arrives when we run out of storage space. The primary reason for this is that storage devices are getting less expensive: Every year you can get more megabytes per dollar when you buy a hard disk. So the 20-MB disk that seemed so boundless in capacity a few years ago is now considered minimal as users are opting for larger hard disks when they purchase their computers.

The increasing demand for disk space is likely to continue as storage prices decline. If you want your computer to be the powerful machine it was intended to be, you need to pay attention to your disk's capacity.

One way of increasing your storage potential is to invest in a compression utility program. SuperDoubler, developed by Symantec Corporation, will compress files to as little as half their size. When the files need to be accessed, SuperDoubler decompresses them back into their normal format. SuperDoubler's enormous popularity is largely due to its ability to compress your files "in the background," so that you never have to go through the steps of compressing and decompressing them. SuperDoubler can nearly double your available disk space, and the process is invisible to you, the user. The only problem with this option is that the activities of compression and decompression require some of your processor's time and can slow the performance of your machine a little.

As an alternative you should consider investing in a larger disk. If you already have an internal hard drive in your Mac and you don't want to replace it, look into an external drive, which resides in a case of its own and sits next to or under your Mac. If you anticipate that your storage needs will continue to grow, you might consider buying a removable hard drive, for which you can purchase indefinitely many 40MB or 80MB disks that pop in and out of the drive, just like 3½-inch disks. If you work heavily with sounds, images, or desktop publications, a removable drive can be of great value to you. A fur-

A removable hard drive can increase the capacity of your system's memory indefinitely with disks that have 40MB or 80MB of memory.

ther advantage of a removable drive is that it facilitates easy porting of huge amounts of data to other machines that have the same kind of drive.

If you do buy a new hard disk, be sure to invest in plenty of extra capacity. The trend of programs and data files getting larger is one that's likely to continue, so planning now will ensure you have enough disk space to last years. A few years ago, a 40-MB hard drive was considered huge; now, many users are buying machines with 80MB, 170MB, 240MB, or even larger drives.

Comparison of Disk and Tape Storage

As you can see, disk storage has many advantages over tape storage. There are those in the industry who wonder why tape is still around at all. Disk does indeed seem the very model of an effective storage medium for the following reasons:

- Disk has high data-volume capacity and allows very fast access.
- Disk is reliable; barring a catastrophe, the data you put there will still be there when you want to retrieve it.
- Disk files permit direct access to read or write any given record. This is the biggest advantage and is basic to real-time systems, such as those providing instant credit checks and airline reservations.

However, tape storage has its own unique advantages. Tape is portable: A reel of tape can be carried or mailed. It is relatively inexpensive: A 2400-foot reel of tape costs less than $15. (Compare this with a full-size disk pack, which costs $300 or more.)

DISCUSSION QUESTION

Compare disk and tape storage.

LECTURE ACTIVITY

Display various kinds of disks and magnetic tapes usable on computers. You might want to include some of historical interest, such as the CPM 8 inch floppy and a magnetic tape reel.

The chief use of magnetic tape today is as a backup medium for disk files. Although a hard disk is an extremely reliable device, the drive is subject to electromechanical failure. With any method of data storage, a **backup system**—a method of storing data in more than one place to protect it from damage or loss—is vital. Backup copies of disk files are made regularly on tape as insurance against disk failure and accidental file deletions. This topic is an important one and will be addressed more fully as a security measure in Chapter 10.

Personal Computer Storage

The market for data storage devices is being profoundly affected by the surge in popularity of personal computers. Storage media are available in two basic forms: diskettes and hard disk; most personal computers today come with both. Let us consider each of these in turn.

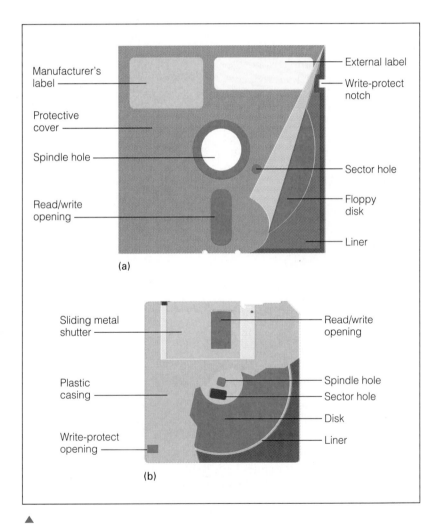

▲
Figure 5-8 Diskettes.
(a) Cutaway view of a 5¼-inch diskette. (b) Cutaway view of a 3½-inch diskette.

Diskettes

Diskettes, sometimes called *floppy disks,* are popular among personal computer users. Diskettes are transferable from one computer to another, provided the density, or capacity, of the borrowed disk does not exceed what the disk drive can handle. Also, diskette drives are relatively inexpensive. The 5¼-inch diskette was popular in the 1980s; however, the newer 3½-inch diskette, which can hold more data, is supplanting the 5¼-inch diskette (Figure 5-8). As a side note, some users prefer to buy a system with both 3½- and 5¼-inch diskette drives, so that their computers can accept data prepared by a computer with either size diskette drive.

The smaller disk is easier to store, and it fits handily into a shirt pocket or purse. Its hard plastic jacket provides better protection for the diskette than does the thin jacket of the larger disk. The higher capacity of the 3½-inch diskette lets users store many files on a disk, so users do not have to shuffle so many disks around. Finally, since the 3½-inch disk drive is small, manufacturers can make their computers smaller, so they take up less desk space.

In a shared computer system, such as computers in a college lab or in an office, users keep their data files on their own diskettes, which can be kept separately from the shared system.

Hard Disks

Personal computer hard disks are 5¼-inch or 3½-inch Winchester disks in sealed modules (Figure 5-9a). The cost of hard disks has come down substantially: A hard disk with a capacity of hundreds of megabytes of

LECTURE HINT

One company kept losing its disks due to disk "crashes." A chemist examined the bad disks and found a thin layer of hair spray on them. The company forbade their employees to use hair sprays until the computer center obtained its own separate air conditioner.

LECTURE HINT

The top and bottom surfaces of a multiplatter disk are more likely to be corrupted by dust and other contaminants than other surfaces, and are not used often.

DISCUSSION QUESTION

Why do most hard disk systems include at least one diskette drive?

▲
Figure 5-9   Hard disks.
Innards of a 3½-inch hard disk with the access arm visible.

TRANSPARENCY ACETATE #28

Figure 5-9

▲
Figure 5-10   Optical disk.

TEST BANK

Mult. Choice 25-26
T/F 74-77
Matching I 84
Matching II 96, 99
Fill In 120-122, 127, 130

DISCUSSION QUESTION

Describe how optical storage works.

LECTURE HINT

A recent trend in the publishing industry is for leading magazine publishers, such as Time Inc., Condé Nast, and Hearst, to create multimedia divisions. The plan is to combine electronic, print, and interactive media. It is not yet known whether the multimedia technology will be online services, CD-ROMs, or both.

LECTURE HINT

Whereas the *Random House Unabridged Dictionary* weighs in at 13 pounds, the entire dictionary can fit on a single CD-ROM disk. The CD-ROM version contains over 315,000 entries from the printed dictionary plus an additional 1000 words not included in the 1987 printed edition. Maps and illustrations, however, are not provided in the disk version.

storage now costs only a few hundred dollars or less, down from several thousand dollars just a few years ago. Winchester disks are extremely reliable because they are sealed against contamination from outside air or human hands.

Hard disks can save you time as well as space. Just the way the hard disk speeds up your computing can make it worthwhile, even if you do not need all the storage hard disk provides. Accessing files on hard disk is significantly faster than on diskettes—up to about 20 times faster. Furthermore, users find that accessing files from a hard disk is more convenient than handling diskettes.Unlike a diskette, however, most hard disk units cannot be transported from one computer to another. For that reason most hard disk systems include at least one diskette drive to provide users with software and data portability.

◢ Optical Storage

Would you like to have an encyclopedia at your fingertips? Such a demand can now be met thanks to the technology that is now upon us: the **optical disk** (Figure 5-10). The explosive growth in storage needs compelled the computer industry to provide high-capacity storage devices that are a demand tailor-made for the optical disk. The contents of a typical encyclopedia fit nicely on a single optical disk.

Optical Disk Technology

Optical storage works like this. A laser beam hits a layer of metallic material spread over the surface of the disk. When data is written to the disk, heat from the laser produces tiny spots on the disk's surface. To read the data, the laser scans the disk and a lens picks up different light reflections from the various spots.

Optical storage technology is categorized according to its read/write capability. Data is recorded on **read-only media** by the manufacturer and can be read from but not written to by the user (you can read it, but you cannot change it). This technology is sometimes referred to as **optical read-only memory (OROM)**. Obviously, you could not use an OROM disk to store your files, but manufacturers could use it to supply software. A current multiple-application, or integrated, package—a product that provides software for word processing, spreadsheets, graphics, and a database—sometimes takes as many as a dozen diskettes; the contents could fit easily on one OROM disk.

Write once, read many (WORM) media may be written to once. When the WORM disk is filled, it becomes read-only media. A WORM disk is nonerasable. For applications demanding secure storage of original versions of valuable documents, such as wills or other legal papers, the primary advantage of nonerasability is clear: Once they are recorded, no one can erase or modify them.

CD-ROM: A New Best-Seller

A popular variation on optical technology is **compact disk read-only memory (CD-ROM)**. CD-ROM has a major advantage over other

Personal Computers
In Action

How to Handle Diskettes

Do not lock your diskette in the trunk of your car on a hot day, leave it on the dashboard in the sun, or stick it to the door of your refrigerator with a magnet. Avoid smoking cigarettes around your computer, since smoke particles caught under the read/write head can scratch the disk surface.

These are only a few of the rules for taking care of diskettes. The main forces hostile to diskettes are dust, magnetic fields, liquids, vapors, and temperature extremes. Although 3½-inch diskettes in their sturdy plastic jackets are not especially fragile, be careful not to bend the metal clips lest a disk gets stuck in the disk drive.

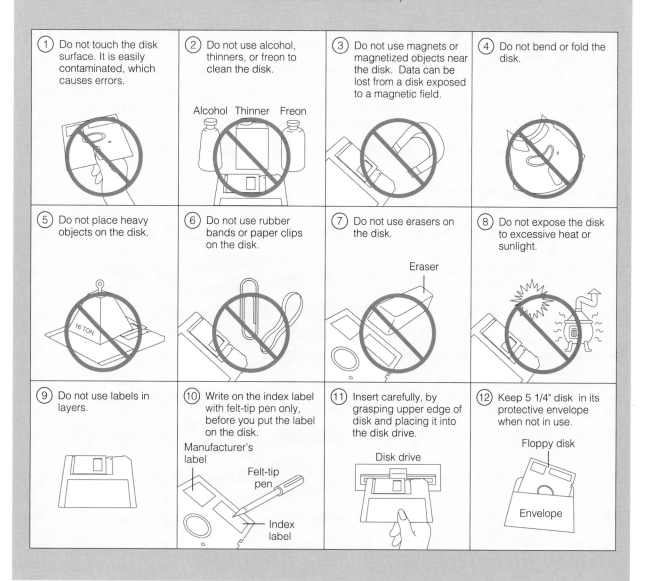

1. Do not touch the disk surface. It is easily contaminated, which causes errors.
2. Do not use alcohol, thinners, or freon to clean the disk.
3. Do not use magnets or magnetized objects near the disk. Data can be lost from a disk exposed to a magnetic field.
4. Do not bend or fold the disk.
5. Do not place heavy objects on the disk.
6. Do not use rubber bands or paper clips on the disk.
7. Do not use erasers on the disk.
8. Do not expose the disk to excessive heat or sunlight.
9. Do not use labels in layers.
10. Write on the index label with felt-tip pen only, before you put the label on the disk.
11. Insert carefully, by grasping upper edge of disk and placing it into the disk drive.
12. Keep 5 1/4" disk in its protective envelope when not in use.

TRANSPARENCY ACETATE #29

Figure 5-PCA

Curling Up with a Good Computer

The computer industry has for years touted reading books from a screen as one of the futuristic advantages of having a computer. However, people seem to prefer sitting in their own comfortable chair and turning paper pages.

Finally, along comes an offering that is so exciting on-screen that it surpasses the paper-only version. A CD-ROM package called From Alice to Ocean includes a well-written, glossy adventure book, lavish color photos, and two digital disks. This material chronicles a six-month trek across Australia's outback by a woman accompanied by four camels and a dog. The beautifully done CD-ROM disks, complete with pictures and text, make the product surpass what the book could have achieved alone.

DISCUSSION QUESTION

What are the hardware requirements for a multimedia system?

optical disk designs: The disk format is identical to that of *audio* compact disks, so the same dust-free manufacturing plants that are now stamping out digital versions of Mozart or Pearl Jam or Reba McEntire can easily convert to producing anything from software to the aforementioned encyclopedia. Since manufacturing CD-ROM disks is simply a matter of pressing out copies from a master disk, it is much more economical than traditional magnetic storage, which makes copies byte by byte. Furthermore, CD-ROM storage is gargantuan—up to 660 megabytes per disk, the equivalent of over 400 3½-inch diskettes.

The popularity of CD-ROM disks is a relatively recent phenomenon. Early uses in the late 1980s focused on reference materials: dictionaries, thesauruses, encyclopedias, and atlases. The key advantage was speed: It is faster and easier to type a key word or two and let the computer look up the subject matter, rather than shuffling through weighty volumes. Early users were mostly businesses who were burdened with massive amounts of information. As interest in CD-ROMs increased, manufacturers expanded the variety of applications, leaning more to the consumer market (Figure 5-11). Of particular interest to college students is Monarch Notes, which provides a computerized set of crib notes for studying literary classics.

The CD-ROM market is being driven by two factors: the flood of enticing new offerings and the falling prices of both the disks and the disk drives. Keep in mind that a CD-ROM disk cannot be used in your magnetic disk drive; you must have a CD-ROM drive installed on your computer. If you have a CD-ROM drive, you could be on your way to one of the computer industry's great adventures: multimedia.

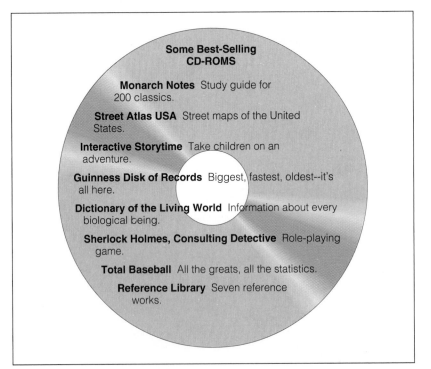

▲
Figure 5-11 Popular CD-ROM software.

Multimedia: The Computer As Centerpiece

Photography, video, music, recorded voice—all these media have something to offer. Now, thanks to the high capacity of CD-ROM disks, these media can be offered on your computer. **Multimedia** is the term used to describe the hardware and software combination that provides access to all these media. Multimedia software typically presents information with text, illustrations, photos, narration, music, animation, and film clips. In addition to a CD-ROM drive, you will need a sound card (installed internally), a set of inexpensive speakers, and the required software to

LECTURE HINT

A CD-ROM disk can store more than 450 times the data of a conventional floppy disk, which is important becausestoring video and sound requires extensive computer code. Although a CD-ROM disk can hold approximately 330,000 printed text pages, it can hold only about 45 minutes of a movie.

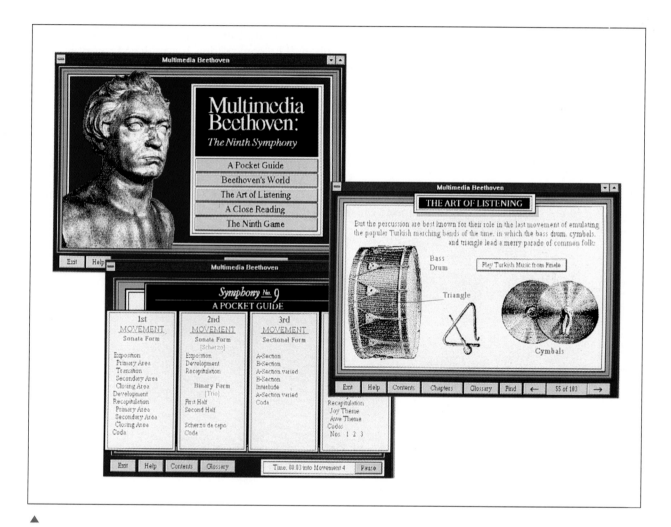

▲

Figure 5-12 Multimedia application.
This educational approach makes learning a pleasure. The name of the application is Multimedia Beethoven: The Ninth Symphony. It contains an overview of the most famous symphony ever written, along with a biography of the composer that places the work in historical context. As the Vienna Philharmonic plays the symphony, the screen text provides a running commentary from which even a sophisticated musician can learn. A user can also highlight passages and have the program repeat a line. The disk also includes a game that doubles as a test of knowledge.

LECTURE HINT

The term *digital convergence,* means the combining of the computer industry with communications and entertainment companies. Numerous alliances are being created, but it is not yet clear which business model will be followed when these companies work together.

CLASS PROJECT

Divide the class into groups and have each group research one of the storage technologies discussed in the chapter. How is each technology used today? How has the technology changed over the years? How will each technology be used in the future?

take advantage of multimedia offerings. (Be sure to examine the multimedia gallery, which describes multimedia in more detail and presents several examples of colorful multimedia offerings.)

A good example of a multimedia program is Sherlock Holmes, Consulting Detective. The program begins with a blast of Victorian-sounding music and an animation sequence showing a book opening. The title page offers three different murder mysteries from which to choose. Pick one, and Sherlock Holmes and Dr. Watson appear in a digitized video clip of an old movie. The video plays right on the computer screen, almost like a television movie. The object of the game is to solve the mystery with as few clues as possible. This kind of application illustrates the somewhat fanciful claim that CD-ROM technology may eventually allow the computer industry and Hollywood to merge (Figure 5-12).

Multimedia is making swift inroads into educational settings, where students can switch from the late President John F. Kennedy's inauguration speech to footage of Martin Luther King's civil rights marches to the first moon landing. The competition for students' interests is so lively and intense today that schools want to get every edge they can in attracting and holding it. Multimedia may be one component of success.

What is the future of storage? Whatever the technology, it seems likely that we will be seeing greater storage capacities in the future. Such capabilities have awesome implications—think of the huge data files for law, medicine, science, education, and government.

To have access to all that data from any location we need data communications, the topic of the next chapter.

Chapter **Review**

Summary and Key Terms

- **Secondary storage,** or **auxiliary storage,** is necessary because primary storage, or memory, can be used only temporarily.
- To be processed by a computer, data represented by characters is organized into fields, records, files, and sometimes databases. A **character** is a letter, digit, or special character (such as $). A **field** is a set of related characters, a **record** is a collection of related fields, a **file** may be a collection of related records, and a **database** is a collection of interrelated files.
- The two main methods of large-scale data processing are **batch processing** (processing data transactions in groups) and **transaction processing** (processing data transactions one at a time).
- Batch processing involves a **master file,** which contains semipermanent data, and a **transaction file,** which contains additions, deletions, and changes to be made to **update** the master file. An advantage of batch processing is the cost savings resulting from processing records in groups; the main disadvantage is the delay of receiving output.
- In transaction processing, the transactions are processed in the order they occur. This is **real-time processing** because the results of the transaction are available quickly enough to affect the activity at hand. Real-time processing requires having the user's terminal **online**—directly connected to the computer. The development of disk storage permitted **interactive** processing—a computer/user dialogue—by providing users with easier access to data.
- **Magnetic tape** is a plastic storage medium coated with iron oxide. A **magnetic tape unit** records and retrieves data by using a **read/write head,** an electromagnet that can convert magnetized areas into electrical impulses (to read) or reverse the process (to write). Before the machine writes, the **erase head** erases any previously recorded data.
- A **hard magnetic disk,** or **hard disk,** is a metal platter coated with magnetic oxide. Several disks can be assembled in a **disk pack.** A **diskette** is a round piece of plastic coated with magnetic oxide.
- The surface of a magnetic disk has tracks on which data is recorded as magnetic spots.
- A disk storage device is a **direct access storage device (DASD)** because the read/write head can directly locate a record on it.
- A **disk drive** rapidly rotates a disk or disk pack as an **access arm** moves a read/write head that detects the magnetized data.
- A **Winchester disk** combines disks, access arms, and read/write heads in a **sealed module**.
- Advantages of disk storage are that it provides high-volume data capacity and allows users to find and update records immediately. Tape storage can be used only for batch processing, but it is portable and less expensive than disk storage.
- A **backup system**—a method of storing data in more than one place to protect it from damage or loss—is vital. Backup copies of disk files are made regularly on tape as insurance against disk failure.
- Diskettes and hard disks are the most common storage media for personal computers. Diskettes are available in 5¼-inch and 3½-inch sizes. A hard disk is more expensive than a diskette and usually cannot be moved from computer to computer, but it does provide more storage and faster processing than using diskettes.

KEY TERMS

access arm
auxiliary storage
backup system
batch processing
CD-ROM (compact disk read-only memory)
character
database
direct access storage device (DASD)
disk drive diskette
disk pack
erase head
field
file
hard disk
hard magnetic disk
interactive
magnetic tape
magnetic tape unit
master file
multimedia
online
optical disk
optical read-only memory (OROM)
read-only media
read/write head
real-time processing
record
sealed module
secondary storage
track
transaction file
transaction processing
update

Winchester disk

write once, read many (WORM)

■ In **optical disk** technology, a laser beam enters data by producing tiny spots on the optical disk's metallic surface. Data is read by having the laser scan the disk surface while a lens picks up different light reflections from the spots.

■ Optical storage technology is categorized according to its read/write capability. The manufacturer records on **read-only media** through a technology sometimes called **optical read-only memory (OROM)**; the user can read the recorded media but cannot change it. **Write once, read many (WORM)** media can be written to once; then the disk becomes read-only. **Compact disk read-only memory (CD-ROM)** disks have the same format as audio compact disks.

■ **Multimedia** is the term used to describe the hardware and software combination that can present information with text, illustrations, photos, narration, music, animation, and film clips.

Student Personal Study Guide

True/False

T   F   1. Real-time processing gives results fast enough to affect the computer user's next action.

T   F   2. Processing data by groups of transactions is called batch processing.

T   F   3. A transaction file contains records to update the master file.

T   F   4. The quickest way to back up a hard disk is to use diskettes.

T   F   5. Another name for magnetic tape is DASD.

T   F   6. Transaction processing systems are usually real-time systems.

T   F   7. A drawback of magnetic tape storage is that it is very expensive.

T   F   8. An optical disk can never be erased.

T   F   9. A field is a set of related records.

T   F   10. Auxiliary storage can be used only temporarily.

Multiple Choice

1. The kind of processing in which data is processed as it occurs:
   a. batch
   b. field
   c. transaction
   d. master

2. A direct access storage device:
   a. optical tape
   b. erase head
   c. magnetic tape
   d. DASD

3. Another name for secondary storage:
   a. auxiliary
   b. drive
   c. memory
   d. master file

4. Semipermanent data:
   a. transaction file
   b. master file
   c. batches
   d. erase head

5. A set of related characters:
   a. database
   b. file
   c. field
   d. record

6. Write once, read many:
   a. backup
   b. OROM
   c. WORM
   d. magnetic tape

7. Several disks assembled together:
   a. database
   b. optical disk
   c. disk pack
   d. diskette

8. Disk, access arms, and read/write heads in a sealed module:
   a. hard drive
   b. diskette
   c. Winchester disk
   d. optical disk
9. A group of related fields comprises a:
   a. database
   b. file
   c. record
   d. field
10. Processing data in groups:
   a. master
   b. field
   c. transaction
   d. batch

Fill-In

1. The two most common media for secondary storage are: _____ and

   _____ .

2. A technique for processing transactions in any order they occur: _____ .

3. DASD stands for: _____ .

4. User/computer dialogue: _____ .

5. Optical storage technology is categorized according to this ability:

   _____ .

6. CD-ROM stands for: _____ .

7. The technology supporting a sealed disk module: _____ .

8. Records that can add, delete, or revise master file records are called: _____ .

9. Data is usually backed up on what media: _____ .

10. The storage technology that uses a laser beam: _____ .

Answers

True/False: 1. T, 2. T, 3. T, 4. F, 5. F, 6. T, 7. F, 8. F, 9. F, 10. F
Multiple choice: 1. c, 2. d , 3. a , 4. b, 5. c, 6. c, 7. c, 8. c, 9. c, 10. d
Fill-In: 1. magnetic tape and magnetic disk, 2. transaction processing, 3. direct access storage device, 4. interactive, 5. read/write, 6. compact disk read-only memory, 7. Winchester, 8. transactions, 9. tape, 10. optical disk

Chapter Overview

LEARNING OBJECTIVES

- Being acquainted with the evolution of data communications systems, from centralized data processing systems to teleprocessing systems to distributed data processing to local area networks
- Knowing data transmission methods
- Differentiating the different kinds of communications links
- Understanding wide area networks and local area networks
- Being acquainted with examples of networking—such as electronic mail, voice mail, teleconferencing, facsimile technology, electronic fund transfers, bulletin boards, Internet—and the contexts in which networking is used—such as in shopping and computer commuting

At age 43, Lucas Eiffert was laid off from his job as a midlevel marketing manager for a toy manufacturer. Even as he sent out résumés and sought out his old contacts, he knew that the whole industry was paring middle management and that his chances of finding something in his current field were slim. Lucas decided to augment one of his job-related skills, computers.

Lucas had no formal computer training except a brief word processing course. He had picked up desktop publishing and a smattering of computer graphics on the job. Even so, he was still very much a user, not a computer professional. Lucas figured out how to survive for a year while both going to school and working part time. He went to his local community college and took the basic courses in programming. He eventually took courses in systems analysis and design, database management, and—the one that captured his interest—data communications. Data communications, he discovered, was basically a marriage of computers and communications links such as the telephone.

As Lucas learned the technical end of data communications, he could see how the technology applied to situations at the toy company. He remembered, for example, the limited number of quality printers and the inconvenience of using someone else's printer. He realized that, using a data communications network in which machines and resources such as printers are hooked together, users could easily share printers. He also recalled the confusion over data duplication and who had what in which disk file; again, a network would let users establish one file for one purpose and give all users access to the same file. Lucas also remembered trying to reach people to set up a meeting; leaving messages by computer was the obvious solution. Finally, he recalled his boss complaining about the expenses of trips to meet with branch managers to plan marketing campaigns. Lucas now knew that, through data communications technology, these meetings could be done by computer, with everyone staying at home.

Lucas served an internship with a networking consultant company. He helped install the hardware and software for several office networks. To continue his job search in his new field, Lucas revamped his résumé and told *everyone* that he was job hunting.

Through an unexpected source (his mail carrier) Lucas found a job with a kitchen products sales company that was about to install a data communications network. Lucas' dual backgrounds in marketing and data communications made a favorable impression. He was hired as an assistant to the personal computer manager, and the two of them soon began planning a data communications network for the office.

All this happened in 1990–1991. Lucas now owns his own data communications consulting company.

Communications

Computer Connections

Sit Back and Relax with Your Laptop

Business travelers used to look forward to flights as a way to get away from the office and maybe catch up on a novel. No more. Now they tote their laptops along and feel guilty if they do not get some work done on the trip.

The airlines are both helping and hindering the effort. On one hand airlines have announced plans to have computers aboard, with the screen imbedded on the back of the seat in front of you. Just bring along your own diskettes and get to work. They even plan to include an air-to-ground system for data communications so you can exchange data with the office. Ah, but there lies the problem.

The problem is that the airlines have some realistic fears about communications from any kind of device interfering with the airplane's navigational systems. At this writing, most airlines prohibit the use of any portable device during takeoff and landing. Back to that novel.

TEST BANK

Mult. Choice 4, 2, 15, 22
T/F 40-41, 45, 72-73
Matching I 91
Fill In 132, 140, 145

TEST BANK

T/F 89

DISCUSSION QUESTION

How does centralized data processing differ from distributed data processing?

Data Communications Now

Merging communications and computers can help you get full value from each technology. Possible benefits include access to services like computer banking and computer shopping and to other workers in a computer network. People who use computer communications technology are just as casual about linking up with a computer in another state or country as they are about using the telephone. The technology that makes it possible is called data communications.

Data communications systems—computer systems that transmit data over communications lines such as public telephone lines or private network cables—have been gradually evolving since the mid-1960s. When computers were still a novelty, users placed everything—all processing, hardware, software, and storage—in one central location, a scheme now called **centralized data processing.** Centralization, however, proved inconvenient. The next logical step was **teleprocessing**—connecting users to a central computer via telephone lines and terminals right in their own offices.

The most innovative scheme, however, is **distributed data processing (DDP),** which is similar to teleprocessing but accommodates both remote *access* and also remote *processing.* Processing and files are dispersed among several remote locations and can be handled by local computers—usually mini- or microcomputers—all hooked up to the central host computer and sometimes to each other as well. A typical application of a distributed data processing system is a business or organization with many locations, branch offices, or retail outlets.

The whole picture of distributed data processing has changed dramatically with the advent of networks of personal computers. A **network** is a computer system that uses communications equipment to connect two or more computers and their resources, such as printers and hard disks. DDP systems are networks. We will examine networking in more detail in later sections of the chapter.

The Complete Communications System: How It All Fits Together

Suppose you work at a sporting goods store. You learn the first day that the store has a computer that is part of a network. The network is connected to the warehouse and to other stores so that you can exchange inventory and other information. What components are in place to help you do your job?

The basic configuration—how the components are put together—is straightforward, but the choices for each component vary, and the technology is ever changing. Assume that you have some data—a message—to transmit from one place to another. The basic hardware components of a data communications system to transmit that message are (1) the sending device, (2) a communications link, and (3) the receiving device. In the sporting goods store, you might want to send a message to the warehouse to inquire about a particular skateboard, an item you need for a customer. In this case the sending device is your terminal or personal computer at the store, the communications link is the phone line, and the receiving machine is the computer at the warehouse. As you will see later, there are many other possible configurations.

There is another often-needed component in this basic configuration, as you can see in Figure 6-1. This component is a modem, which may be needed to convert computer data to signals that can be carried by the communications channel and vice versa.

Let us see how these components work together, beginning with how data is transmitted.

 # Sending Your Data: Data Transmission

If you want to communicate with other computers, you must overcome a significant obstacle: the inherent incompatibility of computers with some communications links. A terminal or computer produces digital signals, and most communications travel along telephone lines, which were built for voice transmission and require analog signals. We will look at these two types of transmissions and then consider modems, which translate between them.

Types of Transmission: Digital and Analog

Digital transmission sends data as distinct pulses, either on or off, and thus can accept computer-generated data directly. However, most communications media—such as telephone lines, coaxial cables, and microwave circuits—are not digital. For most users transmitting via one of these common means is more practical than establishing a means of digital transmission. Furthermore, the common communications media have a common characteristic: They all use analog transmission.

▼
Figure 6-1 Communications system components.
Data originating from (1) a sending device is (2) converted by a modem to data that can be carried over (3) a link and (4) reconverted by a modem at the receiving end before (5) being sent to the receiving computer. Although we show external modems here for the purpose of illustration, most modems are inside the computer's housing.

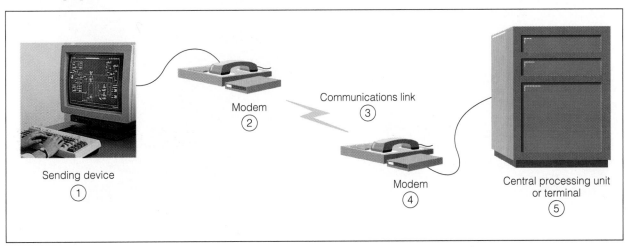

Analog transmission uses a continuous electrical signal in the form of a wave. A digital signal must be converted to analog before it can be sent over analog lines. Conversion from digital to analog signals is called **modulation,** and the reverse process—reconstructing the original digital message at the other end of the transmission—is called **demodulation.** So we see that the marriage of computers to communications is not a perfect one. Instead of just "joining hands," a third party may be needed in between to make signal conversions. This extra device is called a modem.

Making the Switch: Modems

A **modem** is a device that converts a digital signal to an analog signal and vice versa (Figure 6-2a). *Modem* is short for *mo*dulator/*dem*odulator. Once a modem is attached to your computer, all you have to do is send the data; the modem will take care of the translation automatically.

▼

Figure 6-2   Modems.
(a) Modems convert, or modulate, digital data signals to analog signals for traveling over communications links; then they reverse the process, or demodulate, at the other end. (b) This external modem rests under the telephone that hooks the computer to the outside world. (c) This internal modem slips into an expansion slot inside the computer. The phone cord plugs into a jack, accessible through the back of the computer.

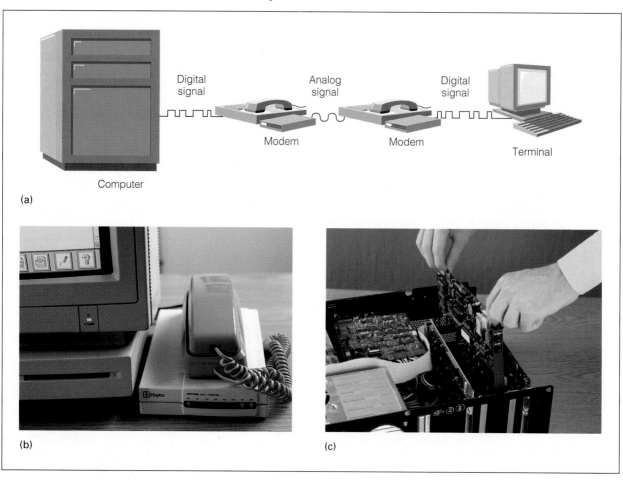

Most modems today are **direct-connect modems,** directly connected to telephone lines by means of telephone jacks. Although some users still use **external modems,** which are placed outside computers (Figure 6-2b), most personal computer users prefer **internal modems,** which can be inserted inside computers (Figure 6-2c).

A modem's speed of transmission is an important consideration. In general, modem users use normal telephone lines to connect their computers and pay telephone charges based on the time they are connected. Thus there is a strong incentive to transmit as quickly as possible. Although some modems still operate at slower speeds, common transmission speeds today are 2400 bits per second (bps) and 9600 bps. At 2400 bps, a modem can transmit a 20-page single-spaced report in five minutes; the same report can be transmitted at 9600 bps in just over one minute. The fastest modem on the market today can transmit data at an amazing 14,400 bps, sending that same report in less than one minute.

Now that we have discussed translating the data and the rates at which it can be sent, let us turn to the media that transmit it.

 # Carrying Your Data: Communications Links

What communications link will you choose to send your data? A communications **link** is the physical medium used for transmission. If your computer is at home, you will doubtless hook up to another computer through the telephone system. Large organizations, on the other hand, have more choices and must consider the cost factor. The cost for linking machines can be substantial (as much as one-third of the data processing budget), so it is worthwhile to examine the communications options.

Among the most common communications media are **wire pairs,** also known as **twisted pairs** (Figure 6-3a). Wire pairs are wires twisted together to form a cable, which is then insulated. Wire pairs are inexpensive and frequently used to transmit information over short distances, such as in a phone system within a metropolitan area.

Known for contributing to high-quality transmission, **coaxial cables** are insulated wires within a shield enclosure (Figure 6-3b). These cables can be laid underground or undersea, and they can transmit data at rates much higher than telephone lines. Coaxial cables have been the mainstay of cable television.

Traditionally, most phone lines have transmitted data electrically over wires made of metal, usually copper. These wires must be protected from water and other corrosive substances. **Fiber optics** technology was developed by Bell Laboratories to solve these and other problems (Figure 6-3c). Instead of using electricity to send data, fiber optics uses light. The cables are made of glass fibers, thinner than a human hair, that guide light beams for miles. Fiber optics can transmit data faster than some technologies, yet the materials are lighter and less expensive than wire cables.

Also popular is **microwave transmission** (Figure 6-4a), which uses line-of-sight transmission of data signals through the atmosphere. Since these signals cannot bend around the curvature of the earth, relay stations—usually antennas in high places such as the tops of mountains,

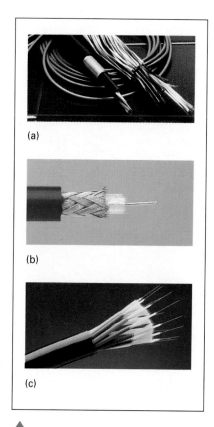

(a)

(b)

(c)

Figure 6-3 Communications links. (a) Wire pairs are twisted together to form a cable, which is then insulated. (b) A coaxial cable. (c) Fiber optics are hairlike glass fibers that carry voice, television, and data signals.

LECTURE HINT

In 1968 the FCC handed down the landmark Carterfone decision, which permitted competitors—many from the data processing industry—to enter the formerly regulated domain of AT&T. The gist of the decision is that other companies can now interface independent equipment with the public telephone network.

TEST BANK

Mult. Choice 3, 6, 32-35
T/F 46- 51, 74, 78, 80, 83
Matching I 90, 92, 98-99
Matching II 106
Fill In 114-115, 131, 133, 142, 144

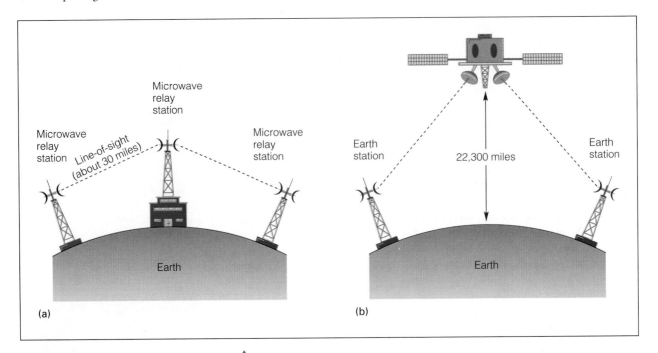

(a)

(b)

▲

Figure 6-4   Microwave transmission.
(a) To relay microwave signals, dish-shaped antennas are placed atop buildings, towers, and mountains. Microwave signals can follow only a line-of-sight path, so stations must relay this signal at regular intervals to avoid interference from the earth's curvature. (b) A satellite acts as a relay station and can transmit data signals from one earth station to another. A signal is sent from an earth station to the relay satellite in the sky, which changes the signal frequency before transmitting it to the next earth station.

towers, and buildings—are positioned at points approximately 30 miles apart to continue the transmission. Microwave transmission offers speed, cost-effectiveness, and ease of implementation.

Communications satellites are very far away: 22,300 miles above the earth. The basic components of **satellite transmission** are the earth stations that send and receive signals and the satellite component, which is called a transponder. The **transponder** receives the transmission from earth, changes the signal, and retransmits the data to a receiving earth station (Figure 6-4b). This entire process takes less than a second.

◤ # Hooking Up to the Big Computer: Wide Area Networks

As noted earlier, computers that are connected so they can communicate among themselves form a network. Two important kinds of networks are wide area networks and local area networks. Wide area networks send data over long distances. Most of these networks use the telephone system, although some companies have implemented their own microwave and satellite networks. Local area networks allow communication among computers linked together in one building or in buildings that are close together. Let us first consider wide area networks.

COMPUTING TRENDS

What Happens When You Charge a Purchase

The good old days of having your credit checked by your friendly local merchant are gone. Say you have just decided to buy a wristwatch from a merchant in Ann Arbor, Michigan. You offer your Visa charge card to pay for the $160 purchase. While you idly chat with a friend or stare out the window, the salesclerk is checking your credit card. Is the card good? Do you really have $160 available in credit to pay for the watch? Only the computer knows for sure.

However, it is not just "the computer" at work here, but a series of machines, all linked together to relay the questions and answers. Follow the trail: (1) The clerk passes your Visa card through a slot on a credit verification terminal and keys in data related to the sale. (2) The data travels by satellite or microwave to the regional computers of a data service clearinghouse in Cherry Hill, New Jersey. (3) From there, the credit inquiry travels to the data service's headquarters computers in Atlanta for processing. The transaction exceeds $50, so it needs a second opinion. (4) The request is turned

over to the Visa computers, which send the query to its mainframe computers in McLean, Virginia. (5) The Visa mainframe determines that the card is from a San Francisco bank and sends the transaction to the bank's computer, which checks to see if there is $160 available credit. The bank's okay retraces the path of the request in reverse order, working its way back to the store in Ann Arbor.

Total time elapsed? Approximately 15 seconds. And you hardly noticed.

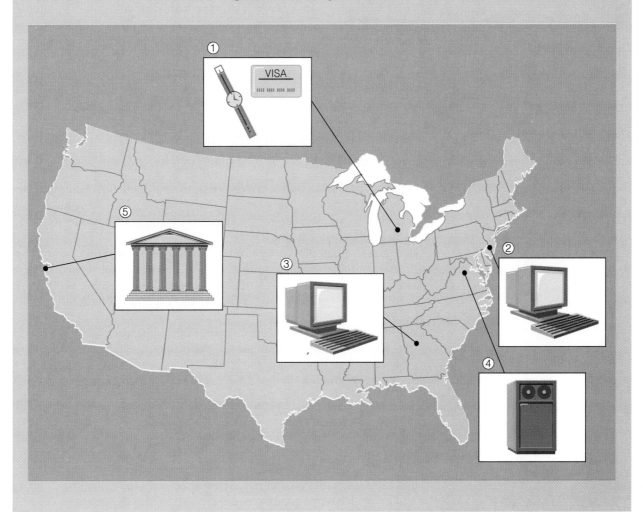

LECTURE HINT

Marshall McLuhan envisioned a world in which communications, television, and radio tied all of the people in the world together, creating a "global village." Thanks to the developments described in this chapter, McLuhan's vision is now becoming a reality.

TEST BANK

Mult. Choice 6-7, 20, 37-39
T/F 62, 79, 82, 85
Matching I 95-97
Matching II 101, 104
Fill In 113, 116, 120, 127-128, 134-135, 138, 147

DISCUSSION QUESTION

What are some typical LAN tasks?

A **wide area network (WAN)** is a network of geographically distant computers and terminals. In business a personal computer sending data any significant distance is probably sending it to a minicomputer or mainframe computer. Since these larger **host** computers are designed to be accessed by terminals, a personal computer can access a minicomputer or a mainframe only if it uses special software called **emulation software** to imitate, or emulate, a terminal. That is, the larger computer must consider the personal computer as just another terminal. Special communications software permits **downloading**—retrieving files from the host computer—or **uploading**—sending files from a personal computer to the host computer.

An alternative network is a local area network, which can communicate information much faster than most wide area networks.

Networking Within the Office: Local Area Networks

A **local area network (LAN)** is a collection of computers, usually personal computers, that share hardware, software, and data. In simple terms, LANs hook personal computers together through communications media so the computers can share resources. Personal computers attached to a LAN are often referred to as **workstations.** All the devices—personal computers and other hardware—attached to the LAN are called **nodes** on the LAN. As the name implies, LANs cover short distances, usually one office or building.

How Users Use Local Area Networks

Here are some typical tasks for which LANs are especially suited:

- A personal computer can read data from a hard disk belonging to another personal computer as if the data were its own. This allows users who are working on the same projects to share word processing, spreadsheet, and database data.
- A personal computer may print one of its files on a printer hooked up to another personal computer. This second computer is usually used especially for printing. (Since few people need exclusive access to a high-quality printer, only a few of the expensive printers need be hooked to the LAN.)
- One copy of an applications program, when purchased with the proper license from the vendor of the program, can be used by all the personal computers on the LAN. This is less confusing and less expensive than purchasing a copy of the program for each user.

LAN usage goes beyond simple convenience; some applications require that the same data be shared by coworkers. Consider, for example, a company that sends catalogs to customers, who can then place orders over the telephone. Waiting at the other end of the phone line are customer-service representatives, who key the order data into the computer system as they are talking to customers.

The service representatives use their own personal computers to enter orders but share common computer files that provide information on product availability and pricing. Having a separate set of files for each representative would lead to trouble because one representative would not know what others had sold. One representative, for example, could accept an order for 20 flannel shirts when, because of recent sales, only five shirts remain in stock.

In this kind of application workers must have access to one central master file that reflects the activities of other workers. LANs make such access possible.

How Local Area Networks Are Set Up

The physical layout of a local area network is called its **topology.** Local area networks come in three basic topologies: star, ring, and bus networks (Figure 6-5). A **star network** has a central host computer that is responsible for managing the LAN. It is to this computer—sometimes called a **server**—that the shared disks and printers are usually attached. The server also provides access to software and monitors the network. In a star network all messages are routed through the server. A ring or bus network also has servers to monitor the system, but messages are routed in a different way.

A **ring network** links all nodes together in a circular manner. Data is passed in one direction around the ring. Since only one node can send data at a time, a system called **token passing** controls the sender. That is, the node possessing the token—a pattern of bits—can send a message, which then goes from node to node in the ring until the proper recipient receives it. Once reception is acknowledged, the token is released to the

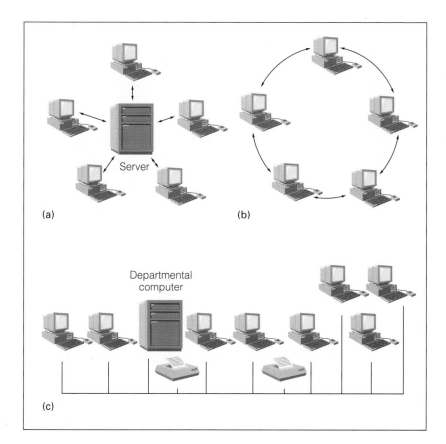

Figure 6-5 LAN topologies.
(a) The star network has a central host computer, and all messages are routed through the host. (b) The ring network connects computers in a circular fashion and uses a token-passing messaging system. (c) The bus network broadcasts messages to all computers, with the addressee acting on the message.

MACINTOSH

Going Public with America Online

There was a time when people equated personal computers with isolation. The classic image was that of the antisocial computer nerd who spent most of his or her hours interacting with machines instead of people. That image is changing, partly because of the friendliness of modern online subscriber services—mainframe computers to which users can connect from thousands of miles away. Among the most popular of such services is America Online.

Established in 1985 by Steve Case, America Online (AOL) is now the world's fastest growing subscriber service, with over 600,000 members. If you own an Apple Macintosh or DOS-based machine with Windows, getting an account on AOL is easy. You will, of course, need to have a modem connected to your computer and some related software. AOL will

a) America Online features a wide variety of services and forums centered around different topics. You can go to a specific department just by clicking on its icon.

send you a free copy of their software, which will manage all the modem settings and connection specifications necessary to begin your membership. Once you've installed the software and provided it with a little information (your name, address, and so forth), connecting to AOL is as simple as clicking a button.

The interface you work with once you've connected to AOL is equally friendly, in the tradition of the Macintosh graphical interface: Choices are presented to you in the form of windows and colorful icons that you activate by pointing and clicking. AOL offers many services but is organized in such a way that you can find the items you want quickly and easily. Each window presented to you by AOL offers you several choices of what to do or where to go next. For instance, when you first log on, you have the choices of reading the top news items of the day, checking any electronic mail you might have received, or going directly to the Departments section. If you choose Departments, you are given a window of choices such as Entertainment, Lifestyles & Interests, and News & Finance.

What lies at the end of this stream of choices? Possibly a display of information; for instance, you can look up a topic in Compton's Encyclopedia or display the day's stock market activities. You can copy files from AOL to your own computer's hard drive—perhaps some computer-scanned works of art from the Smithsonian Department, or interactive

educational programs, or some good games. AOL, like most subscriber services, provides massive software libraries through which you can browse.

Services like AOL are not just software storehouses, though; in fact,

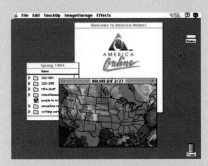

b) Here the user has downloaded a satellite image from AOL's Weather service, just a few hours after the photo was taken.

they're more aptly described as electronic communities. You can send mail to and receive mail from other users of the service, or even users of different services or machines. You can actively participate in a number of different forums—groups of users who exchange messages, post notices, and provide programs and documents to each other. Each forum is organized around some topic of interest, and there are many to choose from.

If you are interested in giving it a try, you can get your free software and a free trial period by consulting a major software retailer or bookstore, or by calling (800) 827-6364.

next node on the ring, which, if it has nothing to send, releases it to the next node, and so on.

A **bus network** configuration consists of a length of cable with nodes attached. A message is broadcast to all nodes. Each node examines the received message to see if it is the addressee; only the addressee(s) will act on the message. A node that wants to send a message waits its turn until the network is clear. Bus networks are the most common configuration; *Ethernet* is a widely used bus network.

Peer-to Peer Networks

A **peer-to-peer network**, which physically cables computers one to another, is commonly used for smaller networks of a dozen or so computers. Messages are grapevined, that is, passed along from one computer to another until the proper recipient is found. Disks and printers are scattered throughout the system. Peer-to-peer network users usually can access a software package on someone else's computer and use it as if it were on their own computers. For example, if just two computers were linked in a peer-to-peer network and one had WordPerfect (word processing) and the other Excel (spreadsheets), each could use the other's software.

 # Using Networks in the Office and Home

Think of it: More than 500 million telephones are installed throughout the world and, theoretically, you can call any one of them. Furthermore, every one of these phones has the potential to be part of a computer network. Although we have discussed other communications media, it is still the telephone that is the basis for networking at home or in the office. Revolutionary changes are in full swing in both places but particularly in the office.

Automation in the office is as variable as the offices themselves. As a general definition, **office automation** is the use of technology to help achieve the goals of the office. Much automated office innovation is based on communications technology. We begin this section with four important office technology topics—electronic mail, voice mail, teleconferencing, and facsimile.

Electronic Mail

Perhaps you have heard about "telephone tag." From your office you call Ms. Chan. She is not in, so you leave a message. You leave your office for a meeting, and when you return you find a message from Ms. Chan; she returned your call while you were out . . . and so it goes. Few of us, it seems, are sitting around waiting for the phone to ring. It is not unusual to make dozens of calls to set up a meeting among just a few people. **Electronic mail** or **e-mail**, is the process of sending messages directly from one computer to another. Electronic mail releases workers from the tyranny of the telephone.

Perhaps a company has employees who find communication difficult because they are geographically dispersed or are too active to be reached easily. Yet these may be employees who need to work together frequently, whose communication is valuable and important. These people are ideal candidates for electronic mail. Through a computer network a user can type messages to a colleague downstairs; a query across town to that person who is never available for phone calls; even memos simultaneously to regional sales managers in Cleveland, Raleigh, and San Antonio. The beauty of electronic mail is that a user can send a message to someone and know that the person will receive it.

Voice Mail

Here is how a typical **voice mail** system works. A user tries to complete a call by dialing the desired number in the normal way. If the recipient does not answer, the caller is then prompted by a recorded voice to dictate his or her message into the system. The voice mail computer system translates the words into digital impulses and stores them in the recipient's "voice mailbox." Later, when the recipient dials his or her mailbox, the system delivers the message in audio form (Figure 6-6).

This may sound like a spoken version of electronic mail. There is one big difference between electronic mail and voice mail. To use electronic mail, you and the mail recipient must have compatible devices and keyboards and be able to use them. In contrast, for voice mail all you need is a telephone; and telephones are everywhere, and everyone knows how to use them.

▼

Figure 6-6   A voice mail system.
The caller's message is stored in the recipient's voice mailbox on disk. Later the recipient can check his mailbox to get the message.

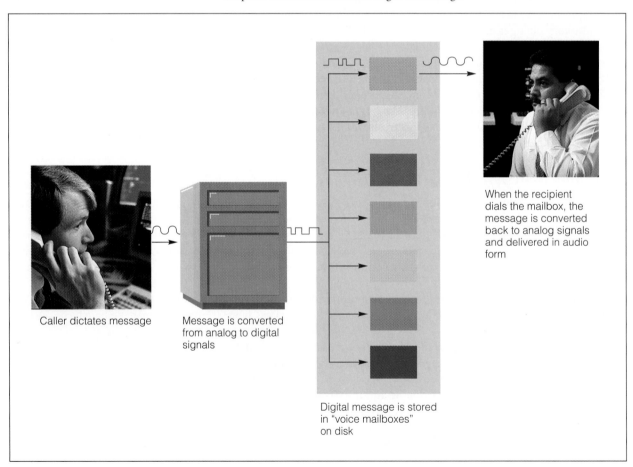

Caller dictates message

Message is converted from analog to digital signals

Digital message is stored in "voice mailboxes" on disk

When the recipient dials the mailbox, the message is converted back to analog signals and delivered in audio form

Teleconferencing

An office automation development with great promise is **teleconferencing,** a method of using technology to bring people and ideas together despite geographic barriers. The technology has been available for years, but the acceptance of it is quite recent.

There are several varieties of teleconferencing. The simplest, **computer conferencing,** is a method of sending, receiving, and storing typed messages within a network of users. Computer conferences can be used to coordinate complex projects over great distances and for extended periods. Participants can communicate at the same time or in different time frames, at the users' convenience.

A computer conferencing system is a single software package designed to organize communication. The conferencing software runs on a network's host computer, be it a micro, mini, or mainframe. In addition to access to the host computer and the conferencing software, each participant needs a personal computer or terminal, a telephone, a modem, and communications network software. Computer conferencing is a many-to-many arrangement; everyone is able to "talk" to everyone else via computer. Messages may be sent to a specified individual or set of individuals or broadcast to all receivers. Recipients are automatically notified of incoming messages.

Would you like your picture broadcast live across the miles for meetings? Add cameras and audio to computer conferencing, and you have another form of teleconferencing called **videoconferencing** (Figure 6-7). The technology varies, but the pieces normally put in place are a large (possibly wall-size) screen, cameras, and a computer system to record communication among participants.

Although this setup is expensive to rent and even more expensive to own, the costs seem trivial when compared to time and travel expenses for in-person meetings.

▼

Figure 6-7   A videoconferencing system.
Geographically distant groups can hold a meeting with the help of videoconferencing. The people shown on the screen are participants in another locale.

TRANSPARENCY ACETATE #34

Figure 6-7

The Revolution Comes Full Cycle

Could it be that we are back where we started? The original idea behind the personal computer was that it was, indeed, *personal.* You were on your own: your computer, your data, your business. Individual users had truly broken away from the large computers that were located elsewhere and used for heavy-duty computer tasks.

Personal computer pioneers smile at that notion now. Personal computer users, whether at home or in the office, are busily connecting their computers to everything in sight. In fact, the very power of a personal computer is coming to be defined in terms of what it is connected to. And what about those big computers, the ones personal computer users left behind? Users now gleefully connect to the big computer to access massive databases, to route messages, and much more.

Users once were willing to isolate themselves on personal computers rather than be an insignificant cog in the large computer system. Now, with networking, they have the best of both worlds.

▲
Figure 6-8   Faxing it.
This facsimile machine can send text and graphics long distance via the telephone in the background.

Facsimile Technology

To save the money and even the time associated with overnight mail service, you can use computers and data communications technology to transmit drawings and documents from one location to another. **Facsimile technology,** operating something like a copy machine connected to a telephone, uses computer technology to send graphics, charts, text, and even signatures almost anywhere in the world. The drawing, or whatever, is placed in the facsimile machine at one end (as shown in Figure 6-8), where it is digitized. Those digits are transmitted across the miles and then reassembled at the other end into the original picture. All this takes only minutes, or less. Facsimile is not only faster than overnight letter services, it is less expensive too. Facsimile is abbreviated **fax,** as in "I sent a fax" and "I faxed the report to the Chicago office." Faxing has become common in many businesses and some home offices.

A variation on the fax machine is the **fax board,** which fits inside a personal computer, thus facilitating transmission of computer-generated text and graphics. (If the document to be sent is on paper, it must be scanned by a scanner and stored in the computer first.) Incoming faxes are stored on the computer's hard disk; later they can be reviewed on screen and, if desired, printed. Another option is a **fax-modem board,** which, as its name indicates, performs the functions of both fax machine and modem.

Electronic Fund Transfers: Instant Banking

You may already be handling some financial transactions electronically instead of using checks. In **electronic fund transfers (EFTs),** people pay for goods and services by having funds transferred from various checking and savings accounts electronically, using computer technology. One of the most visible manifestations of EFT is the ATM—the automated teller machine.

Incidentally, many millions of social security checks have been disbursed by the government directly into the recipients' checking accounts via EFT rather than by mail. Unlike those sent via U.S. mail, such payments are unlikely to be lost. Moreover, EFT payments are traceable—again unlike the ordinary mail. A more recent trend is electronic transfer of salaries from businesses to employees' bank accounts. No more extra trips to the bank on payday. In addition, many people elect to have the bank pay their recurring bills, such as monthly mortgage payments, by electronically debiting their account and forwarding the money to the creditor.

Carrying this one step further, many people use their personal computers to pay all their bills, that is, to transfer funds from their bank accounts to the accounts of their creditors. A record of these transactions is included on the billpayer's monthly bank statement.

Bulletin Boards

Person-to-person data communications is one of the more exhilarating ways of using your personal computer, and its popularity is increasing at breakneck speed. A **bulletin board system (BBS)** uses data communications to link personal computers to provide public access to messages.

Electronic bulletin boards are somewhat like the bulletin boards you see in student lounges or employee lunchrooms. Somebody leaves a message, perhaps selling something, but the person who picks up the message does not have to know the person who left it. To get access to a bulletin board on someone else's computer, all you really have to know is that bulletin board's phone number. You can use any kind of computer, but you need a modem so you can communicate over the phone lines. Users find bulletin boards helpful in all the ways that people can help each other with advice or companionship. In particular, people with questions about their computers can get all sorts of free advice. You just leave the question and come back to pick up the answers. Anyone who has a personal computer can set up a bulletin board: It takes a computer, a phone line, a couple of disk drives, and free or inexpensive software.

Commercial Communications Services

We have talked about specific services, but some companies offer a wide range of services. Users can connect their personal computers to commercial, consumer-oriented communications systems via telephone lines. These services—known as **information utilities**—are widely used by both home and business customers. Three popular information utilities are CompuServe Information Service, Prodigy, and America Online (Figure 6-9). In each case you must take a few minutes to install the system software on your personal computer. Then, for a fee, the world opens up to you via computer.

These three utilities each offer myriad services, including news, weather, shopping, games, educational materials, electronic mail, forums, and financial information. Generally speaking, *CompuServe* is of greatest value to sophisticated users and computer professionals, offering program packages, text editors, a software exchange, and a number of programming languages. *Prodigy* is newer and much more user friendly, mainly because of its splashy graphics screens. Prodigy is also family-oriented, offering services such as meal-planning advice and children's educational games. *America Online*, the newest of these three, offers a superior, easy-to-use graphical environment, with mouse-controlled icons and overlayed screen windows. Macintosh or Windows users are familiar with this type of environment.

Charges for these services vary. Most charge a nominal sum for the initial setup software. The services offer some sort of ongoing package deal, usually a monthly fee that includes all basic services and a certain amount of connection time, with extra charges for extra time. People who live in populated areas can connect to the service at no extra charge through a local phone number. However, be warned: People in remote areas may have to access the service through a long distance phone number, a disadvantage that can generate a shocking phone bill.

Internet

Internet is the largest and most far-flung network system of them all, with more than 20 million users worldwide. Surprisingly, Internet is not really a network at all, but a loosely organized collection of networks. In fact, no one owns Internet and it is run by volunteers. It has no central headquarters, no centrally offered services, and no online index to tell you

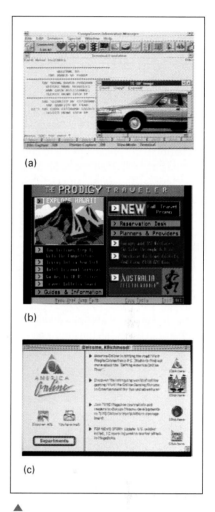

(a)

(b)

(c)

▲

Figure 6-9 Information utilities.
(a) CompuServe. (b) Prodigy. (c) America Online.

LECTURE HINT

Early in 1994 Southern California was hit by a major earthquake. People trying to reach loved ones invariably received a recording saying the call couldn't go through. To help its subscribers, the Prodigy network opened a special area on its electronic bulletin board for users to post messages about the earthquake, which resulted in 4000 messages during the first 6 hours.

DISCUSSION QUESTION

What are some services offered by information utilities?

LECTURE HINT

The 225-year-old Encyclopaedia Britannica is the oldest continuously published encyclopedia in the English language. This massive encyclopedia comprises 32 volumes, 44 million words, and 23,000 illustrations. Encyclopaedia Britannica executives plan to distribute the encyclopedia to universities and selected public libraries over Internet. Eventually the distribution will be expanded to a wider audience.

DISCUSSION QUESTION

What is telecommuting?

CLASS PROJECT

Divide the class into groups and have each group research the different LISTSERV groups or newsgroups available on the Internet.

what information is available. Originally developed by, and still subsidized by the United States government, Internet now connects libraries, college campuses, research labs, and businesses.

The great attraction of Internet for these users is that, once they have paid the sign-up fees, there are no extra charges. Therefore, and this is the key drawing card, electronic mail is free, regardless of the amount of use. In contrast, individuals using Internet must pay ongoing monthly fees. Internet is available to individuals through third-party vendors, such as Delphi or America Online. Alternatively, individuals can install personal computer software and be billed at an hourly rate for access to Internet.

Experts predict exponential growth for Internet in the next few years.

Computer Commuting

A logical outcome of computer networks is **telecommuting**, the substitution of data communications and computers for the commute to work (Figure 6-10). Many in the work force are information workers; if they do not need frequent face-to-face contact to do their jobs, they are candidates for using telecommuting to work at home. Although the number of telecommuters is still small, it is growing. In 1989, 3 million people telecommuted; by 1994 that number had risen to almost 8 million.

Although the original idea was that people would work at home all the time, telecommuting has evolved into a part-time activity. That is, most telecommuters stay home two or three days a week and come into the

▶

Figure 6-10
This telecommuter is wearing a headset to talk to and listen to customers. Her hands are free to input data during the conversation.

Personal Computers In Action

Living Online

Millions of people spend a part of each day online, connected to their favorite network, probably an information utility. Here are some of the things they can do with their connected computers:

Make travel plans. Andy Crowley travels several times a month for his business. He signs onto CompuServe and looks over flights going his way on the American Airlines EAASY SABRE reservation system. He makes his choices, charges them to his credit card, and picks up his tickets at the airport. Andy likes the convenience, but he also likes the chance to comparison-shop routes and prices and get the best deal.

Pay bills. Using Prodigy, Mary Deininger has listed and filed the names and addresses of all her creditors. Once a month she takes a stack of bills, hooks up to Prodigy, and keys in dollar amounts next to the appropriate creditors. Prodigy transfers the money to the creditors' computer systems. For Mary's dentist, Prodigy generates and mails a check. For Mary it is no checks, no envelopes, and no stamps.

Check a bulletin board. Somewhere there is a bulletin board that exactly matches your interests. Here are some samples of existing boards, from the mundane to the bizarre: genealogy, careers, automotive, collecting bottles or baseball cards or teddy bears, peace, astronomy, ecology, beer, atheists. And, lastly, yes it really exists (on Internet), there is a bulletin board devoted to Spam, a canned hamlike product.

Stay in touch. Networking is especially valuable to those in outlying locations. Jackson Qunit, who lives in a remote Alaskan village, relies on Internet to send and receive messages. He notes that it is like having pen pals, except that there is an instant response. Others find friends or even romance. People get acquainted on screen, eventually meet, and—sometimes—marry.

Follow your investments. Most services offer stock quotes and even quotes for your particular portfolio. But Roger Vaughn went a step further on America Online. He entered his individual stocks by price and quantity. Now, whenever he calls up his portfolio, the screen shows one line for each stock: original price, quantity, current price, and profit or loss. On the top of the screen is the total value of the portfolio and the total profit or loss to date.

Do research. Biochemist Barbara Aragona makes extensive use, through Internet, of NSFnet, the heavily used National Science Foundation network that is a key information exchange for scientists. Journalist Dorothy Moore finds the reference library on CompuServe both convenient and useful, especially the listings for business demographics, census data, consumer reports, and government publications.

Shop. Many people do a substantial amount of shopping at the hundreds of stores in the electronic shopping malls. Some find it particularly convenient to select and buy gifts, which the stores will gift wrap and send. Some people even use their computers to check out new cars.

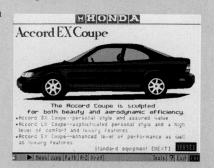

A cross-section of popular shop stops: Lands' End, Books on Tape, Gimmee Jimmy's Cookies, J. C. Penney, Metropolitan Museum of Art, Brooks Brothers, Coca-Cola Catalog, Florida Fruit Shipper, Spiegel, The Flower Shop, Musicworks, and the Contact Lens Replacement Center.

Hang out. Although most people who sign onto one of America Online's "lobbies" are individuals, Jody and Marty Czyzowicz enjoy this activity as a couple. When they click the People Connection icon on the screen, America Online assigns them to a lobby with other people (23 maximum) who will join in the "conversation" that appears on-screen. On one fairly typical evening, these topics were tossed around: the federal budget, a current movie, joining the Marines, Microsoft's multimedia encyclopedia, gays, and the weather. The last item was actually the most interesting, since participants are from all over the country.

Figure 6-11
In perhaps the ultimate in telecommuting, this column writer shows up in the office only once a week for a staff meeting.

office the other days. Time in the office permits the needed personal communication with fellow workers and also provides a sense of participation and continuity.

▼ ▼ ▼

The near future in data communications is not difficult to see. The demand for services is just beginning to swell. Electronic mail already pervades the office, the campus, and the home. Expect instant access to all manner of databases from a variety of convenient locations. Prepare to become blasé about services made available through data communications in your own home, office, and everywhere you go.

Chapter **Review**

Summary and Key Terms

- **Data communications systems** are computer systems that transmit data over communications lines such as public telephone lines or private network cables.
- **Centralized data processing** places all processing, hardware, software, and storage in one central location. In **teleprocessing** systems, terminals at various locations are connected by communications lines to the central computer, which does the processing.
- Businesses with many locations or offices often use **distributed data processing (DDP),** which allows both remote access and remote processing. Processing can be done by both the central computer and the other computers that are hooked up to it.
- A **network** is a computer system that uses communications equipment to connect two or more computers and their resources.
- The components of the simplest data communications system are a sending device, a communications link, and a receiving device.
- **Digital transmission** sends data as distinct on or off pulses. **Analog transmission** uses a continuous electrical signal.
- Computers produce digital signals, but most types of communications equipment use analog signals. Therefore, transmission of computer data involves altering the signal. Digital signals are converted to analog signals by **modulation. Demodulation** is the reverse process; both processes are performed by a device called a **modem.**
- Most modems today are **direct-connect modems,** directly connected to the telephone line by means of a telephone jack. An **external modem** is outside the computer; an **internal modem** can be inserted inside the computer.
- A communications **link** is the physical medium used for transmission. Common communications links include **wire pairs** (also called **twisted pairs**), **coaxial cables, microwave transmission, satellite transmission,** and **fiber optics.** In satellite transmission a **transponder** receives and retransmits the signal.
- A **wide area network (WAN)** is a network of geographically distant computers and terminals. The computer to which the terminal is attached is called the **host** computer. A personal computer can access these larger computers only if it uses special software called **emulation software** to imitate, or emulate, a terminal. Special software allows **downloading** files—retrieving files from the host computer—or **uploading** files—sending files from a personal computer to the host computer.
- A **local area network (LAN)** is a collection of personal computers that share hardware, software, and information. Personal computers attached to a LAN are referred to as **workstations.** All the devices—personal computers and other hardware—attached to the LAN are called **nodes** on the LAN. The physical layout of a local area network is called its **topology.** A **star network** has a central computer that is responsible for managing the LAN; it is to this central computer—sometimes called a **server**—that the shared disks and printers are usually attached. A **ring network** links all nodes together in a circular manner. Since only one node can send data at a time, a system called **token passing** controls the sender; the node possessing the token can send a message. A **bus network** assigns a portion of network management to each computer but preserves the system if one node fails.
- A **peer-to-peer network** physically cables computers one to another and grapevines messages to the recipient.

KEY TERMS

analog transmission

bulletin board system (BBS)

bus network

centralized data processing

coaxial cable

computer conferencing

data communications system

demodulation

digital transmission

direct-connect modem

distributed data processing (DDP)

downloading

electronic fund transfers (EFT)

electronic mail (e-mail)

emulation software

external modem

facsimile (fax) technology

fax board

fax-modem board

fiber optics

host

information utility

internal modem

link

local area network (LAN)

microwave transmission

modem

modulation

network

node

office automation

peer-to-peer network

ring network

satellite transmission

server

star network

telecommuting

teleconferencing

teleprocessing

token passing

topology

transponder

uploading

wide area network
(WAN)

wire pair/twisted pair

workstations

videoconferencing

voice mail

- **Office automation** is the use of technology to help achieve the goals of the office. **Electronic mail (e-mail)** and **voice mail** allow workers to transmit messages to the computer files of other workers. **Teleconferencing** includes **computer conferencing**—in which typed messages are shared among many users—and **videoconferencing**—computer conferencing combined with cameras and screens. **Facsimile (fax) technology** can transmit graphics, charts, and signatures. **Fax boards** can be inserted inside computers. A **fax-modem board** performs the functions of both a fax machine and a modem. In **electronic fund transfers (EFTs)**, people pay for goods and services by having funds transferred from various checking and savings accounts electronically, using computer technology.
- A **bulletin board system (BBS)** uses data communications systems to link personal computers to provide public-access message systems.
- *CompuServe*, *Prodigy*, and *America Online* are three major commercial communications services, or **information utilities.**
- *Internet* is a loosely organized collection of networks whose key drawing card is free electronic mail.
- **Telecommuting** is the substitution of communications and computers for the commute to work.

Student Personal Study Guide

True/False

T F   1. Teleprocessing allows a user to query a central computer a thousand miles away.
T F   2. Analog transmission sends distinct on/off pulses.
T F   3. A modem can be used for either modulation or demodulation.
T F   4. Microwave uses line-of-sight transmission.
T F   5. Fiber optics is a cheaper form of communications link than wire pairs.
T F   6. The majority of LANs use a ring structure.
T F   7. E-mail and voice mail are identical technologies.
T F   8. A ring network has no central host computer.
T F   9. Fax boards can be inserted into computers.
T F   10. Telecommute is a type of network structure.

Multiple Choice

1. Distinct on/off pulse transmission:
   a. analog   c. server
   b. bit pattern   d. digital
2. The topology in which each network computer does some network management:
   a. ring   c. star
   b. any topology   d. bus
3. A personal computer attached to a network:
   a. node   c. token
   b. WAN   d. bus
4. Which is *not* an information utility?
   a. Prodigy   c. CompuServe
   b. Ethernet   d. America Online
5. All processing, hardware, and software in one location:
   a. network processing   c. teleprocessing
   b. centralized processing d. DDP

6. Which is *not* a type of communication link?
   a. coaxial cables   c. microwave transmission
   b. fiber optics   d. modem
7. Computers plus cameras plus screens:
   a. videoconferencing   c. facsimile
   b. BBS   d. star network
8. Analog to digital conversion:
   a. modulation   c. LAN
   b. fax   d. demodulation
9. System that combines computers and communications:
   a. topology   c. centralized processing
   b. data communications   d. network interface
10. Transferring funds via computer:
    a. EFT   c. WAN
    b. BBS   d. LAN

Fill-In

1. The kind of signal most telephone lines require: _____ .

2. Converts a digital signal to an analog signal or vice versa: _____ .

3. Prodigy and CompuServe are examples of: _____ .

4. The general term for the use of technology in the office: _____ .

5. The collection of networks subsidized by the government: _____ .

6. Process of converting analog signals to digital: _____ .

7. The physical medium used for transmission is called: _____ .

8. Networks that share resources in a limited geographical location: _____ .

9. A satellite device to receive and transmit the signal: _____ .

10. BBS stands for: _____ .

Answers

True/False: 1. T, 2. F, 3. T, 4. T, 5. T, 6. F, 7. F, 8. T, 9. T, 10. F
Multiple choice: 1.d, 2. d , 3. a , 4. b, 5. b, 6. d, 7. a, 8. d, 9. b, 10. a
Fill-In: 1. analog, 2. modem, 3. information utilities, 4. office automation, 5. Internet, 6. demodulation, 7. communications link, 8. local area network, 9. transponder, 10. bulletin board system

Interview: Computers at the Bottom of the Ocean

Judith Connor, who works for the Monterey Bay Aquarium Research Institute — usually called MBARI — talks about computer application to ocean sciences.

Tell us a little about the institute first.

MBARI was started in 1987 by David Packard, one of the founders of Hewlett-Packard, and continues to be privately funded. He was really excited about the idea of bringing technology to ocean sciences. MBARI's primary focus is research, although we have a secondary mission of education.

Can you give me an overview of the educational activities at MBARI?

Very generally, we're set up to let the public peek over the shoulders of scientists at work. We have a ship in Monterey Bay that controls a robotic submarine, officially called a remotely operated vehicle, or ROV. The robot, which is about the size of a car, is manipulated from the ship by joysticks. The robot's camera takes video images of the sea life, which are sent by cable back to the ship.

Microwave technology brings the video images from the robot to the aquarium where they are instantly shown on a screen to a public audience. There is only a 3-second delay, so the audience really gets the feeling of looking under water with the scientist.

The physical data that the robot is sensing, such as temperature, salinity, and oxygen, also is sent back to land and later stored on the mainframe. This information is of interest to scientists; we keep extensive database files.

How deep can the robot go down?

The robot itself is capable of withstanding pressures down to 6000 feet, but the cable that connects the robot with the mother ship is only 4000 feet long. Also, they leave a lot of give in the cable. So the deepest they've worked so far with this robot is 3300 feet.

How do you fit into the picture here?

My official title is senior research associate, but I am really a marine biologist. My undergraduate work was in botany and chemistry, but for my first job I ended up living on a boat for three years in the Caribbean doing field research. I came back thinking that this is what I want to do with my life, so I went to

Exploring

graduate school in marine biology.

How did you pick up a computer background?
When I went for my Ph.D. at U.C. Berkeley, the computer science department gave any student who wanted it $300 worth of time on the mainframe computer. Nobody was using it. I used up my $300 and they gave me more, so I wrote my disserta-tion using the mainframe. I had a newborn baby at the time, so I rented a computer and a modem, wrote at home and sent my work to the mainframe. That was my introduction to computers.

How do you keep records from the images that come in from the robot?
We get about 10 video tapes every day that the robot goes out. We want to pare that down to the good stuff, and that's another place the computer comes in. I can put a tape in the VCR and then give the computer a file of time codes. For each time code the computer will automatically steal five image frames and lay them down on a laser disk. Later, instead of spending hours pouring over half-hour tapes to get to individual frames that are interesting, you can put in an hour-long laser disk and zip through it. You can put a disk in the machine and zoom—you're on the ocean bottom, and you can see the animals.

Are you connected to a network?
All our personal computers are tied into a network. We use the network for e-mail and tend not to use the tele-phone. Our real purpose is to focus on research. Phones are an interruption, whereas e-mail can wait. I can check my e-mail when I want to, but sometimes I just wait and do all the messages at the end of the day. And, of course, we hook into Internet, so we have access to colleagues anywhere in the world.

And they to you. Is this infor-mation—all these videos and lasers—can they access them from you through Internet?
Not yet, but maybe down the road. But we definitely con-nect. For example, I have a colleague in Florida who sent me e-mail this morning to ask about our krill sightings, because he is monitoring an animal that might be feeding on krill. So I can go into the database and generate a file

> *You can put a disk in the machine and zoom—
> you're on the ocean bottom, and you can see
> the animals.*

of information that I can e-mail to him the same day.

Any final thoughts?
There's an ethic now that's very strong in scientists that we have a responsibility to give good information to help the decision makers make good decisions. We want to be thoughtful advocates of the environment.

Software

LEARNING OBJECTIVES

- Understanding what programmers do and do not do
- Being acquainted with how programmers define a problem; plan the solution; and then code, test, and document the program
- Knowing fundamental flowcharting techniques and pseudocode
- Understanding the levels of programming languages—machine, assembly, high level, very high level, and natural
- Being acquainted with some important languages—FORTRAN, COBOL, BASIC, Pascal, and C
- Understanding object-oriented programming concepts

Bill Stanhope, trained as a programmer, was hired by a large midwestern auto insurance company. He was well-qualified technically and had some understanding of the process of programming. His management considered the programming process so important that they regularly sent their programmers, Bill among them, for further training.

So Bill had the programming process re-enforced. The first lesson was always the same: Be sure you understand the client's problem before you start solving it. That amused Bill because he knew very well that eager programmers, himself included, are tempted to start writing programs prematurely. The next step in the programming process is to come up with a solution; only then does actual programming begin. Then, once a program is written, it must be tested thoroughly. Finally, and perhaps most important, the programmer must document the program on an ongoing basis, that is, keep records about it.

Programming

Even though Bill was fully indoctrinated on the programming process, he found that he and others in his organization did not always follow it. In particular, in the rush toward deadlines, Bill never quite kept his documentation up-to-date. Eventually, Bill became a supervisor in charge of the claims department. He wanted to do well by both his programmers and his clients, the company's claims adjusters. His programmers were trained in the programming process, but with the ever-mounting pressure of deadlines, Bill did not pay much attention to the formalities. This neglect, as it turned out, cost him dearly. Deadlines drifted, budgets swelled, and clients became irritable.

It all came to a head in a client meeting. Client Sam Mehter made a request for a small change to a program. Bill responded that it would take a long time because the programmer who wrote that program had left the company and no one else understood the program very well. He did not say so, but Bill could have added that the reason no one could understand it was that the program was never documented properly. Sam then attacked the budget overrun, to which Bill replied that mounting expenses were directly related to Sam's constant requests for changes. At this, Sam exploded. Bill and his programmers, he said, had not taken the time to understand what the client needed. He, Sam, was forced to make changes because nothing had been properly understood in the first place. Bill ruefully remembered all the lessons in the programming process and, after some soul searching, realized he had permitted the programmers to forge ahead without a proper understanding of the problem and without proper documentation.

Bill had some serious fence-mending to do with his client, but, more importantly, he realized he was going to have to change the ways he enforced the programming process. In this chapter, as we take a look at programming, we will examine the programming process and why it is so important.

and Languages

A Glimpse of What Programmers Do

Programmers in the Scheme of Things

What kind of people become programmers? What training do they need? What companies do they work for? And, finally, do they like being programmers?

People who become programmers are usually people with logical minds—often, but not always, the same ones who are good at math and who like to solve puzzles. Programmers need some credentials, most often a two- or four-year degree in computer information systems or computer science. Jobs vary by organization and region, but it is fair to say that many programmers work for medium-size to large business organizations such as banks, insurance companies, and retailers. The programmers who write software for personal computers often have a degree in computer science.

As for whether they like being programmers, surveys of programmers consistently report a high level of job satisfaction. There are several reasons for this contentment. One is the challenge—most jobs in the computer industry are not routine. Another is security—established computer professionals can usually find work. Finally, the work pays well—you will probably not be rich, but you should be comfortable.

LECTURE HINT

Programming sharpens your mind, training you to be more precise and analytical. Even if you cannot write elaborate programs, most people can learn enough to write simple programs that may be helpful to them in their daily lives.

TEST BANK

Mult. Choice 4, 7-11, 13-15, 20
T/F 21, 25-31
Matching I 42, 44, 47-50
Matching II 59
Fill In 61-63, 67, 71-74, 79-80

Why Programming?

You may already have used commercial software to solve problems or perform certain tasks. But perhaps now you are ready to learn something about how software is written. As we noted earlier, a **program** is a set of step-by-step instructions that directs the computer to do the tasks you want it to do and produce the results you want. This chapter introduces you to the programming process and what programmers do.

What Programmers Do

TEST BANK

T/F 22-24

Suppose you manage an urban entertainment complex that features movies and various live performances. You need to schedule a year in advance, considering the availability of performers, the time of year, and the need to present a balanced selection. Several factors vary with the type of act and must be considered in the early planning stages, including local props, special lighting effects, union extras, work permits, and so forth. The set of tasks is complex and difficult to coordinate. You need to enlist the aid of a computer because you have work that requires computer power.

The easiest way to get the computer's help is to use an existing commercial software package—a package you can buy off the shelf or from a vendor. Using existing software is also the fastest and least expensive way if the software fits your needs. Commercial scheduling software could solve some of your scheduling problems. But, after consulting with a computer professional, it seems clear that most of your problems are too complicated and too company-specific for commercial software. You need a customized program and someone to write it: a **programmer.**

In general, the programmer's job is to convert a problem solution, such as a scheme for handling the entertainment-complex problems just described, into instructions for the computer. That is, the programmer prepares the instructions of a computer program and runs, tests, and corrects the program. The programmer also documents the way the program works. These activities are all done for the purpose of helping a user fill a need—to manage a business, pay employees, bill customers, admit students to college, and so forth. Programmers help the user develop new programs to solve problems, weed out errors in existing programs, or make changes to programs as a result of new requirements (such as a change in a payroll program to make automatic union dues deductions).

A programmer typically interacts with a variety of people. For example, if a program is part of a system of several programs, the programmer probably coordinates with a systems analyst (see Chapter 9) and other programmers to make sure that the programs operate well together.

Let us turn now from programmers to programming.

The Programming Process

Developing a program requires five steps:

1. Defining the problem
2. Planning the solution

3. Coding the program
4. Testing the program
5. Documenting the program

Let us discuss each of these in turn.

Defining the Problem

Suppose you are a programmer. Users consult with you because they need your services. You meet with users from a client organization to analyze a problem, or you meet with a systems analyst who outlines a project. Eventually, you produce a written agreement that, among other things, specifies the kind of input, processing, and output required. This is not a simple process. It is closely related to the process of systems analysis, which we will discuss in Chapter 9.

Planning the Solution

People spend a lot of time solving problems, often by just talking them over with a friend. But a programmer using a computer to solve a client's problem must use a methodical approach. A solution can be thought of as an ordered set of activities that will convert the given input into the desired output. This is often the most complex part of the entire programming process.

There are many approaches to planning solutions, most of them beyond the scope of this book. Although this chapter is not intended to make you a programmer, we will present two common ways of planning the solution to a programming problem: drawing a flowchart and writing pseudocode. Essentially, a **flowchart** is a symbolic diagram of an orderly step-by-step solution to a problem. It is a map of what your program is going to do and how it is going to do it. **Pseudocode** is an English-like language that you can use to state your solution with more precision than you can in plain English but with less precision than is required when using a formal programming language. We will discuss flowcharts and pseudocode in greater detail later in this chapter.

Coding the Program

As the programmer, your next step is to code the program; you need to express your solution in a language the computer understands—a programming language. You can translate the logic from the flowchart or pseudocode to a programming language. There are many programming languages: BASIC, COBOL, Pascal, FORTRAN, and C are common examples. These languages operate grammatically, somewhat like a simple version of the English language, but they are much more precise. To get your program to work, you have to follow exactly the rules, or **syntax**, of the language you are using. Of course, using the language correctly is no guarantee that your program will work, any more than speaking grammatically correct English means you will actually communicate. The point is that correct use of the language is the required first step. The program must also correctly and logically express the solution. Your coded program must be keyed, often at a terminal, in a form the computer can understand. We will discuss programming languages in more detail later in the chapter.

Tell Us About the Bugs

Computer literacy books are bursting with bits and bytes, disks and chips, and lessons on writing programs in BASIC. All this is to provide quick enlightenment for the computer illiterate. But the average newcomer to computing has not been told about the bugs.

It is a bit of a surprise, then, to find that the software you are using does not always work quite right. Or perhaps the programmer who is doing some work for you cannot seem to get the program to work correctly. Both problems are bugs—errors that were introduced unintentionally into a program when it was written. The term *bug* comes from an experience in the early days of computing. One summer day in 1945, the Mark I computer came to a halt. Working to find the problem, computer personnel actually found a moth inside the computer (see photo). They removed the offending bug, and the computer was fine. From that day forward any mysterious problem was said to be a bug.

DISCUSSION QUESTION

What is the purpose of desk-checking?

DISCUSSION QUESTION

How does a logic error differ from a syntax error?

Testing the Program

Some experts support the notion that a well-designed program can be written correctly the first time. However, the imperfections of the world are still with us, so most programmers get used to the idea that there will be a few errors in the early versions of their programs.

After coding and keying the program, you test it to find the mistakes. Many programmers use these phases: desk-checking, translating, and debugging.

Desk-Checking

In **desk-checking**, you simply sit down and mentally trace, or check, the logic and the syntax of the individual instructions of the program to ensure that the program is error-free and workable. This phase, similar to proofreading, may uncover several errors and possibly save several computer runs. In businesses that account for every second of computer time, this phase is especially important.

Translating

A **translator** is a program that converts your program into language the computer can understand. A by-product of the process is that the translator tells you if you have improperly used the programming language in some way. Such mistakes in programming-language usage are called **syntax errors.** The translator produces descriptive error messages. For instance, if in FORTRAN you mistakenly type N=2*(I+J))—which has two closing parentheses instead of one—you will get a message something like "UNMATCHED PARENTHESES." Programs are most commonly translated by still other software—a compiler or an interpreter. A **compiler** translates your entire program at one time, giving you all the syntax error messages—called **diagnostics**—at once. The compiler usually places these diagnostics in context in a **source program listing,** which is a list of the program, as written by the programmer, that can be used to make any corrections necessary to the program. An **interpreter,** often used for the BASIC language, translates your program one line at a time.

As shown in Figure 7-1, the original program, called a **source module,** is translated to an **object module,** to which prewritten programs may be added during the **link/load phase** to create a load module. The **load module** can then be executed by the computer.

Debugging

A term used extensively in programming, **debugging** is detecting, locating, and correcting bugs (mistakes) by running the program. These bugs are **logic errors,** such as telling a computer to repeat an operation but not telling it how to stop repeating. In this phase you run the program against test data that you devise. You must plan the test data carefully to make sure you test every part of the program.

Documenting the Program

Documentation is a written detailed description of the programming cycle and specific facts about the program. Documenting is an ongoing

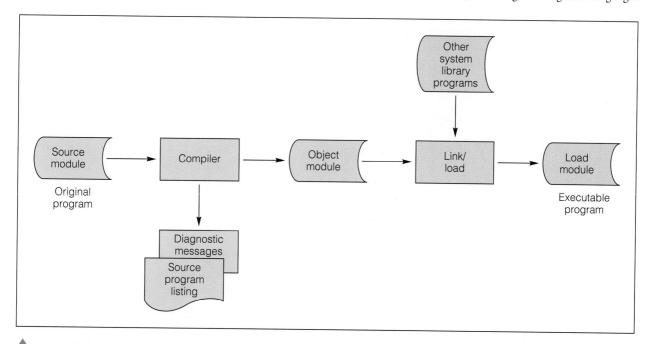

Figure 7-1   Preparing your program for execution.
Your original program, the source module, is translated by the compiler into an
object module, which represents the program in machine language that the computer can understand. The compiler may produce diagnostic messages, indicating
syntax errors. A listing of the source program may also be output from the compiler.
After the program successfully compiles, the object module is linked in the link/load
phase with system library programs as needed, and the result is a load module, or
executable program.　**TRANSPARENCY ACETATE #35**　Figure 7-1

process needed to supplement human memory and to help organize program planning. Also, documentation is critical to communication with
others who have an interest in the program. Typical program documentation materials include the origin and nature of the problem, a brief nar-
rative description of the program, logic tools such as flowcharts and
pseudocode, data descriptions, program listings, and testing results.
Comments embedded in the program itself are also considered an essential part of documentation.

In a broader sense, program documentation could be part of the documentation for an entire system.

Planning the Solution:
A Closer Look at Flowcharts
and Pseudocode

We have described the five steps of the programming process in a general way. We noted that the first step, defining the problem, is related to
the larger arena of systems analysis and design. The last three steps—
coding, testing, and documenting the program—are done in the context
of a particular programming language.

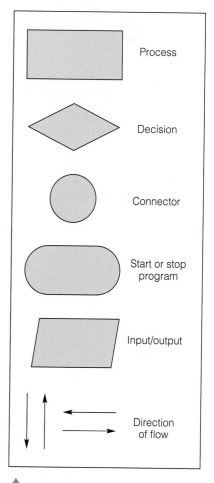

Figure 7-2   ANSI flowchart symbols.

TRANSPARENCY ACETATE #36

Figure 7-2

COMPUTING TRENDS

Can I Afford the Premiums?

A most unwelcome trend, but a trend nonetheless, is liability insurance for programmers. Look at it this way. Does the software you use really work? Are you sure? Did the programmer who wrote it absolutely, positively guarantee that it would never have a glitch that would ruin your work? Some jobs have little room for error or second guessing; the job must be done right the first time. An air traffic controller has such a job; for example, directing a plane to the wrong altitude could have fatal consequences. Programmers, on the other hand, have many opportunities to ponder, to test, to rethink. Given those opportunities, it seems reasonable to hope that the completed software will have a high degree of reliability. In fact, some people think that a programmer should indeed be able to absolutely, positively guarantee that the software works as it is supposed to.

However, reliability has not been the hallmark of computer software. There are several reasons for this.

One is the inherent complexity of most software. The most vexing is that, despite heroic efforts by the programmer or programmers, the nature of the desired software often changes as it is developed, causing time and budget crunches. Finally, as in every field, there are some incompetent people writing computer programs.

Although software may be less than perfect when first tested, programmers usually work out the kinks until it is acceptable. Sometimes, however, unreliable software is inadvertently released to an organization or to the public. This is why some clients are now suing programmers, and why some programmers are taking out insurance.

TEST BANK

Mult. Choice 1, 12
T/F 32-35
Matching I 41, 43, 45-46
Fill In 69, 75

In this section we will study the second step, planning the solution. This discussion will help you understand how program logic is developed. The following sections offer an introduction to flowcharting and pseudocode.

Some standard flowchart symbols have been established and are accepted by most programmers. These symbols, shown in Figure 7-2, are called ANSI flowchart symbols. (**ANSI** stands for American National Standards Institute.) The most common symbols a programmer uses represent process, decision, connector, start/stop, input/output, and direction of flow.

Pseudocode is easy to maintain. Since pseudocode is just words, you can keep it on a computer file and change it easily, using text editing or word processing. Although pseudocode is not a visual tool, it is nevertheless an effective vehicle for stating and following program logic. For these reasons, flowcharts have fallen out of favor among professionals and pseudocode has become popular. But flowcharting is still useful for beginners and in complex programming situations, so we include it here.

Example: Preparing a Letter

Figure 7-3 shows how you might diagram the steps of preparing a letter for mailing. There is usually more than one correct way to design a flowchart; this becomes obvious with more complicated examples.

The rectangular **process boxes** indicate actions to be taken: "Address envelope," "Fold letter," "Place letter in envelope." Sometimes the order in which actions appear is important, sometimes not. In this case the letter must be folded before it can be placed in the envelope.

The diamond-shaped box ("Have stamp?") is a **decision box.** The decision box asks a question that requires a yes or no answer. It has two **paths,** or **branches:** One path represents the response yes, the other no. Note that the decision box is the only box that allows a choice; no other box has more than one exit. Whether you do have a stamp or do not, you take a path that comes back to a circle that puts you on a path to the end. The circle is called a **connector** because it connects the paths. Notice that the flowchart begins and ends with oval **start/stop** symbols.

This example suggests how you can take almost any activity and diagram it in flowchart form—assuming, that is, that you can always express your decisions as choices between yes and no, or something equally specific, such as true or false. Now let us use flowcharting for an example related to computer programming.

Example: Summing Numbers from 1 through 100

Figure 7-4 shows how you might flowchart a program to find the sum of all numbers from 1 through 100. You should observe several things about this flowchart.

First, the program uses two locations in the computer's memory as storage locations, or places to keep intermediate results. In one location is a counter, which might be like a car odometer: Every time a mile passes, the quantity 1 is added to the counter. In the other location is a sum—that is, a running total of the numbers counted. The sum location will eventually contain the sum of all numbers from 1 through 100: $1+2+3+4+5+...+100$.

Second, note that you must initialize the counter and the sum. When you **initialize,** you set the starting values of certain storage locations, called **variables,** usually as program execution begins. For this example the sum is initialized to 0 and the counter to 1.

Third, note the looping. You add the quantity stored in the counter to the sum, add a 1 to the counter, and then come to the decision diamond, which asks if the counter is greater than 100. If the answer is no, the computer loops back around and repeats the process. The decision box contains a **compare operation;** the computer compares two numbers and performs alternative operations based on the comparison. If the result of the comparison is yes, the computer produces the sum as output, as indicated by the print instruction. Notice that the parallelogram-shaped symbol is used for printing the sum because it represents an output process.

A **loop** is the heart of computer programming. The beauty of the loop, which may be defined as instructions causing the repetition of actions under certain conditions, is that you, as the programmer, have to describe certain actions only once rather than describing them repeat-

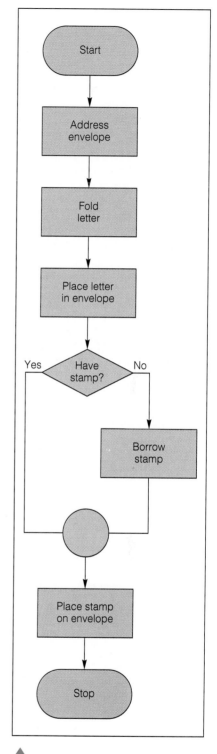

▲
Figure 7-3 A simple flowchart.
This flowchart shows how to prepare a letter for mailing.

TRANSPARENCY ACETATE #37

Figure 7-3

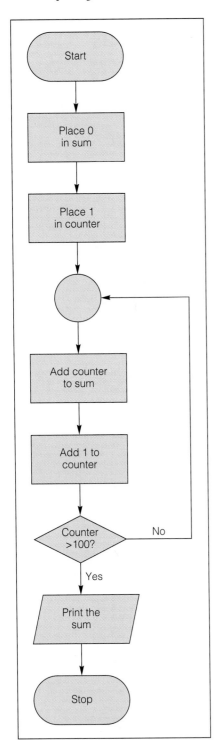

▲
Figure 7-4 Loop example.
This flowchart uses a loop to find the sum of numbers from 1 through 100.

TRANSPARENCY ACETATE #38

Figure 7-4

edly. One trip around the loop is called an **iteration.** Once the programmer has established the loop pattern and the conditions for concluding (exiting from) the loop, the computer begins looping and exits as it has been instructed to do. The flowchart can be modified easily to sum the numbers from 1 to 1000, from 500 to 700, or any other variation.

Example: Student Grades

Now let us see how a flowchart or pseudocode is translated into a program. Figure 7-5 shows a flowchart, pseudocode, and program designed to compute student grades. You could enter this program directly into your computer. The computer would deliver back to you, on the monitor or in printout form, the output shown in Figure 7-5d.

The problem is to compute the student grades (ranging from 0 through 100) for six students, and, second, to count the number of students whose computed scores are lower than 60. The grade points are based on student performance on two tests, a midterm exam and a final exam. These scores have been weighted in a certain way.

The program is written in the programming language called BASIC. There are several dialects of the BASIC language, but for this example we have chosen a version called Microsoft QBASIC.

In Figure 7-5c, the numbers in the far left of each line are called statement numbers. REM stands for remark statement. REM statements are used to document the program, providing a brief description of what the program is supposed to do and a list of all variable names—symbolic names of locations in memory. The PRINT statement tells the computer what message or data to print out, the READ statement reads the data to be processed, and the DATA statements list the data to be read by the computer. The IF statement executes a certain statement (here adding 1 to the count) if the condition is found to be true. The WHILE and WEND statements are used to form a loop: The lines between WHILE and WEND will be executed repeatedly while the condition on the WHILE line (in this case NUM <> -9999) holds true, and then control will transfer to the line following the WEND. In this example, when NUM equals -9999, as it will once the last line of data is read (from program line 480), then control will pass out of the loop to line 390.

BASIC is similar to English in many ways, so you can probably follow the program in a general way, even with no knowledge of BASIC. The following section introduces other programming languages.

TEST BANK
T/F 36
Fill In 70

◤ Programming Languages

What language will a programmer use to communicate with the computer? Surely not the English language, which—like any human language—can be loose and ambiguous and full of slang, variations, and complexities. A programming language is needed. A **programming language**—a set of rules that provides a way of telling the computer what operations to perform—is anything but loose and ambiguous.

A programming language, the key to communicating with the computer, has certain definite characteristics. It has a limited vocabulary. Each "word" in it has precise meaning. Even though a programming language has limitations, it can still be used in a step-by-step fashion to solve complex problems. There is not, however, just one programming language; there are many.

As we will see, the languages in use today tend to meet specific needs, such as programming for scientific or business applications. Before we turn to the discussion of specific languages, however, we need to discuss levels of language.

Levels of Language

Programming languages are said to be low level or high level, depending on whether they are close to the language the computer itself uses (0s and 1s—low level) or to the language people use (more English-like—high level). We will consider five levels of programming language. They are numbered 1 through 5 to correspond to what are called the generations of programming languages. Each generation has improved on the ease of use and capabilities of its predecessors. The five generations of languages are

1. Machine language
2. Assembly languages
3. High-level languages
4. Very high-level languages
5. Natural languages

Figure 7-6 is a time line for language generations. Let us look at each of these categories.

Old and Difficult: Machine Language and Assembly Languages

Humans do not like to deal in numbers alone; we prefer letters and words. But numbers are what machine language is. This lowest level of language, **machine language,** represents information as 1s and 0s—binary digits corresponding to the on and off electrical states in the computer. Each type of computer has its own machine language.

In the early days of computing, programmers had rudimentary systems for combining numbers to represent instructions such as add or compare. Primitive by today's standards, the programs were not at all convenient for people to read and use. The computer industry moved to develop assembly languages.

Today **assembly languages** are considered very low level—that is, they are inconvenient compared to more recent languages, although they have the advantage of executing quickly. At the time they were developed, however, they were considered a great leap forward. Rather than using simply 1s and 0s, assembly languages use abbreviations or mnemonic codes as substitutes for machine language: A for Add, C for Compare, MP for Multiply, and so on.

The programmer who uses an assembly language requires a software translator, called an **assembler program,** to convert his or her assembly language program into machine language. A translator is needed because machine language is the only language the computer can actually exe-

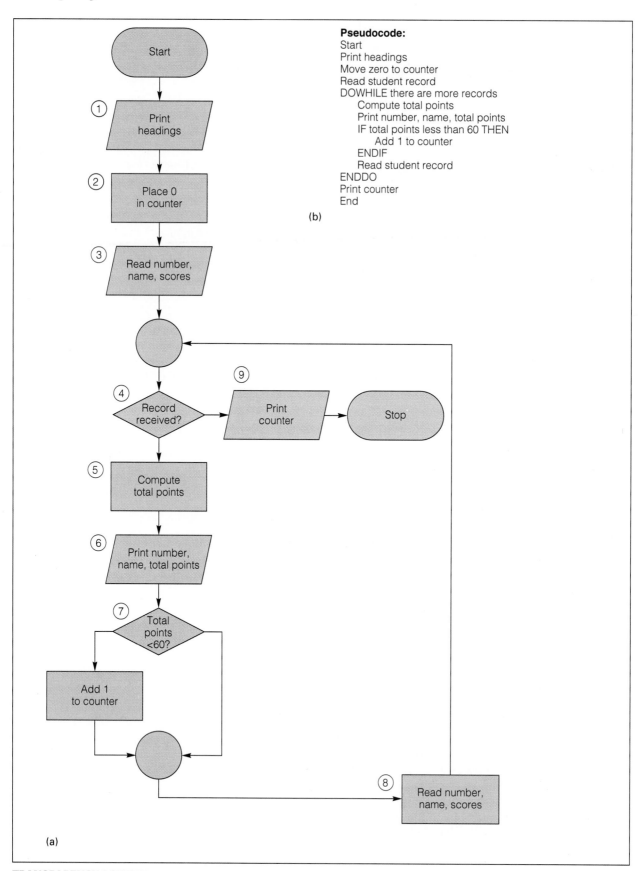

Pseudocode:
Start
Print headings
Move zero to counter
Read student record
DOWHILE there are more records
    Compute total points
    Print number, name, total points
    IF total points less than 60 THEN
        Add 1 to counter
    ENDIF
    Read student record
ENDDO
Print counter
End

(b)

(a)

TRANSPARENCY ACETATE #39

Figure 7-5 a, b

```
10     REM PROGRAM TO COMPUTE STUDENT POINTS
20     REM
30     REM THIS PROGRAM READS, FOR EACH STUDENT,
40     REM    STUDENT NUMBER, STUDENT NAME, AND
50     REM    4 TEST SCORES. THE SCORES ARE TO
60     REM    BE WEIGHTED AS FOLLOWS:
70     REM
80     REM       TEST 1: 20 PERCENT
90     REM       TEST 2: 20 PERCENT
100    REM       MIDTERM: 25 PERCENT
110    REM       FINAL: 35 PERCENT
120    REM
130    REM VARIABLE NAMES USED:
140    REM
150    REM    COUNT    COUNT OF STUDENTS SCORING LESS THAN 60
160    REM    NUM      STUDENT NUMBER
170    REM    NAM$     STUDENT NAME
180    REM    TEST1    SCORE FOR TEST 1
190    REM    TEST2    SCORE FOR TEST 2
200    REM    TEST3    SCORE FOR MIDTERM
210    REM    TEST4    SCORE FOR FINAL
220    REM    TOTAL    TOTAL STUDENT POINTS
230    REM
240    PRINT
250    PRINT "    STUDENT GRADE REPORT"
260    PRINT
270    PRINT "STUDENT","STUDENT","TOTAL"
280    PRINT "NUMBER","NAME","POINTS"
290    PRINT
300    PRINT
310    LET COUNT = 0
320    READ NUM,NAM$,TEST1,TEST2,TEST3,TEST4
330    WHILE NUM <> -9999
340    LET TOTAL = TEST1 + .2 * TEST2 + .25 * TEST3 + .35 * TEST4
350    PRINT NUM,NAM$,TOTAL
360    IF TOTAL < 60 THEN COUNT = COUNT+1
370    READ NUM,NAM$,TEST1,TEST2,TEST3,TEST4
380    WEND
390    PRINT
400    PRINT "NUMBER OF STUDENTS WITH POINTS < 60:";COUNT
410    STOP
420    DATA 2164,ALLEN SCHWAB,60,64,73,78
430    DATA 2644,MARTIN CHAN,80,78,85,90
440    DATA 3171,CHRISTY BURNER,91,95,90,88
450    DATA 5725,CRAIG BARNES,61,41,70,53
460    DATA 6994,RAOUL GARCIA,95 96,90,92
470    DATA 7001,KAY MITCHELL,55,60,58,55
480    DATA -9999,XXX,0,0,0,0
490    END
```

(c)

```
               STUDENT GRADE REPORT

    STUDENT        STUDENT              TOTAL
    NUMBER         NAME                 POINTS


    2164           ALLEN SCHWAB         70.4
    2644           MARTIN CHAN          84.4
    3171           CHRISTY BURNER       90.5
    5725           CRAIG BARNES         56.5
    6994           RAOUL GARCIA         92.9
    7001           KAY MITCHELL         56.8

    NUMBER OF STUDENTS WITH POINTS <60:2
```

(d)

◀

Figure 7-5   Student grades.
The (a) flowchart and (b) pseudocode
for (c) the program that produces (d) a
student grade report.

TRANSPARENCY ACETATE #40

Figure 7-5 c

TRANSPARENCY ACETATE #41

Figure 7-5 d

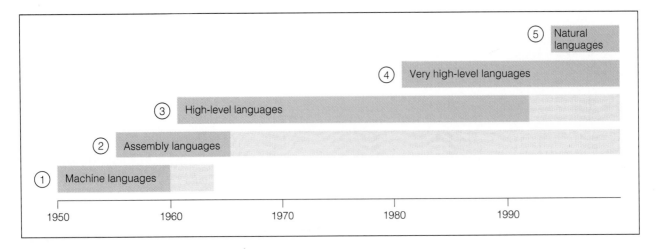

▲
Figure 7-6   Language generations on a time line.
The darker shading indicates the period of greater use by applications programmers; the lighter shading indicates the time during which a generation faded from popular use.

cute. A programmer need not worry about the translating aspect; the translation is taken care of by the computer system.

Although assembly languages represent a step forward, they still have the disadvantage of requiring the programmer to describe in excruciating detail every small step involved in the program.

Readable: High-Level Languages

The first widespread use of **high-level languages** in the early 1960s transformed programming into something quite different from what it had been. The harried programmer working on the nitty-gritty details of assembly language codes became a programmer who, by using a better language, had more time to spend solving the client's problems. Programs in high-level languages were written in an English-like manner, thus making them more convenient to use and to debug.

Of course, a translator was needed to translate the symbolic statements of a high-level language into computer-executable machine language; this translator is usually a compiler.

More Like English: Very High-Level Languages

Languages called **very high-level languages** are often known by their generation number. That is, they are called **fourth-generation languages** or, more simply, **4GLs.** But if the name is easy, the definition is not. There is no consensus about what constitutes a fourth-generation language.

One characteristic of 4GLs is they are somewhat nonprocedural. A **procedural language** tells the computer *how* a task is done: add this, compare that, do this if something is true, and so forth—a very specific step-by-step process. The first three generations of languages are all procedural. In a **nonprocedural language,** the concept changes. Users define only *what* they want the computer to do; the user does not provide the details of just how it is to be done. Obviously, it is a lot easier and faster to just say what you want rather than explain how to get it. This leads us to the issue of productivity, a key characteristic of fourth-generation languages.

Consider this task: Produce a report showing the total units sold for each product, by customer, in each month and year, and with a subtotal for each customer. In addition, each new customer must start on a new page. The 4GL request looks something like this:

TABLE FILE SALES
SUM UNITS BY MONTH BY CUSTOMER BY PRODUCT
ON CUSTOMER SUBTOTAL PAGE BREAK
END

Even though some training is required to do even this much, you can see that it is pretty simple. The third-generation language COBOL, however, would typically require hundreds of statements to fulfill the same request. If we define productivity as producing equivalent results in less time, then fourth-generation languages clearly increase productivity.

Everyday Speech: Natural Languages

The word *natural* has become almost as popular in computing circles as it has in the supermarket. But fifth-generation languages are, as you may guess, even harder to define than fourth-generation languages. Those in the fifth generation are most often called **natural languages** because of their resemblance to the "natural" spoken English language. Instead of being forced to key correct commands and data names in correct order, a manager (programmers are not needed) tells the computer what to do by keying in his or her own words. Figure 7-7 illustrates a natural language.

A manager can say the same thing any number of ways. For example, "Get me tennis racket sales for January" works just as well as "I want Jan-

```
Hello
How may I help you?
        Who are my customers in Chicago?
Just a sec.  I'll see.
The customers in that city are:
I.D.              Name
_____

Ballard           Ballard and Sons, Inc.
Fremont           Henry Fremont Associates
Greenlake         Greenlake Consortium
Wallingford       Wallingford, Inc.
What can I do for you now?
        What is Fremont's balance?
Hang on.  I'll see.
Accounts Receivable    563.47
Unapplied Credit        79.16
            Balance    484.31
What else can I do for you?
        Give me Fremont's phone number!
Please wait while I check the files.
    (312) 789-5562
What can I do for you now?
```

Figure 7-7   A natural language.
This package, called Cash Management System, uses a language that is so "natural" that some might think it is a little too cute, as in "Just a sec."

uary tennis racket revenues." Such a request may contain misspelled words, lack articles and verbs, and even use slang. The natural language translates human instructions—bad grammar, slang, and all—into code the computer understands. If it is not sure what the user has in mind, it politely asks for further explanation.

Some Popular Languages

How does a programmer choose the language in which to write a program? Perhaps a particular language is the standard at the programmer's place of business. Perhaps the manager decrees that everyone on a project will use a certain language.

A sensible approach is to pick the language that is most suitable for the particular program application. The following sections on individual languages provide an overview of the languages in common use. We describe these languages: FORTRAN, COBOL, BASIC, Pascal, and C—all third-generation languages in common use today. Special features of each language are noted, including the types of applications for which they are often used. Table 7-1 summarizes the languages and their applications.

To accompany our discussion of particular languages, we will show a program and its output to give you a sense of what each language looks like. Since we are performing the same task in each program, finding the average of three numbers, you can see some of the differences and similarities among the languages. We do not expect you to understand each line of these programs; they are here merely as illustrations. Figure 7-8 provides a flowchart and pseudocode for the task of averaging numbers.

FORTRAN: The First High-Level Language

Developed by IBM and introduced in 1954, **FORTRAN**, which stands for FORmula TRANslator, was the first high-level language. FORTRAN is a scientifically oriented language; in the early days use of the computer was primarily associated with engineering, mathematical, and

Table 7-1	Applications of some important programming languages.	
Language	Origin	Application
FORTRAN	FORmula TRANslator (1954)	Scientific
COBOL	COmmon Business-Oriented Language (1959)	Business
BASIC	Beginner's All-purpose Symbolic Instruction Code (1965)	Education, Business
Pascal	Named after French inventor Blaise Pascal (1971)	Education, systems programming
C	Invented at Bell Labs (1972)	Systems programming, general use

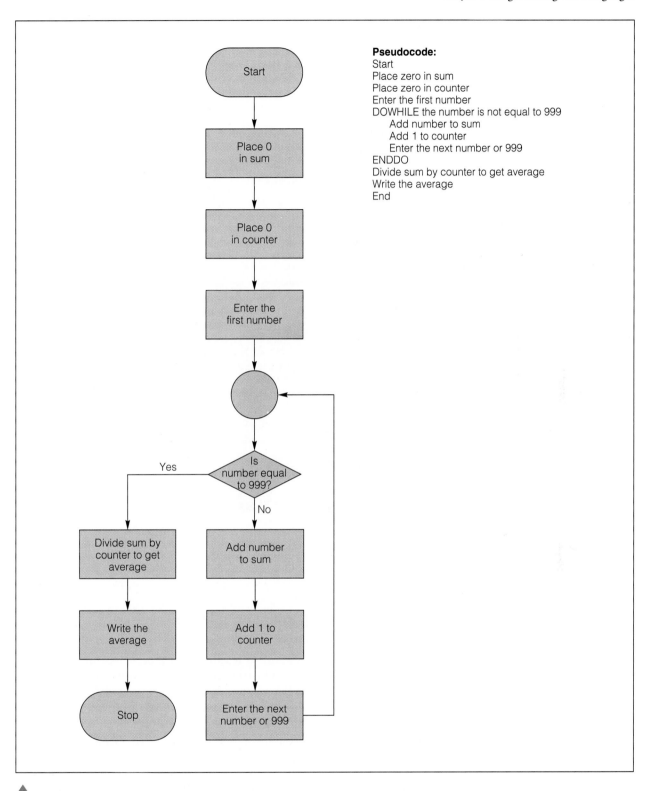

Pseudocode:
Start
Place zero in sum
Place zero in counter
Enter the first number
DOWHILE the number is not equal to 999
    Add number to sum
    Add 1 to counter
    Enter the next number or 999
ENDDO
Divide sum by counter to get average
Write the average
End

▲
Figure 7-8　Flowchart and pseudocode for averaging numbers.
This flowchart and matching pseudocode show the logic for a program to let a user enter numbers through the keyboard; the program then averages the numbers. Any number of numbers can be entered, one at a time; the signal that all data has been entered is 999. The logic to enter the numbers forms a loop: entering the number, adding it to the sum, and adding 1 to the counter. When 999 is keyed, the loop is exited. The average is then computed and displayed on the screen. This logic is used for the programs, in various languages, that follow in Figures 7-9 through 7-12.

Personal Computers In Action

Home Sweet Home

Maybe programmers should work at home. The idea is not new, but new factors are affecting the decision to work at home or in the office. The first factor is the freedom derived from the personal computer, and the second is the newly acknowledged influence of environment on productivity.

First the personal computer. Many programmers in the office still work on terminals that interact with a large mainframe computer. The response time from the mainframe is either uniformly awful or so unpredictable that it becomes difficult to plan work effectively. In contrast, a single-user personal computer provides relatively instant and uniform response times for most programming tasks. A programmer working with a personal computer at home can sit right down and get to business.

Now, what about the environment? Recent studies have shown that a programmer's physical work environment influences his or her

productivity more profoundly than managers had suspected. Although programming productivity has long been known to vary dramatically from one individual to another, these variances have usually been attributed to differences in experience and ability. But studies suggest something quite different. When groups of people in different environments are compared, productivity is improved by such environmental factors as desk size, noise levels, and privacy.

The direction seems clear. Get a personal computer for home use, place it on a large desk in a quiet room, and lock yourself in. Your productivity should soar. Well, it is hardly that simple, but the findings are worthy of consideration by all who want to work at home.

scientific research tasks. FORTRAN is still the most widely used language in the scientific community. A FORTRAN program is shown in Figure 7-9.

COBOL: The Language of Business

The U.S. Department of Defense was interested in creating a standardized business language, and so it called together representatives from government and various industries, including the computer industry, to come up with such a language. This language, called **COBOL,** for COmmon Business-Oriented Language, was introduced in 1959. The principal feature of COBOL is that it is English-like—far more so than FORTRAN. Even if you know nothing about programming, you can still read a COBOL program and have some understanding of its general purpose. COBOL is also renowned for being **machine independent;** that is, a program written in COBOL can be run on different computers. A COBOL program is shown in Figure 7-10.

BASIC: For Beginners and Others

We have already shown **BASIC**—Beginner's All-purpose Symbolic Instruction Code—earlier in the chapter (Figure 7-5c). Developed at

```
C       FORTRAN PROGRAM
C       AVERAGING INTEGERS ENTERED THROUGH THE KEYBOARD
        WRITE (6,10)
        SUM = 0
        COUNTER = 0
        WRITE (6,60)
        READ (5,40) NUMBER
   1    IF (NUMBER .EQ. 999) GOTO 2
        SUM = SUM + NUMBER
        COUNTER = COUNTER + 1
        WRITE (6,70)
        READ (5,40) NUMBER
        GO TO 1
   2    AVERAGE = SUM / COUNTER
        WRITE (6,80) AVERAGE
  10    FORMAT (1X, 'THIS PROGRAM WILL FIND THE AVERAGE OF ',
        'INTEGERS YOU ENTER ',/1X, 'THROUGH THE ',
        'KEYBOARD. TYPE 999 TO INDICATE END OF DATA.',/)
  40  * FORMAT (I3)
  60  * FORMAT (1X, 'PLEASE ENTER A NUMBER ')
  70    FORMAT (1X, 'PLEASE ENTER THE NEXT NUMBER ')
  80    FORMAT (1X, 'THE AVERAGE OF THE NUMBERS IS ',F6.2)
        STOP
        END
```

(a)

```
THIS PROGRAM WILL FIND THE AVERAGE OF INTEGERS YOU ENTER
THROUGH THE KEYBOARD.  TYPE 999 TO INDICATE END OF DATA.
PLEASE ENTER A NUMBER    6
PLEASE ENTER THE NEXT NUMBER     4
PLEASE ENTER THE NEXT NUMBER    11
PLEASE ENTER THE NEXT NUMBER   999
THE AVERAGE OF THE NUMBERS IS    7.00
```

(b)

Figure 7-9 A FORTRAN program and sample output for averaging numbers. This program is interactive, prompting the user to supply data. (a) The first two lines are comments, as they are in the other programs in this chapter. The WRITE statements send output to the screen in the format matching the number in the WRITE parentheses. The READ statements accept data from the user and place it in location NUMBER, where it can be added to the accumulated SUM. The IF statement checks for number 999 and, when it is received, diverts the program logic to statement 2, where the average is computed. The average is then displayed. (b) This screen display shows the interaction between program and user.

TRANSPARENCY ACETATE #44

Figure 7-9

Dartmouth College by John Kemeny and Thomas Kurtz in 1965, BASIC was originally intended for use by students in an academic environment. In the late 1960s it became widely used in universities and colleges. The use of BASIC has extended to all kinds of users, especially those using personal computers. The primary advantage of BASIC is one that may be of interest to many readers of this book: BASIC is relatively easy to learn, even for a person who has never programmed before. There are different versions of BASIC; two popular commercial forms are Quick BASIC and Microsoft BASIC.

DISCUSSION QUESTION

What was the motivation behind the creation of BASIC?

▶

Figure 7-10 A COBOL program and sample output for averaging numbers.
The purpose of this program and its results are the same as those of the FORTRAN program in Figure 7-9, but the look of the COBOL program is very different. (a) Note the four divisions. In particular, note that the logic in the procedure division uses a series of PERFORM statements, diverting logic flow to other places in the program. After a section has been performed, logic flow returns to the statement after the one that called the PERFORM. DISPLAY writes to the screen, and ACCEPT takes the user input. (b) This screen display shows the interaction between program and user.

TRANSPARENCY ACETATE #45

Figure 7-10 a

TRANSPARENCY ACETATE #46

Figure 7-10 b

```
****************************************************************
IDENTIFICATION DIVISION.
****************************************************************
PROGRAM-ID.  AVERAGE.
* COBOL PROGRAM
* AVERAGING INTEGERS ENTERED THROUGH THE KEYBOARD.
****************************************************************
ENVIRONMENT DIVISION.
****************************************************************
CONFIGURATION SECTION.
SOURCE-COMPUTER.          H-P 3000.
OBJECT-COMPUTER.          H-P 3000.
****************************************************************
DATA DIVISION.
****************************************************************
FILE SECTION.
WORKING-STORAGE SECTION.
01 AVERAGE       PIC ---9.99.
01 COUNTER       PIC 9(02)        VALUE ZERO.
01 NUMBER-ITEM   PIC S9(03).
01 SUM-ITEM      PIC S9(06)       VALUE ZERO.
01 BLANK-LINE    PIC X(80)        VALUE SPACES.
****************************************************************
PROCEDURE DIVISION.
****************************************************************
100-CONTROL-ROUTINE.
    PERFORM 200-DISPLAY-INSTRUCTIONS.
    PERFORM 300-INITIALIZATION-ROUTINE.
    PERFORM 400-ENTER-AND-ADD
            UNTIL NUMBER-ITEM = 999.
    PERFORM 500-CALCULATE-AVERAGE.
    PERFORM 600-DISPLAY-RESULTS.
    STOP RUN.
200-DISPLAY-INSTRUCTIONS.
    DISPLAY
      "THIS PROGRAM WILL FIND THE AVERAGE OF INTEGERS YOU ENTER".
    DISPLAY
      "THROUGH THE KEYBOARD. TYPE 999 TO INDICATE END OF DATA.".
    DISPLAY BLANK-LINE.
300-INITIALIZATION-ROUTINE.
    DISPLAY "PLEASE ENTER A NUMBER".
    ACCEPT NUMBER-ITEM.
400-ENTER-AND-ADD
    ADD NUMBER-ITEM TO SUM-ITEM.
    ADD 1 TO COUNTER.
    DISPLAY "PLEASE ENTER THE NEXT NUMBER".
    ACCEPT NUMBER-ITEM.
500-CALCULATE-AVERAGE.
    DIVIDE SUM-ITEM BY COUNTER GIVING AVERAGE.
600-DISPLAY-RESULTS.
    DISPLAY "THE AVERAGE OF THE NUMBERS IS ",AVERAGE.
```

(a)

```
           THIS PROGRAM WILL FIND THE AVERAGE OF
           INTEGERS YOU ENTER THROUGH THE KEYBOARD.
           TYPE 999 TO INDICATE END OF DATA.

           PLEASE ENTER A NUMBER
           6
           PLEASE ENTER THE NEXT NUMBER
           4
           PLEASE ENTER THE NEXT NUMBER
           11
           PLEASE ENTER THE NEXT NUMBER
           999
           THE AVERAGE OF THE NUMBERS IS    7.00
```

(b)

Pascal: The Language of Simplicity

Named for Blaise Pascal, the 17th-century French mathematician, **Pascal** was developed as a teaching language by a Swiss computer scientist, Niklaus Wirth, and first became available in 1971. Since that time it has become quite popular, first in Europe and now in the United States, particularly in universities and colleges offering computer science programs.

The foremost feature of Pascal is that it is simpler than most other languages: It has fewer features and is less wordy than most. Because of its limited input/output capabilities, however, it is unlikely to have a serious impact on the business community in its present form. Figure 7-11 presents an example of a Pascal program.

C: A Sophisticated Language

C was invented by Dennis Ritchie at Bell Labs in 1972. Its unromantic name evolved from earlier versions called A and B. C lends itself to sophisticated programming as well as to more mundane programming tasks. Further, C produces code that approaches assembly language in efficiency while still offering high-level language features.

Although C is simple and elegant, it is not particularly simple to learn. C was originally developed for professional programmers, and, except for elementary tasks, requires a serious learning period. Figure 7-12 shows an example of a C program and sample output.

 # Object-Oriented Programming

Imagine having to write an inventory program for a large manufacturer. Using a conventional programming language, such as those described in the previous section, a programmer would have to write a line of program code for the tiniest detail of the system. Actually, this would probably take many programmers many months to write many thousands of lines of code. But what if the programmers could take a shortcut? What if they could use some code already written—and tested—for another program? In other words, what if they did not have to reinvent the wheel every time they sat down to write a new program? Many people in the computer industry have asked these questions.

In recent years a new approach to writing programs has emerged. **Object-oriented programming (OOP)** means building a new program from standardized, precoded modules (Figure 7-13). Those precoded modules, together with the data to be processed, are called **objects.** Each object performs a certain function and is self-contained. Steve Jobs, a founder of Apple Computer, likes to use a laundry example. He lists the normal procedures for doing laundry at the laundromat: sort clothes, load washer, select temperature, input quarters, add detergent, and so forth. If, for some reason, this same information should be needed repeatedly, it could be stored as an object, perhaps called CLEAN. When next needed, rather than start from scratch, the object CLEAN could be invoked.

Currently, the two most widely used languages that embody object-oriented programming are **Smalltalk** and **C++.** Proponents of Smalltalk

```
PROGRAM AVERAGE (INPUT, OUTPUT);
(* PASCAL PROGRAM *)
(* AVERAGING INTEGERS ENTERED THROUGH THE KEYBOARD *)
VAR
    COUNTER, NUMBER, SUM : INTEGER;
    AVERAGE : REAL;
BEGIN
WRITELN ('THIS PROGRAM WILL FIND THE AVERAGE OF INTEGERS YOU ENTER');
WRITELN ('THROUGH THE KEYBOARD. TYPE 999 TO INDICATE END OF DATA.');
WRITELN;
SUM := 0;
COUNTER := 0;
WRITELN ('PLEASE ENTER A NUMBER');
READ (NUMBER);
WHILE NUMBER <> 999 DO
    BEGIN
    SUM :=SUM + NUMBER;
    COUNTER := COUNTER + 1;
    WRITELN ('PLEASE ENTER THE NEXT NUMBER');
    READ (NUMBER);
    END;
AVERAGE := SUM / COUNTER;
WRITELN ('THE AVERAGE OF THE NUMBERS IS',AVERAGE :6:2);
END.
```

(a)

```
THIS PROGRAM WILL FIND THE AVERAGE OF INTEGERS YOU ENTER
THROUGH THE KEYBOARD. TYPE 999 TO INDICATE END OF DATA.

PLEASE ENTER A NUMBER
6
PLEASE ENTER THE NEXT NUMBER
4
PLEASE ENTER THE NEXT NUMBER
11
PLEASE ENTER THE NEXT NUMBER
999
THE AVERAGE OF THE NUMBERS IS   7.00
```

(b)

TRANSPARENCY ACETATE #47
Figure 7-11

Figure 7-11 A Pascal program and sample output for averaging numbers.
(a) Comments are from (* to *). Each variable name must be declared. The symbol := assigns a value to the variable on the left; the symbol <> means not equal to. WRITELN by itself puts a blank line on the screen. (b) This screen display shows the interaction between program and user.

```
/* C PROGRAM */
/* AVERAGING INTEGERS ENTERED THROUGH THE KEYBOARD */
main()
{ float average;
  int counter = 0; number = 0; sum = 0;
printf("THIS PROGRAM WILL FIND THE AVERAGE OF INTEGERS YOU ENTER\n");
printf("THROUGH THE KEYBOARD. TYPE 999 TO INDICATE END OF DATA. \n\n");
printf("PLEASE ENTER A NUMBER");
scanf("%d",&number);
while (number != 999)
    {
        sum = sum + number;
        counter ++ ;
        printf("PLEASE ENTER THE NEXT NUMBER");
        scanf("%d",&number);
    }
  average = sum / counter;
  printf("THE AVERAGE OF THE NUMBERS IS ",AVERAGE);
}
```
(a)

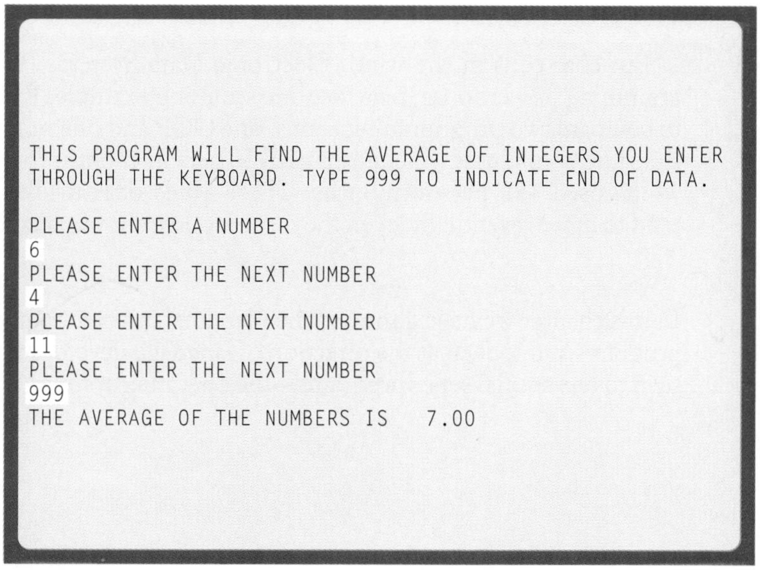

```
THIS PROGRAM WILL FIND THE AVERAGE OF INTEGERS YOU ENTER
THROUGH THE KEYBOARD. TYPE 999 TO INDICATE END OF DATA.

PLEASE ENTER A NUMBER
6
PLEASE ENTER THE NEXT NUMBER
4
PLEASE ENTER THE NEXT NUMBER
11
PLEASE ENTER THE NEXT NUMBER
999
THE AVERAGE OF THE NUMBERS IS   7.00
```
(b)

▲
Figure 7-12   A C program and sample output for averaging numbers.
(a) Comments are between /* and */. The command printf sends output to the
screen, and the scanf command accepts data from the user. (b) This screen display
shows the interaction between program and user.

TRANSPARENCY ACETATE #48
Figure 7-12

say it is the only "pure" OOP language, but supporters of C++, chiefly
programmers who develop commercial software products, see its extension from the C language as an advantage. Despite its popularity in theory and in the press, large-scale use of object-oriented programming is
still far from common. Two reasons for hanging back are the decades-
long entrenchment of COBOL programs and the rather steep learning
curve to change the programming orientation of an entire organization.

LECTURE HINT

Ridding a program of errors, or bugs, can be both time-consuming and costly. It has been estimated that 50 percent of a programmer's time is spent debugging programs. Fortunately, software has been developed to help simplify the debugging process. A debugger is a program that helps locate and correct programming errors.

TRANSPARENCY ACETATE #49

Figure 7-13

CLASS PROJECT

Divide the class into groups and assign to each group one of the programming languages available in the computer lab. For each language the students should record the following: (1) Is the language compiled or interpreted? (2) What are the hardware system requirements (e.g., RAM, monitors)? (3) What are the software system requirements (e.g., operating system, editor)?

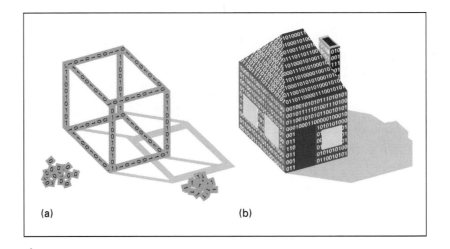

(a)   (b)

Figure 7-13   Object-oriented programming.
(a) In traditional programming, programmers typically divide up the task and write thousands of lines of program code from scratch. (b) In an object-oriented approach, a programmer searches a library of objects (precoded chunks of software) and incorporates those that are useful to the task.

But change is in the wind. Electronic Data Systems (EDS), a programming powerhouse, provides one stunning example. EDS ran a test to compare two programming teams, one OOP and one not, performing the same task. Guess which team used 10 person-months for the task and which used 152 person-months. These kinds of real-life illustrations tend to move, eventually, even the most recalcitrant organizations.

In this chapter we have glimpsed the planning and care required to write programs and looked at the direction of language development. We now turn to one special set of programs—the operating system.

Chapter **Review**

Summary and Key Terms

- A **programmer** converts solutions to the user's problems into a **program,** or instructions for the computer, by defining the problem, planning the solution, coding the program, testing the program, and documenting the program.
- Defining the problem means discussing it with the users to determine the necessary input, processing, and output.
- Planning can be done by using a **flowchart,** which is a pictorial representation of the step-by-step solution, and by using **pseudocode,** which is an English-like language.
- Coding the program means expressing the solution in a programming language.
- Testing the program consists of desk-checking, translating, and debugging. The rules of a programming language are referred to as its **syntax. Desk-checking** is a mental checking or proofreading of the program before it is run.
- In translating, a **translator** program converts the program into language the computer can understand and in the process detects programming-language errors, which are called **syntax errors.** Two types of translators are a **compiler,** which translates the entire program at one time and gives all the error messages **(diagnostics)** at once, and an **interpreter,** which translates the program one line at a time. The compiler also produces a **source program listing.** The original program, called a **source module,** is translated to an **object module,** to which prewritten programs may be added during the **link/load phase** to create an executable **load module.**
- **Debugging** is running the program to detect, locate, and correct mistakes, called **logic errors.**
- **Documentation** is a detailed written description of the program and the test results.
- The standard symbols used in flowcharting are called **ANSI** (American National Standards Institute) symbols. The rectangular **process box** shows an action to be taken. The diamond-shaped **decision box**—with two **paths,** or **branches**—is the only symbol that allows a choice. The **connector** is a circle that connects paths. The oval **start/stop symbol** is used at the beginning and end of a flowchart.
- To **initialize** is to set the starting values of certain storage locations, or **variables,** before running a program.
- A **loop** is a set of instructions causing the repetition of actions under certain conditions. An **iteration** is one trip through the loop. The computer can recognize the conditions by performing a **compare operation.**
- Pseudocode allows a programmer to plan a program, without being concerned about the rules of a specific programming language.
- A **programming language** is a set of rules for instructing the computer what operations to perform.
- **Machine language,** the lowest-level programming language, represents information as 0s and 1s.
- **Assembly languages** use letters as abbreviations or mnemonic codes to replace the 0s and 1s of machine language. An **assembler program** translates assembly language into machine language.
- **High-level languages** consist of English-like words. A compiler translates high-level languages into machine language.

procedural language

process box

program

programmer

programming
language

pseudocode

Smalltalk

source module

source program
listing

start/stop symbol

syntax

syntax errors

translator

variable

very high-level
language

- **Very high-level languages,** also called fourth-generation languages or **4GLs,** are basically nonprocedural. A **nonprocedural language** only defines *what* the computer should do, without detailing the procedure. A **procedural language** tells the computer specifically *how* to do the task.
- Fifth-generation languages are often called **natural languages** because they resemble natural human language.
- The first high-level language, **FORTRAN** (FORmula TRANslator), is a scientifically oriented language.
- **COBOL** (COmmon Business-Oriented Language) is a standard programming language for business that is considered **machine independent** because a COBOL program can be run on different computers.
- When introduced, **BASIC** (Beginner's All-purpose Symbolic Instruction Code) was intended for instruction, but its uses now include business and personal-computer systems.
- **Pascal** is popular in college computer courses.
- **C** offers high-level language features while producing efficient code.
- **Object-oriented programming (OOP)** means building a new program from standardized, precoded modules. The precoded modules, together with the data to be processed, are called **objects.** Each object performs a certain function and is self-contained. Two popular object-oriented languages are **Smalltalk** and **C++.**

Student Personal Study Guide

True/False

T F 1. Process boxes in flowcharting have two exits called paths.
T F 2. Lower-level languages are closer to the language the computer uses than are higher-level languages.
T F 3. A flowchart is an example of pseudocode.
T F 4. Desk-checking is the first phase of testing a program.
T F 5. A translator is hardware that translates a program into language the computer can understand.
T F 6. The highest-level languages are called, simply, high-level languages.
T F 7. Debugging is the process of locating program errors.
T F 8. Expressing a problem solution in Pascal is an example of coding a program.
T F 9. An advantage of pseudocode is that it can be used both to plan and execute a program.
T F 10. A 4GL increases clarity but reduces productivity.

Multiple Choice

1. A scientific language:
   a. 4GL   c. FORTRAN
   b. BASIC   d. COBOL
2. A programming language often used to teach programming to beginners:
   a. C   c. BASIC
   b. assembly language   d. pseudocode
3. Which is not part of testing a program?
   a. debugging   c. initializing
   b. desk-checking   d. diagnostics

4. The highest level of programming languages:
   - a. assembly
   - b. natural
   - c. high range
   - d. machine
5. A popular business-oriented language:
   - a. assembly
   - b. COBOL
   - c. Pascal
   - d. FORTRAN
6. Mentally "proofreading" the program:
   - a. desk-checking
   - b. compiling
   - c. linking
   - d. translating
7. The standard used for flowchart symbols:
   - a. key
   - b. magnetic tape
   - c. ANSI
   - d. syntax
8. Which is *not* a type of flowchart box?
   - a. syntax
   - b. process
   - c. connector
   - d. decision
9. A detailed written description of the program and the test results:
   - a. coding
   - b. link/loading
   - c. compiling
   - d. documentation
10. Which is not output from the compiler:
   - a. load module
   - b. object module
   - c. source program listing
   - d. diagnostics

Fill-In

1. Translates high-level languages into machine language: _____ .

2. Two common methods of planning the solution to a problem: _____ .

3. A language written by Niklaus Wirth: _____ .

4. A language specifically designed to write systems software: _____ .

5. The standard symbols used in flowcharting are called: _____ .

6. A kind of language that states *what* needs to be done, not *how*: _____ .

7. Languages that resemble spoken languages are called: _____ .

8. Type of language that builds programs from objects: _____ .

9. The error messages a translator provides are: _____ .

10. One trip through a loop: _____ .

Answers

True/False: 1. F, 2. T, 3. F, 4. T, 5. F, 6. F, 7. T, 8. T, 9. F, 10. F
Multiple choice: 1. c, 2. c, 3. c , 4. b, 5. b, 6. a, 7. c, 8. a, 9. d, 10. a
Fill-In: 1. compiler, 2. flowcharting, pseudocode, 3. Pascal, 4. C, 5. ANSI symbols, 6. non-procedural, 7. natural, 8. object-oriented, 9. diagnostics, 10. iteration

LEARNING OBJECTIVES

- Appreciating the need for operating systems
- Understanding that there are differences among operating systems for personal computers
- Becoming familiar with operating systems for personal computers
- Understanding operating environments

When Felicia Lee was taking a night class in applications software at a community college four years ago, she did not have to worry much about the operating system—the necessary software in the background. The college personal computers were on a network that managed all the computers. As Felicia sat down to begin work, the computer screen showed a menu of numbered choices reflecting the software packages available: 1. WordPerfect, 2. Microsoft Word, 3. Lotus 1-2-3, and so forth. At the bottom of the screen, Felicia was instructed to type the number of her chosen selection; if she typed 1, for example, the system put her into Word-Perfect. Felicia did have to learn operating system commands to prepare her own diskettes and save data on them so she could take her work with her, but she had little other contact with the operating system.

Operating

For her job as a supervisor in airport freight, Felicia needed to use word processing, spreadsheets, and database software packages on her IBM personal computer. But no one had set up a menu shortcut here, so, with a little advice from colleagues, she learned what she needed to know about the operating system called MS-DOS. She learned, among other things, to execute the software she needed to use and to take care of her data files—copying files from one disk to another and sometimes renaming or deleting them. She eventually felt fairly comfortable with her operating system knowledge.

Eighteen months later, Felicia was informed by the company personal computer manager that all personal computers were going to be switched to Microsoft Windows, a sort of overlay for the operating system. Despite assurances that the new system would be colorful and easy to use, Felicia was less than thrilled to be making another change. But she did not say so. She knew that being a computer user meant being willing to adjust to change. So Felicia learned to use a mouse and mastered icons, overlapping windows, pull-down menus, and other mysteries.

Approximately six months later, Felicia took a job at another airline freight

company. Part of the reason she was hired was her response to the revelation that the new company used Macintosh computers, which, she knew, used another operating system altogether. Felicia said, "Oh, I have learned several systems. It shouldn't be any problem learning another." She was right, of course. In fact, she thought the Macintosh operating system was the easiest of them all.

Systems

The Underlying Software

Operating Systems: Powerful Software in the Background

An **operating system** is a set of programs that allows the computer to control and manage its own resources, such as the central processing unit, memory, and secondary storage. Figure 8-1 gives a conceptual picture of operating system software as an intermediary between the hardware and applications programs, such as word processing and database programs. Much of the work of an operating system is hidden from the user; many necessary tasks are performed behind the scenes. In other words, whether or not you are aware of it, using any software application requires that you invoke, or call into action, the operating system as well. As a user you must be able to interact with an operating system at some level, however rudimentary.

Operating systems for mainframe and other large computers are complex indeed, since they must keep track of several programs from several users all running in the same time frame. Although some personal computer operating systems—most often those found in business or learning environments—can support multiple programs, many are concerned only with a single user running a single program at a given time. This chapter focuses on the interaction between a user and a personal computer operating system.

Operating Systems for Personal Computers

If you peruse software offerings at a retail store, you will generally find the software grouped according to the computer, probably IBM or Macintosh, with which the software can be used. But the distinction is actu-

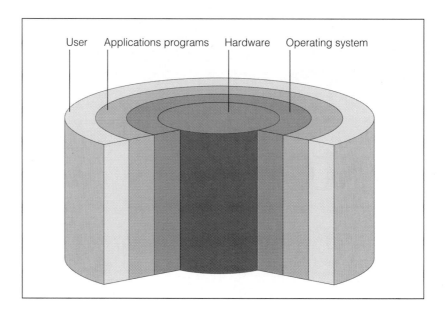

ally finer than the differences among computers: Applications programs—word processing, spreadsheets, games, or whatever—are really distinguished by the operating systems on which they can run.

Generally, an application program can run on just one operating system. Just as you cannot place a Nissan engine in a Ford truck, you cannot take a version of WordPerfect designed to run on an IBM machine and run it on an Apple Macintosh. IBM personal computers and others like them use Microsoft's operating system, called MS-DOS (for Microsoft Disk Operating System). Macintoshes use an entirely different operating system called System 7, which is produced by Apple. Most personal computers are limited to one of these two. The operating systems are different because the central processing units are different. Software makers must decide for which operating system to write a software package, although some make versions of their software for each operating system.

Users do not set out to buy operating systems; they want computers and the applications software to make them useful. Since the operating system determines what software is available for a given computer, many users observe the high volume of software available for MS-DOS machines and make their computer purchases accordingly. Others prefer the user-friendly style of the Macintosh operating system and choose Macs for that reason.

Although operating systems differ, many of their basic functions are similar. We will show some of the basic functions of operating systems by examining MS-DOS.

Getting Started with MS-DOS

Most users today have a computer with a hard disk drive. When the computer is turned on, the operating system will be loaded from the hard disk into the computer's memory, thus making it available for use. (Users without a hard disk drive must load the operating system from a diskette each time they use the computer.) The process of loading the operating system into memory is called bootstrapping, or **booting**, the system. The word *booting* is used because, figuratively speaking, the operating system pulls itself up by its own bootstraps. When the computer is switched on, a small program (in ROM—read-only memory) automatically pulls up the basic components of the operating system from the hard disk.

The net observable result of booting MS-DOS is that the characters C> (or possibly C:\>) appear on the screen. (Users without a hard drive will see A>). The C refers to the disk drive; the > is a **prompt**, a signal that the system is prompting you to do something. At that point you must give some instruction to the computer. Perhaps all you need to do is key certain letters to make the application software take the lead. But it could be more complicated than that because C> is actually a signal for direct communication between the user and the operating system.

Although the prompt is the only visible result of booting the system, MS-DOS also provides the basic software that coordinates the computer's hardware components and a set of programs that lets you perform the many computer system tasks you need to do. We will consider some of these tasks now.

Windows 95: The Latest and Greatest

As 50 million users can attest, the operating environment called Windows is an unqualified success. But even a popular software product can be improved. Here are some highlights of Windows 95:

User convenience. You can't miss it: the message "Click here to begin" bounces along the bottom, near the Start button in the lower left corner. From this launch, you can find a program or a file. And, by the way, all actions use only a single click of a mouse. Want to revise a memo? Just click its file name to retrieve it—the word processing program is automatically invoked too. As another example of convenience, long file names, up to 255 characters, are permitted.

Information center. Windows 95 puts all communications activities—e-mail, downloads, and so forth—in a single screen icon. Furthermore, Windows 95 includes software that makes it easier to configure computers for networks and the Internet.

Plug and play. Anyone who has added a new component—perhaps a modem or a sound card—to an existing computer knows that it may not work correctly right away. This is because the new component must be configured to the system, a process that may involve some tricky software and even hardware moves. Windows 95 supports plug and play, a concept that lets the computer configure itself when a new component is added. However, for plug and play to become a reality, hardware components must also feature the plug and play standard.

TEST BANK

Mult. Choice 1-3, 9, 12, 17-18

T/F 29-31, 34-37, 48

Matching 52, 58, 60

Fill In 61-62, 70, 72, 75-80

DISCUSSION QUESTION

What are some typical tasks you can accomplish using DOS commands?

 # Using MS-DOS

We will now refer to MS-DOS by its abbreviated name, DOS, pronounced to rhyme with *boss*. Recall that an operating system is actually a *set* of programs. To execute a given DOS program, a user must issue a **command,** a name that invokes a specific DOS program. Whole books have been written about DOS commands, but we will consider only the commands you need to use applications software. There are dozens of commands, but most people need just a few for ordinary activities. Here are some typical tasks you can do with DOS commands:

- Access files using DOS commands
- Prepare (format) new diskettes for use
- List the files on a disk
- Copy files from one disk to another
- Erase files from a disk

See the "Personal Computers in Action" box on page 167 for more details.

A Brief Disk Discussion

Since many DOS commands involve files on disk, we are particularly concerned about disk drives in this chapter.

Disk Drive Configuration

There are two kinds of disk drives associated with a personal computer: a diskette drive and a hard disk drive. A common configuration is a diskette drive as drive A and the hard drive as drive C. If you have a second diskette drive (perhaps one for 3½-inch diskettes and one for 5¼-inch diskettes), the second disk drive will be drive B. If you are lucky enough to have a CD-ROM drive, that will probably be drive D. Configurations vary, but the four most common are shown in Figure 8-2.

The Default Drive

Consider the DOS command DIR, which displays a list of files. How does DOS know which drive to look at when you type DIR? Just which set of files do you want? If you do not specify a particular drive, DOS will look at the default drive.

DISCUSSION QUESTION

How does DOS remind you which drive is the current drive?

The **default drive,** also called the **current drive,** is the drive that the computer is currently using. Only one disk drive at a time can be the default drive. If you have a hard disk drive, then that drive—drive C—starts out as the current drive and usually stays as the current drive. DOS uses the prompt to remind you which drive is the current drive. If you see C> on the screen, then the current drive is C.

You can change the default to another drive if you wish. After the prompt, type the letter of the desired drive, followed by a colon, and then press Enter. Suppose, for example, that the default drive is currently drive C (as you can see from C> on the screen), but you want to access files on a diskette in drive A. To change the default drive to A, type A: (A followed by a colon) and then press Enter. (You can, by the way, type either an upper- or lowercase A—DOS recognizes both.) Now the screen should show A>.

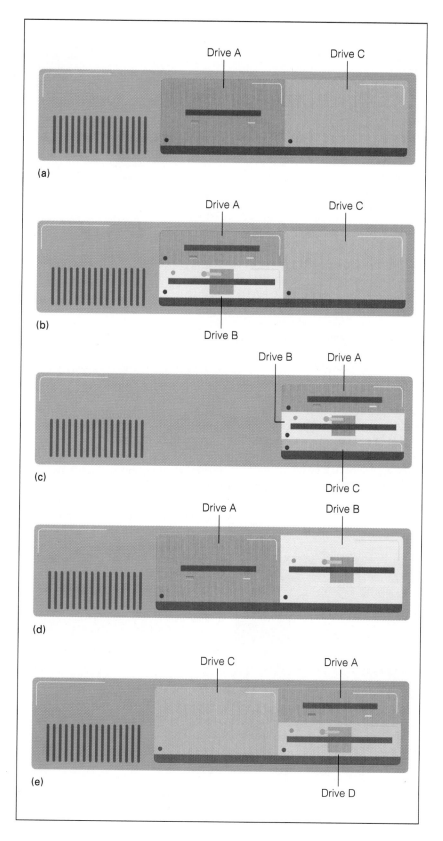

◀

Figure 8-2 Disk drive configurations.
As you use different computers, you may see several different types of disk drive combinations. The following are common. (a) Drive A for 3½-inch diskettes on the left, hard disk drive C on the right. (b) Drive A for 3½-inch diskettes on the top left; drive B for stacked 5¼-inch diskettes on the lower left; hard disk drive C on the right. (c) Drive A for 3½-inch diskettes on the top right; drive B for stacked 5¼-inch diskettes on the lower right; hard disk drive C may be on the bottom right or, in some cases, further back under the housing (in either case the indication that a drive is being used—that is, read or written—is the indicator light on the front panel, no matter where the actual drive is located). (d) On older systems without a hard disk drive, drive A for 3½-inch diskettes is on the left and drive B for stacked 5¼-inch diskettes is on the right. (e) Any of the first three may be complicated by the presence of a CD-ROM drive, which is usually drive D.

TRANSPARENCY ACETATE #51

Figure 8-2

MACINTOSH

The Macintosh Applications Interface

Computers based on the DOS operating system are fundamentally different from Macintosh computers. The main difference has to do with the computer's hardware, especially the design of the processor. But the difference that most users notice first is the Macintosh's graphical user interface (GUI). While DOS-based programs have traditionally employed an interface that is textual (the user has to type in commands), the Mac's interface works by creating a graphical "world," displaying pictures of disks, folders, and even a trash can. Items in this world can be picked up, moved around, dropped, or discarded, using the same intuitive skills of grabbing and handling objects that we learn as children.

A typical GUI makes use of four basic elements: icons (pictures that symbolize items like files or disks); a pointer (a cursor moved around the screen using a mouse); windows (rectangular areas on the screen used to display information, easily moved or resized using the pointer); and pull-down menus (each of which offers a list of commands, which the user can choose from by using the pointer). These four elements together provide an interface that is surprisingly easy to learn. For instance, to copy a file from one disk to another, the user can simply "grab" the file's icon with the pointer and "drag" it onto the destination disk's icon. The Macintosh was the first example of this interface to succeed in the computer market, although its design had been created years earlier by researchers at

XEROX's Palo Alto Research Center. And now Microsoft has provided a similar GUI for DOS-based machines called Microsoft Windows.

Another advantage to using the Mac is consistency. Before these interfaces became popular, every program had its own way of interacting with the user. Some provided menus, but you had to use special keystrokes to activate them. If you wanted to learn a new software package, you could count on having to learn a whole new set of keystrokes and commands. Apple was aware of this problem when they developed the first Macintosh and went about solving it in two ways.

First, they provided a set of programs called the Macintosh Toolbox, which is dedicated to providing standard windows, icons, menus, and pointers. The Toolbox is available for any application to make use of, so that when programmers are creating a new application, they do not have to trouble with the design of windows and menus: The details will be taken care of by the Toolbox. The payoff is that virtually every applica-

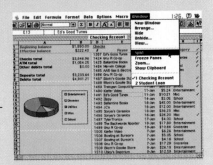

b) This spreadsheet document was created to balance a checkbook but has a look and feel similar to that of the Finder and other applications.

tion will have windows and menus that look and behave in exactly the same way.

In addition to the Toolbox, Apple put forth a set of standards to which applications should adhere. For instance, most Macintosh applications provide File and Edit menus, each of which contains standard commands for working with documents. A newer standard is the availability of Balloon Help. When this feature is activated, the user can get information on different components of an application simply by positioning the pointer over it; a cartoon-style balloon will then appear with a description of that element.

This consistency between applications gives the impression, quite falsely, that all Macintosh software is produced by a single manufacturer. In fact, there are hundreds of companies as well as individuals developing software for the Mac, and virtually all of them make a special effort to adhere to the Macintosh standard interface.

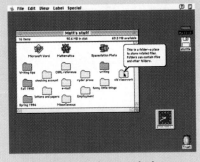

a) When Balloon Help is switched on, a user can get instant descriptions about any object in his environment by positioning the pointer over the object.

Personal Computers
In Action

The MS-DOS Commands You Will Use Most

The instructions here assume you are using a computer with diskette drive A and hard disk drive C. Instructions for you to type are highlighted.

FORMAT (Prepare an unformatted diskette for use). Whether the data you are producing is a document, spreadsheet, database, or graph, you must have some place to keep it. Unless you are fortunate enough to have your own hard disk, the place to keep your data is on a diskette. However, a diskette fresh from the store may need to be formatted before it can be used, and that is the purpose of this command. Caution: *Never* format the hard disk in drive C; formatting destroys all data on a disk.

1. Insert the blank diskette in drive A.
2. `C:\>CD \DOS` (Enter) Change to the DOS directory.
3. `C:\DOS>FORMAT A:` (Enter) Type the command to format.
4. When asked, press Enter to confirm diskette present and also to skip volume label.

DIR (Directory). In no time at all, most computer users have lots of files on lots of disks; forgetting where these files are located is easy. DIR produces an on-screen list of file names. /P and /W add further options.

`C:\>DIR` Lists one line per file, with name, size in bytes, and date/time created.

`C:\>DIR /W` Lists file name only, in five columns across the screen.

`C:\>DIR /P` Lists one line per file, a page at a time; press any key to continue.

`C:\>DIR /W/P` Lists file name only, in five columns, a page at a time.

COPY (Make a copy of a file). One important reason to copy a file is to produce a backup copy. Another is to copy a data file generated on a community (school or office) hard disk to your own diskette. If we assume the file to be copied is on the current drive, in this case drive C, C need not be mentioned in the command. And, if you want the new file to have the same name in its new location, which is usually the case, you need not key it again on the new drive, in this case A.

`C:\>COPY MRKTDATA.SUM A:` Copies file MRKTDATA.SUM on drive C to drive A.

`C:\>COPY *.* A:` Copies all files in the directory to drive A.

DEL or ERASE (Delete a file). When your diskette gets cluttered with files you no longer want, it is time to clean house. Use DEL followed by the name of each file you want to delete.

RENAME (Give a file a new name). If you decide to change a file name, use the RENAME command, followed by the old name and then the new name. Assume that a file named MRKTDATA.SUM is on a diskette in drive A.

`A:\>RENAME MRKTDATA.SUM SSDATA.CHT` New name is SSDATA.CHT.

Other simple commands. These four commands can be invoked by simply keying the commands themselves, without the need for any additional information. **CHKDSK**, meaning check disk, causes a screen display of information about the status of the disk, including number of files, number of bytes used in files, and number of bytes available for use. **CLS** clears the screen. When you key **TIME** the proper time appears on the screen. If you wish, you may key a new time; this is convenient for switching back and forth between daylight savings time and standard time. **VER** will provide the

Types of Files

The three types of files you may use are (1) DOS system files, (2) applications software files, and (3) data files. DOS system files are the operating system programs. Applications software files are the software needed for an application, such as word processing. Data files hold data that is

DISCUSSION QUESTION

What are three types of files you may use?

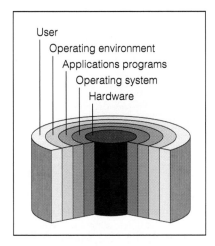

Figure 8-3 An operating environment.
This illustration is identical to Figure 8-1, except that an operating environment layer has been added to shield the user from having to know commands of the operating system.

related to applications software, such as the memo or term paper you typed using word processing.

When are these files used? The DOS system files are used to start the computer system and, as you proceed, to provide services and control of software and files. Generally speaking, unless you invoke some command for a specific need, such as copying a file, you will not deal directly with the operating system files. If you do need to use the operating system files directly, you do so by issuing a command that invokes the program name. Application software files are invoked by you whenever you use that specific application, but again, you will probably have little direct interaction with the files themselves. Data files are used with applications software, either to supply input data or, more likely, to store the files you create.

Data files are different from DOS system and applications software files. To begin with, the DOS and applications software may belong to your school or company and may be used by several people. Input data files may also be files created by the school or company personnel. Output data files, on the other hand, usually contain data created by you and may be used only by you, especially in an academic environment. Once you place your school or personal data files on diskettes, then the files are in your exclusive control, to use, to destroy, or to take home with you.

When you first purchase a data diskette (disk) it contains no files—that is, the disk is empty. Although it is possible to purchase disks that are already formatted, traditionally disks come unformatted. To prepare an unformatted disk to receive the files you will create, you must use the FORMAT command. In contrast, DOS and applications software disks that you purchase already have been formatted, have files on them, and should not be formatted again.

When you use application software to create a data file, you must choose a name for the file. When there are several data files on the disk, you may want to see a list of all the file names. You may want to copy files from one data disk to another so you can have a backup copy. You may want to erase files you no longer need. To do these things, you need to know how to use the appropriate DOS commands, as shown in the "Personal Computers in Action" box.

Operating Environments

There is another, some say *better*, way to interact with the computer's operating system. Figure 8-3 tells the story: Another layer has been added to separate the operating system and the user. This layer is often called a **shell** because it forms a "coating" over the operating system. More formally, this layer is called an **operating environment** because it creates a new way of doing business and even presents a new screen appearance—one more palatable to many users than the C> prompt.

When using an operating environment, you see pictures and/or simply worded choices instead of C> or some other prompt. Instead of having to *know* some command to type, you have only to make a selection from the choices available on the screen. Apple's Macintosh paved the way for simple interfaces between users and the operating system, and

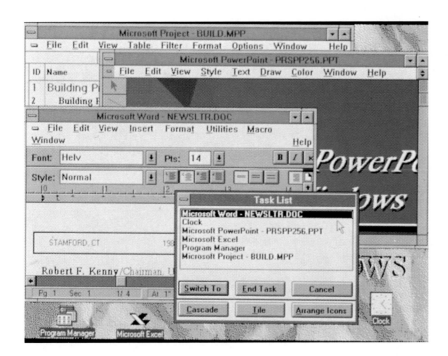

Figure 8-4   Microsoft Windows.
The operating environment provided by Windows, a Microsoft product, can run several programs concurrently and let users follow their progress on screens divided into windows. Windows offers easy-to-use menu systems as well as user-friendly access to the operating system.

TRANSPARENCY ACETATE #53

Figure 8-4

now Microsoft has captured the operating environment standard for DOS-based computers with Microsoft Windows.

Microsoft Windows: An Overview

Microsoft Windows—Windows for short—uses a colorful graphics interface that, among other things, eases access to the operating system (Figure 8-4). Although earlier versions of Windows were not especially successful, Windows 3.0, introduced in 1990 and followed by Windows 3.1 in 1992, received a warm welcome. The recent versions offer many improvements, including sophisticated screen graphics and faster operation. Almost immediately, many businesses large and small converted their personal computer systems to Windows. Now selling briskly, it is clear that Windows has become a new corporate standard. So, what is so special about Windows?

The feature that makes Windows so easy to use is a **graphical user interface** (**GUI**, pronounced "*goo*-ee"), in which users work more with on-screen pictures called **icons** and with **pull-down menus** rather than with keyed commands (Figure 8-5a). Furthermore, icons and menus encourage pointing and clicking with a mouse, an approach that can make computer use both faster and easier.

To enhance ease of use, Windows is usually set up so that the colorful Windows display is the first thing a user sees when the computer is turned on. The user points and clicks among a series of narrowing choices until arriving at the desired software.

Although the screen presentation and user interaction is the most visible evidence of a different kind of operating system, Windows offers changes that are even more fundamental. It is helpful at this point to make a comparison between Windows and traditional operating systems for large computers.

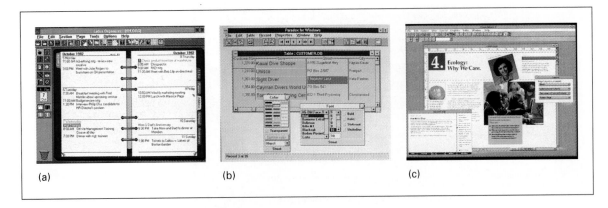

(a)   (b)   (c)

▲
Figure 8-5   Microsoft Windows in Action.
These screens vividly illustrate the Windows graphical user interface (GUI). (a) This organizer program uses the concept of a notebook with tabs. Note also the icons to the left and top. Clicking a mouse on tabs or icons will cause corresponding action. (b) This database program screen demonstrates available color and fonts in different windows. (c) This desktop publishing software can pull together various elements from different windows.

Multiprogramming and Multitasking: Comparing Mainframe Operating Systems to Windows

Is the operating system action the same for big and small computers? The answer is yes—and no. Yes, if you are considering computer action from the perspective of the central processing unit (CPU). No, if you are taking the viewpoint of the user, who accesses the CPU and other computer resources via the operating system.

Large Computers

Considering the CPU for just a moment, recall how a computer executes instructions. The computer usually has a single processor that can do only one thing at a time, that is, one instruction at a time. Since there are invariably other tasks associated with running a program, such as reading from disk or printing, it would be wasteful if the CPU sat idle while these tasks were being accomplished. To maximize CPU use, the large computer's operating system includes a feature called **multiprogramming,** which permits the running of several programs in the same time frame, or **concurrently.** That is, multiprogramming permits several unrelated programs, probably from many different users, to compete for the processor. Remember that we are talking about large computers now— supercomputers, mainframes, and minicomputers.

Although programs are said to run concurrently, this does not mean that they run simultaneously. In fact, the programs take turns using the CPU. For example, one program could be using the CPU while another program prints a record. Amazingly, the operating systems keeps track of everything and makes sure that the programs do not get entangled with each other. From the point of view of the user, a program is executed by the computer just as if the computer and all its resources belong exclusively to that user. (In reality, sometimes a large computer is so overloaded that time delays make the shared nature of the machine more obvious.)

Personal Computers

Personal computers also have a CPU that handles just one instruction at a time. Until quite recently, computers using DOS were limited not only to one user at a time but also to one program at a time. If, for example, a user were using a word processing program to write a financial report and wanted to access some spreadsheet figures, he or she would have to perform a series of arcane steps: exit the word processing program, enter and exit the spreadsheet program, and then re-enter the word processing program to complete the report. This is wasteful in two ways: (1) The CPU is often idle because only one program is executing at a time, and (2) the user is required to move inconveniently from one program to another program.

The solution to this problem is a direct descendant of multiprogramming, an operating system approach called **multitasking.** The idea is the same as multiprogramming: Let several programs compete concurrently for the use of the CPU. In industry jargon, and for all practical purposes, we consider that these programs are running at the same time.

A key feature of Windows is its multitasking capability. From the user's perspective a window on the screen indicates each program currently in operation. Using the financial report example previously described, the user could access the spreadsheet program without closing down or leaving the word processing program. It is possible to run many programs at once in a multitasking environment. In fact, the name Windows refers to the fact that various software tools can be accessed and displayed on the screen in overlapping rectangles that look like windows. It is possible to use one application when you are right in the middle of another (Figure 8-5b).

Applications Software with Windows

Just what will Windows do for your favorite software application? Although you can tell Windows to access your existing software, you will not get the full benefits of Windows unless you use a software version especially designed for use with Windows. Anticipating the popularity of Windows, dozens of software manufacturers have been writing their programs for the Windows environment. Look around your local computer store and you will see an entire section reserved just for software written for Windows.

Reality Check

A Windows user needs a hard disk, and a color monitor is highly recommended. Two other serious considerations for Windows to run efficiently are speed and memory. Decent performance requires a computer with a speedy microprocessor, at least an 80386 and preferably an 80486 or Pentium. Also needed is at least 4 megabytes of memory, preferably 8MB. Many serious users, especially business users, already have such a system in place; those who do not should expect slow going with Windows.

Right This Way, Dummies

An online junkie we will call Helen was hooked up to her favorite information service and had selected an option in which several online users were in the same "room," with their keyed comments showing up on the screen. Helen saw the question "Are there any Windows experts here?" When no one answered right away, Helen keyed "Well, I'm a Windows dummy, if that helps. Try your question." Rather to her surprise, Helen was able to answer the question, something about preserving icon locations.

Helen was not computer illiterate; she had used computers extensively at home. When Windows came along, she picked up a couple of books to ease the transition, a quick reference guide and a book containing thousands of Windows "tips." Unfortunately, she found that neither book met her rather mundane needs; they tended to go into sophisticated aspects such as office networking and optimizing memory use.

Browsing in her computer store, Helen came across the book she needed. She was not embarrassed to report to the checkout counter with *Windows for Dummies.* It turned out to be very helpful, giving her more information on the basics of Windows.

COMPUTING TRENDS

Windows as Far as the Eye Can See

Anyone who has not figured out what the trend is for operating systems has missed the heavy press coverage of billionaire Bill Gates, the still-young founder of the Microsoft Corporation. Mr. Gates has graced the covers of *Time, Fortune,* and any other news magazine you could name (the photos here first appeared in *U.S News and Word Report*). Each time he is interviewed, Mr. Gates makes a pitch for his vision of the future, which features the operating system shell Microsoft Windows, or just Windows for short. (Incidentally, Microsoft was denied a patent on the word *windows;* the word was considered simply too common.)

Mr. Gates can let the numbers speak for themselves. Microsoft's operating system MS-DOS runs 90 percent of the world's personal computers. Windows, the operating environment software designed to run with MS-DOS, is selling one million copies a month.

An early spinoff product was Windows for Workgroups, a software/hardware package that lets users set up peer-to-peer networks with a Windows environment. But perhaps the greatest indicator of

future direction is the product called Windows NT, a sophisticated operating system that will not only run on personal computers but will also power the newest and biggest main-

frame computers. This is the first clear signal that environments for big and small computers will eventually merge.

▼ ▼ ▼

Do I really need to know all about the operating system? The answer to that question depends on how you expect to use a computer. If you use a computer primarily as a tool to complete a specific type of work, then you may have minimum interaction with an operating system. In that case, whether you are using a personal computer or a mainframe, you will learn to access the software of your choice very quickly.

But there are other ways to use a computer. In fact, there are far more options than we are able to present in this introductory chapter. Those who want or need to put the computer to its highest and best use will take direct command of the operating system, because doing so increases their effectiveness and flexibility with the computer. You can learn your way around the operating system of any computer through on-the-job training or manuals that accompany the software.

Chapter **Review**

Summary and Key Terms

■ An **operating system** is a set of programs through which the computer manages its own resources, such as the CPU, memory, secondary storage devices, and input/output devices.

■ Much of the work of an operating system is hidden from the user; many necessary tasks are performed behind the scenes.

■ Operating systems for mainframe and other large computers must keep track of several programs from several users all running in the same time frame.

■ Although some personal computer operating systems can support multiple programs, many are concerned only with a single user running a single program at a given time.

■ In general, an application program can run on just one operating system.

■ IBM personal computers and others like them use Microsoft's operating system, called MS-DOS, for Microsoft disk operating system. Macintoshes use an entirely different operating system, called System 7 and produced by Apple.

■ Most personal computers are limited to either MS-DOS or System 7. The operating systems are different because the central processing units are different. Software makers must decide for which operating system to write a software package, although some make versions of their software for each operating system.

■ Loading the operating system into memory is called **booting** the system.

■ In the on-screen A> and C> prompts, the A and C refers to the disk drive. A **prompt** is a signal that the system is waiting for you to give a command to the computer.

■ To execute a given DOS program, a user must issue a **command,** a name that invokes a specific DOS program. Typical tasks that can be performed with DOS commands are: access files, format new diskettes, list the files on a disk, copy files from one disk to another, and erase files from a disk.

■ The **default drive,** also called the **current drive,** is the drive that the computer is currently using.

■ Diskettes may hold DOS files, applications software files, or data files.

■ Some operating systems provide pictures, worded choices, or both instead of giving a prompt. In effect, these pictures and choices form a user-friendly "coating," or **shell,** over the operating system. They create a comfortable **operating environment** for the user, who does not have to remember or look up the appropriate commands.

■ A key shell product is Microsoft Windows 3.1, software with a colorful **graphical user interface (GUI).** Windows offers on-screen pictures called **icons** and **pull-down menus,** both of which encourage pointing and clicking with a mouse, an approach that can make computer use faster and easier.

■ On mainframe operating systems, **multiprogramming** permits the running of several programs in the same time frame, or **concurrently.** That is, multiprogramming permits several unrelated programs, probably from many different users, to compete for the processor. From the point of view of the user, his or her program is executed by the computer just as if the computer and all its resources belonged exclusively to that user.

■ Using Windows, **multitasking** lets several programs compete concurrently for the use of the CPU; for all practical purposes, these programs are considered to be running at the same time.

- The name Windows refers to the fact that various software tools can be accessed simultaneously and displayed on the screen in overlapping rectangles that look like windows.
- Although software makers are designing products especially for use with Windows, decent performance with Windows requires a fast computer and at least 4 megabytes of memory.

Student Personal Study Guide

True/False

T F   1. The key feature of Microsoft Windows is user–keyboard interaction.
T F   2. FORMAT is an example of a DOS command.
T F   3. C> on the screen means that C is the current drive.
T F   4. The default drive is the current drive.
T F   5. A multiprogramming environment runs programs concurrently.
T F   6. A GUI uses icons.
T F   7. Windows runs well on any computer.
T F   8. An operating system is not needed if a shell is used.
T F   9. The name Windows refers to circular drawings on the screen.
T F 10. Loading the operating system into memory is called booting.

Multiple Choice

1. A graphical interface:
   a. GUI   c. C>
   b. boot   d. prompt
2. The Windows capability for running more than one program at a time:
   a. multiprogramming   c. pull-down menus
   b. interface   d. multitasking
3. Load the operating system:
   a. default   c. prompt
   b. boot   d. command
4. The command to change default drive from C to A:
   a. FORMAT A: c. COPY *. A:
   b. A: d. RENAME C A
5. Which is *not* a resource managed by the operating system?
   a. memory   c. printer
   b. interface   d. CPU
6. Another name for current drive:
   a. default   c. GUI
   b. command   d. boot
7. A signal that the computer is waiting for command from the user:
   a. task   c. prompt
   b. window   d. command
8. Programs running in the same time frame:
   a. commands   c. menus
   b. prompts   d. concurrent operation
9. An operating environment:
   a. shell   c. task
   b. boot   d. command

10. A set of programs to manage the computer's resources:
   a. operating system   c. diskette
   b. disk   d. command

Fill-In

1. Waiting for a command, the computer displays a: _____ .

2. If your computer has a hard drive, the initial default drive is: _____ .

3. Another name for an operating environment: _____ .

4. GUI stands for: _____ .

5. Loading the operating system is called: _____ .

6. Another name for the current drive: _____ .

7. The DOS command to list files: _____ .

8. The DOS command to get a disk ready to accept files: _____ .

9. The DOS command to move a file to another disk: _____ .

10. The DOS command to erase a file: _____ .

Answers

True/False: 1. F, 2. T, 3. T, 4. T, 5. T, 6. T, 7. F, 8. F, 9. F, 10. T
Multiple choice: 1. a, 2. d , 3. b , 4. b, 5. b, 6. a, 7. c, 8. d, 9. a, 10. a
Fill-In: 1. prompt, 2. C, 3. shell, 4. graphical user interface, 5. booting, 6. default, 7. DIR, 8. FORMAT, 9. COPY, 10. DEL or ERASE

Interview: Real Estate by Computer

Mary Ferrari, a real estate agent, talks about using computers in the office and in the field.

It seems to me that the real estate industry is just beginning to exploit personal computers. How long have you been using a personal computer?

I have been using a personal computer about four years. My computing days began when I saw a flyer that advertised software for real estate agents that could be used to pull up every house listed in the area. The screen could show a picture of a house, as well as all pertinent details, such as number of bedrooms and price. And I thought, "Wow!"

So it was like an electronic multiple listing?

Yes, exactly. It piqued my interest because they were promoting the hardware—a laptop computer—and software as a package, and they offered financing in a way that any agent could afford. I went to the seminar and signed up. At the same time, I bought a desktop computer for home use.

The laptop, of course, is for portability. I take it with me on listing appointments and when I go out with buyers to show them houses. It has a modem, too. The office where I work today is fully computerized. I can dial into the multiple listing service at any time of the day or night, and load all the new listings and all of the current sales. The computer at home is the one I use for artwork and editing and the fancy charts we put out for our clients who are selling their homes.

I was impressed that you can personalize the client sheet. You can add your own name to it, so that the client can remember the agent's name.

That's part of the software. The computer really helps us get new business. Suppose someone calls up and says, "Gee, we're thinking about selling our house, and we want you to do a market analysis." I can go to the computer and in a matter of minutes have a personalized handout sheet for that client when we go to their house to discuss the listing. The sheet shows everything that is a similar property to theirs that has sold or is in escrow or is on the market. The software also lets me prepare a personalized cover sheet, which says something such as "This is a presentation exclusively for Mr. and Mrs. John Doe on March 29, 1995," and includes the agent's phone numbers. The customer is blown away by it because it's

Computers

neat, it's clean, and it's very professional-looking.

It sounds as if your clients are intrigued by your use of the computer.
They expect computers in the office. They know that a computer can provide us with information faster, and it's a reliable source in most cases. But they seem to be really surprised when we take out our laptops outside of the office, in the car or at an open house. Suppose a client at an open house says, "You know, I don't really like this, but it's the right amount of money and this is the neighborhood I want to be in." You can use the laptop to show pictures of similar houses on the market. The consumer isn't really aware that you can put all this information into such a small instrument that is so lightweight and so portable. They're really impressed.

How did you get your skills using the computer? Read the manual?

A lot of that. Some classes, too. It was hit or miss. This is going to sound bad, but I learned how to use a mouse by playing computer games. After having fun with that for two successive weekends, I had enough faith in my ability with a mouse to do graphics work.

How does your business routine now compare with your routine before you incorporated the computer?
It was never as professional. The computerization of real estate definitely improves efficiency and professionalism and reliability. Today, the only thing I do in longhand is write an offer or take a listing. Everything else, literally, is through a computer.

The computer has saved us a bunch of money. I can't even begin to say how much. And then the amount of time. Sometimes we get bored by 3 o'clock in the afternoon. We've done all our work. We used to work up until 5:30 or 6:00 at night. And we've determined that it's all on account of the computer.

What are you able to do now with the computer that you would never have hoped to have done before you started using one?
The advertising, the promotional work, the graphs and the charts—all the marketing stuff. I knew we could write letters; I knew about the word processing, no problem. But I had no idea there was the capability to

do all kinds of publishing. For example, if it's a kind of ranch-style house, there's a cowboy that you can put on your marketing piece. Or if you want to send out invitations to an Easter egg hunt or something similar to your clients, you can make your own invitations and, of course, in this program there's an Easter bunny. The

artwork is all done for you. I never had any idea that we could do all of this ourselves.

Last question. What advice would you give about computers to a new real estate agent starting today? Get a laptop?
A real estate agent starting today should not go to work for a real estate office that does not offer state-of-the-

> *Sometimes we get bored by 3 o'clock in the afternoon. We've done all our work. We used to work up until 5:30 or 6:00 at night. And we've determined that it's all on account of the computer.*

art computer equipment. A new agent won't survive without it. A laptop does give you freedom—you can work at home or from a client's house, or from the beach, for that matter.

and Business

LEARNING OBJECTIVES

- Appreciating the pervasive spread of personal computers in the workplace
- Understanding how personal computers have affected workers on the job
- Understanding what the information center can do for the user
- Understanding the functions of the information systems manager
- Understanding the terms *system, analysis,* and *design*
- Becoming familiar with workgroup computing
- Appreciating the role of the user in systems planning

Although most of Mike Simpson's college friends had no idea what they wanted to major in, Mike began his freshman year knowing exactly what field he wanted to get into: television. He majored in communications and, in addition to the standard requirements, set out to take every class he could that would provide hands-on experience. His first year he wrangled an apprenticeship at the campus radio station; the job meant long hours and no pay. He expected to learn a lot about on-air procedures and behind-the-scenes management. He was rather startled to find that the main thing he learned about was computers.

Computers

The station used computers in several ways. One recurring problem at radio stations is that disc jockeys tend to play their own favorites. To ensure variety and reduce repetition, station staff selected songs, including permissible repetition, and then fed the data to the computer, which arranged them in random order and generated a music log. Computers were also used in the news-gathering process. Information from news services such as the Associated Press was transferred directly to the station's own computer, where it could be pulled up on the screen and edited for local broadcast. Finally, the station had developed its own database of contacts. When a story broke, a reporter could enter a few appropriate words, such as *wetlands, community,* and *business,* to get a balanced list of contacts.

Mike could not miss the pervasiveness of computers in business. He added some basic computer courses to his schedule, learning word processing, desktop publishing, spreadsheets, and database management. Now, seven years later, Mike manages a small TV station, KPXX, and has a computer on his desk.

On a typical work morning, Mike turns on the personal computer, which is part of a network of office computers, as soon as he walks into his office. While he unpacks his briefcase, the computer is displaying a list of options. He selects Today's Calendar, and the screen displays "10:30 AM—Daviess meeting re Sat. a.m. slot" and "1:00 PM—lunch with J. Weinstein, Rosarita Cafe." The meeting notice reminds him to ask program manager John McKenna to bring the latest Daviess reports to the meeting. He uses word processing to compose a memo quickly, then sends it to John via the office computer network. Next, he selects the option Read Mail from the screen and checks the list of incoming messages.

As the day moves on, Mike uses the computer to fetch program data from his database, to retrieve information about a sponsor via a data communications system, and to plot client strategies by using spreadsheet software. Finally, he takes home diskettes of office data to work with that evening on his computer at home. Mike uses all this technology as casually as he uses the telephone or the copy machine. Mike is a prime example of a personal computer user on the job.

on the Job
Action and Power

Personal Computers in the Workplace: Where Are They?

It would be easier to say where personal computers are *excluded* from the workplace than it would to list every example of where computers *are* in the workplace. But a partial list of areas in which computers are used is instructive: retailing, finance, insurance, real estate, health care, education, government, legal services, sports, politics, publishing, transportation, manufacturing, agriculture, and construction (Figure 9-1).

Asked how her company used personal computers, one office staffer replied, "You might as well ask how we use telephones. The computers are everywhere. We use them for everything." It was not always this way, however.

▼
Figure 9-1   Personal computer users.
Whether absorbed in work in a private office or working as part of a team, all these workers find the computer a useful tool.

(a)

(b)

(c)

(d)

Evolution of Personal Computer Use

The evolution of personal computers on the job seems to fall into three phases. Personal computers were first used in business by individual users to transform work tasks. The constantly retyped document, for example, became the quickly modified word-processed document. Similarly, the much-erased manual spreadsheet became the automatically recalculated electronic spreadsheet, and overflowing file drawers were transformed into automated databases. This individual productivity boost could be considered the first phase of on-the-job personal computer acceptance. Some organizations are still in phase 1.

Many more organizations have entered the second phase: They have gone beyond the individual and use personal computers to transform a working group or department. This department-oriented phase probably embraces a network and may also include personal computer access to mainframe computers. The second phase requires planning and structure.

The third phase in the evolution of personal computer use in business is the most dramatic, calling for the transformation of the entire business. Practically speaking, however, phase 3 is just an extension of the earlier phases: Each individual and each department uses computers to enhance the company as a whole. Few companies have fully entered phase 3.

This three-stage transformation—individual, department, and business—broadly describes the progress a company makes in blending computers into its business activities.

The Impact of Personal Computers

People who dismiss the impact of the personal computer sometimes say, "It's just another tool." But what a tool! In the decades to come, personal computers will continue to alter the business world radically, much as the automobile did. For more than 50 years, the automobile fueled the economy, spawning dozens of industries from oil companies to supermarkets. Other industries, such as real estate and restaurants, were transformed by the mobility the car provided. Personal computers will have a similar effect for two reasons: (1) Computers are now cost-effective at a level affordable to most businesses, and (2) few businesses without computers can provide the levels of service their computerized competitors provide.

Computers are changing the way individuals and organizations work. By providing timely access to data, computers let us spend less time checking and rechecking data and more time getting work done. In addition to increasing overall productivity, computers have had a fundamental impact on the way some people approach their jobs.

◤ Who's Running the Information Revolution?

Before the widespread use of personal computers, anyone who needed computer services made a formal request to the computer professionals.

DISCUSSION QUESTION

What does the term *information system* mean today?

LECTURE HINT

Some companies choose to lease their computer systems instead of buying them outright. By leasing their equipment they can distribute the costs over time. Moreover, service agreements often are included in leasing contracts. Nevertheless, over time leasing is more expensive than purchasing, and the income tax deductions are more desirable when the computer systems are owned by the company.

DISCUSSION QUESTION

What are the problems managers faced when personal computers were introduced to their businesses, and how have managers begun to solve these problems?

We begin this section with a brief look at those professionals and then move on to examine the diversified control of computing power.

The Information Systems Manager

An **information system (IS)** may be defined as a set of business procedures designed to provide information for an organization. Today the term *information system* usually means a system that includes at least one computer as a major component. Information serves no purpose unless it gets to its users in a timely way; the computer can act quickly to produce and distribute information.

An information system uses computer technology to solve problems for an entire organization, instead of attacking problems piecemeal. Although in some companies a complete information system is still only an idea, the scope of information systems is expanding rapidly.

The **information systems manager** runs the information systems department. For many years, this meant managing systems running on mainframe computers. The advent of personal computers has changed the role of the information systems manager significantly.

Breaking Away

In the early days of personal computers, users saw the personal computer as their ticket to independence from the computer professionals. Personal computers burst on the business scene in the early 1980s, with little warning and even less planning. People who saw the value of personal computers for their work were able to buy inexpensive computers out of existing budgets, so they did not have to ask anyone's permission. Some managers began to see that personal computers were providing workers with the computer power the information systems department was not. By mastering software for word processing, spreadsheets, and database access, many users were able to declare their freedom from the information systems department.

Soon, however, managers were faced with several problems. The first was incompatibility. The new computers came in an assortment of brands and models that did not mesh well. Software that worked on one machine did not necessarily work on another. In addition, users were not as independent of the information systems department as they had thought; they needed assistance in a variety of ways. In particular, they needed data from the information systems department, and they needed it in formats compatible with their personal computers. Finally, no one person was in charge of the headlong plunge into personal computers. Many organizations began to solve these management problems in the following ways:

- They addressed the compatibility problem by establishing hardware and software acquisition standards and policies.
- They solved the assistance problem by creating information centers that provided, among other things, in-house training.
- They eliminated the management problem by creating a new position, often called the personal computer manager.

In addition to these problems and their solutions, many companies today have impacted the personal computer scene further by downsiz-

COMPUTING TRENDS

Don't Leave Home Without It

Your computer, that is. Many workers attribute their success to plain hard work—and they want to be able to take their work with them wherever they go. The trend today is that taking work along means taking the computer along. Early laptop users were workers for whom travel was a key component: sales people, executives, insurance adjusters, and reporters. Now laptops have reached a much broader market and include just about anyone who wants to have computer access, whether in the office, at home, or on the road.

The Tools of Portability. The portable worker typically needs a laptop computer equipped with a lightweight nickel-hydrade battery and a recharger, a keyboard with a trackball, a screen, a hard disk drive with sufficient space to hold software and data, a diskette drive, and a modem. Some users may need color screens, which are available on some models. If you absolutely need hard copy on the road, consider a lightweight—about three pounds—printer. Another possibility is to use a fax modem and just fax output to a

nearby plain-paper fax machine. In addition to standard software packaging, such as word processing, software made especially for computer-savvy travelers helps users to plan routes, pick hotels, and even prevent jet lag by giving you a timed regimen for eating, sleeping, and exposure to light.

Tips for traveling with a computer.

✓ Never check your laptop computer as baggage and do not carry it through metal detectors.
✓ Make sure your batteries are sufficiently charged so that you can boot the computer, to show airport authorities that it is not just an empty shell.
✓ Do not use your laptop during takeoff and landing.
✓ Since you may not be able to find an outlet near the desk in your hotel room, carry an extension cord.
✓ If you plan to use a modem, ask in advance for a hotel room with removable phone jacks.
✓ To avoid running out of battery time, carry an extra battery and, of course, a recharger.
✓ Save and back up data often.
✓ Copy your critical data to diskettes.

Free at last. Some say that computing portability goes beyond convenience, that a better word is *liberation.* Liberation from the confines of the office. Liberation from the 9-to-5 day with a commute on each end. Liberation from "telephone tag." Liberation from time-zone barriers. When you own a portable computer, you decide when and where you work. Workers can, for all practical purposes, stay in touch with the office and the action where and when they choose—24 hours a day, 7 days a week—from almost any location.

---

ing—moving applications from big to small computers—and by teaming personal computer users into workgroups.

Let us examine the issues of acquisition, the information center, the personal computer manager, downsizing, and workgroups, respectively.

Personal Computer Acquisition

In an office environment managers know they must control the acquisition and use of personal computers. Consider this example: A user's budget process may call for certain data that resides in the files of another worker's personal computer or perhaps output incorporating the figures produced by yet a third person. If the software and machines these workers use are different, accessing or outputting the data may become a major problem. Most companies avoid this problem by purchasing uniform hardware and software and, most probably, hook the computers together in a network so that data can be shared.

The Information Center

If personal computer users compared notes, they would probably find that their experiences are similar. The experience of budget analyst Manuella Lopez is typical. She convinced her boss to let her have her own personal computer so she could analyze financial data. She learned to use a popular spreadsheet program. She soon thought about branching out with other products. She wanted a statistics software package but was not sure which one was appropriate. She thought a modem for data communications would be useful and wanted to discuss the features of the various modems available on the market. Most of all, Manuella felt her productivity would increase significantly if she could access the data in the corporate data files.

The company **information center** is the solution to these kinds of needs. Although no two centers are alike, all information centers are devoted exclusively to giving users service. Best of all, user assistance is often immediate, with little or no red tape.

Information centers often offer the following services:

■ **Software selection.** Information center staff members help users determine which software packages suit their needs.

■ **Data access.** If appropriate, the staff helps users get data, in formats compatible with the users' own computers, from the large corporate computer systems.

■ **Training.** Education is a principal reason for an information center's existence. Classes are usually small, frequent, and on a variety of topics (Figure 9-2).

■ **Technical assistance.** Information center staff members are ready to assist in any way possible, short of actually doing the users' work for them. That help includes aiding in the selection and use of software, finding errors, helping submit formal requests to the information systems department, and so forth.

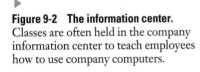

DISCUSSION QUESTION

Describe the various services provided by information centers.

▶

Figure 9-2   The information center.
Classes are often held in the company information center to teach employees how to use company computers.

To be successful, the information center must be placed in an accessible location. The center should be equipped with personal computers and terminals, a stockpile of software packages, and perhaps a library. It should be staffed with people who have technical backgrounds but whose explanations feature plain words that the user can understand. Their mandate must be that the user comes first.

The Personal Computer Manager

The benefits of personal computers for individual users have been clear almost from the beginning: increased productivity, worker enthusiasm, and easier access to information. But once personal computers move beyond entry status, standard corporate accountability becomes a factor; large companies are spending millions of dollars on personal computers, and top-level managers want to know where all this money is going. Company auditors begin worrying about data security. The company legal department begins to worry about workers illegally copying software. Before long, everyone is involved, and it is clear that someone must be placed in charge of personal computer use. That person is the **personal computer manager,** also known as the **microcomputer manager.** In addition, if computers are networked, there may be a separate position called the **network manager.**

Four key areas need the attention of the personal computer manager:

- **Technology overload.** The personal computer manager must maintain a clear vision of company goals so that users are not overwhelmed by the massive and conflicting claims of aggressive vendors. Users engulfed by phrases like *network topologies* or *file gateways* or a jumble of acronyms can turn to the personal computer manager for guidance with their purchases.
- **Cost control.** Many people who work with personal computers believe the initial costs are paid back rapidly, and they think that should satisfy managers who hound them about expenses. But the real costs entail training, support, hardware and software extras, and communications networks—much more than just the cost of the computer itself. The personal computer manager's role includes monitoring *all* the expenses.
- **Data security and integrity.** Access to corporate data is a touchy issue. Many personal computer users find they want to download data from the corporate mainframe to their own machines, and this presents an array of problems. Are they entitled to the data? Will they manipulate the data in new ways and then present it as the official version? Will they expect the information systems department to take the data back after they have done who-knows-what with it? The answers to these perplexing questions are not always clear-cut, but at least the personal computer manager will be tuned in to the issues.
- **Computer junkies.** What about the employees feverish with the new power and freedom of the computer? Some users, unable to resist the allure of their machines, overuse them and neglect their other work. These user-abusers are often called "junkies" because their fascination with the computer seems like an addiction. Personal computer managers usually respond to this problem by working with managers to set guidelines for computer use.

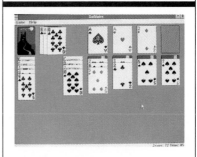

Honestly, Only on My Lunch Hour

Should you be playing solitaire on your personal computer at the office? Maybe. The game was included as an extra in Microsoft Windows™, partly to promote friendliness to home users. Rather to the surprise of its author, Wes Cherry, people have spent hours and hours playing the game at work. This was also a surprise, not an especially pleasant one, to the companies whose employees are using Windows.

Some managers have adopted the attitude that a little relaxation with a computer game relieves stress, but many more have reacted negatively, prohibiting employees from playing games at the office. Some have gone so far as to remove all games from the company's personal computers.

LECTURE HINT

Although an increasing number of executives are using Internet as an alternative telephone service, postal system, and research library, many executives are overwhelmed by Internet's complexity. Fortunately, a number of Internet books, newsletters, and publications designed for businesses are now available, such as the "Internet Letter," a newsletter published by Net Week, Inc.; "Internet World," a magazine published by the Meckler Corporation; and "Doing Business on the Internet," a book published by Van Nostrand Reinhold.

The person selected to be the personal computer manager is usually from the information systems area. Ideally, he or she has a broad technical background, understands both the potential and limitations of personal computers, and is well known to a diverse group of users. In small companies the personal computer manager may be a jack-of-all-trades, as long as the trade is computers. That is, in addition to the duties listed here, the personal computer manager may handle computer acquisitions and fill the functions normally assumed by information center personnel.

Downsizing

A new and interesting challenge facing established companies is **downsizing,** the process of shifting mainframe applications to a system of smaller computers, often a local area network (LAN) of personal computers. (*Downsizing* has also been used as a generic term to describe reducing a company's workforce; this is not the topic here.) Simply put, companies are dumping their big expensive computers in favor of smaller, less expensive computers. Downsizing has considerable allure because modern personal computers now have substantial power at a fraction of the cost of mainframes.

The downsizing craze began in earnest in the 1980s, but many larger corporations are only now taking the plunge. Switching to a smaller system ultimately has its rewards, but it is not a neat and tidy process. The snags generally fall into two categories: technical and political. Programmers find that they are lacking the same tools they once had on the larger systems. Security and file backup may be more difficult and time-consuming. Politically, entrenched information systems managers tend to fight the changes and cause delays that boost costs. But perhaps the biggest problem is knowing when to downsize, and when not to. For example, applications that use very large databases that must respond quickly to user requests need the resources provided by the mainframe.

Finally, consider the social aspects of downsizing. Until recently, despite the inroads made by personal computers, the power structure of computing was locked in on mainframes. Downsizing, more than any other personal computer phenomenon, has brought power to the people—*office* people.

Workgroups

First the hype: Using workgroups, worker productivity doubles and quality skyrockets. Employees communicate easily, and peace and harmony descend on the company. These statements are, of course, overblown rhetoric, but not so very far from the promises being made, and fulfilled, for workgroup computing. Loosely defined, **workgroup computing** refers to every aspect of a related group of workers (perhaps a department) using computer technology to meet a common goal.

A large factor in workgroup computing is **groupware**—software specifically designed to help groups work together. Groupware allows teams of workers on a network to swap information and collaborate on projects. For example, different users can access the same document and leave notes or suggestions for each other on the same computer file. Lotus Notes™ is the runaway application leader in this market (Figure 9-3), with Windows for Workgroups™ approaching the same task via a

DISCUSSION QUESTION

What is workgroup computing?

DISCUSSION QUESTION

How does groupware help groups work together?

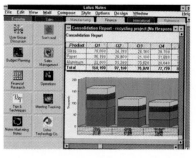

Figure 9-3   Lotus Notes.

variation on the operating system. Eventually, groupware will probably control most of the document-management tasks that users do on networks, from retrieving electronic news clippings to tracking customer service to engaging in user focus groups.

What about worker productivity? Recent surveys show that, despite anticipated setbacks, the return on investment in workgroup computing—hardware, software, and administrative costs—has been over 100 percent.

The Distribution of Power

As access to computers has been expanded, so has the power, both technical and political, that goes with it. Distribution of power has come in a variety of ways. For example, placing minicomputers in remote locations, such as branch offices, gave computer users better access and more control. But the biggest change was made by placing personal computers directly in the hands of users. Connecting personal computers in networks, downsizing, and adding workgroup software has further increased power at the user level.

In many companies the role of those in the information systems department is changing. They used to be caretakers of large computers; now they are becoming supporters of personal computers and their users. Their support is offered right in the user's environment. Some companies choose to spin off a new department, usually called something like user computing support, to focus on personal computer use. In effect, even the management style of the information systems manager is changing to meet the challenges of personal computers.

 # Systems

The original idea of personal computers emphasized the *personal* concept—one person, one computer, an island alone. Although this idea remains largely unchanged in the home environment, it has changed in a number of ways in business. Today, in companies large and small, personal computers may be linked in a network to each other and/or to a larger computer. As soon as a personal computer becomes part of a larger world in this way, it is part of a system. Furthermore, the personal computer user will deal with a person who plans systems—the systems analyst.

Personal Computers In Action

Art in the Numbers

All kinds of publications, from business to computers to sports, want to give their readers charts of numbers that provide information about their particular subjects. These days, numbers often are presented in the form of lively computer-produced graphics. Here are three different exam-

ples. The report card illustration, from *Registered Representative* magazine is used to portray "Grades" awarded to different investment firms. *PickWorld* magazine uses graphics to illustrate the relationship between the two operating systems PICK and DOS. *Runners' World* magazine uses cartoons to show informa-

tion about lactate threshold, oxidative enzymes, and muscle glycogen.

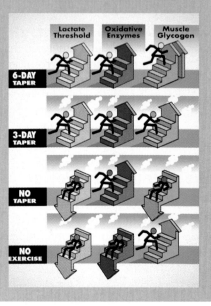

The System and the Systems Analyst

A **system** is an organized set of related components established to accomplish a certain task. There are natural systems, such as the cardiovascular system, but many systems have been planned and deliberately put into place by people. For example, the forms you fill out and the tests you take at the Department of Motor Vehicles compose a system to get your driver's license. A **computer system** is a system that has one or more computers as components.

A **systems analyst** analyzes existing systems and plans new, improved systems. **Systems analysis** is the process of studying an existing system to determine how it works and how effectively it meets user needs; **systems design** is the process of planning a new system.

Classic Systems-Development Life Cycle

For many years systems analysts have created a new system or revised an existing system by using the **systems-development life cycle (SDLC)** model, which consists of five phases (Figure 9-4):

1. Preliminary investigation—determining the problem
2. Analysis—understanding the existing system

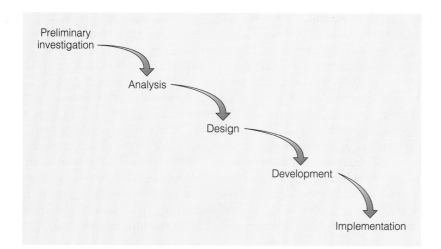

◄

Figure 9-4 Systems development life cycle.

TRANSPARENCY ACETATE # 57

Figure 9-4

3. Design—planning the new system
4. Development—doing the work to bring the new system into being
5. Implementation—converting to the new system

The first two phases, preliminary investigation and systems analysis, lay the groundwork for improvements to a system. The analysis involves an investigation, which usually involves establishing relationships with the client for whom the analysis is being done and with the users of the system. The **client** is the person or organization retaining the analyst to have the work done. The **users** are the people who will have contact with the system, usually employees and customers. For instance, in a college registration system the client is the administration and the users are the school employees and the students. The system to be analyzed may be a manual system or an already-automated system. In either case computers will be components of the new system.

Systems design, the third phase, is the process of developing a plan for an improved system, based on the results of the systems analysis. Once the design of the new system is approved, it can be developed—a process that includes purchasing software or perhaps writing and testing custom software. During the implementation process, the old system is phased out and the new system phased in.

Although describing them is beyond the scope of this book, we must at least mention that, in addition to the classic life cycle noted here, there are many modern approaches, sometimes used in conjunction with the classic life cycle, that differ in approach and implementation.

Life Cycle Example

Consider this example. Systems analyst Walter Dinteman responded to a request from Pacific Sound Technology, a chain of stores carrying a broad selection of television sets, VCRs, and sound system components. The company manager, Amy Nguyan, was disturbed about inventory problems, which caused frequent stock shortages and increased customer dissatisfaction. Although the company had a minicomputer at the headquarters office, Ms. Nguyan envisioned a more sophisticated technology to track inventory.

Mr. Dinteman first did a preliminary investigation, talking to company employees and studying records. He and Ms. Nguyan agreed that

LECTURE HINT

The personal qualities that are desirable in a systems analyst are an analytical mind, good communication skills, self-discipline, self-direction, organization skills, and the ability to work without tangible results.

the system warranted further study, so Mr. Dinteman proceeded to phase two. Analysis techniques vary, but in this case he studied written records and used interviews and questionnaires to analyze the system. His analysis uncovered several problems: a lack of information about inventory supplies; a tendency for stock to be reordered only when the shelf was empty; and, finally, no way to correlate order quantities with past sales records, future projections, or inventory situations. The system needed improvement, which called for the third phase, systems design.

Working with the users, Mr. Dinteman designed a new system that featured personal computers in the individual stores. The personal computers were hooked together in a network and could communicate with each other and the headquarters computer. Information about inventory could now be collected in each store. Information about oversupply could be shared with the other stores but, more important, the reordering process could begin before the shelves were empty.

Once the new design was approved, Mr. Dinteman was ready to move to the next phase, development. In this case he was able to procure commercial software packages that met the needs of the planned system. Finally, Mr. Dinteman, again working closely with the users over a period of several weeks, moved though the fifth phase, and the new system was implemented.

The Pacific Sound Technology example is greatly oversimplified, but it does demonstrate two important points: (1) The old system must be analyzed before a new system can be designed, and (2) users of the system must be involved in both analysis and design.

The User's Role

DISCUSSION QUESTION

What is meant by the phrase "the systems analyst fills the role of change agent"?

CLASS PROJECT

Divide the students into groups and have each group investigate the information center at different local companies to determine the following: (1) services provided, (2) job descriptions of staff members, (3) hardware, and (4) software.

The systems analyst fills the role of **change agent.** That is, even though the initial idea may come from the boss, the analyst is the catalyst who overcomes the natural inertia and reluctance to change within an organization. The key to the analyst's success is involving the people of the client organization in the development of the new system. The common industry phrase is **user involvement,** and nothing could be more important to the success of a system. The finest system in the world will not suffice if users do not perceive it as useful.

If you are a user, it is to your advantage to work with the systems analyst to make the system what you want it to be. Keep in mind that you know the subject matter intimately because you work with it on a daily basis. The systems analyst knows the technical end but not how your business or department works. That is, the systems analyst depends heavily on the user to supply information and to help design a new system that meets user needs.

▼ ▼ ▼

Someone once remarked, somewhat facetiously, that all top management—presidents, chief executive officers, and so forth—should be drawn from the ranks of computer specialists. After all, the argument went, computers pervade the entire company, and people who work with computer systems can bring broad experience to any job. Today, most presidents and CEOs still come from legal, financial, or marketing backgrounds. But as the computer industry and its professionals mature, that pattern could change.

Chapter **Review**

Summary and Key Terms

- Some businesses in which personal computers are used include retailing, finance, insurance, real estate, health care, education, government, legal services, sports, politics, publishing, transportation, manufacturing, agriculture, and construction.
- The evolution of personal computers seems to fall into three phases, involving the transformations of individuals, departments, and businesses.
- Personal computers are radically altering the business world for two reasons: (1) Computers are now cost-effective at a level affordable to most businesses, and (2) few businesses without computers can provide the levels of service their computerized competitors provide.
- An **information system (IS)** is a set of business systems, usually with at least one computer among its components, designed to provide information for decision making.
- The **information systems manager,** a person familiar with both computer technology and the organization's business, runs the information systems department.
- If the software and machines workers use are different, accessing or outputting data may become a problem. Most companies avoid this problem by purchasing uniform hardware and software in volume and, most probably, connecting the computers in a network.
- An **information center** typically offers employees classes on a variety of computer topics, advice on selecting software, help in getting data from corporate computer systems, and technical assistance on such matters as hardware purchases and requests to the information systems department.
- The main concerns of a **personal computer manager,** also known as a **microcomputer manager,** are (1) avoiding technology overload, (2) monitoring all the expenses connected with personal computers, (3) being aware of potential data security problems when users download data from the corporate mainframe to their own personal computers, and (4) setting guidelines for personal computer use to combat user-abusers.
- A person designated to run the network is called the **network manager.**
- **Downsizing** is the process of shifting mainframe applications to a system of smaller computers, often a local area network of personal computers.
- **Workgroup computing** refers to every aspect of a group of workers using computer technology to meet a common goal. **Groupware** refers to a kind of software that allows teams of workers on a network to swap information and collaborate on projects.
- As soon as a personal computer becomes part of a network, it is part of a **system**—an organized set of related components established to accomplish certain tasks. A **computer system** is a system that has one or more computers as components.
- A **systems analyst** studies existing systems and plans new, improved systems. **Systems analysis** is the process of studying existing systems to determine how they work and how they meet users' needs; **systems design** is the process of planning new systems.
- The **systems-development life cycle (SDLC)** model consists of five phases: (1) preliminary investigation—determining the problem, (2) analysis—understanding the existing system, (3) design—planning the new system, (4) development—doing the work to bring the new system into being, and (5) implementation—converting to the new system.

KEY TERMS

change agent

client

computer system

downsizing

groupware

information center

information system (IS)

information systems manager

microcomputer manager

network manager

personal computer manager

system

systems analysis

systems analyst

systems design

systems-development life cycle (SDLC)

user

user involvement

workgroup computing

■ The **client** is the person or organization contracting to have a system modified or created. The **users** are the people who will have contact with the system, usually employees and customers of the client organization. For instance, in a college registration system, the client is the administration and the users are the school employees and the students.

■ The systems analyst fills the role of **change agent**—the catalyst who overcomes reluctance to change within an organization. The key to a system's success is **user involvement.**

Student Personal Study Guide

True/False

T F 1. A systems analyst's role is to design and then analyze systems.

T F 2. The information systems manager and the personal computer manager are usually the same person.

T F 3. In an organization, a client and a user could be the same person but usually are not.

T F 4. There are no security risks when applications are downsized.

T F 5. One function of an information center is to do users' work for them when they get overloaded.

T F 6. An information system usually has one or more computers as components.

T F 7. The SDLC has seven phases.

T F 8. In business, personal computers are usually found only in formal office environments.

T F 9. A systems analyst, sometimes called a change agent, overcomes an organization's reluctance to change.

T F 10. To be cooperative, a user should let the systems analyst decide how a new system should work.

Multiple Choice

1. The person who runs the computer network:
   a. systems analyst
   b. systems designer
   c. network manager
   d. information systems manager

2. Which is *not* a phase of the systems development life cycle?
   a. analysis
   b. information center
   c. implementation
   d. preliminary investigation

3. Software that allows network users to collaborate:
   a. groupware
   b. downsize
   c. SDLC
   d. workware

4. Which assistance, typically, is *not* a function of the information center?
   a. software selection
   b. implementation
   c. training
   d. hardware purchases

5. Shifting mainframe applications to smaller computers:
   a. designing
   b. downsizing
   c. implementing
   d. grouping

6. The analyst's role to overcome resistance to change:
   a. worker
   b. change agent
   c. downsizer
   d. designer

7. People who only have contact with a system:
   a. users
   b. client
   c. designer
   d. analyst

8. The final phase in the evolution of personal computers is the transformation of:
   a. individuals
   b. businesses
   c. divisions
   d. departments

9. Moving data from the corporate computer to a personal computer:
   a. grouping
   b. analyzing
   c. downsizing
   d. downloading

10. Workers collaborating on a project over a network:
   a. downsizing
   b. workgroup computing
   c. downloading
   d. designing

Fill-In

1. An organized set of components to accomplish a task: _____ .

2. The entity retaining an analyst to create or modify a system : _____ .

3. Number of phases in the classic SDLC: _____ .

4. A set of business procedures, with computers as components: _____ .

5. Computer abusers on the job are sometimes called: _____ .

6. A person who analyzes and designs systems: _____ .

7. The first phase of the systems development life cycle: _____ .

8. Studying an existing system with an eye to improving it: _____ .

9. The person who monitors expenses of company personal computers:

   _____ .

10. Planning a new computer system: _____ .

Answers

True/False: 1. F, 2. F, 3. T, 4. F, 5. F, 6. T, 7. F, 8. F, 9. T, 10. F
Multiple choice: 1. c, 2. b , 3. a , 4. b, 5.b, 6. b, 7. a, 8. b, 9. d, 10. b
Fill-In: 1. system, 2. client, 3. five, 4. information system, 5. computer junkies, 6. systems analyst, 7. preliminary investigation, 8. systems analysis, 9. personal computer manager, 10. systems design

Chapter Overview

LEARNING OBJECTIVES

- Being aware of the problem of computer crime, including types of crimes, and the difficulties of discovery and prosecution
- Being aware of the need for security, including disaster recovery plans, software and data security, and security legislation
- Understanding the importance of privacy and how it is affected by the Computer Age
- Understanding the importance of ethics as related to a computer environment

Beth Daultry is the administrative assistant to the head of the Business Division at Southwind Community College. Her responsibilities include setting up meetings, coordinating classes and classrooms, assisting faculty and students, and supervising two secretaries. For these and other tasks, Beth uses word processing, spreadsheet, and scheduling software on her personal computer, producing dozens of files each week.

Security,

Beth knew that she was responsible for the safety and well-being of her computer files. In fact, she had attended training seminars on this very subject. In particular, she learned that it is prudent to make extra copies of her files, so that her work will not be impaired if the original files on hard disk are accidentally destroyed. As a class assignment Beth wrote down all the reasons a person might neglect to back up files properly. Her list was as follows: (1) It takes too much time. (2) It is too boring, just nuisance work. (3) I have more pressing tasks. (4) I have used this computer for a year and nothing has gone wrong yet. But, somehow, know-

ing what she should do was not enough. On a sunny Thursday afternoon, Beth's hard disk drive crashed, and the files on her hard disk were destroyed. Subsequent inspection revealed that less than 40 percent of her files had been backed up—copied to another place.

Beth asked herself just one question: Why? Why, indeed! How could she have been so careless, so thoughtless? While Beth castigates herself, we can reflect on human nature. We tend to think that bad things happen to other people, not us. It is hard to perform consistently the chores that help us avoid the *possibilty* of something bad happen-

ing. Instead, we spend our time on other tasks and put our files at risk.

The good news is that users in a business setting today are likely to have procedures in place for regular file backup. The users most at risk are individuals who use computers in other environments, probably at home or at school. Although this chapter covers a variety of threats to computer systems, the most common by far is the loss of files due to improper backup techniques.

Privacy, and Ethics
Protecting Hardware, Software, and Data

LECTURE HINT

Tiger teams, made up of computer security experts, conduct commando-style raids on computer centers to expose security weaknesses. Most of the companies in the Fortune 100 use tiger teams. One team found that the guard had "stepped out" for a moment; he and his security company were replaced in less than one hour.

LECTURE HINT

Two similar but different examples of computer crime are unauthorized access and unauthorized use. Using a computer system without permission is called unauthorized access. Using a computer system for an unapproved activity is called unauthorized use.

LECTURE HINT

Disgruntled employees have found a new way to get back at their employers–by computer sabotage. The most common crime is to wipe out company records.

 # Computer Crime

It was 5 o'clock in the morning, and 14-year-old Randy Miller was startled to see a man climbing through his bedroom window. "FBI," the man announced, "and that computer is mine." So ended the computer caper in San Diego, California, where 23 teenagers, ages 13 to 17, had used their home computers to invade systems as far away as Massachusetts. The teenagers were **hackers**—people who attempt to gain access to computer systems illegally, usually from a personal computer, via a data communications network.

The term *hacker* used to mean a person with significant computer expertise, but the term has taken on the more sinister meaning with the advent of computer miscreants, particularly teenagers. In the case of Randy Miller, he and his fellow hackers did not use the system to steal money or property. They did change system passwords, however, preventing legitimate access to the computer accounts. They also created fictitious accounts and destroyed or changed some data files. The FBI's entry through the window was calculated—they figured that, given even a moment's warning, the teenagers were clever enough to alert each other via computer.

This story—except for the name—is true. Hackers ply their craft for a variety of reasons: to show off for their peers, to harass people they do not like, to get computer services without paying, and sometimes to get information they can sell. However, hackers are only a small fraction of the security problem. The most serious losses are caused by electronic pickpockets who are usually a good deal older and not so harmless. Consider the following examples:

- A Denver brokerage clerk sat at his terminal and, with a few taps of the keys, transformed 1700 shares of his own stock worth $1.50 each to the same number of shares in another company worth ten times that much.
- A Seattle bank employee used her electronic funds transfer code to move certain bank funds to an account held by her boyfriend as a "joke"; both the money and the boyfriend disappeared.
- In an Oakland department store, a keyboard operator changed some delivery addresses to divert several thousands of dollars worth of store goods into the hands of accomplices.
- A stockbroker used the company's computer system to buy and sell cocaine.

These stories point out that computer crime is not always the flashy, front-page news about geniuses getting away with millions of dollars. Computer systems have been used to steal valuable information, software, phone service, and credit card numbers. These thieves pass along or sell their services and techniques to others—including organized crime.

The problems of computer crime have been aggravated in recent years by increased access to computers (Figure 10-1). More employees now have access to computers in their jobs. In fact, computer crime is often just white-collar crime with a new medium: Every time an employee is trained on the computer at work, he or she gains knowledge that could be used to harm the company.

Disgruntled or militant employee could

- Sabotage equipment or programs
- Hold data or programs hostage

Competitor could

- Sabotage operations
- Engage in espionage
- Steal data or programs
- Photograph records, documentation, or CRT screen displays

Data control worker could

- Insert data
- Delete data
- Bypass controls
- Sell information

Clerk/supervisor could

- Forge or falsify data
- Embezzle funds
- Engage in collusion with people inside or outside the company

System user could

- Sell data to competitors
- Obtain unauthorized information

Operator could

- Copy files
- Destroy files

User requesting reports could

- Sell information to competitors
- Receive unauthorized information

Engineer could

- Install "bugs"
- Sabotage system
- Access security information

Data conversion worker could

- Change codes
- Insert data
- Delete data

Programmer could

- Steal programs or data
- Embezzle via programming
- Bypass controls

Report distribution worker could

- Examine confidential reports
- Keep duplicates of reports

Trash collector could

- Sell reports or duplicates to competitors

▲

Figure 10-1   The perils of increased access.
By letting your imagination run wild, you can visualize numerous ways in which people can compromise computer security. Computer-related crime would be far more rampant if all the people in these positions took advantage of their access to computers.

TRANSPARENCY ACETATE # 58

Figure 10-1

A Glossary of Computer Crime

Although the emphasis in this chapter is on preventing rather than committing crime, it is worthwhile being familiar with computer criminal terms and methods.

Data diddling: Changing data before or as it enters the system.

Data leakage: Obtaining copies of data from the system—without leaving a trace.

Logic bomb technique: Sabotaging a program by setting up a trigger that is activated by certain conditions—usually at a later date, perhaps after the perpetrator has left the company.

Piggybacking: Using another person's identification code or using that person's files before he or she has logged off.

Salami technique: Using a large financial system to embezzle small "slices" of money that may never be missed.

Scavenging: Searching trash cans for printouts and carbons containing not-for-distribution information.

Trapdoor technique: Leaving illicit instructions within a completed program; the instructions allow unauthorized, and undetected, entry.

Trojan horse: Tricking a user into running a destructive program by giving it the name of a trusted program.

Zapping: Bypassing all security systems with an illicitly acquired software package.

DISCUSSION QUESTION

Describe the three basic categories of computer crime.

TEST BANK

Mult. Choice 2-7, 10, 12, 16-18
T/F 27-33, 35-40, 44-45, 50
Matching 51-55, 57, 60
Fill In 64-66, 68-70, 73-75

What motivates the computer criminal? The causes are as varied as the offenders; however, a few frequent motives have been identified. A computer criminal is often a disgruntled employee, possibly a long-time, loyal worker out for revenge after being passed over for a raise or promotion. In another scenario, an otherwise model employee may commit a crime while suffering from personal or family problems. Not all motives are emotionally based. Some people are simply attracted to the challenge of the crime. In contrast, it is the ease of the crime that tempts others. In many cases the criminal activity is unobtrusive; it fits right in with regular job duties. The risk of detection is often quite low. Computer criminals think they can get away with it, and some have.

Types and Methods of Computer Crime

Computer crime falls into three basic categories:

■ Theft of computer time, either for personal use or with the intention of making a profit. Miscreants may, for example, perform computer tasks for outside clients; work on personal projects, such as a hobby club budget or newsletter; or even write software for personal profit.
■ Theft, destruction, or manipulation of programs or data.
■ Alteration of data stored in a computer file.

Though it is not our purpose to be a how-to book on computer crime, the margin note called "A Glossary of Computer Crime" mentions some criminal methods.

Discovery and Prosecution

Prosecuting the computer criminal is complicated by the fact that discovery is often difficult. Most computer crimes simply go undetected, and those that are detected are usually discovered by accident. Furthermore, an estimated 85 percent of the time, crimes that are detected are not reported to the authorities. By law, banks have to make a report when their computer systems have been compromised, but other businesses do not. Often they choose not to report because they are worried about their reputations and credibility in the community.

Even if a computer crime is detected, a prosecution is by no means assured. There are a number of reasons for this. First, some law enforcement agencies do not fully understand the complexities of computer-related fraud. Second, few attorneys are qualified to handle computer crime cases. Third, judges and juries are not educated in the ways of computers and may not understand the value of data to a company.

This situation is changing, however. In 1986 Congress passed the latest version of the **Computer Fraud and Abuse Act** to fight the problem on the national level. Furthermore, most states have passed some form of computer crime law.

Security: Keeping Everything Safe

As you can see from the previous section, the computer industry has been vulnerable in the matter of security. Computer security once meant the physical security of the computer itself—guarded and locked doors. However, locking up the computer by no means prevents access, as we have seen.

What is security? We can define it as follows: **Security** is a system of safeguards designed to protect a computer system and data from deliberate or accidental damage or access by unauthorized persons. That means safeguarding the system against such threats as burglary, vandalism, fire, natural disasters, theft of data for ransom, industrial espionage, and various forms of white-collar crime.

Who Goes There? Identification and Access

How does a computer system detect whether you are a person who should be allowed access to it? Various means have been devised to give access to authorized people without compromising the system. The means fall into four broad categories: what you have, what you know, what you do, and who you are.

- **What you have.** You may have a key or a badge or a plastic card to give you physical access to the computer room or a locked-up terminal. A credit card with a magnetized strip, for example, can give you access to a gas pump at your local station. Taking this a step further, some employees begin each business day by donning an **active badge,** a clip-on identification card with an embedded computer chip. The badge signals its wearer's location—legal or otherwise—by sending out infrared signals that are read by sensors sprinkled around the building. The active badge, which is becoming increasingly common, presents a challenging problem: balancing an employee's privacy against a corporation's desire for efficiency and control.
- **What you know.** Standard what-you-know items are a system password or an identification number for your bank cash machine. Cipher or combination locks on doors require that you know the correct combination of numbers
- **What you do.** Your signature is difficult but not impossible to copy. Signature-access systems are better suited to human interaction than machine interaction. That is, humans can check a signature on sight, a feat more difficult for a computer.
- **What you are.** Now it gets interesting. Some security systems use **biometrics,** the science of measuring individual body characteristics. Fingerprinting is old news, but handprint geometry and voice recognition are relatively new. Even newer is the concept of identification by the retina of the eye, which has a pattern that is harder to duplicate than a voiceprint (Figure 10-2).

Some systems use a combination of these four categories. For example, access to an automated teller machine requires both something you have—a plastic card—and something you know—a personal identification number (PIN).

When Disaster Strikes: What Do You Have to Lose?

In California a poem, a pansy, a bag of Mrs. Field's cookies, and the message "Please have a cookie and a nice day" were left at the Vandenberg Air Force Base computer installation—along with five demolished mainframe computers. Computer installations of any kind can be struck by

▲

Figure 10-2   Identification by retina. The eye can be a means of personal identification. A user first keys a unique identification code number. The security system then matches the person's unique retinal pattern to the individual's computer-stored retina pattern, for conclusive identification of authorized users.

Some Gentle Advice on Security

Being a security expert is an unusual job because, once the planning is done, there is not a lot to do except wait for something bad to happen. Security experts are often consultants who move from company to company. Their advice usually includes long and detailed checklists: Do this, do that, and you will be OK. We cannot offer a long set of lists, but here is a brief subset that includes some of the most effective approaches.

- Beware of disgruntled employees. Ed Street was angry. Seething. How could they pass over him for a promotion again? Well, if they were not going to give him what he deserved, he would take it himself.... Ah, the tale is too common. Be forewarned.

- Sensitize employees to security issues. Most people are eager to help others. They must be taught that some kinds of help, such as assisting unauthorized users with passwords, are inappropriate.

- Call back all remote-access terminals. Don't call us, we'll call you. If, before your system accepts a call, it must check a list of phone numbers to ensure that the caller has valid access, you eliminate most intruders. In such an arrangement your computer has to call the user back for the user to gain remote access, and your computer will do so only if the user's number is valid.

- Keep personnel privileges up-to-date. Furthermore, we might add, make sure they are enforced properly. Some of the biggest heists have been pulled by people who *formerly* had legitimate access to secured areas. In many cases they can still get in because the guard has known them by sight for years.

natural or man-made disasters that can lead to security violations. What kinds of problems might this cause an organization?

Your first thoughts might be of the hardware—the computer and its related equipment. But loss of hardware is not a major problem in itself; the loss can be covered by insurance, and hardware can be replaced. The true problem with hardware loss is the diminished processing ability that exists while managers find a substitute facility and return the installation to its former state. Loss of software should not be a problem if the organization has heeded industry warnings, and used common sense, to make backup copies.

A more important problem is the loss of data. Imagine trying to reassemble lost or destroyed master files of customer records, accounts receivable, or design data for a new airplane. The costs would be staggering. We continue with an overview of disaster recovery and then consider software and data security, worms and viruses that may affect files, and the all-important backing up of files.

Disaster Recovery Plan

A **disaster recovery plan** is a method of restoring data processing operations if those operations are halted by major damage or destruction. Preparing for such a loss is somewhat like installing smoke alarms or wearing seat belts: You hope you will never need them. There are various approaches to disaster recovery planning. Some organizations revert temporarily to manual services, but life without the computer can be difficult indeed. Others arrange to buy time at a service bureau, but this may be inconvenient for companies in remote or rural areas. If a single act, such as a fire, destroys your computing facility, it is possible that a mutual aid pact will help you get back on your feet. In such a plan two or more companies agree to lend each other computing power if one of them has a problem. This would be of little help, however, if there were a regional disaster and many companies needed assistance.

Banks and other organizations whose survival depends on computers sometimes form a **consortium**—a joint venture to support a complete computer facility. Such a facility is completely available and routinely tested but used only in the event of a disaster.

Computer installations regularly practice emergency drills. At some unexpected moment a notice is given that "disaster has struck," and the computer professionals must run the critical systems at some other site.

Software Security

According to a recent court case, Meredith England, a programmer, stands accused of using her key card to slip into the office at 3 o'clock in the morning and take some disks home with her. The problem is that Ms. England had been recently fired and the disks she allegedly took contained proprietary software worth about $15 million. Although Ms. England says she was on the premises merely to clean out her desk, a legal search of her home produced the copied disks.

Who owns custom-made software? Is the owner the person who writes the program or the company for which the author wrote the program? The answer to this question is well established. If a programmer is in the employ of an organization, the program belongs to the organization, not the programmer. If the programmer does her own work on her

Personal Computers
In Action

Your Own Security Checklist

With the subject of security fresh in your mind, now is a good time to consider a checklist for your own home computer and its software:

- Do not eat, drink, or smoke near the computer.
- Do not place the computer near open windows or doors.
- Do not subject the computer to extreme temperatures.
- Clean equipment regularly, following manufacturer's directions.
- Place a cable lock on the computer. In particular, cable-lock your laptop to any nearby immovable object.
- Use a surge protector, a device that prevents electrical problems from affecting data files. The computer is plugged into the

surge protector, which is plugged into the outlet.
- Store disks properly in a locked container.
- Maintain backup copies of all files.
- Store copies of critical files off site.
- Scan a diskette for viruses before use.

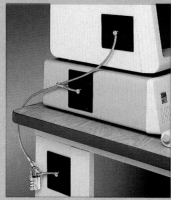
(a)

(b)

Security devices.
(a) Locking up your computer can help minimize theft. (b) A surge protector can protect your computer system and files from unpredictable electrical problems.

own computer on her own time, for no recompense, the program belongs to her.

Commercial software, especially software for personal computers, presents a different problem. Although specifically prohibited by law, software is copied as blatantly as music or video tapes. We will examine this issue more closely when we consider ethics later in the chapter.

Data Security

In addition to the possible loss of data, there are problems related to data safety. What steps can be taken to prevent theft or alteration of data? Several data protection techniques are in common use; these will not individually (or even collectively) guarantee security, but at least they make a good start.

Secured Waste

Discarded printouts, printer ribbons, and the like can be sources of information to unauthorized persons. This kind of waste can be made secure by the use of shredders or locked trash barrels.

Passwords

Passwords are the secret words or numbers that must be typed on the keyboard to gain access to a system or some part of a system. In some installations the passwords are changed so seldom that they become known to many people. Good data protection systems change passwords often and also compartmentalize information by passwords, so that only authorized persons can have access to certain data. Cracking passwords is the most prevalent method of illicit entry to computer systems. If you are able to choose your own password, do not name your password after your child or pet poodle. Recommended password creation techniques include using at least six characters, embedding at least one nonalphabetic character, and even mixing upper- and lowercase; for example, PIN*curve.

Internal Controls

Internal controls are controls that are planned as part of the computer system. One example is a transaction log—a file of all accesses or attempted accesses to certain data.

Auditor Checks

Most companies have auditors who go over the financial books. In the course of an audit, auditors with special training may also review computer programs and data. From a data security standpoint, for example, auditors might check to see who has accessed data during periods when that data is not usually used.

DISCUSSION QUESTION

Why is data encryption necessary?

Cryptography

Data being sent over communications lines may be protected by scrambling the messages—that is, putting them in code that can be broken only by the person receiving the message. The process of scrambling messages is called **encryption.** The American National Standards Institute has endorsed a process called the **Data Encryption Standard (DES),** a standardized public key that senders and receivers can use to scramble and unscramble their messages. Although the DES code has been broken, companies still use it because the method makes it quite expensive to intercept coded messages, forcing interlopers to use methods of gathering data that carry a greater risk of detection.

Worms and Viruses

These rather unpleasant terms have entered the jargon of the computer industry to describe some of the insidious ways that computer systems and programs can be invaded. A **worm** is a program that transfers itself from computer to computer over a network and plants itself as a separate file on the target computer's disks. One newsworthy worm, originated by student Robert Morris at Cornell University, traveled the length and breadth of the land through an electronic mail network, shutting down thousands of computers. The worm was injected into the network and multiplied uncontrollably, clogging the memories of infected computers until they could no longer function.

A virus, as its name suggests, is contagious. That is, a **virus,** a set of illicit instructions, passes itself on to other programs with which it comes in contact. Viruses seem to show up when least expected. In one instance, a call came to the company's information center about 5:00 p.m.; the caller's computer was making a strange noise. With the exception of an occasional beep, computers performing routine business chores do not usually make noises. Soon calls came in from all over the company, all with "noisy" computers. One caller said that it might be a tune coming from the computer's small internal speaker. Finally, one caller recognized a tinny rendition of Yankee Doodle, confirmation that an old virus had struck once again. The Yankee Doodle virus, once attached to a system, is scheduled to go off at 5:00 p.m. every eight days. Viruses, once considered merely a nuisance, are costing American businesses collectively over $2 billion a year. Unfortunately, viruses are easily transmitted.

Transmitting a Virus

Consider this typical example. A programmer secretly inserts a few viral instructions into a game called Kriss-Kross, which she then offers free to others via a bulletin board. Any takers download the game to their own computers. Now, each time a user runs Kriss-Kross—that is, loads it into memory—the virus is loaded, too. The virus stays in memory, infecting any other program that is loaded. The virus now has spread to other programs, and the process can be repeated again and again. In fact, each newly infected program becomes a virus carrier. Although many viruses are transmitted just this way over bulletin boards, the most common method is by passing diskettes from computer to computer (Figure 10-3).

More insidious viruses attach to the operating system. One virus, called Cascade, causes random text letters to "drop" to a pile at the bottom of the screen (Figure 10-4). Viruses attached to the operating system itself have greater potential for mischief.

▼

Figure 10-3   An example of a virus invasion.

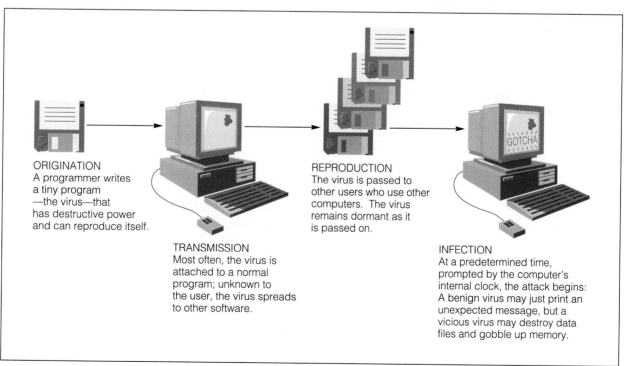

ORIGINATION
A programmer writes a tiny program —the virus—that has destructive power and can reproduce itself.

TRANSMISSION
Most often, the virus is attached to a normal program; unknown to the user, the virus spreads to other software.

REPRODUCTION
The virus is passed to other users who use other computers. The virus remains dormant as it is passed on.

INFECTION
At a predetermined time, prompted by the computer's internal clock, the attack begins: A benign virus may just print an unexpected message, but a vicious virus may destroy data files and gobble up memory.

▶

Figure 10-4 The Cascade virus.
This virus attaches itself to the operating system itself and causes random letters in text to "drop" to a pile at the bottom of the screen display.

TRANSPARENCY ACETATE # 60

Figure 10-4

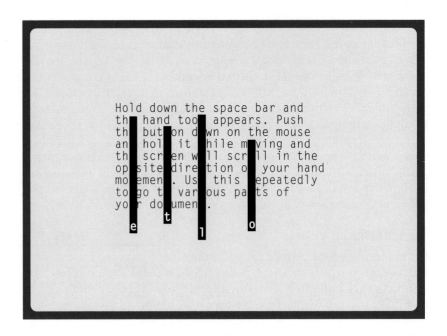

LECTURE HINT

The summer of 1993 marked the beginning of a dramatic increase in Internet break-ins. Computer security experts believe the break-ins were an organized effort to crack Internet's security system. The intruders succeeded in obtaining passwords for hundreds, and possibly thousands, of computers around the world. All users were advised to change their passwords immediately and regularly.

DISCUSSION QUESTION

How can computer viruses be avoided?

Damage from Viruses

The Yankee Doodle virus described earlier is relatively benign, as is the virus that simply displays a peace message. But many viruses do significant damage, often including destruction of files.

Most viruses remain dormant until triggered by some activity. For example, a virus called Jerusalem B activates itself every Friday the 13th and proceeds to erase any file you may try to load from your disk. Another virus includes instructions to add 1 to a counter each time the virus is copied to another disk. When the counter reaches 4, the virus erases all data files. But this is not the end of the destruction, of course; the three copied disks have also been infected.

Prevention

A word about prevention is in order. Although viruses are most commonly passed via diskettes, viruses use many other means to propagate—bulletin boards, local area networks, and electronic mail. If your personal computer has a disk drive, a modem, or a network connector, it is vulnerable. Furthermore, viruses are rampant on some college campuses and a source of considerable annoyance to students. Use these commonsense approaches to new files.

- Never install a program unless the diskette comes in a sealed package.
- Be especially wary of software that arrives unexpectedly from companies with whom you have not done business.
- Use virus-scanning software to check any file, no matter what the source, before loading it onto your hard disk.
- If your own diskette was used in another computer, scan it to see if it caught a virus.

Although there have been isolated instances of viruses in commercial software, viruses tend to show up on free software acquired from friends or through electronic bulletin board systems. Antivirus software can be installed to scan your hard disk every time you boot the computer or, if you prefer, at regularly scheduled intervals.

Prepare for the Worst: Back Up Your Files

During an impassioned speech, a computer expert said, "If you are not backing up your files regularly, you *deserve* to lose them." Strong words. One wonders why, with continuous admonishments and readily available procedures, some people still leave their precious files unprotected.

What Could Go Wrong?

A hard disk could physically malfunction, making your files inaccessible. This is not too likely, but it certainly does happen. It is even less likely that you lose your hard disk to fire or flood, but this is also possible. It is most likely that you will accidentally delete some files yourself. One fellow gave a command to delete all files with the file name extension BAK—there were four of them—but accidentally typed BAT instead, inadvertently wiping out 57 files. There is also the very real possibility of your files being infected with a virus. Experts estimate that average users experience a significant disk loss every year.

Ways to Back Up Files

Some people simply make another copy of their hard drive files on diskette. This is not too laborious if you do so as you go along. If you are at all vulnerable to viruses, you should back up all your files on a regular basis.

A better way is to back up all your files on a tape. Backing up to a tape drive is safer and faster. You can also use software that will automatically back up all your files at a certain time of day or on command. Sophisticated users place their files on a mirror hard disk, which simply makes a second copy of everything you put on the original disk; this approach, as you might expect, is expensive.

Keep backed up files in a cool, dry place off site. For those of you with a home computer, this may mean keeping copies of your important files at a friend's house.

 # Privacy: Keeping Personal Information Personal

Think about the forms you have willingly filled out: paperwork for loans or charge accounts; orders for merchandise through the mail; magazine subscription orders; applications for schools, jobs, and clubs; and so on. There may be some forms you filled out with less delight—for taxes, military draft registration, court petitions, insurance claims, or a stay in the hospital. Furthermore, consider all the checks you have written and the people who may have taken your name and address from them—retailers, fund-raisers, advertisers, petitioners, and others. We have only skimmed the possible sources of data, but we can say with certainty where all this data went: straight to computer files.

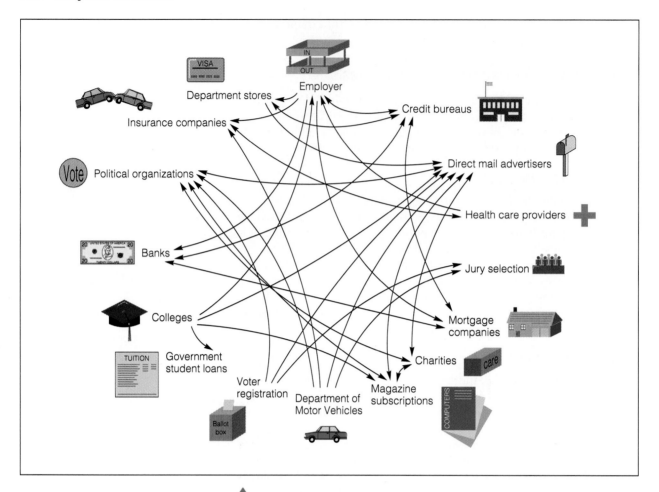

▲
Figure 10-5   Potential paths of data.
When an organization acquires information about you, it is often shared with, or
sold to, other organizations.

Where is that data now? Is it passed around? Who sees it? Will it ever
be expunged? Or, to put it more bluntly, is anything private anymore?
Much of the data is passed around, as anyone with a mailbox can attest.
As for who sees your personal data, the answers are not comforting (Figure 10-5). Furthermore, about 20 states allow their motor vehicle
departments to sell names and addresses, and sometimes even heights
and weights, to anyone who pays a fee. Some states even sell computer
tapes of their entire files to marketers, insurance companies, and other
businesses.

There are matters you want to keep private. You have the right to do
so. Although there is little you can do to stop data about you from circu-
lating through computers, there are laws that give you access to some of
it.

Significant legislation relating to privacy began with the **Fair Credit
Reporting Act** in 1970. This law allows you to have access to and gives
you the right to challenge the information in your credit records. In fact,
this access must be given to you free of charge if you have been denied
credit.

COMPUTING TRENDS

You Have No Privacy Whatever

No privacy on the company e-mail, that is. The company can snoop into messages you send or receive even if you think you erased it. But wait. A federal court recently has ruled that the Privacy Protection Act of 1980 applies to electronically stored information. So, just which way is this trend going?

Companies often failed to convey the message that e-mail, as a company conduit, is not private. Employees were often startled, after the fact, to discover that their messages had been invaded. Furthermore, some people specialize in extracting deleted messages for use as evidence in court. E-mail can be a dangerous time bomb in every corporation

because litigators argue that, more than any other kind of written communication, e-mail reflects the real, unedited thoughts of the writer.

What to do? It is certainly degrading to have something you thought was private waved in front of you as evidence of malingering. As one computer expert put it, if nothing is private, just say so. Companies have begun doing exactly that. The company policy on e-mail is—or should be—expressed in a clear, written document.

How does the Privacy Protection Act fit into this? For now the courts have addressed only government trespassing, not internal company prying. The current trend is clear: You have no privacy on company e-mail. None whatever.

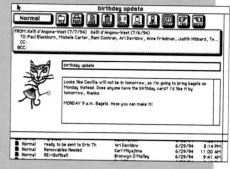

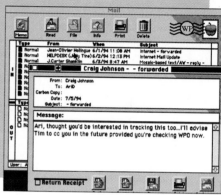

Businesses usually contribute financial information about their customers to a community credit bureau, which gives them the right to review a person's prior credit record with other companies. Before the Fair Credit Reporting Act, many people were turned down for credit, without explanation, because of inaccurate financial records about them. Now people may check their records to make sure they are accurate. The **Freedom of Information Act** was also passed in 1970. This landmark legislation allows ordinary citizens to have access to data about them that was gathered by federal agencies.

The most significant legislation protecting the privacy of individuals is the **Federal Privacy Act** of 1974. This act stipulates that there can be no secret personal files; individuals must be allowed to know what is stored in files about them, to know how the information is used, and to be able to correct it. The law applies not only to government agencies but also to private contractors dealing with government agencies. These organizations cannot obtain data willy-nilly for no specific purpose; they must justify obtaining it.

A more recent law is the **Video Privacy Protection Act** of 1988, which prevents retailers from disclosing a person's video rental records without a court order; privacy supporters want the same rule for medical and insurance files. Another step in that direction is the **Computer Matching and Privacy Protection Act** of 1988, which prevents the government from comparing certain records in an attempt to find a matchup. However, most comparisons are still unregulated. For example, the government routinely compares IRS records with draft registration records to catch those who have failed to register.

A Matter of Ethics

The fact that professional computer personnel have access to files has always presented the potential for problems. In theory, those with access could do something as simple as snooping into a friend's salary on a payroll file or as complex as selling military secrets to foreign countries. The problem has become more tangled as everyday people—not just computer professionals—have daily computer contact. They also have access to important files. As we noted earlier, data is the resource most difficult to replace, so increased access is the subject of much concern among security officers.

Where do you come in? As a student you could easily face ethical problems involving access and much more. Consider some of these examples. A nonstudent friend wants to borrow your password to get access to the school computer. Or you know of a student who has bypassed computer security and changed grades for himself and some friends. Perhaps a "computer jock" pal collects software and wants you to copy a software disk used in one of your classes.

The problems are not so different in the business world. You will recognize that, whether you are a computer professional or a user, you have a clear responsibility to your own organization and its customers to protect the security and privacy of their information. Any compromise of data, in particular, is considered a serious breach of ethics. Many corporations have formal statements stating as much and present them to employees individually for their signatures.

Copying Software

Let us move from general ethical principles to a very individual problem: copying software. Have you ever copied a friend's music CD or tape onto your own blank tape? Many people do so without much thought. It is also possible to photocopy a book. These acts are clearly illegal, although it is legal to copy a few pages of a book for educational purposes. There is much more fuss over individual illegal software copying than over copying music or books. Why is this? Well, to begin with, few of us are likely to undertake the laborious task of reproducing *War and Peace* on a copy machine. The other part of the issue is money. A pirated copy of a top-20 tape will set the recording company and the artist back about $10. On the other hand, pirated software may be valued at hundreds of dollars. The problem of stolen software has grown right along with the personal computer industry. Before we discuss industry solutions, we must distinguish among various kinds of software, based on its availability to the public.

OK If I Copy that Software?

Some software will not cost you a penny because it is free to all. Such software, considered in public domain, is sometimes called **freeware**. It is free because its generous maker, probably an individual at home or an educator, chooses to make it free. A variation on this theme is **shareware,** which may also be given away free. However, the shareware maker hopes for voluntary monetary compensation—that is, the author requests that, if you use it, you send a contribution. Some shareware is available only on a trial basis, in which a user must pay for the software after an evaluation period. Freeware and some shareware may be copied freely and given to other people. However, the software that people use most often, such as a word processing or spreadsheet package, is **licensed software**—software that costs money and may not be copied without permission from the manufacturer.

Making illegal copies of licensed software is called **software piracy.** It is considered stealing because software makers do not get the revenues to which they are entitled. Furthermore, if software developers are not properly compensated, they may not find it worthwhile to develop new software.

Thinking of Copying? Think Again

Copying software is not always illegal; there are lots of legitimate reasons for copying. To begin with, after paying several hundred dollars for a piece of software, you will definitely want to make a backup copy in case of disk failure or accident. You will certainly want to copy the program onto a hard disk and use it, more conveniently, from there. Software publishers have no trouble with any of these types of copying. However, thousands of computer users copy software for another reason: to get the program without paying for it. And therein lies the problem. Pirated software costs the industry over $12 billion annually worldwide.

Software publishers first tried to solve the problem by placing on their software **copy protection**—a software or hardware roadblock that makes it difficult or impossible to make pirated copies. In effect, these devices punish the innocent with the guilty. There was vigorous opposition from software users, who argued that it was unfair to restrict paying customers just to outsmart a few thieves. Most software vendors have now dropped copy protection from their software, but they are still vigilant about illegal copies. Vendors have taken imaginative approaches to protecting their products and, at the same time, keeping customers happy. The most popular approach is site licensing.

Licensing Big Customers

An approach favored by some software makers is site licensing. Although there is no clear definition industrywide, in general a **site license** permits a customer to make multiple copies of a given piece of software. The customer needing all these copies is usually a corporation or a university, which can probably obtain a significant price discount for volume buying. The exact nature of the arrangement between the user and the software maker can vary considerably. Typically, however, a customer obtains the right to make a maximum number of copies of a product, agrees to keep track of who uses it, and takes responsibility for copying and distributing manuals to its own personnel.

Some software makers, however, oppose site licensing; they do not want to be bogged down in licensing negotiations. Industry leaders

Don't Copy that Floppy

The Software Publishers Association has made mighty efforts to educate the public. Specifically, they would like people to stop making illegal copies of copyrighted software. The SPA made a video directed to young people, in which a rapper (accompanied by drums) intones the following:

> Did I hear you right?
> Did I hear you sayin'?
> That you're gonna make a copy of a
>   game without payin'?
> You say I'll just make a copy for me
>   and a friend.
> Then he'll make one and she'll make
>   one
> and where will it end?

The verses continue, with the theme that if no one pays, eventually manufacturers will stop producing software.

DISCUSSION QUESTION

Why have most software vendors dropped copy protection?

Microsoft Corporation and the Lotus Development Corporation favor **concurrent licensing,** a system that charges a fee based on the number of users at a given time or perhaps at peak periods. Suppose, for example, that 20 users are on a network, but a maximum of 10 would be using Lotus at a given time. The company could pay for just 10 copies of the software. However, once 10 of the users are using the software at a given moment, an 11th potential user would be locked out.

Finally, the software industry persuaded Congress to amend the **Copyright Act** to raise software piracy from a misdemeanor to a felony. Under the 1992 law, a convicted pirate faces the possibility of up to five years' jail time and $250,000 in fines.

▼ ▼ ▼

The issues raised in this chapter are often the ones we think of after the fact, that is, when it is too late. The security and privacy factors are somewhat like insurance that we wish we did not have to buy. We buy insurance for our homes, cars, and lives because we know we dare not risk being without it. The computer industry also knows that it cannot risk being without safeguards for security and privacy. As a computer user, in whatever capacity, you can take comfort in the fact that the computer industry recognizes their importance.

Chapter **Review**

Summary and Key Terms

- A **hacker** is a person who gains access to computer systems illegally.
- Three basic categories of computer crime are (1) theft of computer time; (2) theft, destruction, or manipulation of programs or data; and (3) alteration of data stored in a computer file.
- In 1984 Congress passed the **Computer Fraud and Abuse Act,** which is supplemented by local laws in most of the states.
- **Security** is a system of safeguards designed to protect a computer system and data from deliberate or accidental damage or access by unauthorized persons.
- The means of giving access to authorized people are divided into four general categories: (1) what you have (a key, badge, or plastic card), (2) what you know (a system password or identification number), (3) what you do (signing your name), and (4) who you are (making use of **biometrics,** the science of measuring individual body characteristics such as fingerprints, voice, or retina). An **active badge,** with its embedded computer chip, signals its wearer's location by sending out infrared signals that are read by sensors sprinkled around the building.
- A **disaster recovery plan** is a method of restoring data processing operations if they are halted by major damage or destruction. Common approaches to disaster recovery include relying temporarily on manual services; buying time at a computer service bureau; making mutual assistance agreements with other companies; or forming a **consortium**—a joint venture with other organizations to support a complete computer facility.
- Common means of protecting data are securing waste, passwords, internal controls, auditor checks, and cryptography.
- Data sent over communications lines can be protected by **encryption**—the process of scrambling messages. The American National Standards Institute has endorsed a process called the **Data Encryption Standard (DES).**
- A **worm** is a program that transfers itself from computer to computer over a network, planting itself as a separate file on the target computer's disks. A **virus** is a set of illicit instructions that passes itself on to other programs with which it comes in contact.
- Files are subject to various types of losses and should be backed up on disk or tape.
- The security issue also extends to the use of information about individuals that is stored in the computer files of credit bureaus and government agencies. The **Fair Credit Reporting Act** allows individuals to check the accuracy of credit information about them. The **Freedom of Information Act** allows people access to data that federal agencies have gathered about them. The **Federal Privacy Act** allows individuals access to information about them that is held not only by government agencies but also by private contractors working for the government. Other recent laws supporting privacy are the **Video Privacy Protection Act,** which prohibits retailers from disclosing a customer's video rental records, and the **Computer Matching and Privacy Protection Act,** which regulates comparison of records held by different branches of government.
- Software in the public domain, called **freeware,** is free because its maker chooses to make it free. **Shareware** software is also free, but the maker hopes for voluntary monetary compensation. **Licensed software** costs money and may not be copied without

KEY TERMS

active badge

biometrics

Computer Fraud and Abuse Act

Computer Matching and Privacy Protection Act

concurrent licensing

consortium

copy protection

Copyright Act

Data Encryption Standard (DES)

disaster recovery plan

encryption

Fair Credit Reporting Act

Federal Privacy Act

Freedom of Information Act

freeware

hacker

licensed software

security

shareware

site license

software piracy

Video Privacy Protection Act

virus

worm

permission from the manufacturer. Making illegal copies of copyrighted software is called **software piracy.**

- **Copy protection** is a software or hardware roadblock that makes it difficult or impossible to make pirated copies of software.
- Many software publishers offer a **site license,** which permits a customer to make multiple copies of a given piece of software. **Concurrent licensing** allows a customer to use only a limited number of copies of a software product simultaneously.
- In 1992 Congress amended the **Copyright Act** to raise software piracy from a misdemeanor to a felony, with possible penalties of five years' jail time and $250,000 in fines.

Student Personal Study Guide

True/False

T F   1. One category of computer crime is alteration of stored data.
T F   2. Computer security is achieved by physically restricting access.
T F   3. The loss of hardware is the most serious potential security problem.
T F   4. A disaster recovery plan is a scheme to anticipate major software piracy.
T F   5. It is legitimate to make a copy of software for backup.
T F   6. Software piracy is a felony.
T F   7. Retailers are prohibited by law from disclosing a customer's video rentals.
T F   8. The American National Standards Institute has endorsed an encryption standard.
T F   9. Making a copy of a friend's software is generally considered acceptable.
T F   10. Approximately 90 percent of computer crimes are detected and prosecuted.

Multiple Choice

1. Software that may not be copied without permission:
   a. shareware   c. licensed software
   b. encrypted software   d. pirated software
2. Software that can be copied for voluntary compensation:
   a. shareware   c. licensed software
   b. encrypted software   d. pirated software
3. Illegal copies of copyrighted software:
   a. pirated software   c. shareware
   b. licensed software   d. video software
4. Measuring individual body characteristics:
   a. biometrics   c. virus
   b. encryption   d. active badge
5. Illegal program transferred over a network:
   a. backup   c. encryption
   b. worm   d. Trojan horse
6. Permission to make multiple copies of licensed software:
   a. site license   c. encryption
   b. worm evader   d. consortium
7. Gaining access to computer system illegally:
   a. key card   c. hacking
   b. consorting   d. biometrics
8. Illicit instructions copied from program to program:
   a. worm   c. network
   b. encryption   d. virus

9. Which is *not* a method of protecting data?
   a. auditor checks   c. passwords
   b. cryptography   d. worms
10. Which is *not* an approach to disaster recovery?
   a. manual services   c. encryption
   b. buying computer time   d. consortium

Fill-In

1. The most serious potential loss is loss of: _____ .

2. Computer system protection from damage or unauthorized access: _____ .

3. Unauthorized copying of software: _____ .

4. Legislation that allows people to check their credit rating: _____ .

5. Software in the public domain: _____ .

6. A permit to make multiple copies of software: _____ .

7. Legislation that allows access to data from federal agencies: _____ .

8. A joint venture for a computer facility: _____ .

9. A method of restoring computer facilities: _____ .

10. Scrambling messages over communications lines: _____ .

Answers

True/False: 1. T, 2. F, 3. F, 4. F, 5. T, 6. T, 7. T, 8. T, 9. F, 10. F
Multiple choice: 1. c, 2. a , 3. a , 4. a, 5. b, 6. a, 7. c, 8. d, 9. d, 10. c
Fill-In: 1. data, 2. security, 3. software piracy, 4. Fair Credit Reporting Act, 5. freeware, 6. site license, 7. Freedom of Information Act, 8. consortium , 9. disaster recovery plan , 10. encryption

Chapter Overview

LEARNING OBJECTIVES

- Appreciating the progression of artificial intelligence studies
- Understanding the key issues in the artificial intelligence debate
- Becoming familiar with the use of expert systems in business
- Appreciating the various uses of robots
- Understanding virtual reality concepts

Polina Troy worked as a credit consultant for Nordstrom, a chain of stores selling high-quality clothing. Polina had developed significant expertise over a period of years. Consider this example. A customer came to the store, selected a $300 coat, and handed her charge card to the sales clerk. However, the customer's credit limit was just $1000, and she had existing unpaid credit of $875. Should the customer be allowed to charge the coat anyway, or should the clerk adhere strictly to the credit limit? This ticklish question was turned over to Polina who, after quickly reviewing the customer's records, was able to grant the extra charge.

Computers on

Although this seems like a system that works pretty well, Nordstrom recently converted the whole process to an expert system—a computer system in which the computer plays the role of expert. Why go to all that trouble and expense? Why not just stick with human experts? Well, there are problems with human experts. They are typically expensive, subject to biases and emotions, and they may even be inconsistent. Also, there have been occasions when experts have resigned or retired, leaving the company in a state of crisis. But the biggest problem is that the expertise of one individual is not readily available to multiple users at the same time. The computer, however, is ever present and just as available as the telephone.

When the new expert system was being developed at Nordstrom, computer specialists approached Polina to ask her how she made her decisions. Some experts cling to the notion that their decisions are based on instinct, some kind of gut reaction. Study always reveals, however, that their "instincts" are based on certain rules, possibly so embedded in their brains that the experts themselves are not even aware of them. Polina was able to articulate most of her procedures to the computer specialist. In the case of the customer

buying the coat, the purchaser's records showed that she consistently paid her bill on time, that her average monthly balance was usually low, and that she had a good job. These insights, along with many other rules, became part of the new expert system.

What about Polina? Is she now out of a job? No. With the installation of the computerized system, her role as expert changed. She is now a consultant to the expert system, which needs constant updating and monitoring. Polina also has been assigned some management responsibilities and, generally, has a more interesting job than she had before.

the Cutting Edge
Artificial Intelligence, Expert Systems, Robotics, and Virtual Reality

DISCUSSION QUESTION

Describe the various subsets of artificial intelligence.

 # Artificial Intelligence

Artificial intelligence (AI) is a field of study that explores how computers can be used for tasks that require the human characteristics of intelligence, imagination, and intuition. Computer scientists sometimes prefer a looser definition, calling AI the study of how to make computers do things that, at the present time, people can do better. The phrase "at the present time" is significant because artificial intelligence is an evolving science: As soon as a problem is solved, it is moved off the artificial intelligence agenda. A good example is the game of chess, once considered a mighty AI challenge. However, now that most computer chess programs can beat most human competitors, chess is no longer an object of study by AI scientists.

Today the term *artificial intelligence* is an umbrella expression that encompasses several subsets of interests (Figure 11-1):

- **Problem solving,** which covers a broad spectrum, from playing games to planning military strategy
- **Natural languages,** which involve a person—computer interface in unconstrained English language
- **Expert systems,** which present the computer as an expert on some particular topic
- **Robotics,** which endows computer-controlled machines with machine equivalents of vision, speech, and touch

Although considerable progress has been made in these sophisticated fields of study, success has not come easily. Before we examine current advances in these areas, let us pause to consider some moments in the development of artificial intelligence.

Early Mishaps

In the early days of artificial intelligence, scientists thought that the computer would experience something like an electronic childhood, in which it would gobble up the data in the world's libraries and then begin generating new wisdom. Few people talk like this today because the problem of simulating intelligence is far more complex than just stuffing facts into the computer. Facts are useless without the ability to interpret and learn from them.

One grand failure of artificial intelligence was the attempt to translate human languages via computer. Although scientists were able to pour vocabulary and rules of grammar into the machine, the literal word-for-word translations the machine produced were often ludicrous. In one infamous example, the computer was supposed to demonstrate its prowess by translating a phrase from English to Russian and then back to English. Despite the computer's best efforts, the phrase "The spirit is willing, but the flesh is weak" came back as "The vodka is good, but the meat is spoiled."

An unfortunate result of this widely published experiment was the ridicule of artificial intelligence scientists; they were considered dreamers who could not accept the limitations of a machine. Funding for AI research disappeared, plunging the artificial intelligence community into a slump from which it did not recover until expert systems emerged in

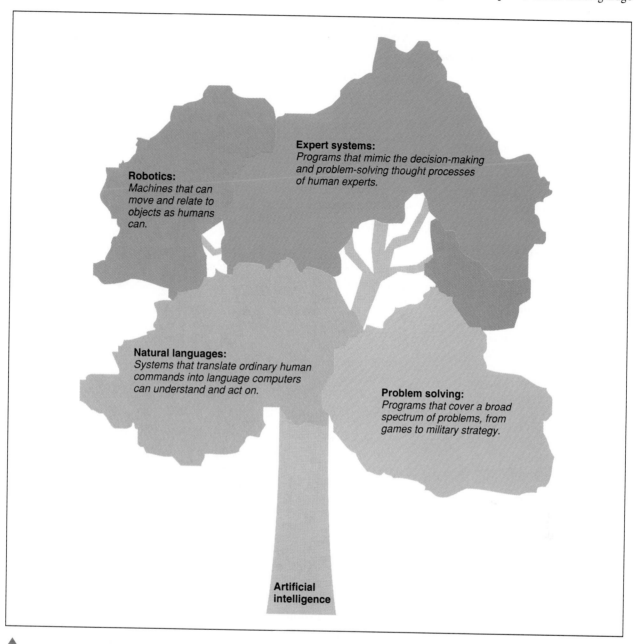

Robotics:
Machines that can move and relate to objects as humans can.

Expert systems:
Programs that mimic the decision-making and problem-solving thought processes of human experts.

Natural languages:
Systems that translate ordinary human commands into language computers can understand and act on.

Problem solving:
Programs that cover a broad spectrum of problems, from games to military strategy.

Artificial intelligence

Figure 11-1   The artificial intelligence family tree.

the 1980s. Nevertheless, a hardy band of scientists continued to explore artificial intelligence, focusing on how computers learn.

How Computers Learn

The study of artificial intelligence is predicated on the computer's ability to learn and to improve performance based on past errors. One approach uses the two key elements called the knowledge base and the inference engine. A **knowledge base** is a set of facts and a corresponding set of rules about those facts. An **inference engine** accesses, selects, and inter-

Eliza

In the 1960s a computer scientist named Joseph Weizenbaum wrote a little program as an experiment in natural language. He named the program after Eliza Doolittle, the character in *My Fair Lady* who wanted to learn to speak proper English. The software allows the computer to act as a benign therapist who does not talk much but, instead, encourages the patient—the computer user—to talk.

The Eliza software has a storehouse of key phrases that the user's input triggers. For example, if a patient types "My mother never liked me," the software—cued by the word *mother*—can respond, "Tell me more about your family." If the patient's input does not contain a word the software can respond to directly, the computer responds neutrally with a phrase such as "I see" or "That's very interesting" or "Why do you think that?" If a patient gives yes or no answers, the computer may respond, "I prefer complete sentences." With party tricks like these, the program is able to move along quite nimbly from line to line.

Weizenbaum was astonished to discover that people were taking his little program seriously, pouring out their hearts to the computer. In fact, what he viewed as misuse of the computer radicalized Weizenbaum, who spent the next several years giving speeches and writing articles against artificial intelligence.

prets a set of rules. The inference engine applies the rules to the facts to make up new facts—thus, the computer has learned something new. Consider this simple example:

Fact: Kim is Hiroshi's wife.

Rule: If X is Y's wife, then Y is X's husband.

The computer—the inference engine—can apply the rule to the fact and come up with a new fact: Hiroshi is Kim's husband. Although the result of this simplistic example may seem of little value, it is indeed true that the computer now knows two facts instead of just one. Rules, of course, can be much more complex and facts more plentiful, yielding more sophisticated results. In fact, artificial intelligence software is capable of searching through long chains of related facts to reach a conclusion—a new fact.

Further explanation of the precise way computers learn is beyond the scope of this book. However, we can use the learning discussion as a springboard to the question that most people ask about artificial intelligence: Can a computer really think?

The Artificial Intelligence Debate

To imitate the human mind, a machine must be able to examine a variety of facts, address multiple subjects, and devise a solution to a problem by comparing new facts to its existing storehouse of data from many fields. So far, artificial intelligence systems cannot match a person's ability to solve problems through original thought instead of familiar patterns.

There are many arguments for and against crediting computers with the ability to think. Some say, for example, that computers cannot be considered intelligent because they do not compose like Beethoven or write like Shakespeare; the rejoinder is that neither do most ordinary human musicians or writers. You do not have to be a genius to be considered intelligent.

Look at it another way. Suppose you rack your brain over a problem, and then—Aha!—the solution comes to you all at once. Now, how did you do that? You do not know, and nobody else knows either. A big part of human problem solving seems to be that jolt of recognition, that ability to see things suddenly as a whole. Experiments have shown that people rarely solve problems by using step-by-step logic, the very thing that computers do best. Most modern computers still plod through problems one step at a time. The human brain beats a computer at the "Aha!" type of problem solving because the brain has millions of neurons working simultaneously. Now some scientists are taking that same approach with computers, in the form of neural networks.

Brainpower: Neural Networks

A microprocessor chip is sometimes referred to as the "brain" of a computer. However, a computer has not yet come close to matching the human brain, which has trillions of connections between billions of neurons. What is more, the most sophisticated conventional computer does not "learn" the same way the human brain learns. To understand this, let us consider an unconventional computer, one whose chips are actually

COMPUTING TRENDS

My Computer Life: The New Revolution

A compelling trend today is the availability of computer technology in most phases of everyday life. Here are some samples:

- **Couch potato bliss.** Video on demand means that a cable user can select a movie from the TV screen index. Unseen, the request is relayed to a central location where a robotic arm plucks the tape that holds the film from archival storage and feeds it to a disk drive, from which it travels back to your home screen.
- **The new yellow pages.** Your networked computer gives you fingertip access to buying books,

gifts, clothing, music and videos, and so much more.

- **See and hear.** The multimedia arena offers sight and sound on an ever-broadening array of topics. Self-education at home is more dramatic than at any time in history.
- **Handy information.** Missed the news? Interested in the progress of a specific bill before Congress? Need quick medical or legal information? All this and more is as close as your connected computer.
- **Pocket communicator.** Part phone, part computer, your go-everywhere device—a personal digital assistant or possibly something even smaller—can alert you to appointments, store phone numbers and notes, send faxes, call your home or office com-

puter, link up to electronic mail, and accept input in your own handwriting or by voice command.

- **ID card.** Wallet too fat? It will soon be much slimmer, as you use just a few chip-based cards for identification, credit, health care, membership, voting, work access, and more.
- **Automated house.** You will maintain computer control over house functions such as lighting, heating, air conditioning, and even cooking.
- **Virtual entertainment.** In the not-too-distant future, you will be able to don a head-mounted display and simulate rock and roll, country line dancing, or your choice of entertainment.

designed to mimic the human brain. These computers are called **neural networks,** or simply neural nets.

If a computer is to function more like the human brain and less like an overgrown calculator, it must be able to experiment and to learn from its mistakes. Researchers are developing computers with a few thousand brain-like connections that form a grid, much like a nerve cell in the brain. The grid enables the computer to recognize patterns rather than simply follow step-by-step instructions. For instance, a neural network with optical sensors could be "trained" to recognize the letter *A*. At best, today's neural networks consist of only a few thousand connections—still a far cry from the billions found in the human brain.

Meanwhile, scientists are getting rather good at developing related areas of artificial intelligence. We will focus on some of the more visible results of recent research in natural languages, expert systems, and robotics.

 The Natural Language Factor

The language people use on a daily basis to write and speak is called a **natural language.** Natural languages are associated with artificial intelligence because humans can make the best use of artificial intelligence if they can communicate with the computer in their own language. Furthermore, understanding natural language is a skill thought to require intelligence.

DISCUSSION QUESTION

In what way are natural languages associated with artificial intelligence?

TEST BANK

Mult. Choice 6, 14
T/F 30
Matching 49
Fill In 58, 66

Some natural language words—such as *horse*, *chair*, and *mountain*—are easy to understand because they represent a definable item. Other words, however—such as *justice*, *virtue*, *beauty*—are much too abstract to lend themselves to straightforward definitions. However, abstractness is just the beginning. Consider the word *hand* in these statements:

Raoul had a hand in the robbery.

Raoul had a hand in the cookie jar.

Raoul is an old hand at chess.

Raoul gave Kevin a hand with his luggage.

Raoul asked Laurie for her hand in marriage.

All hands on deck!

Look, Ma! No hands!

The word *hand* has a different meaning in each statement. So you can see that natural language abounds with inconsistency. In contrast, sometimes statements that appear to be different really mean the same thing, as in the following:

Denzel sold Kelly a pen for two dollars.

Kelly bought a pen for two dollars from Denzel.

Kelly gave Denzel two dollars in exchange for a pen.

The pen that Kelly bought from Denzel cost two dollars.

LECTURE HINT

Translating computers that rely exclusively on the substitution of words to translate documents from one language to another often have less than satisfactory results. A new approach to providing more accurate translations is to use a concept dictionary, which describes words as part of a hierarchy as well as the relationships between concepts.

DISCUSSION QUESTION

Why is providing the computer with context one of the most frustrating tasks for AI scientists?

It takes very sophisticated software (not to mention enormous computer memory) to unravel all these statements and see them as equivalent. A key function of the AI study of natural languages is to develop a computer system that can resolve such problems.

Feeding computers the vocabulary and grammatical rules they need to know is a step in the right direction. However, as we saw earlier in regard to the language translation fiasco, true understanding requires more: Words must be taken in context. Humans begin acquiring a context for words from the day they are born. Consider the statement "Jack cried when Alice said she loved Pedro." From our own context, we could draw several possible conclusions: Jack is sad, Jack probably loves Alice, Jack probably thinks Alice does not love him, and so on. These conclusions may not be correct, but they are reasonable interpretations based on the context we supply. On the other hand, it would *not* be reasonable to conclude from the statement that Jack is a flight attendant or that Alice has a new refrigerator.

One of the most frustrating tasks for AI scientists is providing the computer with context. Scientists have attempted to do this on specific subjects and found the task daunting. For example, a computer scientist who wrote software so the computer could have a dialogue about restaurants had to feed the computer hundreds of facts that any small child would know, such as the fact that restaurants serve food and that you are expected to pay for it.

A less formidable task is to give a computer enough information to answer specific questions on a given topic. For instance, a stockbroker's computer does not need to know what a stock is, only if associated numbers indicate it is time to buy or sell. Such systems, which are categorized in a subset of artificial intelligence, are called expert systems.

Expert Systems

An **expert system** is software used with an extensive set of organized data that presents the computer as an expert on a particular topic. For example, a computer could be an expert on where to drill oil wells, what stock purchase looks promising, or how to cook soufflés. The user is the knowledge seeker, usually asking questions in a natural—that is, English-like—language format. An expert system can respond to an inquiry about a problem with both an answer and an explanation of the answer. The expert system works by figuring out what the question means and then matching it against the facts and rules that it "knows" (Figure 11-2). These facts and rules, which reside on disk, originally come from a human expert.

Expert Systems in Business

For years, expert systems were no more than bold experiments found only within the medical and scientific communities. These special programs could offer medical diagnoses, search for mineral deposits, or examine chemical compounds. In the early 1980s expert systems began to make their way into commercial applications. Today expert systems are slowly finding their place in big business. Consider these examples:

- Factory workers at The Boeing Company use an expert system to assemble electrical connectors for airplanes. In the old days workers had to hunt through 20,000 pages of cross-referenced specifications to find the right parts, tools, and techniques for the job—approximately 42 minutes per search. The expert system lets them do the same thing in about 5 minutes.

Figure 11-2   An expert system on the job. This expert system helps Ford mechanics track down and fix engine problems.

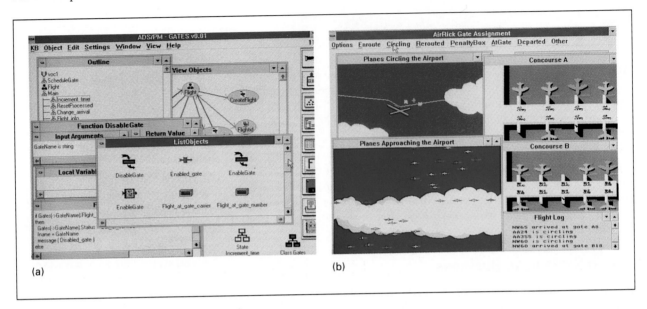

(a)   (b)

▲
Figure 11-3   Airline-scheduling program produced with the aid of an expert system.
This system offers a graphical user interface to help solve a complex airport-scheduling problem. (a) This screen illustrates the system's ability to display multiple views of objects in the knowledge-based system and the relationships between them. (b) Various screen windows show planes circling the airport, the number of planes circling the airport, gate information, and two concourses with planes at their gates.

- Employees at Coopers & Lybrand, a Big Eight accounting firm, use an expert system called ExperTax, which makes the knowledge of tax experts available to financial planners. The knowledge is, in fact, as close as their computers.
- About 400 flights per day land or take off from one of the 50 gates at the United Airlines terminal at O'Hare Airport in Chicago. Factors that complicate routing the traffic include the limitations of jumbo jets (which do not maneuver easily into some gates), weather, and heavy runway use, which can affect how quickly planes can get in and out. Airline employees used to track planes on a gigantic magnetic board. Now they keep track of gate assignments with an expert system that takes all factors into account (Figure 11-3).

The cost of an expert system can usually be justified in situations where there are few experts but great demand for knowledge. An expert system can be especially worthwhile where there is no margin for human failings, such as fatigue, stress, or sickness.

Building an Expert System

Some organizations choose to build their own expert systems to perform well-focused tasks that can easily be crystallized into rules. A simple example is a set of rules for a banker to use when making decisions about whether to extend credit. Very few organizations are capable of building an expert system from scratch. The sensible alternative is to buy an **expert shell**—a software package that consists of the basic structure used to find answers to questions. It is up to the buyer to fill in the actual

Personal Computers In Action

Robot Tales

Like computers before them, robots will soon be everywhere. Here are some examples.

- **My doctor the robot.** If you have orthopedic surgery, you may find that a key player alongside the surgeon is a robot. For example, to make room for a hip implant, a robotic arm drills a long hole in a thigh bone. Robotic precision improves the implant, reduces pain after surgery, and speeds healing.
- **Lending a hand.** Robots may soon be of significant use to the disabled. Researchers have already developed a robot for quadriplegics. The machine can respond to dozens of voice commands by answering the door, getting the mail, serving soup, or performing other tasks.
- **Road maintenance.** In California, road signs may soon say

"Robots at Work." Robots use lasers to spot cracks in the pavement and dispense the right amount of patch material. Soon robots will also be painting the road stripes.

- **Robots making computers.** It seems most fitting that robots should be hard at work in factories that manufacture computers—and indeed they are. For example, in an IBM assembly plant, robots place memory boards inside computers, mount disk drives, screw in power supplies, and more.
- **Robots on display.** If you care to see robots in the workplace, here is your chance. At the General Motors manufacturing plant in Flint, Michigan, 216 state-of-the-art robots labor side-by-side with their human coworkers on an assembly line. One of the most advanced robots places car seats on a conveyor belt, using its electronic eye to match each seat with

the appropriate car model. Tours are available for the public every Tuesday and Thursday.

- **Homer Hoover (see photo).** Robots as vacuum cleaners have always been the ultimate robot joke, but now we can stop laughing. A robot is being developed that can "see" its way around the house, vacuuming as it goes and carefully avoiding sucking up the cat.

knowledge on the chosen subject. You could think of the expert shell as an empty cup that becomes a new entity once it is filled—a cup of coffee, for instance, or a cup of apple juice.

In many cases the most challenging task of building an expert system is deciding who the appropriate experts are and then trying to pin down their knowledge. The person ferreting out the information, sometimes called a **knowledge engineer,** must have a keen awareness and the skills of a diplomat. Sometimes cameras and tapes are used to observe the expert in action.

Once the rules are uncovered, they are formed into a set of IF-THEN rules, which will probably run into hundreds or even thousands. Here is an example: IF the customer has exceeded a credit limit by no more than 20 percent and has paid the monthly bill for six months, THEN extend further credit. After the system is translated into a computerized version, it is reviewed, changed, tested, and changed some more. This repetitive

DISCUSSION QUESTION

What is the most challenging aspect of building an expert system?

process of revision could take months or even years. Finally, it is put into the same situations the human expert would face, where it should give equal or better service but much more quickly.

 # Robotics

Many people smile at the thought of robots, perhaps remembering the endearing R2D2 of *Star Wars* fame and its "personal" relationship with humans. But vendors have not made even a small dent in the personal robot market—the much-heralded domestic robots have yet to materialize. So, where are robots today? Mainly in factories.

Robots in the Factory

Most robots are in factories, spray-painting, welding, and assembling parts. The Census Bureau, after two centuries of counting people, has branched out and today is counting robots. About 15,000 robots existed in 1985, and double that number in 1990. What do robots do that merits all this attention?

A loose definition of *robot* is a type of automation that replaces human presence. A **robot** is more formally defined as a computer-controlled device that can physically manipulate its surroundings. Some robots, as we will see, can also manipulate themselves. Robots vary greatly in size and shape; each design is created with a particular use in mind. Often, a robot's job is a function that would be tedious or even dangerous for a human to perform. The most common industrial robots sold today are mechanical devices with five or six axes of motion so the machines can rotate into proper position to perform their tasks (Figure 11-4).

▼

Figure 11-4   Industrial robots.
(a) These standard robots are used in the auto industry to spray-paint new cars. (b) This robot is not making breakfast. Hitachi uses the delicate egg, however, to demonstrate that its visual-tactile robot can handle fragile objects. Its sensors detect size, shape, and required pressure, attaining sensitivity almost equal to that of a human hand.

(a)

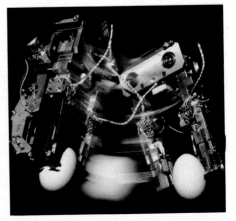

(b)

Color
Graphics
Computers at their Best

1

Computer Art

The screen that opens this gallery was produced by photo imaging, a process that uses the computer to combine photos and sometimes artwork. The photos must first be scanned into the computer, where they can then be manipulated by the artist. Here, photos were added to artwork to produce a "message" computer graphic called *Car Crash*.

On these two pages we will recognize the artists by name.
1. Marc Yankus named this rendering *Pilgrim Road.*
2, 3, 4. These three abstract works were produced by Gregory MacNicol.
5. Bill Frymire won first prize in the annual Corel Draw (a software package) contest with this work.
6. John Fitzgerald leaves this scene untitled.
7. Joseph Maas developed a series of works based on what he calls *Glass Avenue.* This one is *Glass Avenue at Dusk.*

2

3

4

Whimsy and Imagination

The works assembled on these pages were chosen because they so clearly show the unfettered imaginations of the various artists.

8. Artist Tom Cushaw figuratively looks out the window.
9. Greg Buchman made this presentation of a ship sailing in a thunderstorm.
10. Steve Lyons won a prize for his version of *Horse Man*.
11. Called *Key Note*, this was produced by Joseph Maas.

10

12

13

14

15

16

17

12. Artist Lilla Rogers calls this bright montage *Red Bull on Big Red.*
13. This rendition of the letter A is just the first of a set of 26 letters.
14. As is often the case with artworks on canvas, this is untitled.
15, 16, 17. These screens were all created by Marc Yankus.

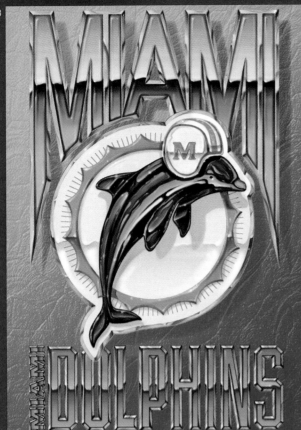

Commercial Applications

Whether the colorful work before your eyes is in a magazine, on a poster, or on television, chances are that it was created on a computer by a computer graphic artist. Here are some samples of their work.

18. This poster was created for the Miami Dolphins professional football team.
19. This design was created for the cover of *Art Direction* magazine.
20. This poster was designed to entice travelers to visit Venice.
21. A graphic artist has used his talents to advertise his own wares, proclaiming that his clients will be a "big fish" in his "small pond."
22. In a process called morphing, the computer is used to give the appearance of converting one photo to another. Here, Exxon wants to show the world what happens when you put a "tiger in the tank."
23. This simple but bright graphic is effective for selling Colgate toothbrushes.
24. A dramatic Academy Awards screen is prepared for the annual presentation.
25. This logo mock–up demonstrates the kinds of graphics available to foundations.
26. A graphic artist used a credit-card theme for the cover of a corporate annual report.

22

23

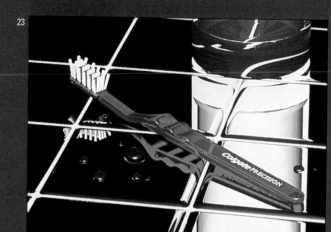

24

25

FOUNDATIONS
FOR THE
F·U·T·U·R·E

26

27

29

Photo Imaging

The opening gallery screen showed photos appended to computer-generated artwork. The works on this page show what can be done with photos alone. Begin with **27,** a photo of a building interior. Then consider **28,** which shows photos of strolling tourists, a statue, and a painting. These four photos have been scanned into the computer and manipulated to become **29,** a museum with artworks and tourists to view them. Note, in particular, the adjusted shape of the painting and the computer artist's addition of clouds in the skylight.

30. Here is the intriguing result of computer imaging four photos. The original photos were of trees, a sunset, a swan, and a red world logo.

31. The artist has produced various computer-manipulated versions of an original photo of a child.

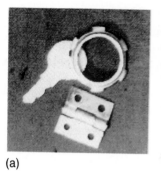 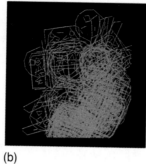  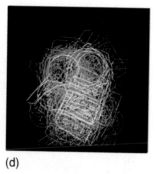

(a) (b) (c) (d)

Figure 11-5 The seeing robot.
Robots "see" by casting light beams on objects and identifying them by matching their shapes to those of "known" objects. In this machine-vision sequence, (a) objects are seen by the robot, (b) the objects are matched to known shapes, (c) inappropriate shapes are eliminated, and (d) the objects are recognized.

We mentioned spray-painting and welding as jobs for robots. Robots that can perform these kinds of repetitive tasks are merely "dumb" robots. A more intelligent robot can adapt to changing circumstances. For example, with the help of a TV-camera eye, a robot can "see" components it is meant to assemble. It is able to pick them up, rearrange them in the right order, or place them in the right position before assembling them.

Robot Vision

Vision robots have been taught to see in living color—that is, they can recognize multicolored objects solely from their colors. This is a departure from the traditional approach, whereby robots recognized objects by their shapes (Figure 11-5) and from vision machines that see a dominant color only. For example, a robot in an experiment at the University of Rochester was able to pick out a box of Kellogg's Sugar Frosted Flakes from 70 other cereal boxes. Among the anticipated benefits of such visual recognition skills is faster supermarket checkout. You cannot easily barcode a squash, but a robot might be trained to recognize it by its size, shape, and color.

Field Robots

Just think of some of the places you would rather not be: inside a nuclear power plant, next to a suspected bomb, at the bottom of the sea, or in the middle of a chemical spill. Robots readily go all those places. Furthermore, they go there to do some dangerous and dirty jobs. These days robots "in the field"—called **field robots**—inspect and repair nuclear power plants, dispose of bombs, inspect oil rigs for undersea exploration, clean up chemical accidents, and much more. Space researchers look forward to the day when "astrobots" can be stationed in orbit, ready to repair faulty satellites.

Only a few years ago, there were just a handful of field robots commercially employed. Now there are thousands. Field robots may be equipped with wheels, tracks, legs, fins, or even wings (Figure 11-6).

Figure 11-6 Flying robot.
Can a robot really fly? Yes. Flying robots have both military and civilian uses. This Sentinel robot can soar up to 10,000 feet to spy on an enemy or to inspect high-voltage wires or spot forest fires.

Commuting Is Getting Easier All the Time

How would you like to sit in the passenger seat reading the paper, or even in the back seat catching a few extra winks, while your car drives itself from your house to work? Yes, that's right: no human driver. Working models of this robotic car already exist.

It works this way. The on-board computer "learns to drive" by mimicking human drivers and matching what it sees through its electronic eyes. If the road curves to the left and the driver thus turns to the left, the computer learns to do the same thing. So far, the model car (a converted Army Humvee) does well on main roads, even in rainstorms. But it still gets lost and confused on off-the-road jaunts.

TEST BANK

Mult. Choice 15, 17
T/F 34
Fill In 52

DISCUSSION QUESTION

What is virtual reality?

Enough computer power can be packed into a field robot to enable it to make most decisions independently. Field robots need all the power they can get. Unlike factory robots, which are bolted to the ground and do the same tasks over and over again, field robots must often contend with highly unstructured environments.

Although robots seem sophisticated, they cannot do many of the simple tasks that humans can do. Robots cannot yet tie shoelaces.

Virtual Reality

The concept of **virtual reality** is to immerse a user in a computer-created environment, so that the user physically interacts with the computer. This is made possible by sophisticated computers and optics that deliver to a user's eyes a three-dimensional scene in living color, complete with motion. The user's body movements can cause interaction with the virtual (artificial) world the user sees, and the computer-generated world responds to those actions. Sensors on the user's body send signals to the computer, which then adjusts the scene viewed by the user.

Travel Anywhere, But Stay Where You Are

At the University of North Carolina, computer scientists have developed a virtual reality program that lets a user walk through an art gallery. A user puts on a head-mounted display that focuses the eyes on a screen and shuts out the rest of the world. If the user swivels his head right, pictures on the right wall come in to view; similarly, the user can view any part of the gallery by just making head movements. This action/reaction presents realistic continuing changes to the user. Although actually standing in one place, the user feels as if he or she is moving and then must stop short as a pedestal appears in the path ahead. It is as if the user is actually walking around inside the gallery.

In another example scientists have taken data about Mars, sent back by space probes, and converted it to a virtual reality program. Information about hills, rocks, and ridges of the planet are used to create a Mars landscape, whose images are projected on the user's head screen.

Getting Practical

An embryonic technology such as virtual reality is filled with hype and promises. We must look to the practical commercial applications for real-world users to see where this technology might lead. Some applications under development include the following:

- Wearing a head-mounted display, consumers can browse for products in a "virtual showroom." From a remote location a consumer will be able to maneuver and view products along rows in a warehouse.
- Similarly, from a convenient office perch, a security guard can patrol corridors and offices in remote locations.
- Air traffic controllers may someday work like this: Microlaser scanner glasses project computer-generated images directly into the controller's eyes, immersing the controller in a three-dimensional scene

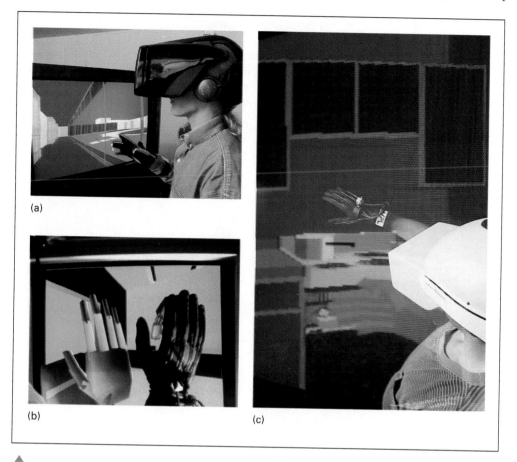

Figure 11-7 Virtual reality.
(a) Users can "tour" a building by physically reacting—a turn of the head shows a different scene. (b) The data glove in the foreground has fiber optic sensors to interact with a computer-generated world. (c) Virtual reality technology can be used to let people who are in wheelchairs design their own apartments.

showing all the aircraft in the area. To establish voice contact with the pilot of the plane, the controller merely touches the plane's image with a sensor-equipped glove (Figure 11-7).

■ Using virtual reality headsets and gloves, doctors and medical students will be able to experiment with new procedures on simulated patients rather than real ones.

Any new technology has its drawbacks. In addition to rather clumsy physical equipment, today's virtual reality pioneers are faced with daunting costs. Many hurdles remain in the areas of software, hardware, and even human behavior before virtual reality can reach its full potential.

▼ ▼ ▼

The immediate prospect for expert systems and robots is growth and more growth. We can anticipate both increased sophistication and more diverse applications. The progress in the more esoteric applications of artificial intelligence will continue to be relatively slow. No one need

GROUP PROJECT

Divide the class into groups and have each group research a different application of artificial intelligence. Possible areas are: medicine, the military, meteorology, mining, business, and industry.

worry just yet that any computer can capture the wide-ranging sophistication of the human mind.

However, even today computer professionals must sometimes convince people that computers cannot "take over." Will intensified publicity about intelligent computers and robots revive these concerns? If so, the answer remains the same: People are in charge of computers, not the other way around.

Chapter **Review**

Summary and Key Terms

- **Artificial intelligence** (**AI**) is a field of study that explores how computers can be used for tasks that require the human characteristics of intelligence, imagination, and intuition. AI has also been described as the study of how to make computers do things that, at the present time, people can do better.

- *Artificial intelligence* is considered an umbrella term to encompass several subsets of interests, including problem solving, natural languages, expert systems, and robotics.

- In the early days of AI, scientists thought it would be useful just to stuff facts into a computer; however, facts are useless without the ability to interpret and learn from them.

- An early attempt to translate human languages via a computer using vocabulary and rules of grammar was a failure because the machine could not interpret context. This failure impeded the progress of artificial intelligence.

- Artificial intelligence applications are predicated on the computer's ability to learn—in particular, to improve performance based on past errors.

- A **knowledge base** is a set of facts and a corresponding set of rules about those facts. An **inference engine** accesses, selects, and interprets a set of rules. The inference engine applies rules to the facts to make up new facts.

- People rarely solve problems by using the step-by-step logic used by most computers. The brain usually beats computers at solving problems, because it has millions of neurons working simultaneously.

- Computers whose chips are designed to mimic the human brain are called **neural networks**.

- **Natural language**—the language people use on a daily basis to write and speak—is associated with artificial intelligence because humans can make the best use of artificial intelligence if they can communicate with the computer in their own language. Furthermore, understanding natural language is a skill thought to require intelligence.

- A key function of the AI study of natural languages is to develop a computer system that can resolve linguistic ambiguities.

- An **expert system** is software used with an extensive set of organized data that presents the computer as an expert on a specific topic. The expert system works by figuring out what the question means and then matching it against the facts and rules that it "knows."

- For years, expert systems were the exclusive property of the medical and scientific communities, but in the early 1980s they began to make their way into commercial applications.

- Some users buy an **expert shell**—a software package that consists of the basic structure used to find answers to questions. It is up to the buyer to fill in the actual knowledge on the chosen subject.

- A person working to obtain information from a human expert is sometimes called a **knowledge engineer.**

- A **robot** is a computer-controlled device that can physically manipulate its surroundings. Most robots are in factories.

- **Vision robots** recognize objects by their shapes or colors.

- **Field robots** do jobs in environments that are too dangerous or unpleasant for humans.

- **Virtual reality** immerses a user in a computer-created environment, so that the user physically interacts with the computer-produced three-dimensional scene.

Student Personal Study Guide

True/False

T   F   1. An expert shell presents the computer as an expert on a specific topic.
T   F   2. A human expert usually explains decision making to the robot replacement.
T   F   3. Field robots are used mostly for farm assistance.
T   F   4. Artificial intelligence is a broad field of study.
T   F   5. An expert system is hardware that is an expert on some topic.
T   F   6. Artificial intelligence software can rely on vocabulary and rules of grammar for language translation.
T   F   7. Artificial intelligence is predicated on the computer's ability to produce knowledge it is given.
T   F   8. A robot is computer-controlled.
T   F   9. Natural language ambiguities have largely been solved.
T   F 10. An inference engine is part of an expert system.

Multiple Choice

1. Computers whose chips are designed to mimic the human brain:
   a. neural nets
   b. inference engines
   c. expert systems
   d. AI
2. The person who extracts information from a human expert:
   a. system manager
   b. expert robot
   c. system expert
   d. knowledge engineer
3. Which is *not* a subset of artificial intelligence?
   a. chess
   b. robotics
   c. natural language
   d. expert systems
4. A robot that can recognize shapes and colors:
   a. vision robot
   b. knowledge robot
   c. field robot
   d. labor robot
5. A software package with which to build an expert system:
   a. expert shell
   b. neural network
   c. word processing
   d. natural language
6. A computer-controlled device that can manipulate its surroundings:
   a. expert system
   b. robot
   c. inference engine
   d. knowledge engineer
7. A robot that must react to changing surroundings:
   a. vision robot
   b. knowledge robot
   c. field robot
   d. labor robot
8. A set of facts and rules about these facts:
   a. natural language
   b. expert shell
   c. AI
   d. knowledge base
9. Interaction with a computer-created 3-D environment:
   a. inference engine
   b. knowledge base
   c. vision robot
   d. virtual reality
10. Which is *not* related to neural networks?
    a. simultaneous operations
    b. recognize patterns
    c. mimic the brain
    d. step-by-step process

Fill-In

1. The person who extracts what a human expert knows: _____ .

2. The language people use on a daily basis: _____ .

3. The study of how computers can do human tasks: _____ .

4. Software that presents the computer as an expert on a topic: _____ .

5. Software that accesses, selects, and interprets rules: _____ .

6. Software that offers the structure needed to find answers to questions:

   _____ .

7. A robot that can inspect a nuclear power plant: _____ .

8. A set of facts and rules for an expert system: _____ .

9. Computers that mimic the human brain: _____ .

10. A robot that recognizes an object by shape or color: _____ .

Answers

True/False: 1. F, 2. F, 3. F, 4. T, 5. F, 6. F, 7. F, 8. T, 9. F, 10. T

Multiple choice: 1. a, 2. d , 3. a , 4. a, 5. a, 6. b, 7. c, 8. d, 9. d, 10. d

Fill-In: 1. knowledge engineer, 2. natural language, 3. artificial intelligence, 4. expert system, 5. inference engine, 6. expert shell, 7. field robot, 8. knowledge base, 9. neural networks, 10. vision robot

Interview: Computers Creating Building Designs

John Mirk is an architect who works out of his own home in Ojai, California.

Why did you decide to work at home?

Architecture is a very strange business in that it's kind of on-again, off-again. The business goes through great peaks and valleys, and it's common for firms to hire lots of people when they have lots of work, and then to lay everybody off when they don't have lots of work. I calculated that in the 20 years that I've been in California, I have had 13 different jobs. So I went out on my own with the hope that I would have more control over my destiny.

I see your children are at home sometimes. Was that a factor in your decision?

Yes. My wife and I very much wanted to have at least one parent at home all the time, and that was a major factor in my deciding to work on my own at home.

When did you start using computers?

I took a course in college called Computers in Architecture. This was in 1972, and the computer was extremely clunky and stupid. I remember spending an entire semester getting the computer to draw the floor plan of one house, and we all sort of said, "Oh, this is never going to work for architecture."

Did you come across computers in architectural firms?

Years later, there was a lot of talk about computers and architecture. I worked for a big firm, and we spent many months deciding to buy a computer. They finally bought one computer, and it was this very special thing that sat in its own little room, and only certain people who had been trained were allowed to touch it.

On my very next job they had three computers in the office, and the first thing they said was, "Here, sit down at this computer and figure out how to use it." These were early personal computers. We bought a computer-aided design—CAD—program. It was a very simple program that allowed you to draw components such as lines and arcs. As I learned how to use the program, I remember spending six weeks on one drawing. That was a long time, but the sheet was so beautiful that I framed it and put it up on the wall.

So that's when you really began applying the computer to architecture.

Yes. In my next job they had a more enhanced version of the same computer program, and by then computers were getting faster. We did all our projects on the CAD system. For example, we did a whole set of drawings for a hospital. With the computer we could put in the oxygen lines, the electrical lines, and the air conditioning, layered on top of one another to make sure they all fit together.

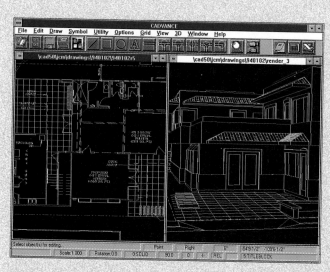

Can you mention some advantages and disadvantages as an architect approaching the computer?
It's difficult to sit at the computer and really think about how a project is going to go together. You really have to do the initial design by hand, so I guess that's a disadvantage. Another disadvantage is that you are dependent on the technology. I worry about

Tell us about the advantages.
It's been wonderful to be a one-man office and be able to produce stuff that looks like it was produced by four people. And everything looks real nice because it's done by a computer, and computers very much shorten the whole process. I just finished a preliminary design for a project. In about a week I

How do you use the computer in your work?
When I went out on my own, the first job that I got was from a developer who had already laid out general plans using CAD on his own computer. He wanted someone to take his computer files and complete the detailed plans. So I went out and bought a computer and the CAD software so I could do that project. Since then I have used the computer for

all my work. I do everything else on it as well, including my correspondence.

So then you're using more that just a CAD program? Word processing too?
Yes, and a spreadsheet program also. I use the computer for virtually everything I do in the business. I keep all my billing on there, generate all the expense reports I need for taxes, all my correspondence. Everything.

> *As I learned how to use the program, I remember spending six weeks on one drawing. That was a long time, but the sheet was so beautiful that I framed it and put it up on the wall.*

the safety of my files. I make copies of my files and keep them in a safe deposit box. Also, I have all my drawings in the computer, so if I want to sit down with a client and talk about them, I have to print everything out. That can be fairly time-consuming.

was able to do the elevation and site plans, which probably would have taken me a month to do by hand.

Applications

Chapter Overview

LEARNING OBJECTIVES

- Appreciating the need for word processing
- Understanding the basic features of word processing programs
- Becoming familiar with the standard programs that are related to word processing, such as spelling checkers and thesaurus programs
- Appreciating the advantages of desktop publishing
- Understanding desktop publishing terminology
- Understanding hardware and software requirements for desktop publishing

Jane Duffin, a physical therapist in the Mount Tahoma School District, appreciates the interaction between computers and her students. In particular, she has observed them using software specially designed to help physically challenged students communicate. Until recently, however, Jane has done most of her own paperwork by hand. Other paperwork, primarily the dreaded end-of-year reports, were typed and retyped by a secretary.

Word Processing and

typing on paper. You are not really typing on the screen, of course; the screen merely displays what you are entering into memory. As you type, the program displays a **cursor** to show where the next character you type will appear on the screen. Although this chapter examines word processing in a general way, we will occasionally illustrate a point, as here, with Microsoft Word (Figure 12-1). The cursor is usually a blinking dash or line or rectangle that you can easily see.

You can move the cursor around on the screen by using either the cursor-movement keys on the right side of the keyboard (Figure 12-2) or a mouse. The **cursor-movement keys** are labeled with arrows that show the direction of cursor movement—up, down, left, and right. The up and down arrow keys move the cursor up or down one line at a time. The left and right arrow keys move the cursor one character at a time across a line. The **PgUp** and **PgDn** keys let you move the cursor up or down either a whole page at a time or a whole screenful at a time, depending on the word processing software package. To change the location of the cursor by using a **mouse,** move the mouse until the pointer is positioned where you want the cursor to be, and then click the mouse button.

Scrolling

A word processing program lets you type page after page of material. Most programs show a horizontal line on the screen to mark where one printed page will end and another will begin; this line does not appear on the printed document. Most word processing programs also display, at the bottom of the screen, the number of the page on which you are currently typing and also an indicator of the line, either by line number or by inches from the top of the printed page.

▼

Figure 12-1 Entering text with word processing software.
As you type in your text, the position of the cursor (the vertical line just to the right of the last word on the screen) shows where the next character will be placed.

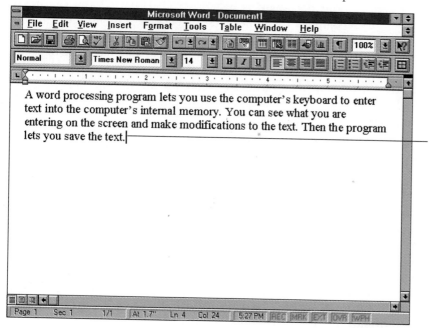

cursor (or insertion point)

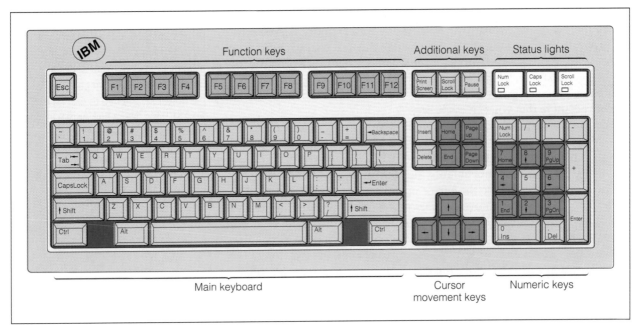

▲

Figure 12-2   A personal computer keyboard.
The cursor-movement (arrow) keys let you move the cursor around on the screen. Note function keys F1 through F12 across the top of the keyboard.

Although the screen display size is limited, your document size is not. As you add new lines at the bottom of the screen, the lines you typed earlier move up the screen, that is, they are "scrolled up." Eventually, the first line you typed disappears off the top of the screen. The line has not disappeared from the document or from the computer's memory.

To see a line that has disappeared from the top using your cursor-movement keys, move the cursor up to the top of the screen and press the up arrow key; the line that had disappeared drops back down onto the screen. Your document is being "scrolled down." You can use a mouse to accomplish the same thing by clicking a mouse over the up arrow of the scroll bar to the right of the screen. The program treats the text you are typing as if it were on a long roll of paper like a roll of paper towels or a scroll. You "roll the scroll" by moving the cursor, making different portions of the document visible on the screen. This process, called **scrolling,** lets you see any part of the document—but only one screen at a time (Figure 12-3).

No Need to Worry About the Right Side

After you start to type the first line of a document, you will eventually get to the right side of the screen. The word processing program watches to see how close you are to the edge of the "paper" (the right margin). If there is not enough room at the end of a line to complete the word you are typing, the program automatically starts that word at the left margin of the next line down. You never have to worry about running out of space on a line; the word processing program plans ahead for you. This feature is called **word wrap.** With word wrap you do not have to push a carriage return key (on the computer, Enter) at the end of each line as you would with a typewriter; in fact, you should *not* press Enter at the

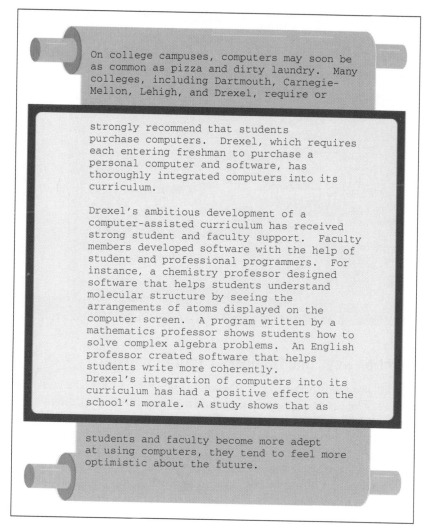

Figure 12-3 Scrolling through a document.
Although most documents contain many lines of text, the screen can display only a limited number at one time. You can use the cursor-movement keys or a mouse to scroll up and down through the document.

TRANSPARENCY ACETATE # 66

Figure 12-3

end of a line, or the word wrap feature will not work properly. You should only press Enter when you want a blank line or to signal the end of a paragraph.

Easy Corrections

What if you make a mistake while you are keying? No problem: Move the cursor to the position of the error and make the correction. Use the **Backspace key** to delete characters to the left of the cursor or the **Del key** to delete the character under the cursor or just to the right of the cursor. Word processing programs let you delete characters or whole words or lines that you have already typed, and the resulting spaces are closed up automatically.

You can also insert new characters in the middle of a line or a word, without typing over (and erasing) the characters that are already there. The program automatically moves the existing characters to the right of the insertion as you type the new characters. However, if you wish, the word processing program also lets you *overtype* (replace) characters you typed before. We will discuss these correction techniques in more detail later in this chapter.

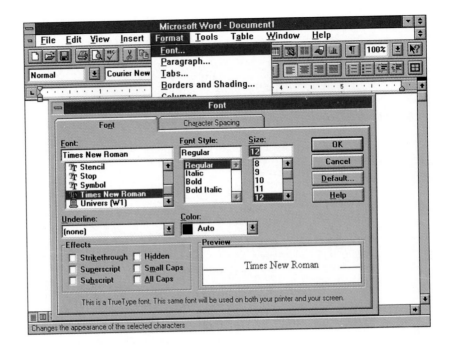

Figure 12-4   Pull-down menus.
When the Format menu is clicked with a mouse, a submenu of choices appears. Some of those submenus have their own submenus; here, the submenu Font has further selections. Note also the vertical scroll bar on the right side of the screen. When a mouse is used to click the up or down arrow on the scroll bar, the document moves down or up, respectively. A mouse can also move the square within the scroll bar up or down, causing rapid movement through the document.

TRANSPARENCY ACETATE # 67

Figure 12-4

Function Keys and Menus: At Your Command

The keyboard's **function keys,** shown in Figure 12-2, can save you a lot of time. The result of pressing each function key differs according to the word processing program you use. Generally, the function keys are pre-programmed to perform certain tasks, such as setting up columns or saving a file, with a minimum of keystrokes.

Users who prefer a mouse use word processing packages (probably under Microsoft Windows or on a Macintosh computer) that permit commands to be issued through a series of **menus,** a series of choices normally laid out across the top of the screen. The menus are called **pull-down menus** because each initial choice, when clicked with a mouse, reveals lower-level choices that "pull down" like a window shade from the initial selection at the top of the screen. For example, an initial selection of Format may reveal several submenus; the submenu Font has its own set of selections (Figure 12-4).

WYSIWYG

Pronounced "wizzy-wig," WYSIWYG is an acronym that stands for *what you see is what you get.* That is, the document you see on the screen is exactly what you get when the document is printed. In contrast, there was a time when a word processing package might show *bf*bold example*bf* on the screen—the *bf* indicating that the phrase was to be bold-faced—but **bold example** on the printed page. Now, **bold example** shows as boldfaced on both screen and printed page. Other formerly hidden features, such as text size changes and footnotes, now appear on the screen the same way as on the page. Since the newer versions of word processing packages work exactly this way, WYSIWYG has become the standard, and the term *wizzy-wig* as a distinguishing feature should fall into disuse.

Personal Computers In Action

Writers Throw Off Their Chains

Although some resist, most people who write for a living have taken the plunge into word processing. So do people who write reports, memos, and so forth, as a component of their jobs. The statements of these people tell the story:

Mike Royko, columnist. The machine terrifies me but I know enough to write my column on it. When the first typewriter came out, a lot of newspaper guys said they'd never write with "that monster." They'd rather write with a pen. When my newspaper brought in its [computer] system, I was the last guy writing with a typewriter; I didn't

Mike Royko

have time to learn to use the system. Then another reporter explained enough to me in simple English so I could do my columns.

Alice Kahn, author. For me, getting a computer meant the difference between being an amateur and a pro. I used to write on yellow pads and scribble the changes into the margin before I would even go near the typewriter. Now I turn out two pieces a week, and my writing income has increased 800 percent.

Andrew Tobias, author. The PC has changed my life in several respects. I was already an established writer, but the computer has added a whole new dimension to my career. It would be dishonest of me not to acknowledge that it has bought me a vacation house and a lot of other nice things...I didn't expect it to turn out that way, but it has.

Chris Pray, television writer. I have a war with machines. I don't even drive. I have a Stone Age psychology and even have a Stone Age computer: no modem, no hard disk. The first month I had my computer, I found myself thinking like a computer after I turned it off: I'd think about deleting dumb remarks I'd made in a conversation, or inserting things, or moving things around.

Esther Dyson, editor and publisher. The first PC I ever knew was a Wang word processor I single-

Esther Dyson

handedly brought into the Wall Street firm where I was working. Everyone in the office was very suspicious of the machine, but by the time I left they were all standing in line to use it.

Harvey Rosenfield, head of Ralph Nader's access to justice. The special interests, with their infinitely greater resources, had access to computerized press lists and word processing. Then came the PC. Sensing vaguely what it could do for us, I took out a loan and bought a PC. It was a revolution among the revolutionaries. Suddenly, a position paper could quickly become legislative testimony; a press release, a newsletter. Most important, it helped even the odds for the consumer movement.

 ## Word Processing Features

As we have noted, the most important advantages of word processing are the ability to separate keying from printing, and the need to key only the changes to an existing document rather than retype the entire document. All word processing users begin by learning the basics: Invoke the word processing software, key in the document, change the document, and save and print the document. However, most users also come to appreciate the various features offered by word processing software. Figure 12-5 depicts some of the features available for word processing documents.

Formatting

The most commonly used features are those that control the **format**—the physical appearance of the document. *Format* refers to centering, margins, tabs and indents, justification, line spacing, emphasis, and all the other factors that affect appearance. Formatting is not a trivial matter. In fact, one of the most appealing aspects of word processing is the capability it gives you to adjust a document's appearance. With this capability you can present your company—or yourself—on paper in the best possible light. Note the examples in Figure 12-5 as we discuss some formatting options.

Vertical Centering

Once a document has been keyed in, it is often easy to see that its appearance could use some improvement. For example, a short document such as a memo is typically bunched at the top of the page. **Vertical centering** adjusts the top and bottom margins so the text is centered vertically on the printed page. This eliminates the need to calculate the exact number of lines to leave at the top and bottom, a necessary process if you are using a typewriter.

Line Centering

Any line can be individually **centered** between the left and right margins of the page. Headings and titles are usually centered; other lines, such as addresses, may also be appropriately centered.

Margins

Feature settings as automatically used by the word processing program, unless overridden by the user, are called **default settings.** The default left and right margins and the top and bottom margins are usually 1 inch wide. Documents are often typed using the default margin settings. However, if the document would look better with narrower or wider margins, the margin settings can be changed accordingly. You can even vary the margin settings in different parts of the same document. Typical margin adjustments are to widen the left and right margins to make a short document look longer and slimmer, or to shorten side or bottom margins to accommodate a long line or long document.

When the margin settings are changed, word processing software automatically adjusts the text to fit the new margins. This process is called **automatic reformatting.**

Tabs and Indentation

It is common to **tab** just once to begin a paragraph. Some users need a set of tab positions across the page to make items align. It is also possible to **indent** an entire paragraph, and even to indent it from two sides, so it stands out. Both tabs and indents are easy options in any word processing software.

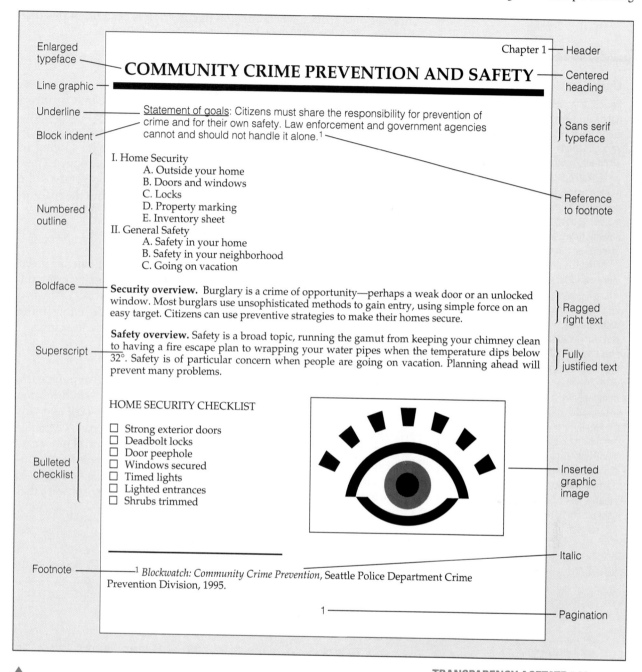

Enlarged typeface

Line graphic

Underline

Block indent

Numbered outline

Boldface

Superscript

Bulleted checklist

Footnote

Header

Centered heading

Sans serif typeface

Reference to footnote

Ragged right text

Fully justified text

Inserted graphic image

Italic

Pagination

Chapter 1

COMMUNITY CRIME PREVENTION AND SAFETY

<u>Statement of goals</u>: Citizens must share the responsibility for prevention of crime and for their own safety. Law enforcement and government agencies cannot and should not handle it alone.[1]

I. Home Security
    A. Outside your home
    B. Doors and windows
    C. Locks
    D. Property marking
    E. Inventory sheet
II. General Safety
    A. Safety in your home
    B. Safety in your neighborhood
    C. Going on vacation

Security overview. Burglary is a crime of opportunity—perhaps a weak door or an unlocked window. Most burglars use unsophisticated methods to gain entry, using simple force on an easy target. Citizens can use preventive strategies to make their homes secure.

Safety overview. Safety is a broad topic, running the gamut from keeping your chimney clean to having a fire escape plan to wrapping your water pipes when the temperature dips below 32°. Safety is of particular concern when people are going on vacation. Planning ahead will prevent many problems.

HOME SECURITY CHECKLIST

☐ Strong exterior doors
☐ Deadbolt locks
☐ Door peephole
☐ Windows secured
☐ Timed lights
☐ Lighted entrances
☐ Shrubs trimmed

[1] *Blockwatch: Community Crime Prevention,* Seattle Police Department Crime Prevention Division, 1995.

1

▲
Figure 12-5 Word processing features.
Although it not possible to show all word processing features on a single page, this page shows several formatting and other features.

Justification

A document of several paragraphs is often most attractive if it is **fully justified,** that is, has an even margin down each side. In most word processing programs, a single command justifies the document as specified from that point on. The program adjusts each line separately, usually leaving spaces within the line. There are occasions, perhaps to spot any

Updating Software

Periodically, software makers offer new and improved versions of their software. If you are using an older version when a new version is made available, you have a decision to make: You can stick with the old or update to the new. Your decision will depend on a number of factors, including cost, the value to you of the new features, and the time constraint of learning the new version.

Money is not necessarily the primary consideration. Suppose you share files with a colleague who upgrades. Although your files—made with the older version—will probably still work with the upgraded version, files created by your colleague with the upgraded version may not work with your older version. This lack of compatibility is a powerful incentive to upgrade software.

Finally, are you willing to expend the time it takes to learn the new version? If you are well acquainted with the old version, the learning curve for the new version is usually not too steep. The decision is yours. Most users, both businesses and individuals, elect to update.

DISCUSSION QUESTION

How can you give certain words and phrases special emphasis?

LECTURE ACTIVITY

Illustrate with printed handouts or with a computer some of the key differences of the popular word processing programs. In addition you can contrast DOS, Windows, and Macintosh versions of the same software.

unintentional spaces, when only left justification is desired; in this case the unjustified right side is referred to as **ragged right** text.

Line Spacing

Most of the time you will want your documents—letters, memos, reports—to be single spaced. But there are occasions when it is convenient or necessary to double space or even triple space a document. Word processing lets you do this with ease. In fact, a word processing program lets you switch back and forth from one type of spacing to another. A writer, for example, can print one single-spaced copy of a new chapter for his or her own use. Then a double-spaced copy of the same document can be printed for the editor, who will appreciate the space to make suggested changes.

Boldface, Italic, and Underlining

Certain words or phrases, or even entire paragraphs, can be given emphasis by using a darker text known as **boldface** text, or by using the slanted type called *italic*, or by underlining important words. All word processing software packages make these options easy to do, either as the document is being typed or as changes to the completed document.

Typefaces

Most word processing packages offer several typefaces. A **typeface** is a set of characters—letters, punctuation, and numbers—of the same design. Everyday typefaces can generally be grouped into serif and sans serif typefaces (*sans* means without). On a **serif** typeface, each character includes small marks, the serifs, thought to help the eye travel more easily from character to character, making reading easier. A **sans serif** typeface is clean and stark, with no serif marks (Figure 12-6). The typefaces in word processing packages can be augmented by separate software that offers an amazing variety of typefaces (Figure 12-7).

Other Important Features

Popular word processing packages offer more features than most people use. We cannot discuss every feature here, but we want to mention a few that you may find handy.

Search

Imagine working with a 97-page study called *Western Shorebirds*, all nicely prepared as a word-processed document. There has been an additional sighting of the white-rumped sandpiper, and it has fallen to you to make a change in the report. You could, of course, leaf through the printed report to find out where to put the change. Alternatively, you could scroll the report on the screen, hoping to see the words *white-rumped sandpiper* pass by. The fast and easy way is to use the **search command.** Just invoke the search command, key in the word or words you are looking for, and the exact page and place where it is located will appear on the screen.

Search and Replace

Suppose you type a long report in which you repeatedly spell the name of a client as *Mr. McDonald*. After you submit the report to your boss, she

(a) The quick brown fox jumped over the lazy dog.

(b) The quick brown fox jumped over the lazy dog.

Figure 12-6 Comparing serif and sans serif typefaces.
(a) This popular serif typeface is called Times New Roman. (b) This sans serif typeface is called Arial.
TRANSPARENCY ACETATE # 69
Figure 12-6

this typeface is called Libra.

This typeface is called Briem Script.

This typeface is Commercial Script.

This typeface is called Cloister Black.

This typeface is called Bell Bottom.

THIS TYPEFACE IS BREMEN.

This typeface is called Mambo.

THIS TYPEFACE IS CALLED SnoKone.

THIS IS THUNDERBIRD.

THIS TYPEFACE IS CALLED STAR TREK CLASSIC.

Figure 12-7 Various typefaces.
These typefaces, just ten of dozens of possibilities, can serve a purpose or just whimsy. As you can see, some are more readable than others.
TRANSPARENCY ACETATE # 70
Figure 12-7

sends it back to you with this note: "Our client's name is MacDonald, not McDonald. Please fix this error and send me a corrected copy of the report."

You could search for each individual *McDonald*, replacing each incorrect *Mc* with the correct *Mac*. There is, however, a more efficient way—using the **search and replace** function. You make a single request to replace one word or phrase with another. Then, search and replace quickly searches through the entire document, finding each instance of the word or phrase and replacing it with the word or phrase you designated. Most word processing programs also offer **conditional replace,** which asks you to verify each replacement before it takes place.

Pagination

Displaying page numbers in a document is a normal need for most users. Word processing programs offer every imaginable paging option, permitting the page number to be located at the top or bottom of the page, and to the left, right, or center, or even alternating left and right.

Print Preview

Many users call this their favorite feature. With a single command, a user can view on the screen an entire page or even two facing pages. This gives a better overall view than the limited number of lines available on a screen.

Footnotes

Any student or professional who has had to type a formal research paper on a typewriter knows how tedious it is to add footnotes. The typist must plan ahead to make sure that sufficient room is left at the bottom of the page to hold the footnotes. Furthermore, footnotes must be numbered consecutively, so it is discouraging to add one in the middle. This grim scenario becomes brighter when we switch from typing to word processing. A user need only give the footnote command and type the footnote. The word processing program keeps track of space needed and automatically renumbers if a new footnote is added.

Headers and Footers

Unlike footnotes, which appear once, headers (top of the page) and footers (bottom of the page) appear on every page of a document (see Figure 12-5). A number of variations are available, including placement, size, and typeface.

Text Blocks: Moving, Copying, and Deleting

Text block techniques comprise a powerful set of tools. Since they are slightly more complex than other commands, we give them their own special section. A **text block** is a unit of text in a document. A text block can consist of one or more words, phrases, sentences, paragraphs, or even pages. Text blocks can be used in many ways; in particular, they can be moved, copied, or deleted. To appreciate the power of text-block commands, imagine trying to move a paragraph to another place in a document if your only tool were a typewriter.

Consider this example. Robert Merino is the manager of the Warren Nautilus Club, a fitness center just seven blocks from the state university he attends. Last December, just before the student holidays, Robert used word processing to dash off a notice to the members, informing them of changes in the holiday schedule (Figure 12-8a). He keyed in the notice, watching it appear on the screen as his document actually went to the computer's memory. When he was satisfied with the document, he saved it on a data diskette and printed it.

Now, four months later, Robert wants to produce a similar notice regarding schedule changes during spring break. Rather than beginning anew, Robert will retrieve his old document from the diskette and key in the changes. After Robert has placed the diskette in the disk drive and given the command to retrieve the document, the current version of the notice, just as he saved it on his data diskette, is loaded into memory and displayed on the screen.

Robert plans to make changes so that the new notice will be as shown in Figure 12-8b. Robert begins by deleting *assistant* so that his title reflects his recent promotion to manager. He next uses the search and replace command to change each mention of December to March. He

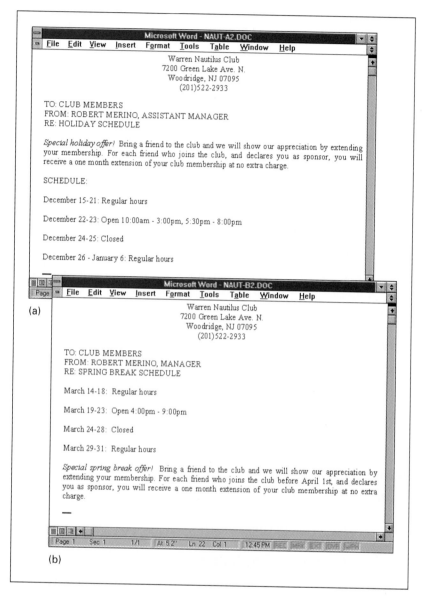

(a)

(b)

◄
Figure 12-8   Moving a text block.
(a) Robert's original memo. (b) Robert's revised memo, with a moved text block and other changes.

TRANSPARENCY ACETATE # 71
Figure 12-8 a

TRANSPARENCY ACETATE # 72
Figure 12-8 b

takes a few moments to delete the old dates and times, add the new ones, and add *April 1st* as the deadline for the new member promotion. Finally, since the notice is supposed to be about the changed schedule, he wants to move the special offer paragraph to the end of the notice. He will use text block commands to move the paragraph.

Marking a Text Block

Whenever action is to be taken on a block of text, that block must first be **marked,** which is a form of identification. Marking a block of text is done in different ways with different word processing software. In general, marking involves moving the cursor to the beginning of the chunk of text that constitutes the block and then pressing a function key to mark the beginning of the block; similarly, the end of the block is also marked. Mouse users will place the cursor at the beginning of the block

LECTURE HINT

The leading word processing programs for Windows are Microsoft Word, WordPerfect, and Ami Pro. These packages are updated regularly. Although new and improved features are added with each new version, the advances come at a cost that is not just financial—the packages require 6 megabytes of memory to operate properly.

and drag the mouse to the end of the block. In Robert's memo the block to be marked is the paragraph with the special offer. On the screen the marked block is now highlighted, probably by **reverse video**—the print in the marked text is the color of the normal background and the background is the color of the normal text. Once the block is marked, it can be subject to a variety of block commands.

Moving a Text Block

Once the text block is marked, Robert can use a set of move commands. Moving a block of text removes it from its original location and places it in another location. The block still appears only once in the document. Moving a block from one location to another is also called **cutting and pasting,** a reference to what literally would have to be done if you were using a typewriter. Some word processing programs use the actual words *cut* and *paste* as command names: The cut command removes the block from its old location, and the paste command places the block in its new location. Once the block is marked, the cut command will remove it. Then Robert must move the cursor to the desired new location before invoking the paste command.

Copying a Text Block

Copying a block of text is different from moving a block of text. As we noted, moving deletes a block from its original location and places it in a new location. The copy command leaves the block intact in its original location, but also inserts it in a designated new location; now there are two copies of the block. Typical commands for copying a block are copy and paste.

Deleting a Text Block

Deleting a block of text is easy. In fact, we have already described it. Once a block is marked and cut, it is effectively deleted. An easy alternative is to mark a block and then press the Del key.

And Other Features Too Numerous to Mention

Well, we will at least mention them. Users can use word processing to present text in columns, can dress up reports with graphic images, retrieve other documents to be put in the middle of the current document, switch uppercase to lowercase and vice versa, allow a subscript or superscript, permit a forced page break, and automatically create a table of contents or outline or bulleted list (see Figure 12-5).

Clearly, word processing is a powerful and convenient tool.

TEST BANK

Mult. Choice 6, 26
T/F 41, 66
Matching I 92
Fill In 133, 148, 157

 # Extra Added Attractions

The popularity of word processing has encouraged the development of some very helpful programs that are used in conjunction with word processing software. These programs analyze text that has already been entered. The most widely used programs of this type check spelling or offer a thesaurus.

Spelling Checker Programs

A **spelling checker** program finds spelling errors you may have made when typing a document. The program compares each word in your document to the words it has in its dictionary—a list of from 20,000 to 100,000 correctly spelled words. If the spelling checker program finds a word that is not in its list, it assumes that you have misspelled or mistyped that word. The spelling checker draws attention to the offending word in some way, perhaps by reversing the screen colors. Then it displays words from its dictionary that are close in spelling or sound to the word you typed (Figure 12-9). If you recognize the correct spelling of the highlighted word in the list you are given, you can replace the incorrect word with the correct word from the list. If the word the program reads as misspelled is correct, you may leave it unchanged and signal the spelling checker to ignore the word and continue searching through your document.

Spelling checkers often do not recognize proper names (such as *Ms. Verwys*), or acronyms (*NASA*), or technical words specific to some disciplines (*orthotroid*). So you must decide if the word is actually misspelled. If it is, you can correct it easily with the word processing software. If the word is correct, the software lets you signal that the word is acceptable and, if you wish, even add it to the dictionary.

Thesaurus Programs

Have you ever chewed on the end of your pencil trying to think of just the right word—a better word than the bland one that immediately came to mind? Perhaps you were energetic enough to get a thesaurus to help you. A **thesaurus** is a book that offers synonyms (words with the same meaning) and antonyms (words with the opposite meaning) for common words. But never mind the big books. Now you can have a great vocabulary at your fingertips—electronically, of course. Word processing software often includes a thesaurus program.

LECTURE HINT

One of the new features of Microsoft Word 6.0 is Auto Correct, which is able to fix common mistakes, such as transposed letters and double-capital letters. The feature also capitalizes the first letter of a sentence. Moreover, it can be trained to recognize a typist's common mistakes and can even be trained to translate shorthand notations into full text (such as *CPU* into *central processing unit*).

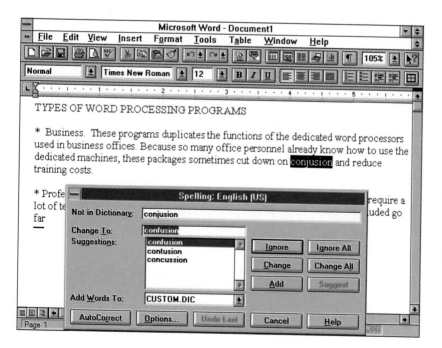

Figure 12-9 Spelling checker.
The highlighted word, *conjusion*, is misspelled, so the spelling checker offers some alternatives. In this case pressing Change replaces the misspelled word with the correct spelling. Note, however, that spelling checkers have limitations. On the second line, for example, the word *duplicates* is correctly spelled, so would not be caught by the spelling checker, even though it is gramatically incorrect.

TRANSPARENCY ACETATE # 73

Figure 12-9

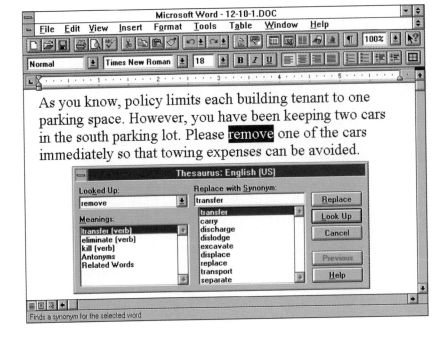

Suppose you find a word in your document that you have used too frequently or that does not seem suitable. Place the cursor on the word. Then press the key to activate the thesaurus program. The program immediately provides a list of synonyms for the word you want to replace (Figure 12-10). You can then replace the word in your document with the synonym you prefer. It is easy, and it is even painlessly educational.

Grammar/Style Programs

Do you make grammatical errors? Certainly not. And your writing style is all right...isn't it? Most people get a bit of a shock when they first submit their writing to a **grammar/style program,** which checks for common grammar and writing errors. In search of grammatical errors, the program points out mismatched subjects and verbs (*they wasn't going*), split infinitives (*to quickly run*), incorrect punctuation (*the country of Estonia: which has a rich culture*) and much more. The most common complaints from a grammar/style program are long sentences and the tendency to write in a passive voice (*The car was driven by Leigh*) rather than active voice (*Leigh drove the car*).

Grammar/style programs carry less weight than a spelling checker. Although they make myriad suggestions, many are just that—suggestions. You may feel they can be ignored.

 # Desktop Publishing: An Overview

Would you like to be able to produce well-designed pages that combine elaborate charts and graphics with text and headlines in a variety of typefaces? Would you like to be able to do all this at your desk, without a

◄
Figure 12-11 Desktop publishing.
With desktop publishing software and a
high-quality laser printer, you can create
professional-looking newsletters and
documents.

TRANSPARENCY ACETATE # 75

Figure 12-11

ruler, pen, or paste? You can, with a technology called **desktop publishing.** You can use desktop publishing software to design sophisticated pages and, with a high-quality printer, print a professional-looking final document (Figure 12-11).

Before desktop publishing, people who wanted to publish had just two alternatives—the traditional publishing process or word processing. Both processes have significant limitations. In the mid-1980s the development of desktop publishing offered a new solution to the publishing problems of both large companies and individuals.

Consider the case of Marianne Bernotsky. Marianne is an independent investment counselor who wants to send a newsletter to her clients. She wants to use the newsletter to outline conditions in investment markets, make investment recommendations, and describe some client success stories. In the past Marianne tried to publish a newsletter by hiring conventional publishing services. But timing was a problem: By the time the newsletter was printed, the investment advice was out of date. Furthermore, using outside help to produce the newsletter was expensive. Marianne wanted an easy way to produce the newsletter herself.

LECTURE HINT

Some cautions about desktop publishing. Consider avoiding:

- Underlining text
- Setting headings in all capital letters
- Putting long stretches of copy in italic or boldface
- Making column width wider than 40 characters
- Crowding out all white space.
- Getting "boxitis"
- Using more than three typefaces on a page

Principles of Good Design

Desktop publishing programs put many different fonts and images at your disposal, but you can overwhelm a document if you crowd too much onto a page. The guidelines that follow will help get favorable reviews for you and your document:

- Do not use more than two or three typefaces in a document.
- Be conservative: Limit the use of decorative or unusual typefaces.
- Use different sizes and styles of one typeface to distinguish between different heading levels, rather than several different typefaces.
- Avoid cluttering a document with fancy borders and symbols.
- Do not use type that is too small to read easily just to fit everything on one page.

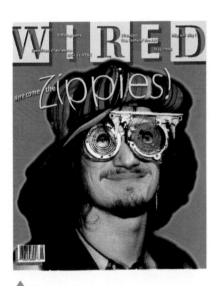

▲

Figure 12-12 High-end desktop publishing.
This magazine cover was produced with computer software. The art was created with graphics software. The photo was digitized with imaging software. The type and layout were produced with desktop publishing software, which was also used to combine the text and art. In a separate step the magazine cover was printed by a color printer.

With desktop publishing Marianne can now produce a newsletter that looks professional, without the cost and delay of going to an outside service. Unlike word processing, desktop publishing gives the personal computer user the ability to do **page composition.** That is, Marianne can decide where she wants text and pictures on a page, what typefaces she wants to use, and what other design elements she wants to include. Desktop publishing fills the gap between word processing and professional typesetting (Figure 12-12).

The Publishing Process

Sometimes we take the quality appearance of publications for granted. A great deal of activity goes on behind the scenes to prepare a document for publication. Writers, editors, designers, typesetters, and printers all contribute their knowledge and experience to complete a finished document. When you begin to plan your own publications, you will play several roles.

Desktop publishing gives the user full control over the editing and design of the document. Desktop publishing also eliminates the time-consuming measuring and cutting and pasting involved in traditional production techniques.

The Art of Design

Word processing programs can generate lines of text that look like a typed page, but if you are producing a brochure or newsletter, a more sophisticated appearance is expected. One part of the design is **page layout**—how the text and pictures are arranged on the page. For example, magazine publishers have found that text organized in columns and separated by a solid vertical line is an effective page layout. If pictures are used, they must be inserted into the text. Picture size needs to be adjusted for proper fit on the page. In addition to page layout, designers must take into account such factors as headings, type sizes, and typefaces. Are general headings used? Do separate sections or articles need their own subheadings? Does the size of the type need to be increased or decreased to fit a story into a predetermined space? What is the best typeface to use? Should there be more than one kind of typeface used on a page?

To help you understand how some of the decisions are made, we need to discuss some of the publishing terminology involved.

Typefaces: Sizes and Styles

The type that a printer uses is described by its size, typeface, weight, and style. **Type size** is measured by a standard system that uses points. A **point** equals about 1/72 inch. Point size is measured from the top of the letter that rises the highest above the baseline (a letter such as *h* or *l*) to the bottom of the letter that descends the lowest (a letter such as *g* or *y*). The text you are now reading was typeset in 10.5-point type; margin notes, however, were set in 9-point type. Figure 12-13 shows type in different sizes.

Helvetica (12 pt)

Helvetica (18 pt)

Helvetica (24 pt)

Helvetica (36 pt)

Helvetica (48 pt)

The shapes of the letters and numbers in a published document are determined by the typeface selected. Recall that a **typeface** is a set of characters of the same design. A typeface can be printed in a specific **weight**—such as boldface, which is darker than usual—or in a specific **style**—such as italic. Changes in typeface provide emphasis and variety. A **font** is a complete set of characters in a particular size, typeface, weight, and style.

As shown in Figure 12-14a, varying the size and style of the type used in a publication can improve the appearance of a page and draw attention

Figure 12-13   Different point sizes.
This figure shows a variety of different point sizes in the typeface called Helvetica.

TRANSPARENCY ACETATE # 77

Figure 12-13

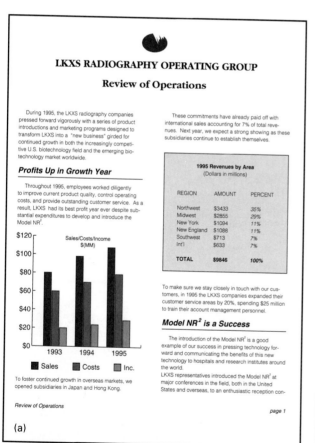

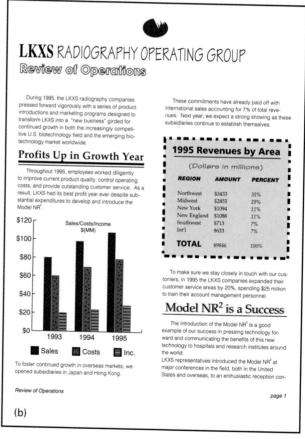

Figure 12-14   Sample designs.
(a) This example uses complementary typefaces to produce a professional-looking document. (b) The same page created with clashing typefaces.

to the most important sections. However, using too many different fonts or using clashing fonts can create a page that is unattractive and hard to read (Figure 12-14b). Combine fonts with discretion.

Most printers used in desktop publishing store a selection of fonts in a ROM chip in the printer. These are called the printer's **internal fonts.** Also, most desktop publishing programs provide a **font library** on a disk. A font library contains a wide selection of type fonts called **soft fonts.** A soft font can be sent—downloaded—from the library disk in the computer's disk drive to the computer, which then can be sent to the printer.

Leading and Kerning

Two terms you will encounter when you begin desktop publishing are *leading* and *kerning*. **Leading** (pronounced "ledding") refers to the spacing between the lines of type on a page. Leading is measured vertically from the base of one line of type to the base of the line above it. The greater the leading, the more white space between lines. Leading, just like type size, is measured in points.

Kerning refers to adjusting the space between the characters in a word. In desktop publishing software each font has a default kerning. Occasionally, you might want to change the kerning to improve the appearance of the final typeset work. An example of kerning is shown in Figure 12-15.

Halftones

Halftones, which resemble photographs, appear in newspapers, magazines, books, and documents produced by desktop publishing. Halftones are representations made up of black dots printed on white paper. Varying the number and size of dots in a given space produces shades of gray. As you can see in Figure 12-16, the smaller the dot pattern used, the clearer the halftone. At present only the most expensive printers used in desktop publishing produce halftones that meet professional standards.

Now let us put this publishing background to work by examining desktop publishing in more detail.

(a) Unkerned:

WAVE

(b) Kerned:

WAVE

▲

Figure 12-15　Kerning.
(a) In this example the space between the characters is not altered. (b) Kerning, or adjusting the space between the characters, can improve the overall appearance of the word.

▶

Figure 12-16　Halftones.
Halftones consist of a series of dots. Reducing the size of the dots makes the resulting halftone clearer.

MACINTOSH

Desktop Publishing at Its Best

If there is one application that sets the Macintosh apart from other personal computers, it is desktop publishing (DTP). Combining a page layout program with a laser printer, DTP lets users create attractive publications, from brochures to newsletters to full-size books. Since you can easily move text and graphics around on the screen, Macintosh software simulates what graphic artists do when they cut and paste on a drafting table.

But buying DTP software does not turn a person into a graphic designer. For one thing, DTP programs are generally more complex than word processing packages. Since the user is given more power and control over the page, he or she will have to learn more about the software before being able to use it effectively and creatively. In the long run, DTP software makes more effective use of time than non-electronic methods, but getting started involves an investment of time in learning the software.

And the acquirement of basic software skills is only part of it; there is also the requisite talent for being able

to compose a page that is visually attractive. Just as word processing software will not in itself make you a good writer, so DTP and graphics software do not make artists. And while many of us pick up a little something about drawing and mixing colors in school, design literacy is not a hot topic on the national education agenda. But perhaps more important than making a page attractive is making it *effective*. Page designers should strive for layouts that organize the textual and graphical information in a way that is clear and easy to read.

But the software does not leave us helpless as graphic designers. To get inexperienced users off to a good start, many software companies offer *templates*—professionally created page layout files into which you can incorporate your own text and graphics. For example, PageMaker—

the leading DTP application for Macs—comes with several templates for creating brochures, calendars, and labels. You can also purchase packages that are templates for newsletters, business cards, letterheads, and envelopes. As a beginning designer you can use these templates to produce high-quality documents with a minimum of effort. More importantly, you can use them as examples, experimenting with the templates and altering them, developing step-by-step your own unique style.

Desktop Publishing Software

TEST BANK
Mult. Choice 29
T/F 69
Fill In 139, 151

Desktop publishing systems consist of the following software:

1. A word processing program to create the text of the publication
2. A graphics program to create and manipulate the graphics of the publication
3. A page composition program

The page composition program is the key ingredient of a desktop publishing system.

Page composition programs, also called **page makeup programs** or **desktop publishing programs,** let you design each page on the com-

COMPUTING TRENDS

It Used to Be So Easy to Tell Them Apart

Perhaps you have seen proposals or newsletters or contracts done with desktop publishing. They look so good. You want your work to look good, too—crisp, professional, as if it just came from the typesetter. You want desktop publishing. Or do you?

Many people who think they want desktop publishing are actually attracted to quality printing—the output from a laser printer. Those same people may want only a few of the tricks of the trade—putting the word *memo* in inch-high letters across the top of the page, or perhaps putting a heavy line across the bottom of the page followed by the page number. These users may not want to switch to desktop publishing; it may not be worth their time or money. Word processing vendors, recognizing a need, are upgrading their products to include some desktop publishing features in their products.

First there was word processing and then there was desktop publishing. What will the hybrid be called? High-end word processing? Super-processing? Word publishing?

puter screen. You can determine the number and the width of the columns of text to be printed on the page. You can also indicate where pictures, charts, graphs, and headlines are to be placed.

Once you have created the page design, you use the page composition program to combine the text files created by your word processing program with the graphics you produced with your graphics program. The page composition program inserts them into the page design you laid out. Page composition programs also let you move blocks of text and pictures around on your page. If you are not satisfied with the way the page looks, you can change the size of the type or the pictures.

Some desktop program packages offer **templates,** predetermined page designs that you can use quickly by filling in your own text. Templates typically offered include those for newsletters, flyers, greeting cards, banners, calendars, and even business forms.

Page composition programs can also integrate **clip art**—images already produced by professional artists for public use—into your publication to enliven your text. Most desktop publishing programs include a library of clip art. You can purchase disks of additional clip art. Figure 12-17 shows examples of illustrations in a clip art library.

Desktop Publishing: The Payoff

The design, typesetting, and printing costs incurred by company publications are a major business expense. Many companies spend hundreds of thousands of dollars annually on publishing. Publications are a major expense for nonprofit organizations as well.

Desktop publishing users value the time and money savings the programs provide, but what they value even more is the control—the ability to see for themselves exactly how a change in the type size or layout looks by observing the results immediately on a computer screen. No more company newsletters filled with typos and amateurish drawings; most offices are moving to the greener pastures of desktop publishing.

▲
Figure 12-17   Clip art.
A variety of clip art software can be purchased and used to improve the appearance of a document. Most clip art is mundane—standard sketches of everyday items such as cars, flags, food, and household implements. The items pictured here offer a little more visual enhancement than the usual clip art.

TRANSPARENCY ACETATE # 81

Figure 12-17

▼ ▼ ▼

We hope you are convinced that word processing is a great time-saver, that it is easy to learn, and that it is one of the best software tools for personal computers. Most of all, we hope you are convinced that word processing is probably essential for your career and that desktop publishing is a valuable tool for individuals as well as businesses.

Some people, however, are more interested in software that works with numbers rather than words. We are talking, of course, about spreadsheet software. This important tool is the subject of our next chapter.

CLASS PROJECT

Divide the class into groups and have each group research the various word processors used on campus. The word processors should be compared in terms of the following: cost, ease of use, hardware requirements, and capabilities.

Chapter **Review**

Summary and Key Terms

■ **Word processing** is the creating, editing, formatting, storing, retrieving, and printing of a text document.

■ A *text document* is any text that can be keyed in, such as a memo. *Creation* is the original composing and keying in of the document. *Editing* is making changes to the document to fix errors or improve its content. *Formattting* refers to adjusting the appearance of the document to make it look appropriate and attractive. *Storing* the document means saving it on a data disk, so that it can be accessed on demand. *Retrieving* the document means bringing the stored document from disk back into computer memory so it can be used again, or changed in some way. *Printing* is producing the document on paper, using a printer connected to the computer.

■ The advantages of word processing over typing are that word processing lets you see on the screen what you type before your print it, remembers what you type and lets you change it, and prints the typed document at your request.

■ Two notable differences between using a word processing program and using a typewriter are the separation of typing from printing and the ability to make changes as you go along, or even at some later time, and print out a revised copy. Only the changes themselves are retyped, not the entire document.

■ As you type, the screen displays a **cursor** to show where the next character you type will appear; you can move the cursor by using **cursor-movement keys** or a mouse. The **PgUp** and **PgDn** keys move the cursor up or down a page or screen at a time. A **mouse** also can be used to position the cursor.

■ Most word processing programs show a horizontal line on the screeen to mark where one printed page will end and another will begin; this line does not appear on the printed document. Most word processing programs also display, on the bottom of the screen, the number of the page on which you are currently typing and also an indicator of the line, either by line number or by inches from the top of the printed page.

■ **Scrolling,** done by moving the cursor, lets you display any part of the document on the screen.

■ **Word wrap** automatically starts a word on the next line if it does not fit on the previous line.

■ Use the **Backspace key** to delete characters to the left or the **Del key** to delete the character under the cursor or to the right of the cursor.

■ The command issued by pressing a **function key,** or some combination of keys, differs according to the word processing program you use. Mouse users issue commands through a series of **menus,** called **pull-down menus,** which offer initial choices and submenus.

■ After entering text and making corrections, save the document on a data diskette.

■ The **format** is the physical appearance of the document.

■ **Vertical centering** adjusts the top and bottom margins so that the text is centered vertically on the printed page.

■ Any line can be individually **centered** between the left and right margins of the page.

■ Feature settings automatically used by the word processing program, unless overridden by the user, are called **default settings.**

■ The default left and right margins and the top and bottom margins are usually 1 inch wide. The **margin** settings can be changed. When the margin settings are changed, word processing software adjusts the text to fit the new margins; this process is called **automatic reformatting.**

- Users can **tab** just once to begin a paragraph or **indent** an entire paragraph.
- **Full justification** means a document has an even margin down each side. Left justification causes an unjustified right side, which is referred to as **ragged right** text.
- **Line spacing** can vary. Documents can be single spaced, double spaced or even triple spaced.
- Certain words or phrases, or even entire paragraphs can be given special emphasis by using a darker text known as **boldface** text, or by using the slanted type called *italic*, or by underlining the important words.
- A **typeface** is a set of characters—letters, punctuation, and numbers—of the same design. On a **serif** typeface, each character includes small marks, the serifs. A **sans serif** typeface is clean and stark, with no serif marks.
- The **search command** displays on the screen the exact page and place where a word or phrase is located.
- The **search and replace function** searches through a document to find each instance of a certain word or phrase and replaces it with another word or phrase. A **conditional replace** asks you to verify each replacement.
- Word processing programs offer various **pagination** options, permitting the page number at the top or bottom of the page, and to the left, right, or center, or even alternating left and right.
- With a single command, a user can see a **print preview** of an entire page or even two facing pages.
- A user need only give the **footnote** command and type the footnote. The word processing program keeps track of space needed and automatically renumbers if a new footnote is added.
- **Headers** (top) and **footers** (bottom) appear on every page of a document. A number of variations are available, including placement, size, and typeface.
- A **text block** can be moved, copied, or deleted. To manipulate a block of text, you must first **mark** the block, which then usually appears in **reverse video** (in which the background color becomes the text color and vice versa).
- The **block move** command moves the text to a different location. A block move is also known as **cut and paste.** The **block copy** command copies the block of text into a new location, leaving the text in its original location as well. **Block delete** removes the block entirely.
- A number of special programs work in conjunction with a word processing package, analyzing text that has been entered already. These programs include a **spelling checker** program, which includes a built-in dictionary, and a **thesaurus** program, which supplies synonyms and antonyms. A **grammar/style program** checks for common grammar and writing errors. Common errors pointed out by grammar/style programs are mismatched subjects and verbs, split infinitives, incorrect punctuation, long sentences and the tendency to write in a passive voice.
- A **desktop publishing** program lets you produce professional-looking documents containing both text and graphics.
- One part of the overall design of a document is **page layout**—how text and pictures are arranged on the page. Adding text to a layout is called **page composition.**
- Printers offer a variety of type. Type is described by **type size, typeface, weight,** and **style.** Type size is measured by a standard system based on the **point.** A **font** is a complete set of characters in a particular size, typeface, weight, and style.
- Most printers used in desktop publishing contain **internal fonts** stored in a ROM chip. Most desktop publishing programs provide a **font library** on disk, containing additional fonts called **soft fonts.**
- **Leading** refers to the spacing between the lines of type on a page. **Kerning** refers to adjusting the space between the characters in a word.

page makeup

pagination

PgDn

PgUp

point

print preview

pull-down menu

ragged right

reverse video

sans serif

scrolling

search and replace function

search command

serif

soft font

spelling checker

style

tab

template

text block

thesaurus

typeface

type size

vertical centering

weight

word processing

word wrap

- A **halftone**—a photographic representation made up of dots—can be produced by desktop publishing printers.
- The software requirements for desktop publishing include a word processing program, a graphics program, and a page composition program. **Page composition** programs, also called **page makeup** programs or **desktop publishing** programs, enable the user to design the page layout. Some desktop program packages offer **templates,** predetermined page designs that you can use by filling in your own text. Page composition programs also allow the incorporation of electronically stored **clip art**—professionally produced images for public use.

Student Personal Study Guide

True/False

T F   1. Formatting refers to adjusting the appearance of a document to make it look attractive.

T F   2. A spelling checker program can detect spelling errors and improper use of language.

T F   3. A serif typeface is clean and stark.

T F   4. The default settings for side margins are one-half inch.

T F   5. Text is centered vertically by adjusting the right margin.

T F   6. A conditional replace goes through the program and automatically replaces each instance of a repeated error.

T F   7. Text can be marked to be underlined.

T F   8. Most desktop publishing systems include an inexpensive dot-matrix printer.

T F   9. Once a page layout has been planned using desktop publishing, the layout is very difficult to change.

T F   10. Kerning refers to the space between lines.

Multiple Choice

1. The formal word for adding page numbers:
   a. serif
   b. format
   c. grammar
   d. pagination
2. Seeing on the screen an entire page as it will be printed:
   a. print preview
   b. page layout
   c. scrolling
   d. marking
3. An image made up of dots:
   a. halftone
   b. block
   c. headers
   d. pull-down menu
4. The automatic feature settings unless overridden:
   a. layout
   b. default
   c. indents
   d. pagination
5. Moving a block:
   a. word wrap
   b. reformatting
   c. cut and paste
   d. conditional replace
6. Software that comments on your writing style:
   a. desktop publishing
   b. spelling checker
   c. thesaurus
   d. grammar/style checker
7. Left justification causes:
   a. ragged right
   b. scrolling
   c. reverse video
   d. block delete

8. Centers document on the page:
   a. print preview
   b. line spacing
   c. vertical centering
   d. justification
9. Automatically starts word on next line if it does not fit this line:
   a. word wrap
   b. page composition
   c. vertical centering
   d. full justification
10. Adjusting text to fit new margins:
   a. marking text block
   b. automatic reformatting
   c. vertical centering
   d. word wrap

Fill-In

1. A complete set of characters in a particular size, typeface, weight, and style is called:

   _____ .

2. A set of art work stored on disk: _____ .

3. The fonts stored in the printer are called: _____ .

4. A feature allowing user to move through document: _____ .

5. You can make a document shorter and wider by resetting the: _____ .

6. The feature that finds and changes text: _____ .

7. Words in darker type are: _____ .

8. Before a block of text can be copied or moved, it must be: _____ .

9. The computer's adjustment to fit text in new margin settings: _____ .

10. Italic is an example of this typeface characteristic: _____ .

Answers

True/False: 1. T, 2. F, 3. F, 4. F, 5. F, 6. F, 7. T, 8. F, 9. F, 10. F
Multiple choice: 1. d, 2. a, 3. a, 4. b, 5. c, 6. d, 7. a, 8. c, 9. a, 10. b
Fill-In: 1. font, 2. clip art, 3. internal fonts, 4. scrolling, 5. margins, 6. search and replace, 7. boldface, 8. marked, 9. automatic reformatting, 10. style

LEARNING OBJECTIVES

- Appreciating the need for spreadsheets
- Understanding the underlying principles of electronic spreadsheet use
- Becoming acquainted with the features provided by electronic spreadsheets
- Understanding the types of data represented by different graphs

Tom Shaffer earned his degree in accounting just before the revolution—the Computer Revolution, that is. He learned to balance corporate budgets by using a desktop calculator, a paper ledger, and a pencil with an eraser.

After he had been on the job for several years, Tom saw an electronic spreadsheet for the first time at a business convention. The convention crowd focused on the Apple exhibit, where the black-and-white screen of an Apple II computer displayed VisiCalc, the first widely available electronic spreadsheet software.

Spreadsheets and

Tom was not impressed at first. The little Apple screen showed only a few rows and columns of numbers. The only way to see the whole ledger at once was to print it. Yes, the machine-printed ledger was attractive. But a secretary could type a table of numbers on a type-writer and make it look even better. Nevertheless, Tom began to listen to the sales representative.

The first advantage of electronic spreadsheets that Tom noticed was that no erasers were required. When the sales rep made a mistake or wanted to make a change, she just backspaced over it and entered the correct number. However, the greater advantage was one that had not been at all apparent at first. The sales representative pointed out that not all the numbers in the spreadsheet had been keyed in manu-ally; several of the columns of numbers had been calculated automatically by the computer. As the sales rep made changes to some of the manually entered numbers, Tom watched the automatically calculated figures change accordingly. A change in one number—an interest rate, for instance—could result in the automatic updating of half the numbers in the spreadsheet.

Back at the office, Tom lobbied hard for a desktop computer and electronic spreadsheet software. Now Tom works on a personal computer 50 times more powerful than his first Apple II, and with spreadsheet software many times more sophisticated than VisiCalc. He moves rows and columns of data with the click of the mouse. A color screen shows him high-quality graphs automatically con-structed from the spreadsheet data.

Tom went from skeptic to computer enthusiast in one afternoon. Not every-one is that quick at seeing how to apply a computer-based tool to a particular line of work. However, once experi-enced, it is hard to live without the com-puter advantage.

Business Graphics

Facts and Figures

TEST BANK

Mult. Choice 2, 10
T/F 21, 31, 38, 40
Matching 41-42
Fill In 51-52, 64

LECTURE HINT

VisiCalc was the first electronic
spreadsheet. It was introduced in 1979
for the Apple computer. Before Visi-
Calc personal computers were mainly
used in the home and in schools. Visi-
Calc illustrated that personal computers could be used for business applications.

▶
**Figure 13-1 Manual versus electronic
spreadsheets.**
(a) This manual spreadsheet is a typical
spreadsheet consisting of rows and
columns. (b) The same spreadsheet created with a spreadsheet program.

TRANSPARENCY ACETATE # 82

Figure 13-1

The Nature of Spreadsheets

A worksheet that presents business data in a grid of rows and columns is called a **spreadsheet** (Figure 13-1a). The manually constructed spreadsheet has been used as a business tool for centuries. Spreadsheets can be used to organize and present business data, thus aiding managerial decisions. However, spreadsheets are not limited to businesses. Personal and family budgets, for example, are often organized on spreadsheets. Furthermore, nonfinancial or even nonnumerical data can be analyzed in a spreadsheet format.

Unfortunately, creating a large spreadsheet manually is time-consuming and tedious, even when you use a calculator or copy results from a computer printout. Another problem with manual spreadsheets is that making a mistake is too easy. If you do not discover the mistake, the consequences may be serious. If you discover the mistake after the spreadsheet is finished, you must manually redo all the calculations that used the wrong number.

	JAN.	FEB.	MAR.	APR.	TOTAL
SALES	1750	1501	1519	1430	6200
COST OF GOODS SOLD	964	980	932	943	3819
GROSS MARGIN	786	521	587	487	2381
NET EXPENSE	98	93	82	110	383
ADM EXPENSE	77	79	69	88	313
MISC EXPENSE	28	45	31	31	135
TOTAL EXPENSES	203	217	182	229	831
AVERAGE EXPENSE	68	72	61	76	277
NET BEFORE TAXES	583	304	405	258	1550
FEDERAL TAXES	303	158	211	134	806
NET AFTER TAX	280	146	194	124	744

(a)

File Edit View Insert Format Tools Data Window Help	Jan	Feb	Mar	Apr	Total
Sales	1750	1501	1519	1430	6200
Cost of Goods Sold	964	980	932	943	3819
Gross Margin	786	521	587	487	2381
Net Expense	98	93	82	110	383
Adm. Expense	77	79	69	88	313
Misc. Expense	28	45	31	31	135
Total Expenses	203	217	182	229	831
Average Expense	68	72	61	76	277
Net Before Tax	583	304	405	258	1550
Federal Taxes	303	158	211	134	806
Net After Tax	280	146	194	124	744

(b)

Electronic Spreadsheets

An **electronic spreadsheet,** or **worksheet,** is a computerized version of a manual spreadsheet (Figure 13-1b). Working with a spreadsheet on a computer eliminates much of the toil of setting up a manual spreadsheet. In general, an electronic spreadsheet works like this: You enter the data you want on your spreadsheet and then key in the types of calculations you need. The electronic spreadsheet program automatically does all the calculations for you, completely error-free, and produces the results. You can print a copy of the spreadsheet and store the data on your disk so that the spreadsheet can be used again. By far the greatest labor-saving aspect of the electronic spreadsheet is that, when you change one value or calculation on your spreadsheet, all dependent values on the spreadsheet are **automatically recalculated** to reflect the change.

"What-If" Analysis

Automatic recalculation has several advantages. For example, if a mistake is made in entering a number in a manually created spreadsheet, and that number is used to calculate other numbers, then the results of all the calculations will be incorrect. In an electronic spreadsheet, when the one erroneous number is corrected, all resulting calculations will be automatically corrected at the same time. Similarly, if a number is changed—not because it is incorrect but because a user wants to see different results—related calculations will also be changed at the same time. This ability to change a number and have the change automatically reflected throughout the spreadsheet is the foundation of **"what-if" analysis**—the process of changing one or more spreadsheet values and observing the resulting calculated effect.

Consider these examples:

- What if a soap manufacturer were to reduce the price of a certain brand by 5 percent; how would the net profit be affected? How about 10 percent? 15 percent?
- What if a general contractor were to subcontract with several workers, but one of them reneges and the contractor has to hire someone more expensive; how will that affect the total cost? Or, what if there is an increase in cost of materials or a delay from a strike; how do these affect the total cost?
- What if the prime lending rate were raised or lowered; how will this affect interest monies for the bank or the cost of a loan for bank customers?
- What if the commission rate for the insurance sales staff were raised a quarter of a percent; how much would that increase each salesperson's commission?

Once the initial spreadsheet is set up, any of these "what-if" scenarios can be answered automatically.

 # Spreadsheet Fundamentals

Before you can learn how to use a spreadsheet, you must understand some basic spreadsheet features. The characteristics and definitions that follow are common to all spreadsheet programs.

Planning Your Spreadsheet

Unless you are an experienced spreadsheet user, you will want to take time to plan your spreadsheet before you invoke the spreadsheet software.

1. Determine the results you want to display on your spreadsheet by mapping it out on paper.
2. Determine the data you have to input to your spreadsheet to calculate the results you want.
3. Write down the names of the input and output values that you will use in your spreadsheet and the equations you will use. Record the exact form in which you will enter them in your spreadsheet.
4. Write down the formulas for converting the spreadsheet's inputs to its outputs.

DISCUSSION QUESTION

What is the greatest labor-saving aspect of an electronic spreadsheet?

DISCUSSION QUESTION

Describe the process of "what-if" analysis.

LECTURE HINT

Mitch Kapor founded the Lotus Development Corporation, which pioneered Lotus 1-2-3, the first integrated spreadsheet package, in 1981. Lotus became, for a time, the number one software house in the world. In 1986 Kapor announced that he was leaving Lotus to "pursue other endeavors."

TEST BANK

Mult. Choice 1, 3-9, 11-13
T/F 22, 25-30, 36, 39
Matching 45, 48-50
Fill In 53-58, 59-62, 65

C O M P U T I N G   T R E N D S

Spreadsheets in the Home

Family budgeting is the most common home use for spreadsheets. However, some people are more interested in "what-if" scenarios, for which spreadsheets are the perfect tool. Here are some examples users have dreamed up:

- **What if I go back to work**...is it really worth it? You can factor in all the expenses of employment—travel, wardrobe, child care, and other disbursements—and compare the total against the income received.
- **What if I save $100 a month**...how soon can I buy a car? What if I save $125 or $150 per month? You can also play out

other varied possibilities such as interest rates and price of car to see what time periods result.

- **What if I start my own business**...can I make a go of it? Although estimates may be sketchy at best, a budding entrepreneur can approximate expenses (for materials, tools, equipment, office rental, and so forth) and compare them to anticipated revenues from clients over different periods of time.
- **Should I jump into the stock market**...or stick to a more conservative investment approach? A popular sport among investors is running dollar amounts and anticipated growth rates of various investment opportunities through

spreadsheets. The results may give them a glimpse of their future financial picture.

- **What if I buy the house by the lake**...instead of the house near work? The houses have different price tags and different expenses. These factors and others can be built into a spreadsheet and used to calculate monthly payments and other related expenses, such as transportation.
- **What if I save $50 per month for my child's education**...how much money would be saved (with accumulated interest) by the time the child is 18? What if I were to save $75 or $100 per month?

LECTURE HINT

In 1993 Borland International, Inc., dramatically lowered the price of Quattro Pro for Windows from $495 to $49. It was Borland's belief that the new low price would get users of Lotus and Excel for DOS who were in the process of switching to a Windows version to switch to Quattro Pro instead. Yet Borland's market research surprisingly showed that 41 percent of the sales were actually to first-time spreadsheet buyers.

Cells and Cell Addresses

Figure 13-2 shows one type of spreadsheet—a teacher's grade sheet. Notice that the spreadsheet is divided into rows (horizontal) and columns (vertical). The rows have *numeric labels* and the columns have *alphabetic labels*. There are actually more rows and columns than you can see on the screen. Some spreadsheets have thousands of rows and hundreds of columns—probably more than you will ever need to use.

The intersection of a row and column forms a cell. A **cell** is a storage area on a spreadsheet. When referring to a cell, you use the letter and number of the intersecting column and row. For example, in Figure 13-2, cell B7 is the intersection of column B and row 7—in this example, the grade of 25 for Vedder on Quiz 1. This reference name is known as the **cell address.** Notice that the alphabetic column designation always precedes the row number: B7, not 7B.

On a spreadsheet one cell is always known as the **active cell,** or **current cell.** When a cell is active you can enter data or edit that cell's contents. Typically, the active cell is marked by highlighting in reverse video or with a heavy border drawn around it. The active cell in Figure 13-2 is cell A1.

You can use the cursor-movement (arrow) keys to move one row or column at a time. In fact, you can also use the cursor-movement keys to scroll through the spreadsheet both vertically and horizontally. Most spreadsheet packages also let you use a mouse to move from cell to cell on the screen.

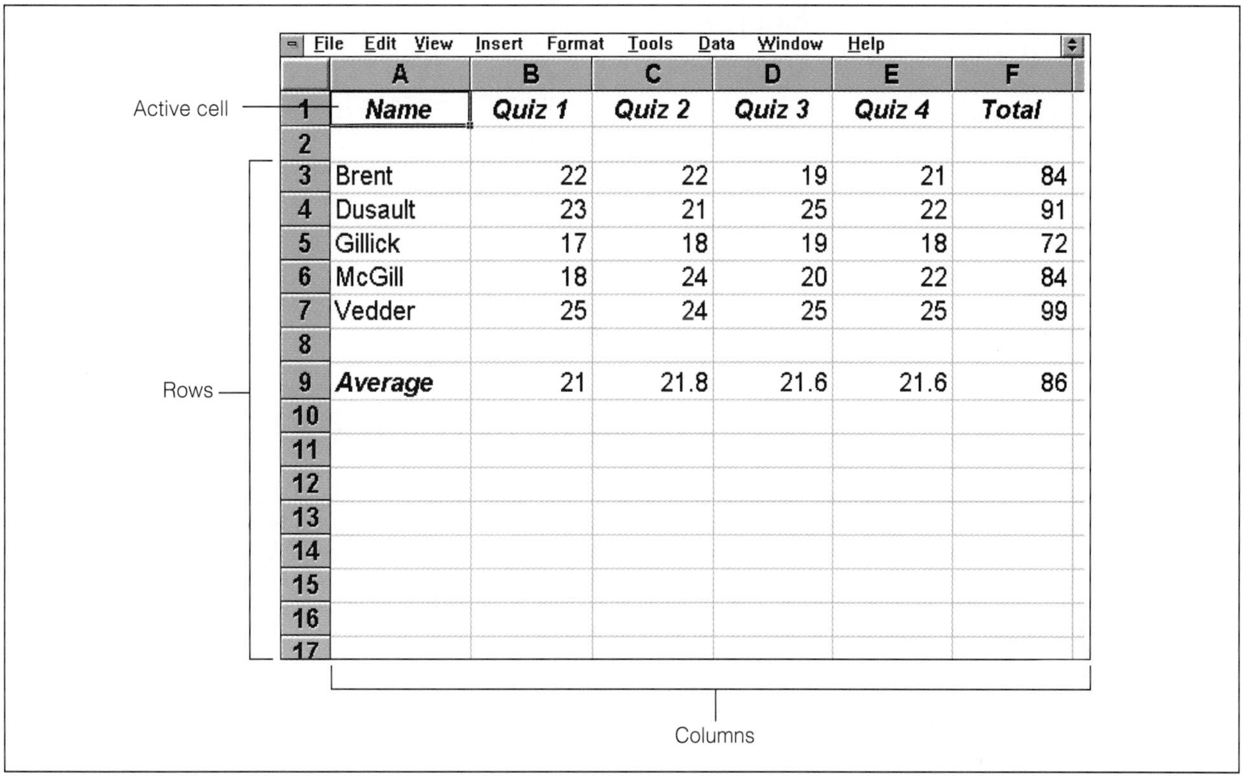

	A	B	C	D	E	F
1	**Name**	**Quiz 1**	**Quiz 2**	**Quiz 3**	**Quiz 4**	**Total**
2						
3	Brent	22	22	19	21	84
4	Dusault	23	21	25	22	91
5	Gillick	17	18	19	18	72
6	McGill	18	24	20	22	84
7	Vedder	25	24	25	25	99
8						
9	*Average*	21	21.8	21.6	21.6	86
10						
11						
12						
13						
14						
15						
16						
17						

Active cell

Rows

Columns

File   Edit   View   Insert   Format   Tools   Data   Window   Help

Figure 13-2   Anatomy of a spreadsheet screen.
This screen shows a typical spreadsheet—a teacher's grade sheet. It shows space for 17 rows numbered down the side and seven columns labeled A through F. The intersection of a row and column forms a cell. Here, cell A1 is the active cell—the cell into which a user may key data. Only one cell may be active at a given time.

TRANSPARENCY ACETATE # 83

Figure 13-2

DISCUSSION QUESTION

What are the three types of information contained in a spreadsheet cell?

Contents of Cells: Labels, Values, and Formulas

Each cell can contain one of three types of information: a label, a value, or a formula. A **label** provides descriptive text information about entries in the spreadsheet, such as a person's name. A cell that contains a label is not generally used to perform mathematical calculations. For example, in Figure 13-2, cells A1, A9, and F1, among others, contain labels.

A **value** is an actual number entered into a cell to be used in calculations. In Figure 13-2, for example, cell B3 contains a value.

A **formula** is an instruction to the program to calculate a number. A formula generally contains cell addresses and one or more arithmetic operators: a plus sign (+) to add, a minus sign (-) to subtract, an asterisk (*) to multiply, and a slash (/) to divide. When you use a formula rather than entering the calculated result, the software can automatically recalculate the result if you need to change any of the values on which the formula is based.

In addition to the types of calculations just mentioned, a formula can include one or more functions. A **function** is like a preprogrammed formula. Two common functions are the *sum* function, which adds numbers together, and the *average* function, which calculates the average of a group of numbers. Most spreadsheet programs contain many functions for a variety of uses, from mathematics to statistics to financial applications.

Formulas and functions do not appear in the cells; instead, the cell shows the result of the formula or function. The result is called the **displayed value** of the cell. The formula or function is the **content** of the cell.

LECTURE HINT

Spreadsheet formulas typically follow precedence rules that determine the order of operation for the various operations. Multiplication and division are done from left to right. Then addition and subtraction are done from left to right. If there are any parentheses, operations within parentheses are done first.

TEST BANK

T/F 34-35
Fill In 63

LECTURE HINT

In large spreadsheets requiring many changes, automatic recalculation can be time consuming, because each time a user changes the spreadsheet, the user has to wait until all recalculations have been made before continuing work on the spreadsheet. Instead, the user can delay recalculation until all changes have been made.

TRANSPARENCY ACETATE # 84

Figure 13-3

Ranges

Sometimes it is necessary to specify a range of cells in order to build a formula or perform a function. A **range** is a group of one or more cells occurring in a rectangular shape; the program treats the range as a unit during an operation. Figure 13-3 shows some ranges. To define a range, you must indicate the upper-left and lower-right cells of the block. Depending on the particular spreadsheet software you are using, the cell addresses are separated by a colon or by two periods. For example, in Figure 13-2, the Quiz 1 range is B3:B7 (or B3..B7), and the Brent quiz range is B3:E3 (or B3..E3).

 # Spreadsheet Features

Once spreadsheet users master the basics, they are usually eager to learn the extra features that make their work more useful or attractive. Most spreadsheet software packages offer a variety of features that enhance the basic spreadsheet.

Formatting

Users format their data in different ways to make it more readable and even more appealing. Formatting features take a worksheet beyond the historically plain sheet of numbers. Here is a partial list of features you will probably find included with spreadsheet software:

- **Wide columns.** In particular, columns containing labels—words—usually need to be wider than a column for numbers. Note, for exam-

▼

Figure 13-3   Ranges.
A range is a group of one or more cells arranged in a rectangle. You can name a range or refer to it by using the addresses of the upper-left and lower-right cells in the group.

□	File	Edit	View	Insert	Format	Tools	Data	Window	Help		⬍
	A	**B**	**C**	**D**	**E**	**F**	**G**	**H**		**I**
1										
2										
3	A3:A3									
4						F4:H4				
5										
6										
7										
8			C2:C15							
9										
10					E7: F14					
11										
12										
13										
14										
15										
16										
17										
18										
19										
20										
21										
22										
23										

ple, that column A in Figure 13-1 is wider than the other columns to accommodate the data. (Incidentally, although less common, it is also possible to alter the height of a row.)

- **Headings.** If a heading is desired, it can be invoked as a wide column and can even be centered.
- **Number symbols.** If appropriate, a number value can be shown with a dollar sign ($), percent sign (%), and commas and decimal places, as desired.
- **Appearance of data.** Spreadsheet data can be presented in one of many proffered fonts and in boldface or italic. Furthermore, data can be centered within the cell, or justified right or left within the cell. Often an entire column of cells will be justified right or left. In Figure 13-2, for example, all data in column A is left justified, whereas data in columns B through F are right justified.
- **Printing.** When a user is developing and experimenting with a spreadsheet, he or she is looking at the spreadsheet on the screen. But the finished product, or even a series of variations of the product, will probably be printed for distribution and examination. Spreadsheet software offers several printing options. For example, a spreadsheet may be centered on the printed page. Margins may be altered. The entire page may be printed sideways, that is, horizontally instead of vertically. Vertical and horizontal grid lines may be hidden on the printed spreadsheet.
- **Decoration.** Many spreadsheet packages include decorative features, such as borders and color options.

Finally, perhaps in the "super-extras" category, we can mention that cells in rows or columns or in an entire spreadsheet may be sorted in ascending or descending order, that a spelling checker may be invoked, and that a zooming feature can be used to focus on an enlarged section of the spreadsheet.

Graphics

The change from numbers to pictures is a refreshing variation. Fortunately, most spreadsheet software makes the switch from numbers to pictures a fairly easy transition. That is, once you prepare a spreadsheet, you can show your results in graphics form. We will discuss the value of business graphics in detail later in the chapter.

 # A Problem for a Spreadsheet

Dawn Kosanovich, at age eight, was an entrepreneur. One hot summer day she borrowed some sugar and lemons from the kitchen and stirred up a pitcher of lemonade, which she proceeded to sell from a stand in front of her house. By the end of the day, she had gone through three pitchers and had taken in $6.25. Her joy, however, subsided when her mother explained that a business person has to pay for supplies—in this case, the sugar and lemons. But Dawn was not deterred long. In her growing up years, she sold bird houses, a neighborhood newsletter, and sequined hair barrettes. In the process, she learned that it was important to keep good business records.

Getting Help on the Phone

Sooner or later, most computer users need some technical help. That help is usually available over the phone from staff employed by the software maker. Typically, assistance is free for a certain time period, perhaps 90 days from the first phone call, but then there is a charge to the user. To make the best use of your time on the phone, do some advance preparation.

Before you call:

- Have your software documentation handy.
- Place your phone near your computer.
- Know your computer type and model and the version of your software package.
- Write down the exact wording of any error messages.

When you call:

- Give identifying information when asked.
- State the problem clearly.
- Tell the technician what you have already tried.
- Be ready to explore solutions on the computer as you talk.

LECTURE HINT

Some applications of spreadsheets are (1) budget management, (2) competitive bidding, (3) investments, and (4) grade computation.

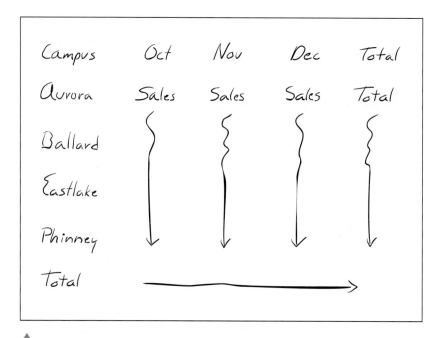

▲

Figure 13-4   Spreadsheet planning.
This sketch of a spreadsheet is useful before invoking the software. The plan includes one row per campus and month total, and one column for campus name, each month's sales, and campus totals.

A New Business

When Dawn attended Ballard Community College, she noticed that the only beverages available were milk, coffee, and canned soft drinks. Thinking back to her early days, Dawn got permission to set up a lemonade stand on campus. In addition to fresh lemonade, she sold bagels and homemade cookies. The stand was soon successful, and eventually Dawn hired other students to manage stands on nearby campuses: Aurora, Eastlake, and Phinney.

Using Spreadsheets for the Business

When Dawn took a computer applications course at the college, she decided that spreadsheets were appropriate for keeping track of her business. She began by comparing sales for the four campuses for the fourth quarter of the year. She sketched her spreadsheet on paper (Figure 13-4). As she invoked the spreadsheet software, Dawn decided that she also would add some headings. In her first cut at the spreadsheet, Dawn keyed in the campus names in column A and the campus sales for each of the three months in columns B, C, and D (Figure 13-5).

Dawn does not, of course, have to compute totals—the spreadsheet software will do that. In fact, the obvious solution is to key formulas using the SUM function to compute both column and row totals. In cell E6, for example, Dawn keys =SUM(B6:D6). The software thus has been instructed to sum the values in cells B6, C6, and D6, and place the resulting sum in cell E6. Even though she typed a formula in the cell, the result is a value, in this case 4671 (Figure 13-5). Keep in mind that the resulting value in any cell containing a formula will change if any of the

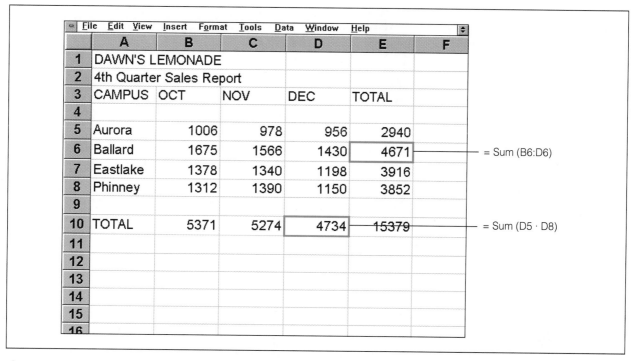

Figure 13-5 First draft of sales spreadsheet.
This initial look at Dawn's spreadsheet shows the headings and data keyed in to the spreadsheet. Dawn keyed formulas that include the SUM function in cells E5, E6, E7, E8, B10, C10, D10, and E10. Later, Dawn will make a change to a data item and also format the spreadsheet to improve its appearance.

values in the cells in the formula change. For cell E6, the resulting value would change if there were a change to the values in cells B6, C6, or D6. The other cells containing totals (E5, E7, E8, B10, C10, D10, and E10) also contain formulas that will calculate a value. Cell E10, by the way, could sum up either the E column (=SUM(E5:E8)) or the 10 row (=SUM(B10:D10)). The result is the same either way.

Now that the basic spreadsheet is complete, Dawn saves it on disk and prints it.

Changing the Spreadsheet: Automatic Recalculation

Dawn has discovered an error in her spreadsheet: cell D6, rather than 1430, should be 1502. Again using her spreadsheet software, she needs merely to retrieve the spreadsheet from disk and make the single change to cell D6 (Figure 13-6). Note, however, that cell D6 is used for the totals calculations in cells E6 and D10. Furthermore, recalling that either column E or row 10 was used to compute the final total in E10, then either changed cell E6 or changed cell D10 will cause a change in the value calculated in cell E10. All these changes are made by the spreadsheet software automatically. Indeed, note the changed values in cells E6, D10, and E10—all the result of a single change to cell D6.

Formatting and Printing

Now that Dawn is satisfied with her spreadsheet calculations, she decides to make some formatting changes and then print the spreadsheet. She

▶

Figure 13-6 The altered spreadsheet, reflecting automatic recalculations. Dawn changed the value in cell D6, causing an automatic change to calculated values in cells E6, D10, and E10.

TRANSPARENCY ACETATE # 87

Figure 13-6

File Edit View Insert Format Tools Data Window Help

	A	B	C	D	E	F
1	DAWN'S LEMONADE					
2	4th Quarter Sales Report					
3	CAMPUS	OCT	NOV	DEC	TOTAL	
4						
5	Aurora	1006	978	956	2940	
6	Ballard	1675	1566	1502	4743	
7	Eastlake	1378	1340	1198	3916	
8	Phinney	1312	1390	1150	3852	
9						
10	TOTAL	5371	5274	4806	15451	
11						
12						
13						
14						
15						
16						

LECTURE HINT

Spreadsheet templates are worksheets that are prepared in advance. The cells already contain row and column labels, and prewritten formulas. All you have to add is the data. Prewritten templates can be purchased for common spreadsheet applications, such as tax-form templates.

uses the spreadsheet software to make the changes (to see the changes, you can look ahead to Figure 13-7a). Here is a list of the changes she wants to make:

- Center the two major headings.
- Use a different font on the two major headings, and change them to boldface.
- Center CAMPUS, OCT, NOV, DEC, and both TOTAL labels, each within its own cell, and boldface each label.
- Put each campus name in italic.
- Present the sales figures as currency by adding dollar signs ($) and decimal points.
- Use a vertical double border to separate the campus names from the sales figures, a horizontal double border to separate the headings from the sales figures, and a single horizontal border to separate the top two heading rows from the rest of the spreadsheet.
- Remove the spreadsheet grid lines.

Note that the printed result need not include the alphabetic column labels or the numeric row labels (Figure 13-7a).

A Graph from Spreadsheet Data

Dawn decides to make a chart to contrast the sales totals among the four campuses. These figures already exist in the last column of the spreadsheet, cells E5 through E8. Using the software's charting capability, Dawn can select those cells and then request a three-dimensional pie chart to display them. She decides to specify that the sales figures be shown as percentages of total sales, and that each pie wedge be further labeled with the campus name, supplied from column A on the spreadsheet. After adding a title, COMPARISON BY CAMPUS, Dawn saves and prints the finished chart (Figure 13-7b).

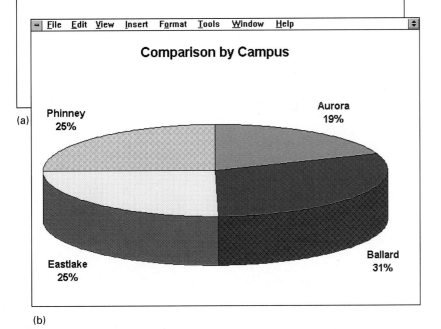

☐ File Edit View Insert Format Tools Data Window Help				⬍
DAWN'S LEMONADE				
4th Quarter Sales Report				
CAMPUS	**OCT**	**NOV**	**DEC**	**TOTAL**
Aurora	$ 1,006.00	$ 978.00	$ 956.00	$ 2,940.00
Ballard	$ 1,675.00	$ 1,566.00	$ 1,502.00	$ 4,743.00
Eastlake	$ 1,378.00	$ 1,340.00	$ 1,198.00	$ 3,916.00
Phinney	$ 1,312.00	$ 1,390.00	$ 1,150.00	$ 3,852.00
TOTAL	$ 5,371.00	$ 5,274.00	$ 4,806.00	$ 15,451.00

(a)

Comparison by Campus

Phinney 25%
Aurora 19%
Eastlake 25%
Ballard 31%

(b)

Figure 13-7 The finished spreadsheet and a matching graph.
(a) On the final version of her spreadsheet, printed here, Dawn has boldfaced and centered the headings and changed their fonts, added vertical and horizontal borders, used italics and boldface on certain cells, and expressed the sales figures as currency. (b) This simple pie chart shows the figures from the rightmost column of the spreadsheet, the campus totals, as percentages of total sales.

TRANSPARENCY ACETATE # 88

Figure 13-7

This completes our discussion of spreadsheet use. Spreadsheet software is much more powerful than we have been able to demonstrate in this small problem. Dawn, for example, will probably expand her spreadsheet repertoire to take a close look at expenses and profits. Furthermore, she can use "what-if" analysis to consider adding new products, hiring more staff, raising or lowering prices, or even adding more lemonade stands. In each "what-if" scenario, Dawn could see the effect of such a change on her profit line. Spreadsheet software makes all these endeavors both possible and uncomplicated.

◥ Business Graphics

Graphics can show words and numbers and data in ways that are meaningful and quickly understood. This is the key reason they are valuable. Personal computers give people the capability to store and use data about their businesses. These same users, however, sometimes find it difficult to convey this information to others—managers or clients—in a

TEST BANK

Mult. Choice 19
T/F 23, 37
Matching 46
Fill In 66

LECTURE HINT

As the number of variables plotted in a bar chart increases, the chart becomes cluttered. A good rule of thumb to use is if more than seven or eight variables are to be plotted, use a line graph instead.

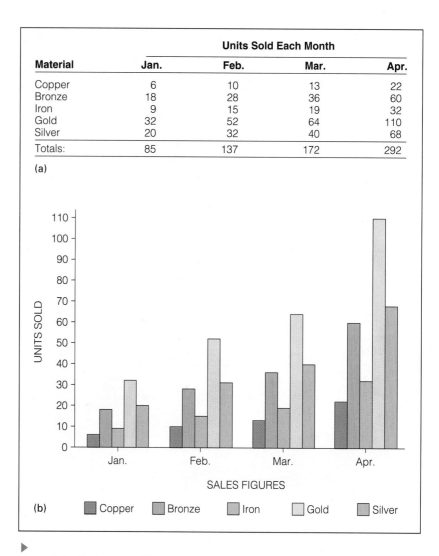

Material	Units Sold Each Month			
	Jan.	Feb.	Mar.	Apr.
Copper	6	10	13	22
Bronze	18	28	36	60
Iron	9	15	19	32
Gold	32	52	64	110
Silver	20	32	40	68
Totals:	85	137	172	292

(a)

(b) ■ Copper ■ Bronze ■ Iron ■ Gold ■ Silver

▶

Figure 13-8 Business graphics.
(a) A large amount of data can be translated into (b) one simple, clear graph.

meaningful way. **Business graphics**—graphics that represent data in a visual, easily understood format—provide an answer to this problem.

Why Use Graphics?

Graphics generate and sustain the interest of an audience by brightening up any lesson, report, or business document. In addition, graphics can help get a point across by presenting numeric data (Figure 13-8a) in one simple, clear graph (Figure 13-8b). What is more, that simple graph can reveal a trend that could be lost if buried in long columns of numbers. In addition, a presenter who uses graphics often appears more prepared and organized than one who does not. To sum up, most people use business graphics software for two reasons: (1) to view and analyze data and (2) to make a positive impression during a presentation. To satisfy these different needs, two types of business graphics programs have been developed: analytical graphics and presentation graphics.

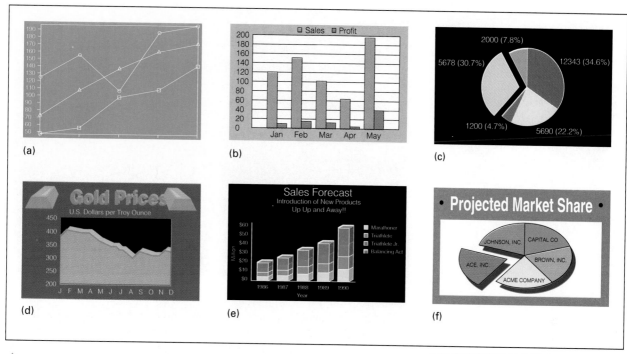

Figure 13-9 Analytical graphics compared to presentation graphics.
Analytical graphics (a, b, and c) are certainly serviceable, but they lack the clarity and appeal of presentation graphics (d, e, and f). Compare the line graphs (a and d), bar graphs (b and e), and pie charts (c and f).

Analytical Graphics

Analytical graphics programs are designed to help users analyze and understand specific data. Sometimes called analysis-oriented graphics programs, these programs use already-entered spreadsheet or database data to construct and view line, bar, and pie chart graphs (Figure 13-9a–c).

Although analytical graphics programs do a good job of producing simple graphs, these programs are too limited and inflexible for a user who needs to prepare elaborate presentations. Analytical graphics programs, for example, let you choose from only a small number of graph types, and the formatting features—graph size, color, and lettering—are limited. These restrictions may be of little concern to some users, but those who require sophisticated graphics will want to consider presentation graphics.

Presentation Graphics

Presentation graphics programs are also called **business-quality graphics.** These programs let you produce charts, graphs, and other visual aids that look as if they were prepared by a professional graphic artist (Figure 13-9d–f). However, you can control the appearance of the product when you create it yourself, and you can produce graphics faster and make last-minute changes if necessary.

Most presentation graphics programs help you do three kinds of tasks:

1. Edit and enhance charts, such as analytical graphs, created by other programs.

DISCUSSION QUESTION

What are the three kinds of tasks performed with presentation graphics?

▶

Figure 13-10 Enhancing graphics with symbols.
Presentation graphics programs provide a library of symbols, from which users can choose. As shown here, such symbols can add appeal to columns of numbers.

TRANSPARENCY ACETATE # 91

Figure 13-10

Economic Growth

	East	Central	West
Government	6%	3%	23%
Manufacturing	29%	-11%	23%
Construction	27%	24%	28%
Mining	9%	16%	48%
Services	40%	42%	18%
Agriculture	15%	27%	4%

Made with 35mm Express software/MAGICorp Network

2. Create charts, diagrams, drawings, and text slides from scratch.
3. Use a library of symbols, drawings, and pictures called clip art (Figure 13-10) that comes with the graphics program. Because the computer produces the "drawings" and manipulates them, even a nonartist can create professional-looking illustrations.

Presentation graphics can increase the impact of your message. They can make the information you are presenting visually appealing, meaningful, and comprehensible. Studies show that high-quality graphics increase both the amount that a listener learns in a presentation and the length of time that the listener retains the information. Also, an audience perceives you as more professional and knowledgeable when your presentation includes overhead graphics or slides. Although graphics hardware requirements vary, be aware that the requirements of presentation graphics include a high-resolution color monitor, possibly a color printer, and some method of transferring your computer-produced results to film.

 Some Graphics Terminology

To use a graphics program successfully, you should know some basic concepts and design principles. Let us begin by exploring the types of graphs you can create.

Line Graphs

One of the most useful ways of showing trends or cycles over a period of time is to use a **line graph.** For example, the graph in Figure 13-11 shows company costs for utilities, supplies, and travel during a five-month period. Line graphs are appropriate when there are many values or complex data. In the business section of a newspaper, line graphs are used to show complex trends in gross national product, stock prices, or employment changes over a period of time. Also, corporate profits and losses are often illustrated by line graphs.

TEST BANK

Mult. Choice 14-18, 20
T/F 24, 32-33
Matching 43-44, 47
Fill In 67-70

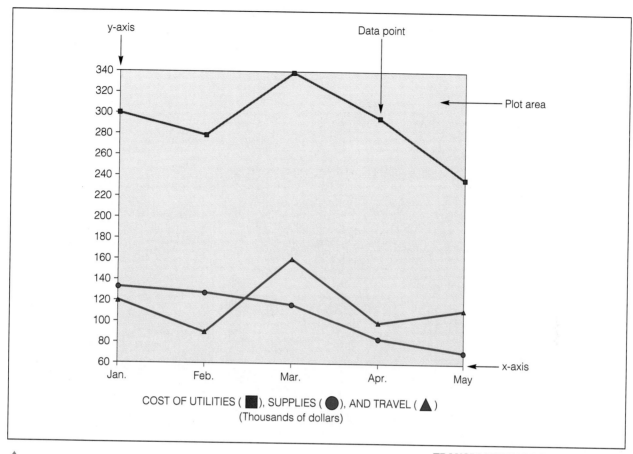

Figure 13-11   A line graph.
Line graphs are useful for showing trends over a period of time. In many analytical programs different symbols are used to show the different types of data being plotted.

Notice the two solid lines in Figure 13-11—one that runs vertically on the left and one that runs horizontally across the bottom. Each line is called an **axis.** (The plural of *axis* is *axes.*) The horizontal line, called the **x-axis,** often represents units of time, such as days, months, or years; it can also represent characteristics, such as model number, brand name, or country. The vertical line, called the **y-axis,** usually shows measured values or amounts, such as dollars, staffing levels, units sold, and so on. The area above and to the right of the axes is called the **plot area**—the space in which the graph is plotted, or drawn.

Graphics programs automatically scale (arrange the units or numbers on) the x-axis and y-axis so the graph of your data is nicely proportioned and easy to read. When you become proficient with a graphics program, you can select your own scaling for the x- and y-axes.

Each dot or symbol on a line graph represents a single numeric quantity called a **data point.** You must specify the data to be plotted on the graph; many graphs are produced from the data stored in the rows and columns of spreadsheet files. This data is usually referred to as the set of *values.* The items that the data points describe are called **variables.** For example, in Figure 13-11 the variable Utilities includes the values 300,

Personal Computers In Action

Presentation Graphics Everywhere

Why are people taking the trouble to get information all gussied up with fancy graphics when the unembellished numbers would be quite acceptable? Graphics are worth the trouble because they can clarify a concept and help the viewer get to the crux of the matter more quickly. Furthermore, studies show that graphics—especially color graphics—increase persuasiveness by as much as 50 percent.

As you can see from these representative samples, colorful graphics can be given a three-dimensional look and can be enhanced with drawings of related objects, such as planes and bottles.

280, 340, 300, and 240; the top line in the plot area shows how these values are graphed.

To make the graph easier to read and understand, **labels** are used to identify the categories along the x-axis and the units along the y-axis. **Titles** summarize the information in the graph and are used to increase comprehension.

Bar Graphs

DISCUSSION QUESTION

What types of data are typically represented by bar graphs?

Bar graphs are used for graphing the same kinds of data that line graphs represent. They are often used to illustrate multiple comparisons, such as sales, expenses, and production activities. Notice in Figure 13-12 that **bar graphs** shade a rectangular area up to the height of the point being plotted, creating a bar. These graphs can be striking and informative when they are simple. Bar graphs are useful for presentations because the comparisons are easy to absorb. However, if there is a lot of data for each of several variables the bars on the graph become narrow and crowded, making a confusing and busy graph. In such a case a line graph may be preferable.

In Figure 13-12 there are three different types of bar graphs. The first is a **single-range bar graph,** in which only one variable is involved; in this example the single variable is monthly expenses. The second type of

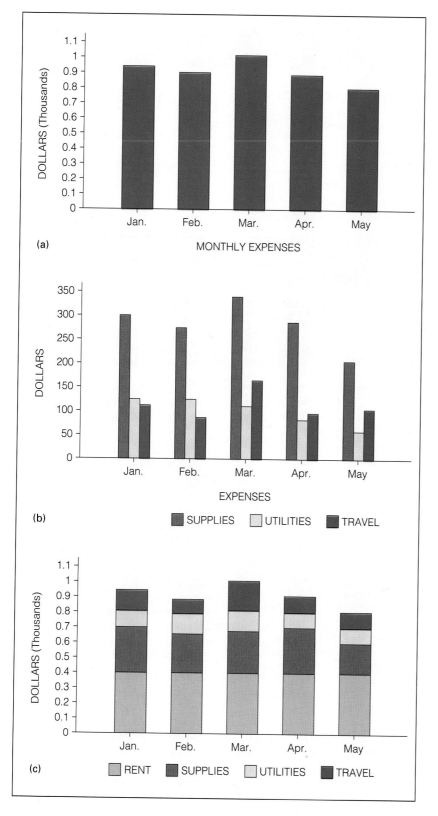

(a)

MONTHLY EXPENSES

(b)

EXPENSES

■ SUPPLIES □ UTILITIES ■ TRAVEL

(c)

■ RENT ■ SUPPLIES □ UTILITIES ■ TRAVEL

Figure 13-12 Types of bar graphs.
(a) A single-range bar graph shows only one variable—in this case, monthly expenses. Multiple-range bar graphs show several variables. The other two graphs in this figure show the two basic types of multiple-range bar graph: (b) A clustered-bar graph shows several variables. (c) A stacked-bar graph shows the different variables stacked on top of one another.

TRANSPARENCY ACETATE # 93

Figure 13-12

MACINTOSH

Presentation Graphics: Mixing Business with Pleasure

The Macintosh is justly famous for its graphics capabilities. Little wonder, then, that the Mac has become the machine of choice for producing high-quality presentation graphics. If you need to make a presentation, graphics can make the difference between communication and confusion. Presentation software for the Mac goes far beyond the mere dressing up of spreadsheet charts. On the contrary, they are highly integrated systems for organizing a presentation, designing illustrations, editing text and visual images, and producing colorful slides, overhead transparencies, and paper materials.

Here are the basic features of good presentation software for the Macintosh:

- Outlining tools supplied with many packages get you off to a good start, helping you organize—and easily reorganize—your thoughts before you commit them to paper.
- A set of standard templates provides basic layouts that you can copy, modify, and reuse. The templates guide you in using logos, titles, text, and illustrations.
- Easy-to-learn tools allow you to create, edit, and embellish graphics that are based on the data in a spreadsheet.

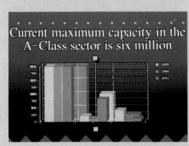

- An overview feature displays 20 or more reduced illustrations on the screen. You can access this feature while working on a specific graphic, and you are free to arrange and rearrange the reduced images in any sequence you like. Most packages also let you create speaker's notes and handouts based on these reduced images.
- Compatibility with a variety of devices allows you a wide range of choices for your final product—from the simplicity of a black-and-white printer to the near-photographic-quality of a high-end laser printer. Service bureaus in most major cities can take the files produced by presen-

tation software and, using machines called film recorders, create dazzlingly clear and colorful 35mm slides.

Also popular are multimedia presentation software packages. With these you don't just create the presentation with the computer, you give the presentation with it. Instead of producing slides and transparencies, these programs provide slide show capabilities, so that images are displayed directly from the computer using a special device placed on an overhead projector. This approach gives you a greater range of expression: you can add sounds, digitized movies, animations, and special effects to wake up your audience.

DISCUSSION QUESTION

What is the purpose of a legend?

bar graph is a multiple-range bar graph called a **clustered-bar graph.** In this graph, data values for three different variables—supplies, utilities, and travel—are plotted next to each other along the x-axis. Since clustered-bar graphs contain so much information, it is important to label each cluster clearly. You can also create a **legend,** or list, that explains different colors, shadings, or symbols in the graph. A legend is used at the bottom of Figures 13-12b and c. The third type of bar graph, the **stacked-bar graph,** is also a multiple-range bar graph. In this graph,

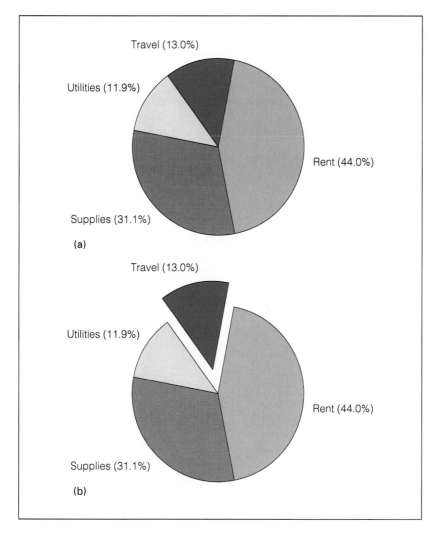

(a)

(b)

◄

Figure 13-13   Types of pie charts.
Pie charts are used to show how various
values make up a whole. (a) A regular pie
chart. (b) An exploded pie chart.

TRANSPARENCY ACETATE # 94

Figure 13-13

however, the different variables are stacked on top of one another. All the data common to a given row or column appear in one bar.

Pie Charts

Representing just a single value for each variable, a **pie chart** shows how various values make up a whole. These charts really look like pies; the whole amount is represented by a circle, and each wedge of the pie—a portion of the whole—represents a value. Figure 13-13a shows a pie chart.

Pie charts can show only the data for one time period, such as a single month, as shown in Figure 13-13. However, of all the graphics, the pie chart does the best job of showing the proportion of all expenses (the whole pie) that goes for rent, supplies, and so forth during that one month. Notice that pie charts often have the written percentage shown by each separate wedge of the pie. It is best to keep pie charts simple; if the pie contains more than eight wedges, you might consider using a bar graph or line graph instead.

Figure 13-13b shows one of the wedges pulled slightly away from the pie, for emphasis. This type of pie chart is called an **exploded pie chart.**

DISCUSSION QUESTION

What type of data does a pie chart
typically represent?

This technique loses its effectiveness if more than one or two slices are separated. Not all graphics programs have the ability to produce an exploded pie chart.

Of the three applications chapters, the first, word processing and desktop publishing, dealt with communicating with words. This chapter has addressed analyzing and communicating with numbers. The upcoming chapter on databases takes a different approach, offering a way for users to keep and retrieve data conveniently.

Chapter **Review**

Summary and Key Terms

- Forms that are used to organize business data into rows and columns are called **spreadsheets.** An **electronic spreadsheet,** or **worksheet,** is a computerized version of a manual spreadsheet.
- The greatest labor-saving aspect of the electronic spreadsheet is that, when one value or calculation on a spreadsheet is changed, all dependent values on the spreadsheet are **automatically recalculated** to reflect the change.
- **"What-if" analysis** is the process of changing one or more spreadsheet values and observing the resulting calculated effect.
- The intersection of a row and column forms a **cell.** The letter and number of the intersecting column and row is the **cell address.**
- The **active cell,** or **current cell,** is the cell in which you may type data.
- Each cell can contain one of three types of information: A **label** provides descriptive information about entries in the spreadsheet; a **value** is an actual number entered into a cell; and a **formula** is an instruction to the program to perform a calculation. A **function** is like a preprogrammed formula. Sometimes you must specify a **range** of cells to build a formula or perform a function.
- To create a spreadsheet you enter labels, values, formulas, and functions into the cells. Formulas and functions do not appear in the cells; instead, the cell shows the result of the formula or function. The result is called the **displayed value** of the cell. The formula or function is the **content** of the cell.
- Most spreadsheet software packages offer a variety of features that enhance the basic spreadsheet, including formatting, printing, and graphics capabilities.
- **Business graphics** represent business data in a visual, easily understood format.
- **Analytical graphics** programs help users analyze and understand specific data by presenting data in visual form. **Presentation graphics** programs, or **business-quality graphics** programs, produce sophisticated graphics. Presentation graphics programs also contain a library of symbols and drawings called clip art.
- A **line graph,** which uses a line to represent data, is useful for showing trends over time. A reference line on a line graph is an **axis.** The horizontal line is called the **x-axis,** and the vertical line is called the **y-axis.** The area above the x-axis and to the right of the y-axis is the **plot area.** Each dot or symbol on a line graph is a **data point.** Each data point represents a value. The items that the data points describe are called **variables.**
- **Bar graphs** show data comparisons by the lengths or heights of bars. In a **single-range bar graph,** only one variable is involved. A **clustered-bar graph** shows more than one variable. A **stacked-bar graph** also shows multiple variables, but the bars are stacked on top of one another. You can create a **legend** to explain the colors or symbols on a complex graph. **Labels** identify the categories along the x-axis and the units along the y-axis. **Titles** summarize the information in the graph.
- A **pie chart** represents a single value for each variable. A wedge of an **exploded pie chart** is pulled slightly away from the pie for emphasis.

KEY TERMS

active cell

analytical graphics

axis

bar graph

business graphics

business-quality graphics

cell

cell address

clustered-bar graph

content

current cell

data point

displayed value

electronic spreadsheet

exploded pie chart

formula

function

label

legend

line graph

pie chart

plot area

presentation graphics

range

single-range bar graph

spreadsheet

stacked-bar graph

title

value

variable

"What-if" analysis

worksheet

x-axis

y-axis

Student Personal Study Guide

True/False

T F   1. A manual spreadsheet automatically recalculates totals when changes are made.
T F   2. Analytical graphics let you construct line graphs, bar graphs, and pie charts.
T F   3. Presentation graphics appear professionally produced.
T F   4. The vertical axis is the x-axis.
T F   5. Analytical graphics use a library of symbols to enhance output.
T F   6. The active spreadsheet cell is also called the current cell.
T F   7. Labels identify categories along graph axes.
T F   8. On an exploded pie chart, one wedge is slightly removed from the pie.
T F   9. "What-if" analysis is related to automatic recalculation.
T F 10. In a spreadsheet, a label cannot be used for calculations.

Multiple Choice

1. The active cell:
   a. current cell
   b. range
   c. formula
   d. cell address
2. A preprogrammed formula:
   a. function
   b. graph
   c. range
   d. cell
3. A chart that represents only one value for each variable:
   a. function
   b. line
   c. pie
   d. bar
4. Business-quality graphics:
   a. stacked bar
   b. legend
   c. analytic
   d. presentation
5. Intersection of a row and column:
   a. active address
   b. formula
   c. cursor
   d. cell
6. The result of a formula in a cell:
   a. label
   b. value
   c. range
   d. displayed value
7. Text information in a cell:
   a. label
   b. value
   c. formula
   d. cell address
8. A dot or symbol on a line graph:
   a. label
   b. data point
   c. variable
   d. axis
9. Summarizes information related to a graph:
   a. plot area
   b. title
   c. label
   d. axis
10. Computer-prepared art:
    a. cell
    b. analytical
    c. clip art
    d. range

Fill-In

1. The three types of information permitted in a spreadsheet cell are: _____ .

2. A bar graph with more than one variable: _____ .

3. Enhanced graphics are called: _____ .

4. In a spreadsheet the calculated result of a formula is called: _____ .

5. The intersection of a row and column on a spreadsheet: _____ .

6. Plain line graphs are an example of what kind of graphics: _____ .

7. The user can see any part of a spreadsheet by using which keys: _____ .

8. Another name for the active cell: _____ .

9. A spreadsheet preprogrammed formula: _____ .

10. A library of computer-ready symbols: _____ .

Answers

True/False: 1. F, 2. T, 3. T, 4. F, 5. F, 6. T, 7. T, 8. T, 9. T, 10. T
Multiple choice: 1. a, 2. a, 3. c, 4. d, 5. d, 6. d, 7. a, 8. b, 9. b, 10. c
Fill-In: 1. labels, numbers, formulas, 2. cluster graph, 3. presentation, 4. displayed value, 5. cell, 6. analytical, 7. cursor-movement keys, 8. current cell, 9. function, 10. clip art

LEARNING OBJECTIVES

- Appreciating the advantages and disadvantages of databases
- Understanding how relational databases are organized
- Understanding in general how to build and change a database

If you try to imagine the perfect job for a movie fanatic, you might come up with the job Sylvia Herrera-Alaniz has. She is the chief executive and sole employee of Starcom Associates, a firm that provides capsule movie descriptions to newspapers, cable television franchises, and video rental shops.

On an average day Sylvia views four or five movies on TV or videotape, often watching two at a time on separate monitors. While she watches, she takes notes and consults a small library of books on domestic and foreign films. To stay current with new releases, she goes to a movie theater once a day. In addition, Sylvia makes it a point to

Database Management

revise her descriptions once a year to keep them fresh.

Sylvia's job keeps her busy doing the thing she loves most. However, the job also includes organizing the thousands of movie descriptions that make up the Starcom Associates product set. Sylvia soon outgrew her original system, a set of shoeboxes with index cards listing movies in alphabetical order. She bought a personal computer with a high-capacity hard disk and set about creating a database.

Consider some of the data items Sylvia has to track for each movie: movie title, year of release, director, principal artists, supporting artists, quality rating, type (drama, western, comedy, and so on) audience rating (G, PG, PG-13, R, X), a one-sentence description, a two-sentence description, and a one-paragraph description.

Entering all the data is just part of the job. Sylvia must also be able to retrieve the data in convenient ways. Sometimes she has requests for all movies in a certain year or for movies featuring a certain star. Her old filing system, by title only, was ill-suited for this type of request and often led to entire days consumed in the search. Finding data quickly in a variety of ways is a key advantage of databases. Sylvia is now able to respond to such requests in a matter of minutes.

Since computers are now so common in the publishing business, Sylvia has begun to sell her customers copies of her entire database on disk. The purchaser can extract movie descriptions from the disk and enter them directly into computer-generated publications. No intermediate paper version is produced in this process, and the publisher saves the cost of rekeying the information.

Database technology has saved Sylvia many hours. She spends that extra time—yes—watching movies.

Systems
Getting Data Together

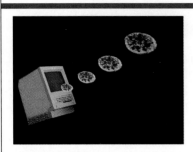

Your Database, My Pizza

You come home after a long day at school or work, tired and hungry. You do not feel like cooking. In some cities you can use your modem-equipped computer for a quick solution. A software package called Delivery Systems lets customers use their home computers to dial up local restaurants and fast-food outlets and make menu choices. The meals are delivered to their homes.

Typically, a customer's call goes to a central phone number that links the customer to a regional order-taking center, where operators route the order to the closest outlet. The only interaction with a human being is when the delivery person comes to the door.

Pizza firms have been leading the charge into computerized home delivery. Domino's, Godfather's, and Pizza Hut have developed large-scale computer systems. Pizza Hut has found that repeat customers order the same pizza 70 percent of the time, so the company keeps a database of customers' previous purchases; this information cuts the normal order-taking time in half. Information in the database is also used to market their products. The database can be interrogated to provide a listing of all customers that have not ordered in the past 60 days. The company then sends them a flyer with an incentive to order.

TEST BANK

Mult. Choice 1, 3
T/F 23, 30-32
Matching 42
Fill In 53, 60

Getting It Together: Database Systems

A **database** is an organized collection of related data. In a loose sense you are using a database when you use a phone book or take papers from a file cabinet. Unfortunately, as the amount of data increases, creating, storing, changing, sorting, and retrieving data become overwhelming tasks.

Answering a Need

Suppose you had a collection of names and addresses, each on a separate index card stored in an index-card file (Figure 14-1). If you had only 25 cards, sorting the cards into alphabetical order or even finding all the people who have the same zip code would be fairly easy. But what if you had 100, or 1000, or 10,000 cards? What if you had several different boxes, one organized by names, one by cities, and one by zip codes? What if different file clerks added more cards each day, not knowing if they were duplicating cards already in the file? And what if another set of clerks were trying to update the data on the cards? As you can see, things might get out of hand. Enter computers and database management software.

A **database management system (DBMS)** is software that helps you organize data in a way that allows fast and easy access to the data. In essence, the program acts as an efficient and elaborate file system. With a database program you can enter, modify, store, and retrieve data in a variety of ways.

Databases Are Different

Before we go on, we should note that database systems are different from word processing or spreadsheet software. Generally, most users have a good understanding of both word processing and spreadsheets. They enter and use the data in the same form as it resides on disk. Data in databases, however, could reside on the disk in ways unknown to a user. In particular, sophisticated database systems, particularly those designed for a mainframe computer environment, are complex, and must be planned and managed by computer professionals. Users of such systems are trained to input data to and retrieve data from the database system, using appropriate software; they can do this successfully without ever having to understand the underlying technology. On the other hand, database software is available for personal computers that a trained user can apply to simple or moderately complex problems. That is, such a user could both set up and use a database on a personal computer.

Advantages and Disadvantages of Databases

Several advantages are generally associated with databases.

■ **Reduced redundancy.** Data carried in separate files, as opposed to a database, tends to repeat some of the same data over and over. A college, for example, needs to have various kinds of information for a student—perhaps financial, academic, and career data. If each of these

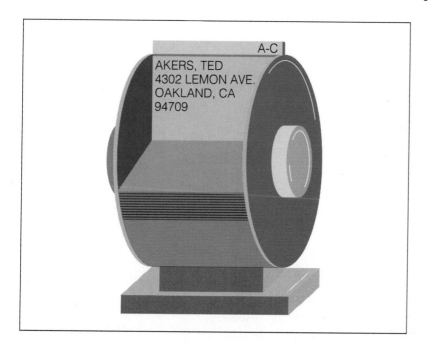

◄

Figure 14-1   An index-card database.
Each card in this index-card file contains one person's name and address. The cards are arranged alphabetically by last name.

TRANSPARENCY ACETATE # 95

Figure 14-1

sets of data is on a separate file, some repetition is inevitable—probably a student's name, address, and social security number or other identification. In a database this information would appear just once.

- **Integrated data.** Rather than being in separate and independent files, data in a database is considered integrated because any item of data can be used to satisfy an inquiry or a report. This advantage is related to the reduced redundancy advantage: Since data can be retrieved from any place in the database, many specific data items need not be repeated.
- **Integrity.** People who maintain any kind of file hope that it has integrity, that is, that the file is accurate and up-to-date. Integrity concerns increase as the sophistication of the data increases. A simple database set up by an individual to keep track of a hobby may not be of great importance, but large databases, especially those involving data about people, must have integrity to keep their value. Reduced redundancy increases the likelihood of data integrity. In the example of a college, the fact that a student's name and address exist for each student in just one place on a database means that these items need to be updated just once, reducing the chance for errors.

Although the advantages far outweigh the disadvantages, databases are not a panacea. As is often the case, the list of disadvantages of databases begins with the expense.

- **Expense.** It can be expensive to set up and maintain a database. If the database is part of a sophisticated operation, probably in a large organization, then employees must be trained to use it properly.
- **Access.** The problem of access refers to people who have improper access to a database. Although keeping data in databases actually reduces snooping by unsophisticated interlopers, databases make data easily available to knowledgeable users, including those who have no right to the information.

Personal Computers
In Action

Plugging in the Public

It is Saturday and you forgot to report that burned-out streetlight during regular working hours. No problem. Just turn to your modem-equipped home computer, and tap into a color screen of icons for city and county government. Dash off a note to the city light department: "The streetlight at 5738 Paisley Dr. N. is out. Can you get it fixed soon?" Click on the Send Mail icon and then on the City Light icon. Done.

Next, you have read that a bill has been introduced in the legislature to expand the use of home incarceration for nonviolent first-time offenders. Again using your computer, you dial up the legislative hotline and have a copy of the bill downloaded to your computer's hard drive for analysis later.

One more matter: You need to pay that parking ticket. Click over to that department and enter your Visa card number.

Finally, you tap into one of the many county databases, this time regarding a business rating system

for local insurance agencies. You read a dozen articles and download three that interest you to your own computer.

Farfetched? Not at all. The technology is available to have a public access system in place today. Local governments are already experimenting with computer systems that give the public two-way communication with just about any government service, department, or agency.

■ **Excess.** Frankly, sometimes organizations carry more data than they should. Consider, for example, a retailer who carries a charge account for you. It is not appropriate for the retailer also to have information about your medical records. We use this ridiculous example to show that it is theoretically possible for a database to carry unsuitable data. Unfortunately, inappropriate data alliances are not always theoretical. There was a time, for instance, when the Internal Revenue Service carried information about 18-year-olds and reported this to the draft board. Today, questionnaires and applications routinely ask questions about age, marital status, and income that have nothing to do with the reason that data is being gathered.

Database Concepts

There are many DBMS programs on the market today. Covering all the operations, features, and functions of each package would be impossible. In this chapter we will look at database management in a generic way. The features we will discuss are common to most database software packages.

Database Models

The way a database organizes data depends on the type, or **model,** of the database. There are three main database models: hierarchical, network, and relational. Each type structures, organizes, and uses data differently. Hierarchical and network databases are usually used with mainframes and minicomputers, so we will not discuss them here. However, relational databases are used with personal computers as well as mainframes.

A **relational database** organizes data in a table format consisting of related rows and columns. Figure 14-2a shows an address list; in Figure 14-2b, this data is laid out as a table.

Fields, Records, and Files

Notice in Figure 14-2b that each box in the table contains a single piece of data, known as a **data item,** such as the name of one city. Each column of the table represents a **field,** which is a type of data item. The specific data items in a field may vary, but each field contains the same

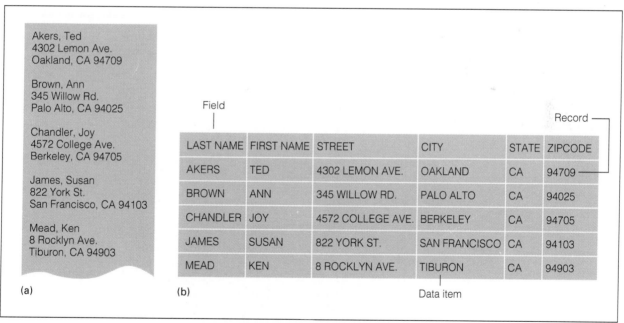

Figure 14-2   A relational database.
In this example the address list in (a) is organized as a relational database in (b). Note that the data is laid out in rows and columns; each field is equivalent to a column, and each record is equivalent to a row.

type of data item—for example, first names or zip codes. The full set of data in any given row is called a **record.** Each record has a fixed number of fields. The fields in a particular record contain related data—for example, the name and address of a person. A collection of related records make up a **file.** In a relational database a file is also called a **relation.** There can be a variable number of records in a given relation; Figure 14-2b shows five records—one for each person. There can also be more than one file in a database.

Database Power

Now that you know what *field*, *file*, and *relation* mean, you are ready to glimpse the real power of databases. The power is in the connection: A relational system can relate data in one file to data in another file, allowing a user to tie together data from several files. To understand how this works, consider the database called MOORE that uses a set of four related files—four relations—to comprise one database. These four files have some fields in common (Figure 14-3). The files are part of a database for Moore Contax, Inc., a company that warehouses computer equipment and supplies. Moore needs to keep track of its sales representatives, customers, orders, and inventory.

Now look at a detailed version of these relations (Figure 14-4). The SALES REPRESENTATIVE FILE has six fields: REP-ID (representative identification), LNAME (last name), FNAME (first name), REGION (geographic area), HDATE (hire date), and PHONE. Similarly, CUSTOMER FILE has four fields, ORDER FILE has four fields,

▶

Figure 14-3 Conceptual diagram of the files in the Moore database.
The files are SALES REP, CUSTOMER, ORDER, and INVENTORY. Note the common fields.

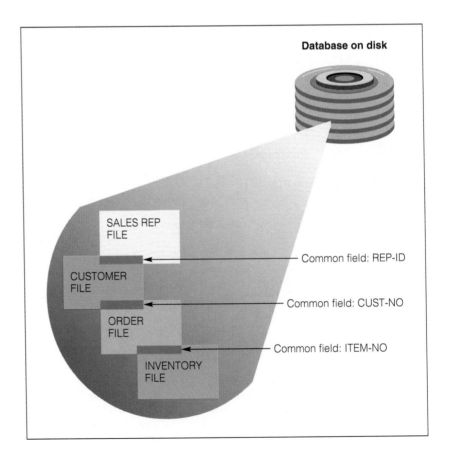

and INVENTORY FILE has three fields (QOH means quantity on hand). The interesting point about these relations is that they are connected. Both the SALES REPRESENTATIVE FILE and the CUSTOMER FILE have a REP-ID field. The CUSTOMER FILE and the ORDER FILE are connected by the field CUST-NO. The ORDER FILE and the INVENTORY FILE are connected by the field ITEM-NO. These sample files are, of course, rather primitive, but they can be useful to illustrate the point of connectivity.

These connections allow users to extract information across several relations, something that would not be possible if each relation was an independent file instead of a file within a database. Suppose, for example, that Anthony Harl, an employee for Moore Contax, receives a phone call inquiring about an order for Computer City. In fact, the folks at Computer City are concerned because a promised order is overdue and they have not heard from their sales representative. Anthony has, of course, a

SALES REPRESENTATIVE FILE

REP-ID	LNAME	FNAME	REGION	HDATE	PHONE
114	Abele	Lori	SW	10-15-86	(602) 624-9384
159	Higgins	Heatheryn	SE	12-16-91	(404) 524-8472
230	Sullivan	Pat	SE	2-21-88	(305) 734-2987
386	Speed	Kristen	MW	6-14-90	(708) 823-8222
349	Demaree	Donn	NW	7-10-93	(206) 634-1955

CUSTOMER FILE

CUST-NO	CNAME	CITY	REP-ID
2934	Ballard Computer	Seattle	349
3007	Computer City	Miami	230
4987	Laser Systems	Atlanta	159
8987	Varner User Systems	Naperville	386
9185	CGI Computers	Spokane	349
9876	Computing Solutions	Tucson	114

ORDER FILE

CUST-NO	DATE	ITEM-NO	QTY
3007	8-12-95	7639	11
4987	8-12-95	6720	15
8987	8-13-95	2378	14
9185	8-10-95	1628	10
9876	8-14-95	6720	20

INVENTORY FILE

ITEM-NO	DESCR	QOH
1628	Hand scanner	191
2378	Modem	453
3457	Hard drive	294
5647	Printer pack	676
6720	3 1/2" disk holder	982
6599	CD-ROM drive	817
7639	Sound card	0
8870	Mouse	296
9037	Monitor	152

Figure 14-4 Records in the four files in the Moore database.
Observe that there are common fields among the files, enabling the files to reference one another.

TRANSPARENCY ACETATE # 98

Figure 14-4

MACINTOSH

HyperCard: Linking Information Electronically

When Apple Computer introduced its HyperCard program for the Macintosh in 1987, a lot of people thought it was just a database manager with a big ego. But HyperCard, distributed free with every Mac sold, is designed to facilitate something beyond databasing. HyperCard is what is sometimes referred to as a *hypertext* program—one geared toward linking information together from a variety of sources.

HyperCard *is* like a database program in many respects. The files you manage with it are called stacks, each of which is a collection of cards, which contain information organized into fields. The intended analogy is a stack of index cards. So cards are like database records, and stacks are like database files. But HyperCard is more flexible than that. Cards can be created with an eye toward appearance as much as functionality, and graphics tools are provided to make a more attractive and user-friendly

stack. Another important option for cards is the use of buttons, which can be clicked on with the pointer in the traditional Macintosh style, and which may have any of a number of effects, depending on the stack you're working in and the way the button has been designed.

But what really distinguishes HyperCard from traditional database managers is its ability to create links between fields, cards, stacks, and even files created by other applications. So you can click on a button in one card to go to a related card, even if the cards are in different stacks. Buttons can also be designed to

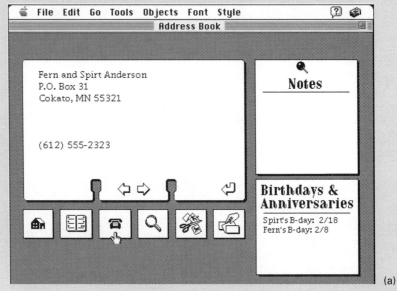

(a)

computer on his desk. Keep in mind that Anthony need not be concerned with how the relations are set up and may not even know what a relation is. From his training, however, he has a pretty good idea what information he can get from the database system.

Anthony can, by using commands appropriate to his database software, ask a question that is the equivalent of this: What is the status of Computer City's order? The database software would look to the CUSTOMER FILE (follow along in Figure 14-4), find CUST-NO 3007 for Computer City, and then go to the ORDER FILE and look up the order lines for CUST-NO 3007. From the 3007 line in the ORDER FILE, the software could pick up ITEM-NO data 7639; using that data and now moving to the INVENTORY FILE, it can be seen that item 7639, sound cards, is out of stock. All this scrambling around is **transparent** to the user; that is, the user is not aware of the specific searches through the files but is merely given a response to the request. Anthony gets a message back on his screen with the net result: On Computer City's order, item 7639, sound cards, is out of stock. Anthony can convey this information to the customer waiting on the line.

access information on other cards, or information within, say, a word-processed document. And like any good database program, HyperCard can sort cards, search for cards or specific field contents, integrate information from several cards into a report, and so forth.

The version of HyperCard that is bundled free with a new Macintosh is designed to give you just an idea of its power. If you choose, you can purchase the fully operative version, which comes with a variety of prefabricated stacks as well as extensive manuals to help you get the most out of the program. And there is a lot to be gotten! You can, if you want, work with HyperCard on a simple *Browsing* level, where your power to change the stack is limited and the ease of using it is enhanced. Deeper than that is the *Authoring* level, where you can create your own stacks, and establish your own buttons and links; you can also modify the prefabricated stacks to better suit your taste. The most sophisticated user level in HyperCard is the *Scripting* level, where you can actually write programs in a language called HyperTalk. Each program, or script, can be associated with a button, so that when the button is clicked, the steps in the program are executed. This gives you the most power in creating stacks; in fact, it becomes more like creating your own software. HyperTalk, is friendlier and more readable than traditional programming languages, and it can be learned and applied in small steps. At the same time, it gives you a high degree of control over the behavior of your stacks.

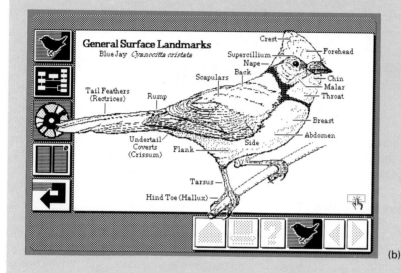

a) Using either a prefabricated stack or one that you create, you can maintain an electronic Rolodex of names and addresses. The buttons beneath the address card allow sorting and searching the stack, as well as switching to related stacks.
b) This card is part of a tailor-made Hyper-Card stack that teaches bird anatomy. Pointing to any part of the the bird's anatomy and clicking the mouse brings up another card with detailed information about that part of the bird.

Furthermore, Anthony can, again by using commands appropriate to his database software, ask about Computer City's sales representative. The database software, looking in the CUSTOMER FILE, can see that Computer City's REP-ID is 230. Moving now to the SALES REPRESENTATIVE FILE, REP-ID 230 is Pat Sullivan, whose phone number is (305) 734-2987. When a message to this effect comes back on the screen, Anthony can pass this information along to the customer on the phone line.

In the real world, company service to customers would probably be more sophisticated than this, but this simple example demonstrates how database files can be connected.

 # A Problem Fit for a Database

In the next sections we will focus on just one database file and see, generally, how data can be planned and entered. MaryLynne Wrye is a convention planner. She lives in Seattle and contracts with various organiza-

LECTURE HINT

Stephen O, a South Korean native, has been rejected by credit card companies twice because his name is too short. It appears the bank computers were not able to process a single-letter last name. After several such problems, Mr. O decided to change his last name to "Oh."

TEST BANK

Mult. Choice 7-8, 9-14, 17, 20
T/F 26-28, 36, 38, 39-40
Matching 41, 43, 46-48
Fill In 54, 59, 63-65, 66-68, 70

DISCUSSION QUESTION

What is the structure of a database?

LECTURE ACTIVITY

Demonstrate in class how to define the structure of a database file, how to enter data into it, how to retrieve information from it through various kinds of queries, how to save it, and how to print parts of it.

TRANSPARENCY ACETATE # 99

Figure 14-5

tions who plan to hold conventions in that city. MaryLynne and her staff of five coordinate every physical aspect of the convention, including transportation, housing, catering, meeting rooms, services, tours, and entertainment.

MaryLynne began moving her files to a computer three years ago. She has found database software useful because of its ability to cross reference several files and, in particular, to answer inquiries about the data. MaryLynne thinks the time is ripe to set up a database file for the tours she offers. She has noticed that clients ask many questions about the tours available, including times, costs, and whether or not food is included. Also, clients want to know if much walking is included on the tour and whether or not there are stairs.

In answer to these kinds of questions, MaryLynne or one of her staff now has to shuffle through a thick folder of brochures and price lists. MaryLynne knows that she will be able to respond more quickly to client inquiries if this information is in her database file.

Creating and Using a Database

There are two steps to creating a database file: (1) designing the structure of the file and (2) entering the data into the file. Look ahead to Figure 14-8 if you want to see what MaryLynne's final database will look like.

File Structure

MaryLynne begins by sketching on paper the **structure** of what will be called the TOUR database—what kind of data she wants in each row and column (Figure 14-5). To create the file structure, she must choose meaningful fields. The fields she chooses should be based on the data she will want to retrieve from the database. After MaryLynne loads the data-

Figure 14-5   Sketch of the structure of the TOUR database.

COMPUTING TRENDS

What About Those 500 Channels?

Entertainment moguls have been talking for some time about the 500 television channels expected sometime in the near future. People who now use their remote control units to channel surf over only a few dozen stations will be busy indeed. There has been endless speculation about just what topics might be featured on all those new channels. A channel dedicated to skiing? Kennedy movies? Artichoke recipes? It is hard to imagine all the possibilities, but it is known that some of those channels will be pay-per-view.

Pay-per-view offers unique challenges. To begin with, it is not much of a bargain. In fact, pay-per-view has been rated as the worst consumer value for dollars spent, just ahead of hospital charges and credit card fees. Another problem is that pay-per-view is an impulse purchase. Viewers decide at the last minute to see the Olympics or WrestleMania or a movie; they must be serviced quickly.

To solve both the cost and speed problems, communications specialists have turned to database technology.

The solution is a memory-resident database of all pay-per-view channel offerings. That is, unlike the usual disk-based database, this database will sit right in the computer's

memory, for quick and easy access. This system is especially lean and fast, partly because there is no wait for disk platters to spin and data to be loaded into memory.

Perhaps customers can anticipate lower costs and faster service. Perhaps.

---

base program and tells the software that she wants to create a file structure, the program will ask for several types of information. Let us take a look at each type.

Field Names

Names of the types of data you want to use are called **field names.** Each field must have a unique name. MaryLynne plans to use these field names for her TOUR database: TOUR-ID (an identifying number for the tour), DESCR (description of the tour), COST (cost of the tour), HOURS (number of hours the tour takes), FOOD (a yes or no on whether food is included in the tour), WALK (yes or no regarding much walking on the tour), and STAIRS (yes or no on whether there are stairs on the tour).

Field Types

There are four commonly used types of fields: character fields, numeric fields, date fields, and logical fields. **Character fields** contain descriptive

DISCUSSION QUESTION

Why must field names be unique?

Figure 14-6 File structure.
These field entries establish the structure of the tour database. Keep in mind that the structure only describes what kind of data will be entered into the database; no actual data has been entered yet.

TRANSPARENCY ACETATE # 100

Figure 14-6

Num	Field Name	Field Type	Width	Dec
1	TOUR-ID	C	2	
2	DESCR	C	20	
3	COST	N	6	2
4	HOURS	N	4	1
5	FOOD	L	1	
6	WALK	L	1	
7	STAIRS	L	1	

DISCUSSION QUESTION

Describe the four commonly used types of fields.

LECTURE HINT

The Wide Area Information Servers (WAIS, pronounced "ways") on Internet enables Internet users to search for information in databases located on computers around the world. Approximately 400 databases on server computers can be searched.

LECTURE ACTIVITY

If the library at your school uses a computerized library catalog, you can demonstrate the system's searching capabilities to your students.

data, such as names, addresses, and telephone numbers. **Numeric fields** contain numbers used for calculations, such as rate of pay. When you enter a numeric field, you must specify the number of decimal places you wish to use. MaryLynne will use two decimal places for COST and one decimal place for HOURS (Figure 14-6). **Date fields** are usually limited to eight characters, including the slashes used to separate the month, day, and year. **Logical fields** accept only single characters. Logical fields are used to keep track of true or false conditions. For example, here, MaryLynne can keep track of which tours include food by making FOOD a logical field; when data for that field is entered, she would enter Y for *yes* or N for *no* (Figure 14-6).

Field Widths

The **field width** determines the maximum number of characters or digits to be contained in the field, including decimal points.

MaryLynne keys in one line for each field in her database (Figure 14-6). With an appropriate command she then signals the database software that she is done defining the structure and names the file TOUR.

Entering the Data

When it is time to key in the data for the records in the file, the screen presents the fields vertically to provide an input form (Figure 14-7). MaryLynne keys the appropriate data next to each field name—14 for TOUR-ID, San Juan Islands for DESCR, and so on. If the data item is shorter than the field length, she presses Enter to move to the next field. However, if the width of the entry is exactly the size of the field, the program automatically advances to the next field. If MaryLynne makes a mistake while she is typing, she can use the Backspace key to make corrections.

After MaryLynne has filled in all the data for the first record, the database program automatically displays another blank input form, so she can enter the data items for the fields in the second record. She will continue this pattern for each of the other records. Eventually, she will signal the database software that she has entered all the records.

If MaryLynne wants to check the enterred records, a database command will let her list the records horizontally on the screen (Figure 14-8).

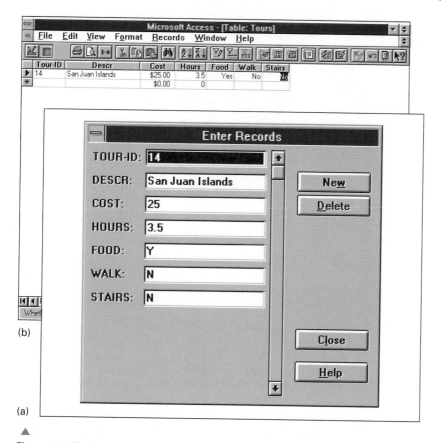

Figure 14-7 The first record for the TOUR database.
(a) The field names are on the left. The data item for each field is keyed in next to the field name. This process is repeated for each record. (b) The completed record as listed across the screen.

Other Options

Since we are not working with a specific software package, it is not practical to demonstrate options that are available to modify the database. The following are descriptions of operations that would be available with any database software package.

■ **List the records.** MaryLynne could ask for a list of all existing records, either displayed on the screen or printed out on paper. If she is displaying the records on screen, the software displays only as many records as will fit on the screen. Scrolling up or down displays additional records. If there were a large number of fields in a record, MaryLynne could **pan**—move horizontally across the screen—to the left or right. Panning is a horizontal version of scrolling.

■ **List specific fields.** In addition to printing all records, MaryLynne has the option of printing just certain fields of each record. Perhaps, to satisfy a customer request, she could print only the DESCR and COST fields for each record. The software also offers the option of printing the fields in any order requested, not just the order in which they appear in the record. For example, MaryLynne could request a list of these fields in this order: DESCR, TOUR-ID, WALK, and HOURS.

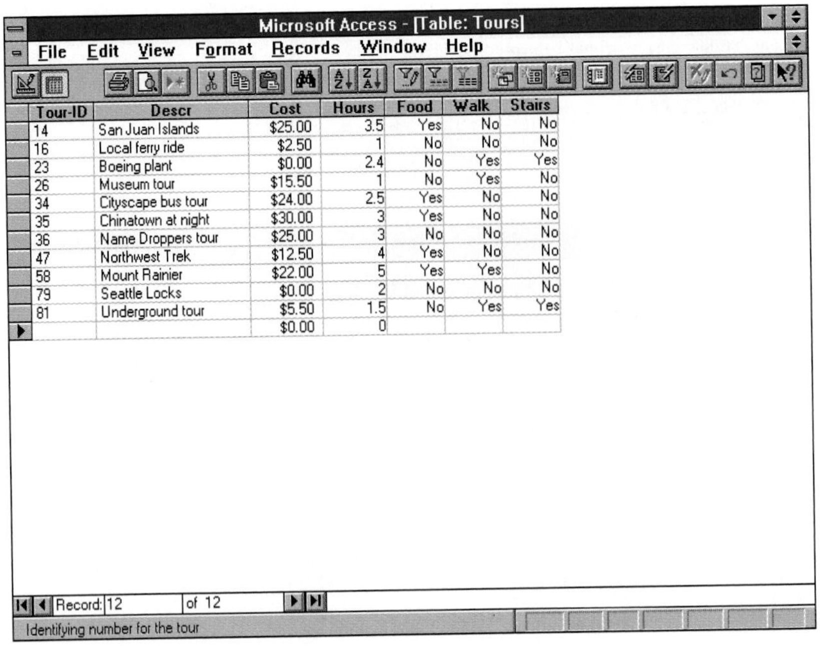

Tour-ID	Descr	Cost	Hours	Food	Walk	Stairs
14	San Juan Islands	$25.00	3.5	Yes	No	No
16	Local ferry ride	$2.50	1	No	No	No
23	Boeing plant	$0.00	2.4	No	Yes	Yes
26	Museum tour	$15.50	1	No	Yes	No
34	Cityscape bus tour	$24.00	2.5	Yes	No	No
35	Chinatown at night	$30.00	3	Yes	No	No
36	Name Droppers tour	$25.00	3	No	No	No
47	Northwest Trek	$12.50	4	Yes	No	No
58	Mount Rainier	$22.00	5	Yes	Yes	No
79	Seattle Locks	$0.00	2	No	No	No
81	Underground tour	$5.50	1.5	No	Yes	Yes
		$0.00	0			

Figure 14-8 The complete set of records for the TOUR database.

TRANSPARENCY ACETATE # 102

Figure 14-8

LECTURE HINT

As databases increase in size, the storage capabilities of personal computers may not be sufficient to hold all of the data. One solution is to store such databases on CD-ROM disks.

LECTURE HINT

In the past large businesses and corporations required mainframe computers to process their data. Now, thanks to networks and the improved processing capabilities of smaller computers, many companies are switching from centralized to distributed databases.

- **Query.** MaryLynne can make a query—ask a question—about the records in the file. She will need to use a **relational operator** when entering instructions that involve making comparisons. Table 14-1 shows the relational operators that are commonly used. These operators are particularly useful when you want to locate specific data items. Suppose, for example, that, based on a client request, MaryLynne wants to find all the tours that cost less than $15. She could issue a query to the database software to find records that meet this requirement by using a command that includes the stipulation COST < 15. The software would respond with a list of all records that meet the requirement, in this case a local ferry ride, the Boeing plant, Northwest Trek, the Seattle Locks, and the underground tour.
- **Add new records.** MaryLynne can add records for new tours at any time.
- **Modify existing records.** MaryLynne may need to change an existing record. In the TOUR file, it would not be uncommon, for example, for the price of a tour to change.

Table 14-1 Relational Operators

Command	Explanation
<	Less than
>	Greater than
=	Equal to
<=	Less than or equal to
>=	Greater than or equal to
<>	Not equal to

■ **Delete records.** Sometimes a record must be removed—deleted—from a database file. In the TOUR file, perhaps a tour no longer exists or MaryLynne, for whatever reason, no longer wants to promote the tour. Database software provides this option.

There are many database options beyond the basic features this chapter discussed. Those options are beyond the scope of this book, but we encourage you to learn all the bells and whistles of whatever database management package you may use in the future. The payoff in timesaving convenience will make your efforts worthwhile.

CLASS PROJECT

Divide the class into groups and have each group research some of the more popular database management software packages at local computer stores; e.g., dBASE, Paradox, Access, and R:Base. The students should compare the database programs in terms of cost, hardware requirement, ease of use, and capabilities.

Chapter **Review**

Summary and Key Terms

- A **database** is an organized collection of related files. A **database management system** (**DBMS**) is software that creates, manages, protects, and provides access to a database.
- Data in databases may reside on the disk in ways unknown to a user. Sophisticated database systems must be planned and managed by computer professionals. Users of such systems are trained to input data to and retrieve data from the database system.
- Advantages of databases are **reduced redundancy, integrated data,** and **integrity.** Potential disadvantages of databases are **expense,** improper **access,** and **excess** of data.
- A database can store data relationships so that files can be integrated. The way the database organizes data depends on the type, or **model,** of database. There are three main database models—hierarchical, network, and relational.
- A **relational database** organizes data in a table format consisting of related rows and columns. Each location in the table contains a single piece of data, known as a **data item.** Each column of the table represents a **field,** which consists of data items. The full set of data in any given row is called a **record.** Related records make up a **file.** In a relational database a file is also called a **relation.**
- Computer activities are considered **transparent** if a user is unaware of them as they are taking place.
- The power of databases is in the connection: a relational system can relate data in one file to data in another file, allowing a user to tie together data from several files.
- There are two steps to creating a file: (1) designing the **structure** of the file and (2) entering the data.
- When a file structure is defined, many database programs require the user to identify the **field types, field names,** and **field widths.** There are four commonly used types of fields: **character fields, numeric fields, date fields,** and **logical fields.** The field width determines the maximum number of letters, digits, or symbols to be contained in the field.
- Once a file structure is defined, it is presented as an input form so that data for each record may be entered.
- Other options that are available with database software allow you to list the records, list specific fields, query, add new records, modify existing records, and delete records.
- At times you may have to **pan**—move sideways across the screen—to view all the fields in a database record.
- A **relational operator** is needed when making comparisons or when entering instructions. Table 14-1 shows the relational operators.

Student Personal Study Guide

True/False

T F   1. A database is an organized collection of related files.
T F   2. The power of a relational database is related to connections among files.
T F   3. There are two commonly used types of fields: character and index.
T F   4. An advantage of databases is that redundancy is reduced.

T F   5. Database records may be entered and modified but not deleted.

T F   6. The pan operation moves sideways across the screen so all fields in a database can be viewed.

T F   7. A record is made up of fields.

T F   8. A sideways move on the screen is called scrolling.

T F   9. The database model most commonly used on personal computers is the hierarchical model.

T F   10. A relational operator—such as =, <, or >—is needed to locate specific data items.

Fill-In

1. The abbreviation for a database management system is: _____ .

2. Advantages of databases : _____ .

3. Disadvantages of databases: _____ .

4. Symbols such as =, >, and < are called: _____ .

5. The way a database organizes data: _____ .

6. In a relational database, another name for a file: _____ .

7. To move sideways across the screen: _____ .

8. The four most common field types: _____ .

9. The rows and columns constitute the: _____ .

10. The database model usually used on personal computers: _____ .

Answers

True/False: 1. T, 2. T, 3. F, 4. T, 5. F, 6. T, 7. T, 8. F, 9. F, 10. T

Fill-In: 1. DBMS, 2. reduced redundancy, integrated data, integrity, 3. expense, access, excess, 4. relational operators, 5. model, 6. relation, 7. pan, 8. character, numeric, date, logical, 9. file structure, 10. relational

Learning Objectives

- Understanding the story of how computer technology unfolded with particular emphasis on the "generations."
- Understanding how people and events affected the development of computers.
- Familiarity with the story of personal computer development.
- Acquaintance with the development of software.

TEST BANK

Mult. Choice 9, 39

T/F 74

Matching I 97

Fill In 115, 141

Although the story of computers has diverse roots, the most fascinating part—the history of personal computers—is quite recent. The beginning of this history turns on the personality of Ed Roberts, whose foundering company took a surprising turn. Ed had already been burned once when he had borrowed heavily to produce microprocessor-based calculators, only to have the chip producers decide to build their own product—and sell it for half the price of Ed's calculator.

History and

Ed's new product was based on a microprocessor too—the Intel 8080—but it was a *computer*—a little computer. The "big boys" at the established computer firms considered computers to be industrial products; who would want a small computer? Ed was not sure, but he found the idea compelling. Ed's small computer and his company, MITS, were given a sharp boost by Les Solomon, who promised to feature the new machine on the cover of *Popular Electronics*. In Albuquerque, New Mexico, Ed worked frantically to meet the publication deadline, and he even tried to make the machine pretty, so it would look attractive on the cover (Figure A-1).

Making a good-looking small computer was not easy. This machine, named the Altair, looked like a flat box. In fact, it met the definition of a computer in only a minimal way: It had a central processing unit (on the chip), 256 characters (a paragraph!) of memory, and switches and lights on a front panel for input/output. No screen, no keyboard, no storage.

But the Altair was done on time for the January 1975 issue of *Popular Electronics,* and Ed made plans to fly to New York to demonstrate the machine for Solomon. He sent the computer on ahead by railroad express. Ed got to New York, but the computer did not—the very first personal computer was lost! There was no time to build a new computer before the publishing deadline, so Roberts cooked up a phony version for the cover picture: an empty box with switches and lights on the front panel. He also placed an inch-high ad in the back of the magazine: Get your own Altair kit for $397. Ed, hoping for perhaps 200 orders, was astonished when 2000 orders came in.

Ed Roberts was an important player in the history of personal computers. Unfortunately, he never made it in the big time; most observers agree that his business insight did not match his technical skills. But other entrepreneurs did make it. In this appendix we will glance briefly at the early years of computers and then examine more recent history.

▲

Figure A-1   The Altair.
The term *personal computer* had not even been invented yet, so Ed Roberts's small computer was called a "minicomputer" when it was featured on the cover of *Popular Electronics*.

Industry

The Continuing Story of the Computer Age

Figure A-2 Charles Babbage's difference engine.
This shows a prototype model. Babbage attempted to build a working model, which was to have been several times larger and steam-driven, but he was unsuccessful.

Figure A-3 The Countess of Lovelace.
Augusta Ada Byron, as she was known before she became a countess, was Charles Babbage's colleague in his work on the analytical engine and has been called the world's first computer programmer.

Babbage and the Countess

Born in England in 1791, Charles Babbage was an inventor and mathematician. When solving certain equations, he found the hand-done mathematical tables he used filled with errors. He decided a machine could be built that would solve the equations better by calculating the differences between them. He set about making a demonstration model of what he called a **difference engine** (Figure A-2). The model was so well received that in about 1830 he enthusiastically began to build a full-scale working version, using a grant from the British government.

However, Babbage found that the smallest imperfections were enough to throw the machine out of whack. Babbage was viewed by his own colleagues as a man who was trying to manufacture a machine that was utterly ridiculous. Finally, after spending its money to no avail, the government withdrew financial support.

Despite this setback, Babbage was not discouraged. He conceived of another machine, christened the **analytical engine**, which he hoped would perform many kinds of calculations. This, too, was never built, at least by Babbage (a model was later put together by his son), but the analytical engine embodied five key features of modern computers:

- an input device
- a storage place to hold the number waiting to be processed
- a processor, or number calculator
- a control unit to direct the task to be performed and the sequence of calculations
- an output device

If Babbage was the father of the computer, then Ada, the Countess of Lovelace, was the first computer programmer (Figure A-3). The daughter of English poet Lord Byron and of a mother who was a gifted mathematician, Ada helped develop the instructions for doing computations on the analytical engine. Lady Lovelace's contributions cannot be overvalued. She was able to see that Babbage's theoretical approach was workable, and her interest gave him encouragement. In addition, she published a series of notes that eventually led others to accomplish what Babbage himself had been unable to do.

Herman Hollerith: The Census Has Never Been the Same

The hand-done tabulation of the 1880 United States census took seven and a half years. A competition was held to find some way to speed the counting process of the 1890 United States census. Herman Hollerith's tabulating machine won the contest. As a result of his system's adoption, an unofficial count of the 1890 population (62,622,250) was announced only six weeks after the census was taken.

The principal difference between Hollerith's and Babbage's machines was that Hollerith's machine used electrical rather than mechanical power (Figure A-4). Hollerith realized that his machine had considerable commercial potential. In 1896 he founded the successful Tabulating Machine Company, which, in 1924, merged with two other companies to form the International Business Machines Corporation—IBM.

Watson of IBM: Ornery But Rather Successful

For over 30 years, from 1924 to 1956, Thomas J. Watson, Sr., ruled IBM with an iron grip. Cantankerous and autocratic, supersalesman Watson made IBM a dominant force in the business machines market, first as a supplier of calculators and then as a developer of computers.

IBM's entry into computers was sparked by a young Harvard professor of mathematics, Howard Aiken. In 1936, after reading Lady Lovelace's notes, Aiken began to think that a modern equivalent of the analytical engine could be constructed. Because IBM was already such a power in the business machines market, with ample money and resources, Aiken worked out a careful proposal and approached Thomas Watson. In one of those make-or-break decisions for which he was famous, Watson gave him $1 million. As a result, a computer named the Mark I was born.

The Start of the Modern Era

Nothing like the **Mark I** had ever been built before. It was 8 feet high and 55 feet long, made of streamlined steel and glass, and it emitted a sound during processing that one person said was "like listening to a roomful of old ladies knitting away with steel needles." Unveiled in

The Computer Museum

The Computer Museum in downtown Boston, Massachusetts, is the world's first and only museum devoted solely to computers and computing. The museum illustrates how computers have affected all aspects of life: science, business, education, art, and entertainment. Over half an acre of hands-on and historical exhibits chronicle the enormous changes in the size, capability, applications, and cost of computers over the past 40 years. Two mini-theaters show computer classics as well as award-winning computer-animated films.

The Computer Museum Store offers a large selection of such unique items as state-of-the-art silicon chip jewelry and chocolate "chips" as well as books, posters, cassettes, and more.

TEST BANK

Mult. Choice 16, 18, 36
T/F 51, 81
Matching I 95, 99
Fill In 127, 132-133, 145

TEST BANK

Mult. Choice 2, 8, 10, 13, 25
T/F 43-44, 50, 52, 87-88
Matching I 91, 93
Matching II 107
Fill In 122, 124-125, 129-130

Figure A-4 Herman Hollerith's tabulating machine.
This electrical tabulator and sorter was used to tabulate 1890 census data.

Figure A-5   The ABC.
John Atanasoff and his assistant, Clifford Berry, developed the first digital electronic computer, nicknamed the ABC for Atanasoff-Berry computer.

1944, the Mark I was never very efficient. But the enormous publicity it generated strengthened IBM's commitment to computer development. Meanwhile, technology had been proceeding elsewhere on separate tracks.

American military officials approached Dr. John Mauchly at the University of Pennsylvania and asked him to build a machine that would rapidly calculate trajectories for artillery and missiles. Mauchly and his student J. Presper Eckert relied on the work of Dr. John V. Atanasoff, a professor of physics at Iowa State University. During the late 1930s Atanasoff had spent time trying to build an electronic calculating device to help his students solve mathematical problems. He and an assistant, Clifford Berry, succeeded in building the first digital computer that worked electronically; they called it the **ABC**, for **Atanasoff-Berry Computer** (Figure A-5).

After Mauchly met with Atanasoff and Berry in 1941, he used the ABC as the basis for the next step in computer development. From this association ultimately came a lawsuit, based on attempts to get patents for a commercial version of the machine Mauchly built. The suit was finally decided in 1974, when a federal court determined that Atanasoff had been the true originator of the ideas required to make an electronic digital computer actually work. (Some computer historians dispute this court decision.) Mauchly and Eckert were able to use the principles of the ABC to create the **ENIAC**, for **Electronic Numerical Integrator and Calculator.** The main significance of the ENIAC is that, as the first general-purpose computer, it was the forerunner of the UNIVAC I, the first computer sold on a commercial basis.

The Computer Age Begins

The remarkable thing about the Computer Age is that so much has happened in so short a time. We have leapfrogged through four generations of technology in about 40 years—a span of time whose events are within the memories of many people today. The first three computer "generations" are pinned to three technological developments: the vacuum tube, the transistor, and the integrated circuit. Each has drastically changed the nature of computers. We define the timing of each generation according to the beginning of commercial delivery of the hardware technology. Defining subsequent generations has become more complicated because the entire industry has become more complicated.

The First Generation, 1951–1958: The Vacuum Tube

The beginning of the commercial Computer Age may be dated June 14, 1951. This was the date the first **UNIVAC**, or **Universal Automatic Computer**, was delivered to a client, the U.S. Bureau of the Census, for use in tabulating the previous year's census. The date also marked the first time that a computer had been built for business applications rather than for military, scientific, or engineering use. The UNIVAC was really the ENIAC in disguise and was, in fact, built by Mauchly and Eckert, who in 1947 had formed their own corporation.

In the first generation, **vacuum tubes**—electronic tubes about the size of light bulbs—were used as the internal computer components

(Figure A-6). However, because thousands of such tubes were required, they generated a great deal of heat, causing many problems in temperature regulation and climate control. In addition, although all the tubes had to be working simultaneously, they were subject to frequent burnout—and the people operating the computer often did not know whether the problem was in the programming or in the machine.

Another drawback was that the language used in programming was machine language, which uses numbers. (Present-day higher-level languages are more like English.) Using numbers alone made programming the computer difficult and time-consuming. The UNIVAC used **magnetic cores** to provide memory. These magnetic cores consisted of small, doughnut-shaped rings about the size of pinheads, which were strung like beads on intersecting thin wires (Figure A-7). To supplement primary storage, first-generation computers stored data on punched cards. In 1957 magnetic tape was introduced as a faster, more compact method of storing data.

The Second Generation, 1959–1964: The Transistor

Three Bell Lab scientists—J. Bardeen, H. W. Brattain, and W. Shockley—developed the **transistor,** a small device that transfers electric sig-

◀

Figure A-6 Vacuum tubes.
Vacuum tubes were used in the first generation of computers. Vacuum tube systems could multiply two ten-digit numbers together in 1/40 second.

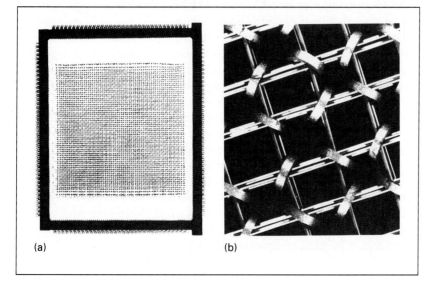

(a)   (b)

◀

Figure A-7 Magnetic cores.
(a) A 6- by 11-inch magnetic core memory. (b) Close-up of a magnetic core memory. A few hundredths of an inch in diameter, each magnetic core was mounted on a wire. When electricity passed through the wire on which a core was strung, the core could be magnetized as either off or on. These states represented a 0 (off) or a 1 (on). Combinations of 0s and 1s could be used to represent data. Magnetic cores were originally developed by IBM, which adapted pill-making machinery to produce them by the millions.

Watson Smart? You Bet!

Just as computers were getting off the ground, Thomas Watson, Sr., saw the best and brightest called to arms in World War II. But he did not just bid his employees a sad *adieu.* He paid them. Each and every one received one quarter of his or her annual salary, in twelve monthly installments. The checks continued to arrive throughout the duration of the war. Every month those former employees thought about IBM and the generosity of its founder.

The result? A very high percentage of those employees returned to IBM after the war. Watson got his brain trust back, virtually intact. The rest is history.

nals across a resistor. (The name *transistor* began as a trademark concocted from *trans*fer plus re*sistor*.) The scientists later received the Nobel prize for their invention. The transistor revolutionized electronics in general and computers in particular. Transistors were much smaller than vacuum tubes, and they had numerous other advantages: They needed no warm-up time, consumed less energy, and were faster and more reliable.

During this generation, another important development was the move from machine language to **assembly languages**—also called **symbolic languages.** Assembly languages use abbreviations for instructions (for example, L for LOAD) rather than numbers. This made programming less cumbersome.

After the development of symbolic languages came **high-level languages,** such as **FORTRAN** (1954) and **COBOL** (1959). Both languages, still widely used today (in updated forms), are more English-like than assembly languages. High-level languages allowed programmers to give more attention to solving problems. Also, in 1962 the first removable disk pack was marketed. Disk storage supplemented magnetic tape systems and enabled users to have fast access to desired data.

All these new developments made the second generation of computers less costly to operate—and thus began a surge of growth in computer systems. Throughout this period computers were being used principally by business, university, and government organizations. They had not filtered down to the general public. The real part of the revolution was about to begin.

The Third Generation, 1965–1970: The Integrated Circuit

One of the most abundant elements in the earth's crust is silicon, a nonmetallic substance found in common beach sand as well as in practically all rocks and clay. The importance of this element to Santa Clara County, which is about 30 miles south of San Francisco, is responsible for the county's nickname: Silicon Valley. In 1965 Silicon Valley became the principal site for the manufacture of the so-called silicon chip: the integrated circuit.

An **integrated circuit** (abbreviated **IC**) is a complete electronic circuit on a small chip of silicon. The chip may be less than 1/8 inch square and contain thousands or millions of electronic components. Beginning in 1965 integrated circuits began to replace transistors in computers. The resulting machines were now called third-generation computers. An integrated circuit was able to replace an entire circuit board of transistors, with one chip of silicon much smaller than one transistor.

Integrated circuits are made of silicon because it is a **semiconductor.** That is, it is a crystalline substance that will conduct electric current when it has been "doped" with chemical impurities implanted in its lattice-like structure. A cylinder of silicon is sliced into wafers, each about 6 inches in diameter, and the wafer is etched repeatedly with a pattern of electrical circuitry. Several layers may be etched on a single wafer. The wafer is then divided into several hundred small chips, each with a complete circuit so tiny it is half the size of a human fingernail, yet under a microscope it looks as complex as a railroad yard.

The chips were hailed as a generational breakthrough because they had desirable characteristics: reliability, compactness, and low cost. Mass-production techniques have made possible the manufacture of inexpensive integrated circuits.

The beginning of the third generation was trumpeted by the IBM 360 series (named for 360 degrees—a full circle of service), first announced April 7, 1964. The System/360 family of computers, designed for both business and scientific use, came in several models and sizes. The equipment housing was blue, leading to IBM's nickname, Big Blue.

The 360 series was launched with an all-out, massive marketing effort to make computers a business tool—to get them into medium-size and smaller business and government operations where they had not been used before. The result went beyond IBM's wildest dreams. The reported $5 billion the company invested in the development of the System/360 quickly repaid itself, and the system rendered many existing computer systems obsolete. Big Blue was on its way.

Software became more sophisticated during this third generation, permitting several programs to run in the same time frame, sharing computer resources. This approach improved the efficiency of computer systems. Software systems were developed to support interactive processing, which put the user in direct contact with the computer through a terminal. This kind of access caused the customer service industry to flourish, especially in areas such as reservations and credit checks.

Large third-generation computers began to be supplemented by minicomputers, which are functionally equivalent to a full-size system but are somewhat slower, smaller, and less expensive. These computers have become a huge success with medium-size and smaller businesses.

The Fourth Generation, 1971–Present: The Microprocessor

Through the 1970s computers gained dramatically in speed, reliability, and storage capacity, but entry into the fourth generation was evolutionary rather than revolutionary. The fourth generation was, in fact, an extension of third-generation technology. That is, in the early part of the third generation, specialized chips were developed for computer memory and logic. Thus, all the ingredients were in place for the next technological development, the general-purpose processor-on-a-chip, otherwise known as the **microprocessor,** which became commercially available in 1971.

Nowhere is the pervasiveness of computer power more apparent than in the explosive use of the microprocessor. In addition to the common applications of digital watches, pocket calculators, and personal computers, microprocessors can be anticipated in virtually every machine in the home or business—microwave ovens, cars, copy machines, television sets, and so on. Computers today are 100 times smaller than those of the first generation, and a single chip is far more powerful than ENIAC.

The Fifth Generation

The term *fifth generation* was coined by Japan to describe its goal of creating powerful, intelligent computers by the mid-1990s. Since then, however, it has become an umbrella term encompassing many research

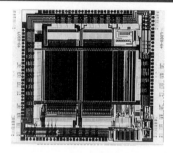

An Invention to Remember

There was a time when an engineer who was also an inventor could look forward to fame as well as fortune. Thomas Edison, for example, was one of the best-known people in the world before he was 35. Today's famous people, however, tend to come from the entertainment industry. So it is that we have lost the names of Jack Kilby and Robert Noyce, who invented the device that operates your watch, oven, calculator, and computer: the integrated circuit. Some have called it the greatest invention ever. Let us make Kilby and Noyce just a little bit famous.

Kilby and Noyce come from America's heartland, Kansas and Iowa, respectively. Both were interested in electronics. But there the similarities end. Jack Kilby flunked the entrance exam at MIT and received only a single job offer when he graduated with an engineering degree from the University of Illinois. Robert Noyce, on the other hand, did get into MIT and stayed around to get a Ph.D.

Kilby and Noyce worked independently, each coming out with the integrated circuit on a chip in 1959—Kilby at Texas Instruments, Inc., and Noyce at Fairchild Semiconductor. Kilby went on to develop the first hand-held calculator, and Noyce founded Intel Corporation to pursue the daring idea of putting the computer's memory on chips.

Personal Computers
In Action

The Software Entrepreneurs

Ever thought you'd like to run your own show? Make your own product? Be in business for yourself? Entrepreneurs are a special breed. They are achievement-oriented; like to take responsibility for decisions; and dislike repetitive, routine work. They also have high levels of energy and a great deal of imagination. But perhaps the key is that they are willing to take risks.

Entrepreneurs often have still another quality—a more elusive quality—that is something close to charisma. This charisma is based on enthusiasm, and it allows them to lead people and to form organizations, and give them momentum. Study these real-life entrepreneurs,

noting their paths to glory and—sometimes—their falls.

Steve Jobs

Of the two Steves who formed Apple Computer, Steve Jobs was the true entrepreneur. Although they both were interested in electronics, Steve Wozniak was the technical genius, and he would have been happy to have been left alone to tinker. But Steve Jobs would not let him alone for a minute; he was always pushing and crusading. In fact, Wozniak had hooked up with an evangelist, and they made quite a pair.

When Apple was getting off the ground, Jobs wanted Wozniak to quit his job so he could work full-time on the new venture. Wozniak refused.

His partner begged and cried. Wozniak gave in. While Wozniak built Apple computers, Jobs was out hustling, finding the best marketing person, the best venture capitalist, and the best company president. This entrepreneurial spirit paid off in a spectacular way as Apple rose to the top of the list of microcomputer companies.

fields in the computer industry. Key areas of ongoing research are artificial intelligence, expert systems, and natural language—topics discussed in detail in Chapter 11.

Japan's original announcement of the fifth generation captivated the computer industry. Some view the fifth generation as a race between Japan and the United States, with nothing less than world computer supremacy as the prize. However, the Japanese budget has been cut significantly in recent years, and enthusiasm over the project has waned somewhat.

TEST BANK

Mult. Choice 3, 6, 26, 34-35
T/F 71-73, 75-80
Matching 98
Matching II 104
Fill In 119-120, 137-138, 142, 149

 # The Special Story of Personal Computers

Personal computers are the machines you can "get closest to," whether you are an amateur or a professional. There is nothing quite like having your very own personal computer. Its history is very personal too, full of stories of success and failure and of individuals with whom we can readily identify.

Bill Gates

When Bill Gates was a teenager, he swore off computers for a year and, in his words, "tried to act normal." His parents, who wanted him to be a lawyer, must have been relieved when Bill gave up the computer foolishness and went off to Harvard in 1974. But Bill started spending weekends with his friend Paul Allen, dreaming about personal computers, which did not exist yet. When the MITS Altair, the first personal computer for sale, splashed on the market in January 1975, both Bill and Paul moved to Albuquerque to be near the action at MITS. But they showed a desire even then to chart their own course. Although they wrote software for MITS, they kept the rights to their work and formed their own company. Their company was called Microsoft.

When MITS failed, Gates and Allen moved their software company to their native Bellevue, Washington. They employed 32 people in 1980 when IBM came to call. Gates recognized the big league when he saw it and put on a suit for the occasion. Gates was offered a plum: the chance to develop the operating system (a crucial set of software) for IBM's soon-to-be personal computer. Although he knew he was betting the whole company, Gates never hesitated to take the risk. He and his crew worked feverishly for many months to produce MS-DOS—Microsoft Disk Operating System. It was this product that sent Microsoft on its meteoric rise.

Mitch Kapor

Kapor did not start out on a direct path to computer fame and riches. In fact, he wandered extensively, from being a disk jockey to piano teacher to counselor. He had done some programming, too, but did not like it much. But, around 1978, he found he did like fooling around with personal computers. In fact, he had found his niche.

In 1983 Kapor introduced a software package called Lotus 1-2-3, and there had never been anything like it before. Lotus added the term *integrated package* to the vocabulary; the phrase described the software's identity as a combination spreadsheet, graphics, and database program. Kapor's product catapulted his company to the top of the list of independent software makers in just two years.

Champions of Change

Entrepreneurs thrive on change. Jobs, Wozniak, and Kapor all left their original companies to start new companies. Stay tuned for future breakthroughs from these and other personal computer entrepreneurs.

I Built It in My Garage

As we noted in the beginning of the chapter, the very first personal computer was the MITS Altair, produced in 1975. But it was a gee-whiz machine, loaded with switches and dials—and no keyboard or screen. It took two teenagers, Steve Jobs and Steve Wozniak, to capture the imagination of the public with the first Apple computer. They built it in that time-honored place of inventors, a garage, using the $1300 proceeds from the sale of an old Volkswagen. Designed for home use, the Apple was the first to offer an easy-to-use keyboard and screen. Founded in 1977, Apple Computer was immediately and wildly successful. When its stock was offered to the public in December 1980, it started a stampede among investors eager to buy in. Apple has introduced an increasingly powerful line of computers, including the Macintosh, which continues to sell well. (Figure A-8 shows early documentation for the first commercial Apple computer.)

The other major player in those early years was Tandy Incorporated, whose worldwide chain of Radio Shack stores provided a handy sales outlet for the TRS-80 personal computer. Other manufacturers who enjoyed more than moderate success in the late 1970s were Atari and Commodore. Their number was to grow.

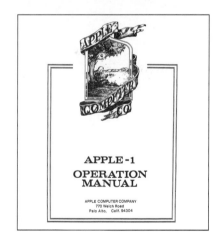

▲
Figure A-8 Apple manual.
Shown here is a collector's item: the very first manual for operation of an Apple computer. Unfortunately, the early manuals were a hodgepodge of circuit diagrams, software listings, and handwritten notes. They were hard to read and understand and almost guaranteed to frighten away all but the most hardy souls.

Semiconductor Drive

This street sign is in Silicon Valley, an area south of San Francisco. As its name indicates, Silicon Valley is noted for silicon chips, also known as semiconductors, and other related computer industries.

The IBM PC Phenomenon

IBM announced its first personal computer in the summer of 1981. IBM captured the top market share in just 18 months and, even more important, its machine became the industry standard (Figure A-9). This was indeed a phenomenal success.

IBM did a lot of things right, such as including the possibility of adding memory. IBM also provided internal expansion slots, so that manufacturers of peripheral equipment could build accessories for the IBM PC. In addition, IBM provided hardware schematics and software listings to companies who wanted to build products in conjunction with the new PC. Many of the new products accelerated demand for the IBM machine.

Other personal computer manufacturers hurried to emulate IBM, producing "PC clones"—copycat computers that can run software designed for the IBM PC. Meanwhile, IBM has offered both upscale and downscale generations of its personal computer.

The story of personal computer history is ongoing, with daily fluctuations reflected in the trade press. The effects of personal computers are far-reaching, and they remain a key topic in the computer industry.

History is still being made in the computer industry, of course, and it is being made incredibly rapidly. A book cannot possibly pretend to describe all the very latest developments. Nevertheless, as we indicated earlier, the four areas of input, processing, output, and storage describe the basic components of a computer system—whatever its date.

Figure A-9 The IBM PC.
Launched in 1981, the IBM PC took just 18 months to rise to the top of the best-seller list.

Appendix **Review**

Summary and Key Terms

- Charles Babbage, is called "the father of the computer" because of his invention of two computation machines: the **difference engine** and the **analytical engine.** Countess Ada Lovelace helped develop instructions for carrying out computations on the analytical engine.
- The first computer to use electrical power instead of mechanical power was Herman Hollerith's tabulating machine, which was used in the 1890 census in the United States. Hollerith founded a company that became the forerunner of International Business Machines Corporation (IBM).
- Thomas J. Watson, Sr., built IBM into a dominant force in the business machines market. He also gave Harvard professor Howard Aiken research funds with which to build an electromechanical computer, the **Mark I,** which was unveiled in 1944.
- John V. Atanasoff, with assistant Clifford Berry, devised the first digital computer to work by electronic means, the **Atanasoff-Berry Computer (ABC).**
- The **ENIAC (Electronic Numerical Integrator and Calculator),** developed by John Mauchly and J. Presper Eckert at the University of Pennsylvania in 1946, was the world's first general-purpose electronic computer.
- The first computer generation began June 14, 1951, with the delivery of the **UNIVAC (Universal Automatic Computer)** to the U.S. Bureau of the Census. First-generation computers required thousands of **vacuum tubes.** The main form of memory was **magnetic core.**
- Second-generation computers used **transistors,** developed at Bell Laboratories. Compared to vacuum tubes, transistors were small, needed no warm-up, consumed less energy, and were faster and more reliable. During the second generation, **assembly languages,** or **symbolic languages,** were developed. They used abbreviations for instructions, rather than numbers. Later, **high-level languages,** such as **FORTRAN** and **COBOL,** were also developed. In 1962 the first removable disk pack was marketed.
- The third generation emerged with the introduction of the **integrated circuit (IC)**—a complete electronic circuit on a small chip of silicon. Silicon is a **semiconductor,** a substance that will conduct electric current when it has been "doped" with chemical impurities.
- With the third generation IBM announced the System/360 family of computers. During this period more sophisticated software was introduced that allowed several programs to run in the same time frame and supported interactive processing, in which the user has direct contact with the computer through a terminal.
- The fourth-generation **microprocessor**—a general-purpose processor-on-a-chip—grew out of the specialized memory and logic chips of the third generation. Microprocessors led to the development of microcomputers, expanding computer markets to smaller businesses and to personal use.
- In 1980 the Japanese announced a ten-year project to develop a fifth generation, radically new forms of computer systems involving artificial intelligence, expert systems, and natural language.
- The first microcomputer, the MITS Altair, was produced in 1975. However, the first successful computer to include an easy-to-use keyboard and screen was offered by Apple computer, founded by Steve Jobs and Steve Wozniak in 1977. IBM entered the microcomputer market in 1981 and captured the top market share in just 18 months.

KEY TERMS

analytical engine

assembly language

Atanasoff-Berry computer (ABC)

COBOL

difference engine

Electronic Numerical Integrator and Calculator (ENIAC)

FORTRAN

high-level language

integrated circuit (IC)

magnetic core

Mark I

microprocessor

semiconductor

symbolic language

transistor

Universal Automatic Computer (UNIVAC)

vacuum tube

Student Personal Study Guide

True/False

T   F   1. The analytical engine embodied the five key concepts of a computer system.
T   F   2. The ENIAC was the world's first electronic digital computer.
T   F   3. The first generation was characterized by the vacuum tube.
T   F   4. The transistor was faster and more reliable than the vacuum tube.
T   F   5. Higher-level languages were developed during the second generation.
T   F   6. Integrated circuits marked the advent of the third generation.
T   F   7. Mauchly and Eckert produced the ENIAC.
T   F   8. IBM's third generation computers were called the IBM PCs.
T   F   9. First generation computers used transistors.
T   F   10. Jobs and Wozniak invented the MITS Altair.

Multiple Choice

1. Aiken's computer at Harvard:
   a. ENIAC   c. UNIVAC
   b. difference engine   d. Mark I
2. The first microcomputer:
   a. MITS Altair   c. Apple
   b. IBM PC   d. Macintosh
3. The first electronic digital computer:
   a. ENIAC   c. Macintosh
   b. ABC   d. Mark 1
4. Second-generation technology:
   a. IC   c. transistors
   b. microprocessor   d. vacuum tubes
5. Father of the computer:
   a. Aiken   c. Hollerith
   b. Atanasoff   d. Babbage
6. A "doped" substance that will conduct electric current:
   a. semiconductor   c. magnetic core
   b. vacuum tube   d. analytical engine
7. Captured the personal computer market in just 18 months:
   a. Apple   c. MITS
   b. IBM   d. Microsoft
8. Babbage's assistant:
   a. Watson   c. Lovelace
   b. Berry   d. Eckert
9. A complete electronic circuit on a silicon chip:
   a. vacuum tube   c. transistor
   b. magnetic core   d. integrated circuit
10. The man who founded a company that became IBM:
   a. Atanasoff   c. Aiken
   b. Watson   d. Hollerith

Fill-In

1. The technology of the second generation: _____ .

2. Built IBM into a dominant force in the business machine market: _____ .

3. The Harvard professor who built the Mark I: _____ .

4. The first commercial computer, delivered in 1951: _____ .

5. The technology used for primary storage in the first generation: _____ .

6. The first personal computer for sale: _____ .

7. Inventor of the difference engine: _____ .

8. Considered the first programmer: _____ .

9. Atanasoff's computer: _____ .

10. Made a machine to tabulate the 1890 census: _____ .

Answers

True/False: 1. T, 2. T, 3. T, 4. T, 5. T, 6. T, 7. T, 8. F, 9. F, 10.F
Multiple choice: 1. d, 2. a, 3. b, 4. c, 5. d, 6. a, 7. b, 8. c, 9. d, 10. d
Fill-in: 1. transistor, 2. Thomas J. Watson, Sr., 3. Howard Aiken, 4. UNIVAC, 5. magnetic core, 6. MITS Altair, 7. Charles Babbage, 8. Ada Lovelace, 9. ABC, 10. Herman Hollerith

Number

Data can be represented in the computer in one of two basic ways: as **numeric data** or as **alphanumeric data.** The internal representation of alphanumeric data—letters, digits, special characters—was discussed in Chapter 3. Recall that alphanumeric data may be represented using various codes; ASCII is a common code. Alphanumeric data, even if all digits, cannot be used for arithmetic operations. Data that is used for arithmetic calculations must be stored numerically.

Data stored numerically can be represented as the binary equivalent of the decimal value with which we are familiar. That is, values such as 1050, 43218, and 3 that we input to the computer will be converted to the binary number system. In this appendix we shall study the binary number system (base 2) and two related systems, octal (base 8) and hexadecimal (base 16).

Systems

Number Bases

A number base is a specific collection of symbols on which a number system can be built. The number base familiar to us is base 10, upon which the **decimal** number system is built. There are ten symbols—0 through 9—used in the decimal system.

Since society uses base 10, that is the number base most of us understand and can use easily. It would theoretically be possible, however, for all of us to learn to use a different number system. This number system could contain a different number of symbols and perhaps even symbols that are unfamiliar.

Base 2: The Binary Number System

Base 2 has exactly two symbols: 0 and 1. All numbers in the **binary** system must be formed using these two symbols. As you can see in column 2 of Table B-1, this means that numbers in the binary system become long quickly; the number 1000 in base 2 is equivalent to 8 in base 10. (When different number bases are being discussed, it is common practice to use the number base as a subscript. In this case we could say $1000_2 = 8_{10}$.) If you were to continue counting in base 2, you would soon see that the binary numbers were very long and unwieldy. The number 5000_{10} is equal to 10011100010000_2.

The size and sameness—all those 0s and 1s—of binary numbers make them subject to frequent error when they are being manipulated by humans. To improve both convenience and accuracy, it is common to express the values represented by binary numbers in the more concise octal and hexadecimal number bases.

Base 8: The Octal Number System

The **octal** number system uses exactly eight symbols: 0, 1, 2, 3, 4, 5, 6, and 7. Base 8 is a convenient shorthand for base 2 numbers because 8 is a power of 2: $2^3 = 8$. As you will see when we discuss conversions, one octal digit is the equivalent of exactly three binary digits. The use of octal (or hexadecimal) as a shorthand for binary is common in printed output of main storage and, in some cases, in programming.

Look at the column of octal numbers in Table B-1. Notice that, since 7 is the last symbol in base 8, the following number is 10. In fact, we can count right through the next seven numbers in the usual manner, as long as we end with 17. Note, however, that 17_8 is pronounced "one-seven," not "seventeen." The octal number 17 is followed by 20 through 27, and so on. The last double-digit number is 77, which is followed by 100. Although it takes a little practice, you can see that it would be easy to learn to count in base 8. However, hexadecimal, or base 16, is not quite as easy.

Base 16: The Hexadecimal Number System

The **hexadecimal** number system uses exactly 16 symbols. As we have just seen, base 10 uses the familiar digits 0 through 9, and bases 2 and 8

Table B-1   Number Bases 10, 2, 8, 16: First Values

Base 10 (decimal)	Base 2 (binary)	Base 8 (octal)	Base 16 (hexadecimal)
0	0000	0	0
1	0001	1	1
2	0010	2	2
3	0011	3	3
4	0100	4	4
5	0101	5	5
6	0110	6	6
7	0111	7	7
8	1000	10	8
9	1001	11	9
10	1010	12	A
11	1011	13	B
12	1100	14	C
13	1101	15	D
14	1110	16	E
15	1111	17	F
16	10000	20	10

use a subset of those symbols. Base 16, however, needs those ten symbols (0 through 9) and six more. The six additional symbols used in the hexadecimal number system are the letters A through F. So the base 16 symbols are: 0, 1, 2, 3, 4, 5, 6, 7, 8, 9, A, B, C, D, E, and F. It takes some adjusting to think of A or D as a digit instead of a letter. It also takes a little time to become accustomed to numbers such as 6A2F or even ACE. Both of these examples are legitimate numbers in hexadecimal.

As you become familiar with hexadecimal, consider the matter of counting. Counting sounds simple enough, but it can be confusing in an unfamiliar number base with new symbols. The process is the same as counting in base 10, but most of us learned to count when we were too young to think about the process itself. Quickly—what number follows 24CD? The answer is 24CE. We increased the rightmost digit by one—D to E—just as you would have in the more obvious case of 6142 to 6143. What is the number just before 1000_{16}? The answer is FFF_{16}; the last symbol (F) is a triple-digit number. Compare this with 999_{10}, which precedes 1000_{10}; 9 is the last symbol in base 10. As a familiarization exercise, try counting from 1 to 100 in base 16. Remember to use A through F as the second symbol in the teens, twenties, and so forth (. . . 27, 28, 29, 2A, 2B, 2C, 2D, 2E, 2F, 30, and so on).

Conversions Between Number Bases

It is sometimes convenient to use a number in a base different from the base currently being used—that is, to change the number from one base to another. Many programmers can nimbly convert a number from one base to another, among bases 10, 2, 8, and 16. We shall consider these conversion techniques now. Table B-2 summarizes the methods.

To Base 10 from Bases 2, 8, and 16

We present these conversions together because the technique is the same for all three.

Let us begin with the concept of positional notation. **Positional notation** means that the value of a digit in a number depends not only on its own intrinsic value but also on its location in the number. Given the number 2363, we know that the appearance of the digit 3 represents two different values, 300 and 3. Table B-3 shows the names of the relative positions.

Using these positional values, the number 2363 is understood to mean:

```
 2000
  300
   60
    3
———
 2363
```

Table B-2 Summary Conversion Chart

	To Base			
From Base	2	8	16	10
2	———	Group binary digits by 3, convert	Group binary digits by 4, convert	Expand number and convert base 2 digits to base 10
8	Convert each octal digit to 3 binary digits	———	Convert to base 2, then to base 16	Expand number and convert base 8 digits to base 10
16	Convert each hexadecimal digit to 4 binary digits	Convert to base 2, then to base 8	———	Expand number and convert base 16 digits to base 10
10	Divide number repeatedly by 2; use remainders as answer	Divide number repeatedly by 8; use remainders as answer	Divide number repeatedly by 16; use remainders as answer	———

Table B-3   Digit Positions

Digit	2	3	6	3
Position	Thousand	Hundred	Ten	Unit

This number can also be expressed as:

$$(2 \times 1000) + (3 \times 100) + (6 \times 10) + 3$$

We can express this expanded version of the number another way, using powers of 10. Note that $10^0 = 1$.

$$2363 = (2 \times 10^3) + (3 \times 10^2) + (6 \times 10^1) + (3 \times 10^0)$$

Once you understand the expanded notation, the rest is easy: You expand the number as we just did in base 10, but use the appropriate base of the number. For example, follow these steps to convert 61732_8 to base 10:

1. Expand the number, using 8 as the base:

$$61732 = (6 \times 8^4) + (1 \times 8^3) + (7 \times 8^2) + (3 \times 8^1) + (2 \times 8^0)$$

2. Complete the arithmetic:

$$61732 = (6 \times 4096) + (1 \times 512) + (7 \times 64) + (3 \times 8) + (2 \times 1)$$
$$= 24576 + 512 + 448 + 24 + 2$$

3. Answer: $61732_8 = 25562_{10}$

The same expand-and-convert technique can be used to convert from base 2 or base 16 to base 10. As you consider the following two examples, use Table 1 to make the conversions. (For example, A in base 16 converts to 10 in base 10.)

Convert $C14A_{16}$ to base 10:

$$C14A_{16} = (12 \times 16^3) + (1 \times 16^2) + (4 \times 16^1) + (10 \times 16^0)$$
$$= (12 \times 4096) + (1 \times 256) + (4 \times 16) + (10 \times 1)$$
$$= 49482$$

So $C14A_{16} = 49482_{10}$.

Convert 100111_2 to base 10:

$$100111_2 = (1 \times 2^5) + (1 \times 2^2) + (1 \times 2^1) + (1 \times 2^0)$$
$$= 39$$

So $100111_2 = 39_{10}$.

From Base 10 to Bases 2, 8, and 16

These conversions use a simpler process but more complicated arithmetic. The process, often called the *remainder method*, is basically a series of repeated divisions by the number of the base to which you are converting. You begin by using the number to be converted as the dividend; succeeding dividends are the quotients of the previous division. The converted number is the combined remainders accumulated from the divisions. There are two points to remember:

1. Keep dividing until you reach a zero quotient.
2. Use the remainders in reverse order.

Consider converting 6954_{10} to base 8:

$$
\begin{array}{rl}
8\underline{|6954} & \\
8\underline{|869} & 2 \\
8\underline{|108} & 5 \\
8\underline{|13} & 4 \\
8\underline{|1} & 5 \\
0 & 1
\end{array}
$$

Placing the remainders backward, $6954_{10} = 15452_8$.

Now use the same technique to convert 4823_{10} to base 16:

$$
\begin{array}{rl}
16\underline{|4823} & \\
16\underline{|301} & 7 \\
16\underline{|18} & 13\ (=D) \\
16\underline{|1} & 2 \\
0 & 1
\end{array}
$$

The remainder 13 is equivalent to D in base 16. So $4823_{10} = 12D7_{16}$.

Convert 49_{10} to base 2:

$$
\begin{array}{rl}
2\underline{|49} & \\
2\underline{|24} & 1 \\
2\underline{|12} & 0 \\
2\underline{|6} & 0 \\
2\underline{|3} & 0 \\
2\underline{|1} & 1 \\
0 & 1
\end{array}
$$

Again placing the remainders in reverse order, $49_{10} = 110001_2$.

To Base 2 from Bases 8 and 16

To convert a number to base 2 from base 8 or base 16, convert each digit separately to three or four binary digits, respectively. Use Table B-1 to make the conversion. Leading zeros—zeros added to the front of the number—may be needed in each grouping of digits to fill out each to three or four digits.

Convert 4732_8 to base 2, converting each octal digit to a set of three binary digits:

4	7	3	2
100	111	011	010

So $4732_8 = 100111011010_2$. Notice that leading zeros were sometimes needed to make three binary digits from an octal digit: for octal digit 3, 11 became 011 and, for octal digit 2, 10 became 010.

Now convert $A046B_{16}$ to base 2, this time converting each hexadecimal digit to four binary digits:

A	0	4	6	B
1010	0000	0100	0110	1011

Thus $A046B_{16} = 10100000010001101011_2$.

From Base 2 to Bases 8 and 16

To convert a number from base 2 to base 8 or base 16, group the binary digits from the right in groups of three or four, respectively. Again use Table 1 to help you make the conversion to the new base.

Convert 111101001011_2 to base 8 and base 16:

In the base 8 conversion, group the digits three at a time, starting on the right:

111	101	001	011
7	5	1	3

So $111101001011_2 = 7513_8$.

For the conversion to base 16, group the digits four at a time, starting on the right:

1111	0100	1011
F	4	B

$111101001011_2 = F4B_{16}$.

Sometimes the number of digits in a binary number is not exactly divisible by 3 or 4. You may, for example, start grouping the digits three at a time and finish with one or two "extra" digits on the left side of the number. In this case just add as many zeros as you need to the front of the binary number.

Consider converting 1010_2 to base 8. By adding two zeros to the front of the number to make it 001010_2, we now have six digits, which can be conveniently grouped three at a time:

001	010
1	2

So $1010_2 = 12_8$.

Glossary

Access arm A mechanical device that can access all the tracks of one cylinder in a disk storage unit.

Accumulator A register that collects the result of computations.

Active badge A badge that, imbedded with a computer chip, signals the wearer's location by sending out infrared signals, which are read by computers distributed throughout the building.

Active cell The cell currently available for use on a spreadsheet. Also called the current cell.

Address A number used to designate a location in memory.

Address register A register that tells where instructions and data are stored in memory.

AI *See* Artificial intelligence.

ALU *See* Arithmetic/logic unit.

America Online (AOL) A major information utility that offers a variety of services.

Analog transmission The transmission of computer data as a continuous electric signal in the form of a wave.

Analytical engine A mechanical device of cogs and wheels, designed by Charles Babbage, that embodied the key characteristics of modern computers.

Analytical graphics Traditional line graphs, bar charts, and pie charts used to illustrate and analyze data.

ANSI American National Standards Institute.

AOL *See* America Online.

Applications software Programs designed to perform specific tasks and functions.

Arithmetic/logic unit (ALU) The electronic circuitry in a computer; it executes all arithmetic and logical operations.

Arithmetic operation Mathematical calculation the ALU performs on data.

Artificial intelligence (AI) The field of study that explores computer involvement in tasks requiring intelligence, imagination, and intuition.

ASCII (American Standard Code for Information Interchange) A coding scheme using 7-bit characters to represent data characters.

Assembler program A translator program used to convert assembly language programs to machine language.

Assembly language A second-generation language that uses abbreviations for instructions.

Atanasoff-Berry Computer (ABC) The first electronic digital computer, designed by John V. Atanasoff and Clifford Berry, in the late 1930s.

ATM *See* Automated teller machine.

Audio-response unit A device that converts data in main storage to sounds understandable as speech to humans. Also called a voice synthesizer or a voice-output device.

Automated teller machine (ATM) An input/output device connected to a computer used by bank customers for financial transactions.

Automatic reformatting In word processing, automatic adjustment of text to accommodate changes.

Auxiliary storage Storage, often disk, for data and programs; separate from the CPU and memory. Also called secondary storage.

Axis A reference line of a graph. The horizontal axis is the x-axis. The vertical axis is the y-axis.

Backup system A method of storing data in more than one place to protect it from damage or loss.

Bar code Standardized pattern (Universal Product Code) of vertical marks that identifies products.

Bar code reader A stationary photoelectric scanner that reads bar codes by means of reflected light.

Bar graph A graph made up of filled-in columns or rows that represent the change of data over time.

BASIC (Beginner's All-purpose Symbolic Instruction Code) A high-level programming language that is easy to learn and use.

Batch processing A data processing technique in which transactions are collected into groups, or batches, for processing.

BBS *See* Bulletin board system.

Binary system A system in which data is represented by combinations of 0s and 1s, which correspond to the two states off and on.

Biometrics The science of measuring individual body characteristics; used in some security systems.

Bit A binary digit.

Block copy command In word processing, the command used to copy a block of text into a new location.

Block delete command In word processing, the command used to erase a block of text.

Block move command In word processing, the command used to remove a block of text from one location in a document and place it elsewhere.

Boldface Printed characters in darker type than the surrounding characters.

Booting Loading the operating system into memory.

Branch In a flowchart, the connection leading from the decision box to one of two possible responses. Also called a path.

Bulletin board system (BBS) Telephone-linked personal computers that provide public-access message systems.

Business graphics Graphics that represent data in a visual, easy-to-understand format.

Business-quality graphics program A program that allows a user to create professional-looking business graphics. Also called a presentation graphics program.

Bus line Electrical path that transports data from one place to another inside the computer.

Bus network A type of local area network that assigns a portion of network management to each computer but preserves the system if one node fails.

Byte A string of bits (usually 8) used to represent one data character—a letter, digit, or special character.

C A sophisticated programming language invented by Bell Labs in 1974.

Cache A small amount of very fast memory that stores data and instructions that are used frequently, resulting in improved processing speeds.

CAD/CAM *See* computer-aided design/computer-aided manufacturing.

Cathode ray tube (CRT) The most common type of computer screen.

CD-ROM *See* Compact disk read-only memory.

Cell The intersection of a row and a column in a spreadsheet. Entries in a spreadsheet are stored in individual cells.

Cell address In a spreadsheet, the column and row coordinates of a cell.

Cell contents The label, value, formula, or function contained in a spreadsheet cell.

Centering The word processing feature that places a line of text midway between the left and right margins.

Centralized data processing Keeping hardware, software, storage, and computer access in one location.

Central processing unit (CPU) The electronic circuitry that executes stored program instructions. It consists of two parts: the control unit and the arithmetic/logic unit.

CGA (color graphics adapter) An early color screen standard with 320 by 200 pixels.

Change agent A systems analyst who, acting as a catalyst, overcomes the reluctance to change within an organization.

Character A letter, number, or special character (such as $).

Client An individual or organization contracting for systems analysis.

Clip art Illustrations stored on disk that are used to enhance a graph or document.

Clustered-bar graph A bar graph comparing several different but related sets of data.

Coaxial cable Bundles of insulated wires within a shielded enclosure that can be laid underground or undersea.

COBOL (COmmon Business-Oriented Language) An English-like programming language used primarily for business applications.

Command A name that invokes the correct program or program segment.

Compact disk read-only memory (CD-ROM) Optical data storage technology using disk formats identical to audio compact disks.

Compare operation An operation in which the computer compares two data items and performs alternative operations based on the comparison.

Compiler A translator that converts the symbolic statements of a high-level language into computer-executable machine language.

CompuServe A major information utility that offers a variety of services.

Computer A machine that accepts data (input) and processes it into useful information (output).

Computer-aided design/computer-aided manufacturing (CAD/CAM) The use of computers to create two- and three-dimensional pictures of manufactured products.

Computer conferencing A method of sending, receiving, and storing typed messages within a network of users.

Computer Fraud and Abuse Act A law passed by Congress in 1984 to fight computer crime.

Computer Matching and Privacy Protection Act A law that regulates comparison of records held by different branches of the government.

Computer literacy Awareness, knowledge of, and interaction with computers.

Computer programmer A person who designs, writes, tests, and implements programs.

Computer system A system that has one or more computers as components.

Concurrent licensing A software licensing agreement in which a customer is permitted to use only a limited number of copies of a software product simultaneously.

Concurrently With reference to the execution of computer instructions, in the same time frame. *See also* Multiprogramming.

Conditional replace A word processing function that asks the user whether to replace copy each time the program finds a particular item.

Connector A symbol used in flowcharting to connect paths.

Consortium A joint venture to support a complete computer facility to be used in an emergency.

Control unit The circuitry that directs and coordinates the entire computer system in executing stored program instructions.

Copy protection A software or hardware block that makes it difficult or impossible to create unauthorized copies of software.

CPU *See* Central processing unit.

CRT *See* Cathode ray tube.

Current cell The cell currently available for use on a spreadsheet. Also called the active cell.

Current drive The disk drive currently being used by the computer system. Also called the default drive.

Cursor A flashing indicator on the screen; it indicates where the next character will be inserted. Also called a pointer.

Cursor-movement keys The keys on the computer keyboard that allow the user to move the cursor on the screen.

Custom software Software specifically tailored to user needs.

Cut and paste In word processing, removing a block of text from one location and placing it in another location.

DASD *See* Direct access storage device.

Data The raw material to be processed by a computer.

Database A collection of interrelated files stored together with minimum redundancy.

Database management system (DBMS) A set of programs that create, manage, protect, and provide access to a database.

Data collection device A device that allows direct data entry in such places as factories and warehouses.

Data communications The process of exchanging data over communications facilities.

Data communications system A computer system that transmits data over communications lines, such as public telephone lines or private network cables.

Data Encryption Standard (DES) The standardized public key by which senders and receivers can scramble and unscramble their messages.

Data item Data in a relational database table.

Data point A single value represented by a bar or symbol in a graph.

DBMS *See* Database management system.

DDP *See* Distributed data processing.

Debugging The process of detecting, locating, and correcting mistakes in a program.

Decision box The standard diamond-shaped box used in flowcharting to indicate a decision.

Default drive The disk drive to which commands refer in the absence of any specified drive. Unless instructed otherwise, an applications program stores files on the memory device in the default drive. Also called the current drive.

Default settings Settings automatically used by a program unless the user specifies otherwise.

Demodulation The process of converting a signal from analog to digital.

DES *See* Data Encryption Standard.

Desk-checking A programming phase in which the logic of the program is mentally checked to ensure that it is error-free and workable.

Desktop publishing The use of a personal computer, special software, and a laser printer to produce very high-quality documents that combine text and graphics. Also called electronic publishing.

Desktop publishing program A software package for designing and producing professional-looking documents. Also called a page composition program or a page makeup program.

Diagnostic message A message that informs the user of programming-language syntax errors.

Difference engine A machine designed by Charles Babbage to solve polynomial equations by calculating the successive differences between them.

Digital transmission A data transmission method that sends data as distinct electrical (on or off) pulses.

Digitizer A graphics input device that converts images into digital data that the computer can accept.

Direct access The immediate access to a record in secondary storage, usually on a disk. Also called random access.

Direct access storage device (DASD) A storage device in which a record can be accessed directly.

Direct-connect modem A modem connected directly to the telephone line.

Disaster recovery plan A method of restoring data processing operations if those operations are halted by major damage or destruction.

Disk drive A device that allows data to be read from a disk and written on a disk.

Diskette A single magnetic disk on which data is recorded as magnetic spots. Available in both 5¼-inch format and 3½-inch format.

Disk pack A stack of magnetic disks assembled together.

Displayed value 1. The calculated result of a formula or function in a spreadsheet cell. 2. A number in a cell; it is displayed according to a user-specified format.

Distributed data processing (DDP) A data processing system in which processing is decentralized, with the computers and storage devices in dispersed locations.

Documentation 1. A detailed written description of the programming cycle and specific facts about the program. 2. The instruction manual for packaged software.

Dot-matrix printer A printer that constructs a character by activating a matrix of pins to produce the shape of a character on paper.

Download The transfer of data from a mainframe or large computer to a smaller computer.

Downsizing The process of shifting mainframe computer applications to smaller computers that are often a local area network of personal computers.

DRAM *See* Dynamic RAM

Dynamic RAM (DRAM) Memory chips that are periodically regenerated, allowing the chips to retain the stored data.

EFT *See* Electronic Fund Transfer.

EGA (enhanced graphics adapter) A color screen standard with 640 by 350 pixels.

Electronic fund transfer (EFT) Paying for goods and services by using electronically transferred funds.

Electronic mail (e-mail) The process of sending messages directly from one terminal or computer to another. The messages may be sent and stored for later retrieval.

Electronic spreadsheet An electronic worksheet used to organize data into rows and columns for analysis.

E-mail *See* Electronic mail.

Emulation software Software that permits a personal computer on a network to imitate a terminal.

Encryption The process of encoding communications data.

End-user A person who buys and uses computer software or who has contact with computers.

ENIAC (Electronic Numerical Integrator and Computer) The first general-purpose electronic computer, which was built by Dr. John Mauchly and J. Presper Eckert, Jr., and was first operational in 1946.

Equal to (=) condition A logical operation in which the computer compares two numbers to determine equality.

Erase head The head in a magnetic tape unit; it erases any previously recorded data on the tape.

Ethernet A popular local area network using a bus topology.

E-time The execution portion of the machine cycle.

Expansion slots The slots inside a computer that allow a user to insert additional circuit boards.

Expert shell Software having the basic structure to find answers to questions; the questions can be added by the user.

Expert system A software package that presents the computer as an expert on some topic.

Exploded pie chart A pie chart with a "slice" that is separated from the rest of the chart.

External modem A modem that is separate from the computer, allowing it to be used with a variety of computers.

Facsimile technology (fax) The use of computer technology to send digitized graphics, charts, and text from one facsimile machine to another.

Fair Credit Reporting Act Legislation passed in 1970; it allows individuals access to and the right to challenge credit records.

Fax board A circuit board that fits inside a personal computer and allows the user, without interrupting other applications programs, to transmit computer-generated text and graphics.

Federal Privacy Act Legislation passed in 1974; it stipulates that no secret personal files can be kept by government agencies and that individuals can have access to all information about them that is stored in government files.

Fiber optics Technology that uses light instead of electricity to send data.

Field A set of related characters. In a database, also called an attribute.

Field name In a database, the unique name describing the data in a field.

Field robot A robot that is used on location to inspect nuclear plants, dispose of bombs, clean up chemical spills, and so forth.

Field type A category describing a field; it's determined by the kind of data the field will accept. Common field types are character, numeric, date, and logical.

Field width In a database, the maximum number of characters that can be contained in a field.

Fifth generation A term coined by the Japanese; it refers to new forms of computer systems involving artificial intelligence, natural language, and expert systems.

File 1. A repository of data. 2. A collection of related records. 3. In word processing, a document created on a computer.

Flash memory Nonvolatile memory chips.

Floppy disk A flexible magnetic diskette on which data is recorded as magnetic spots.

Flowchart The pictorial representation of a step-by-step solution to a problem.

Font A complete set of characters in a particular size, typeface, weight, and style.

Font library A variety of type fonts stored on disk.

Format The specifications that determine the way a document or worksheet is displayed on the screen or printer.

Formula In a spreadsheet, an instruction to calculate a value.

FORTRAN (FORmula TRANslator) The first high-level language, introduced in 1954 by IBM; it is scientifically oriented.

4GL *See* Fourth-generation language.

Fourth-generation language A nonprocedural language. Also called a 4GL or a very high-level language.

Freedom of Information Act Legislation passed in 1970; it allows citizens access to personal data gathered by federal agencies.

Freeware Software that is free.

Full justification In word processing, making both the left and right margins even.

Function A built-in spreadsheet formula.

Function keys Special keys programmed to execute commonly used commands.

GB *See* Gigabyte.

Gigabyte (GB) One billion bytes.

Grammar/style program Software that checks a document for common grammar and writing errors.

Graphical user interface (GUI) A software feature that uses screen icons invoked by pointing and clicking a mouse.

Graphics Pictures or graphs.

Greater than (>) condition A comparison operation that determines if one value is greater than another.

Groupware Software that allows teams of workers on a network to swap information and collaborate on projects.

GUI *See* Graphical user interface.

Hacker A person who gains access to computer systems illegally, usually from a personal computer.

Halftone A reproduction of a black-and-white photograph; it is made up of tiny dots.

Hard copy Printed paper output.

Hard disk An inflexible disk, usually in a pack, often in a sealed module.

Hard magnetic disk A metal platter coated with magnetic oxide and used for magnetic disk storage.

Hardware The computer and its associated equipment.

High-level languages English-like programming language that is easier to use than older symbolic languages.

Host computer The central computer in a network.

Icon A small picture on a computer screen; it represents a computer activity.

Impact printer A printer that forms characters by physically striking the paper.

Inference engine In artificial intelligence systems, software that accesses, selects, and interprets a set of rules.

Information Processed data; data that is organized, meaningful, and useful.

Information center A company unit that offers employees computer and software training, help in getting data from other computer systems, and technical assistance.

Information system (IS) A set of business systems, usually with computers among its components, designed to provide information for decision making.

Information systems manager The person who runs the information systems department.

Information utilities Commercial consumer-oriented communications systems, such as America Online, CompuServe, and Prodigy.

Initialize Set the starting values of storage locations in a program.

Ink-jet printer A printer that sprays ink from jet nozzles onto the paper.

Input Raw data that is put in to the computer system for processing.

Input device A device that puts data in machine-readable form and sends it to the processing unit.

Integrated package A set of software that typically includes related word processing, spreadsheet, database, and graphics programs.

Interactive Data processing in which the user communicates directly with the computer, maintaining a dialogue.

Internal font A font built into the read-only memory of a printer.

Internal modem A modem on a circuit board; it can be installed in a computer by the user.

Internal storage The electronic circuitry that temporarily holds data and program instructions needed by the CPU. Also called memory, main memory, primary memory, primary storage, and main storage.

Internet A loosely organized collection of networks.

IS *See* Information system.

Iteration The repetition of program instructions under certain conditions. Also called a loop.

I-time The instruction portion of the machine cycle.

Joystick A graphics input device that allows fingertip control of figures on a CRT screen.

Justification Aligning text along left or right margins or both.

K *See* Kilobyte.

Kerning Adjusting the space between characters to create wider or tighter spacing.

Keyboard A common input device similar to the keyboard of a typewriter.

Kilobyte (K) 1024 bytes.

Knowledge-based system A collection of information stored in a computer and accessed by natural language.

Knowledge engineer A computer professional who extracts information from a human expert to design an expert system based on that information.

Label In a spreadsheet, data consisting of a string of text characters.

LAN *See* Local area network.

Laptop computer A small portable computer that can weigh less than 10 pounds. Also called a notebook computer.

Laser printer A printer that uses a light beam to transfer images to paper.

LCD *See* Liquid crystal display.

Leading The vertical spacing between lines of type.

Legend The text beneath a graph; it explains the colors, shading, or symbols used to label the data points.

Less than (<) condition A logical operation in which the computer compares values to determine if one is less than another.

Licensed software Software that costs money and must not be copied without permission of the manufacturer.

Light pen A graphics input device that allows the user to interact directly with the computer screen.

Line graph A graph made by using a line to connect data points.

Link A physical data communications medium.

Link/load phase The phase during which prewritten programs may be added to the object module by means of a link/loader.

Liquid crystal display (LCD) The flat display screen found on some laptop computers.

Load module The output from the link/load step.

Local area network (LAN) A network designed to share data and resources among several computers.

Logical field A field used to keep track of true and false conditions.

Logical operations Comparing operations. The ALU is able to compare numbers, letters, or special characters and take alternative courses of action.

Logic error A flaw in the logic of a program.

Loop The repetition of program instructions under certain conditions. Also called iteration.

Machine cycle The combination of I-time and E-time.

Machine language The lowest level of language; it represents information as 1s and 0s.

Magnetic core A flat doughnut-shaped piece of metal used as an early memory device.

Magnetic disk An oxide-coated disk on which data is recorded as magnetic spots.

Magnetic-ink character recognition (MICR) A method of machine-reading characters made of magnetized particles.

Magnetic tape A medium with an iron-oxide coating that can be magnetized. Data is stored on the tape as extremely small magnetized spots.

Magnetic tape unit A data storage unit used to record data on and retrieve data from magnetic tape.

Mainframe A large computer that has access to billions of characters of data and is capable of processing data very quickly.

Main memory The electronic circuitry that temporarily holds data and program instructions needed by the CPU. Also called memory, primary memory, primary storage, main storage, and internal storage.

Main storage The electronic circuitry that temporarily holds data and program instructions needed by the CPU. Also called memory, main memory, primary memory, primary storage, and internal storage.

Mark The process of defining a block of text before performing block commands.

Mark I An early computer; it was built in 1944 by Harvard professor Howard Aiken.

Master file A semipermanent set of records.

MB *See* Megabyte.

Megabyte (MB) One million bytes.

Megahertz (MHz) Millions of machine instructions per second.

Memory The electronic circuitry that temporarily holds data and program instructions needed by the CPU. Also called main memory, primary memory, primary storage, main storage, and internal storage.

Menu An on-screen list of command choices.

MHz *See* Megahertz.

MICR *See* Magnetic-ink character recognition.

Microcomputer The smallest and least expensive class of computer. Also called a personal computer.

Microcomputer manager A person who manages microcomputers. Also called personal computer manager.

Microprocessor A general-purpose processor on a chip; it was developed in 1969 by an Intel Corporation design team headed by Ted Hoff. Also called a logic chip.

Microsecond One-millionth of a second.

Microwave transmission The line-of-sight transmission of data signals through the atmosphere from relay station to relay station.

Millisecond One-thousandth of a second.

Minicomputer A computer with storage capacity and power less than a mainframe's but greater than a personal computer's.

MITS Altair The first microcomputer kit; it was offered to computer hobbyists in 1975.

Model A type of database, each type representing a particular way of organizing data. The three database models are hierarchical, network, and relational.

Modem The term short for *mo*dulate/*dem*odulate. A modem converts a digital signal to an analog signal or vice versa. Used to transfer data over analog communication lines between computers.

Modulation The process of converting a signal from digital to analog.

Monochrome A computer screen that displays information in only one color.

Monolithic Description of a chip because a single unit of storage comprises the circuits on a chip.

Mouse A hand-held computer input device whose rolling movement on a flat surface causes corresponding movement of the cursor on the screen.

Multimedia The multiple sight/sound experience available from a computer that has certain hardware (CD-ROM drive, sound card, speakers) and software.

Multiple-range graph A graph that plots the values of more than one variable.

Multiprogramming A mainframe computer operating system feature under which different programs from different users compete for the use of the central processing unit.

Multitasking A feature of an operating system, in which several programs can compete concurrently for the use of the central processing unit.

Nanosecond One-billionth of a second.

Natural language A programming language that resembles human language.

Network A computer system that uses communications equipment to connect two or more computers and their resources.

Network manager A person designated to manage and run a computer network.

Neural network Computer chips designed to mimic the human brain.

Node A device—such as a personal computer, hard disk, printer, or another peripheral—that is connected to a network.

Nonimpact imprinter A printer that prints without striking the paper.

Nonprocedural language A language that states what task is to be accomplished but does not state the steps needed to accomplish it.

Notebook computer A small portable computer that can weigh less than 10 pounds. Also called a laptop computer.

Object module A machine-language version of a program; it is produced by a compiler or assembler.

Object-oriented programming (OOP) Building a new program from standardized, pre-coded program modules.

OCR-A A standard typeface for optical characters.

OCR devices *See* Optical-character recognition devices.

Office automation The use of technology to help achieve the goals of the office.

OMR devices *See* Optical-mark recognition devices.

Online Processing in which terminals are directly connected to the computer.

OOP *See* Object-oriented programming.

Operating environment An operating system environment in which the user does not have to memorize or look up commands.

Operating system A set of programs through which a computer manages its own resources.

Optical-character recognition (OCR) device An input device that uses a light source to read special characters and convert them to electrical signals to be sent to the CPU.

Optical disk Storage technology that uses a laser beam to store large amounts of data at relatively low cost.

Optical-mark recognition (OMR) device An input device that uses a light beam to recognize marks on paper.

Optical read-only memory (OROM) Optical storage media that cannot be written on but can be used to supply software or data.

Optical-recognition system A system that converts optical marks, optical characters, handwritten characters, or bar codes into electrical signals to be sent to the CPU.

OROM *See* Optical read-only memory.

Output Raw data that has been processed into usable information.

Output device A device, such as a printer, that makes processed information available for use.

Packaged software Software that is packaged and sold in stores.

Page composition Adding type to a page layout.

Page composition program A software package for designing and producing professional-looking documents. Also called a page makeup program or a desktop publishing program.

Page layout In publishing, the process of arranging text and graphics on a page.

Page makeup program A software package for designing and producing professional-looking documents. Also called a page composition program or a desktop publishing program.

Pagination In word processing, including page numbers on printed output.

Pan To move the cursor across a spreadsheet.

Parallel processing Using several processors in the same computer at the same time.

Pascal A structured, high-level programming language named for Blaise Pascal, the 17th-century French mathematician.

Path In a flowchart, the connection leading from the decision box to one of two possible responses. Also called a branch.

Peer-to-peer network A network in which personal computers are physically cabled together.

Pen-based computer A small portable computer that accepts handwritten input on a screen. Also called personal digital assistant.

Peripheral equipment Hardware devices attached to a computer.

Personal computer Generally, the least-expensive class of computer. Also called a microcomputer.

Personal computer manager The manager in charge of personal computer use. Also called a microcomputer manager.

Personal digital assistant (PDA) A small portable computer that accepts handwritten input on a screen. Also called a pen-based computer.

Picosecond One-trillionth of a second.

Pie chart A pie-shaped graph used to compare values that represent parts of a whole.

Pixel A picture element on a computer display screen. Pixels are the individual points of light that make up screen images.

Point A typographic measurement equaling approximately 1/72 inch.

Pointer A flashing indicator on a screen that shows where the next user—computer interaction will be. Also called a cursor.

Point-of-sale (POS) terminal A terminal used as a cash register in a retail setting. It may be programmable or connected to a central computer.

Portable computer A self-contained computer that can be easily carried and moved.

POS terminal *See* Point-of-sale terminal.

Presentation graphics program A program that allows a user to create professional-looking business graphics. Also called a business-quality graphics program.

Primary memory The electronic circuitry that temporarily holds data and program instructions needed by the CPU. Also called memory, primary storage, main storage, internal storage, and main memory.

Primary storage The electronic circuitry that temporarily holds data and program instructions needed by the CPU.

Also called memory, primary memory, main storage, internal storage, and main memory.

Printer A device for generating output on paper.

Print preview In word processing, a feature that permits viewing the page to be printed on the screen before actual printing.

Procedural language A language used to present a step-by-step process for solving a problem.

Process box In flowcharting, a rectangular box that indicates an action to be taken.

Processor The central processing unit (CPU) of a computer.

Prodigy A major information utility that offers a variety of services.

Program A set of step-by-step instructions that directs a computer to perform specific tasks and produce certain results.

Programmable read-only memory (PROM) chips ROM chips that can be changed by ROM burners.

Programmer/analyst A person who performs systems analysis functions in addition to programming.

Programming language A set of rules that can be used to tell a computer what operations to do.

PROM chips *See* Programmable read-only memory chips.

Prompt A signal that the computer or operating system is waiting for data or a command from the user.

Pseudocode An English-like way of representing structured programming control structures.

Public-domain software Software that is free.

Pull-down menu A command menu system in which the click of an initial choice causes a list of subcommands to be "pulled down" like a window shade under the initial selection.

Ragged right margin The nonalignment of text at the right edge of a document.

RAM *See* Random access memory.

Random access The immediate access to a record in secondary storage, usually on a disk. Also called direct access.

Random access memory (RAM) The memory that provides temporary storage for data and program instructions.

Range A group of one or more cells, arranged in a rectangle, that a spreadsheet program treats as a unit.

Raster scan technology A process that forms an image on a computer screen by beaming electrons on a phosphorus-backed screen, causing it to glow.

Read To bring data outside the computer into memory.

Read-only memory (ROM) Memory that can be read only and remains after the power is turned off. Also called firmware.

Read/write head An electromagnet that reads the magnetized areas on magnetic media and converts them into the electrical impulses that are sent to the processor.

Real-time processing Processing in which the results are available in time to affect the activity at hand.

Record A collection of related fields.

Reformatting The readjustment of visual aspects of a word processing document, including the accommodation of additions and deletions.

Register Temporary storage area associated with the CPU that accepts, holds, and transfers instructions or data.

Relation A table in a relational database model.

Relational database A database in which the data is organized in a table format consisting of columns and rows.

Relational model A database model that organizes data logically in tables.

Relational operator An operator (such as <, >, or =) that allows a user to make comparisons and selections.

Resolution The clarity of a video display screen or printer output.

Reverse video The feature that highlights on-screen text by switching the usual text and background colors.

Ring network A circle of point-to-point connections of computers at local sites, with no central host computer.

Robot A computer-controlled device that can physically manipulate its surroundings.

ROM *See* Read-only memory.

ROM burner Used to change instructions on ROM chips; these chips are known as programmable read-only memory (PROM) chips.

Sans serif typeface A typeface that is clean, without the small marks of a serif typeface.

Satellite transmission Data transmission from earth station to earth station via communications satellites.

Scanner A device that reads text and images directly into the computer.

Screen A television-like output device that can display information.

Scrolling A word processing feature that allows the user to move to and view any part of a screen document in 24-line chunks.

SDLC *See* Systems development life cycle.

Sealed module A sealed disk drive containing disks, access arms, and read/write heads. Also called a Winchester disk.

Search and replace function A word processing function that finds and changes each instance of a repeated item.

Secondary storage Additional storage, often disk, for data and programs; it is separate from the CPU and memory. Also called auxiliary storage.

Security A system of safeguards designed to protect a computer system and data from deliberate or accidental damage or access by unauthorized persons.

Semiconductor A crystalline substance that conducts electricity when it is "doped" with chemical impurities.

Semiconductor storage Data storage on a silicon chip.

Serif typeface A typeface in which each character includes small marks that make the eye travel easily from one character to the next.

Server The central computer in a network; it is responsible for managing the LAN.

Shareware Software that is given away free, although the maker hopes that satisfied users will voluntarily pay for it.

Shell An operating environment layer that separates the operating system from the user.

SIMM *See* Single in-line memory module.

Single in-line memory module (SIMM) A board containing memory chips that can be plugged in to a computer expansion slot.

Single-range bar graph A graph that plots the values of only one variable.

Site license A license permitting a customer to make multiple copies of a piece of software.

Soft copy Computer output displayed on a screen.

Soft font A font that can be downloaded from disk files in a personal computer to a printer.

Software Instructions that tell a computer what to do.

Software piracy Unauthorized copying of computer software.

Source data automation The use of special equipment to collect data and send it directly to a computer.

Source document Data, on paper, to be prepared as input to a computer.

Source module A program as originally coded, before being translated into machine language.

Source program listing The printed version of a program as the programmer wrote it.

Speaker dependent A data input method in which a speech recognition system "learns" the voice of a speaker.

Speaker independent A data input method in which a speech recognition system can recognize commands from any speaker.

Speech recognition The process of presenting input data to the computer through the spoken word.

Speech recognition device A device that accepts the spoken word through a microphone and converts it into digital code that can be understood by a computer.

Speech synthesis The process of enabling machines to talk to people.

Spelling checker program A word processing program that checks the spelling in a document.

Spreadsheet An electronic worksheet divided into rows and columns that can be used to analyze and present business data.

Stacked-bar graph A bar graph in which all data common to a given row or column appears stacked in one bar.

Star network A network consisting of one or more smaller computers connected to a central host computer.

Start/stop symbol An oval symbol used to indicate the beginning and end of a flowchart.

Storage register A register that temporarily holds data that is taken from memory or about to be sent to memory.

Style The way a typeface is printed, for example, in *italic*.

Submenu An additional set of options related to a prior menu selection.

Supercomputer The largest and most powerful category of computers.

Supermicro A multiuser, multitasking microcomputer that has a high-speed microprocessor, increased memory, and hard-disk storage.

Supermini A minicomputer at the top end of capacity and price.

Surge protector A device that prevents electrical problems from affecting data files.

SVGA (super VGA) A superior screen standard with 800 by 600 pixels or 1024 by 768 pixels.

Syntax The rules of a programming language.

Syntax errors Errors in the use of a programming language.

System An organized set of related components established to perform a certain task.

System software The operating system; the underlying computer software.

Systems analysis The process of studying an existing system to determine how it works and how it meets user needs.

Systems analyst A person who plans and designs individual programs and entire computer systems.

Systems design The process of developing a plan for a system, based on the results of a systems analysis.

Systems development life cycle (SDLC) A model for developing a computer system.

Tape drive The drive on which reels of magnetic tape are mounted when their data is ready to be read by the computer system.

Telecommuting The home use of telecommunications and computers as a substitute for working outside the home.

Teleconferencing A system of holding conferences by linking geographically dispersed people through computer terminals or personal computers.

Terminal A device that consists of an input device, an output device, and a communications link to the main terminal.

Text block In word processing, a continuous section of text in a document.

Thesaurus program With a word processing program, this program provides a list of synonyms and antonyms for a word in a document.

Title The caption on a graph that summarizes the information in the graph.

Token passing In a ring network, the node possessing the token is permitted to send a message.

Topology The physical layout of a local area network.

Touch screen A computer screen that accepts input data by letting the user point at the screen to select a choice.

Trackball A ball used as an input device; it can be hand manipulated to cause a corresponding movement of the cursor on the screen.

Transaction file A file that contains all the changes to be made to a master file: additions, deletions, and revisions.

Transaction processing The technique of processing transactions one at a time in the order in which they occur.

Transistor A small device that transfers electrical signals across a resistor.

Translator A program that translates programming language into machine language.

Transponder A device in a communications satellite that receives a transmission from earth, amplifies the signal, changes the frequency, and retransmits the data to a receiving earth station.

Twisted pairs Wires twisted together in an insulated cable. Twisted pairs are frequently used to transmit information over short distances. Also called wire pairs.

Typeface A set of characters—letters, symbols, and numbers—of the same design.

Type size The size, in points, of a typeface.

Underlining Underscoring text.

UNIVAC (UNIVersal Automatic Computer) The first computer built for business purposes.

Universal Product Code (UPC) A code number, unique to a product, represented on the product's label in the form of a bar code.

Update To keep files current by changing data as appropriate.

Upload To send a file from one computer to a larger computer.

User A person who uses computer software or has contact with computer systems.

User friendly Refers to software that is easy for a novice to use.

User involvement The participation of users in the systems development life cycle.

Vacuum tube An electronic tube used as a basic component in the first generation of computers.

Value In a spreadsheet, data consisting of a number representing an amount, a formula, or a function.

Variable 1. A storage location in memory. 2. On a graph, the items that the data points describe.

Vertical centering A word processing feature that adjusts the top and bottom margins so that text is midway between the top and the bottom of the page.

Very high-level language A nonprocedural language. Also called a 4GL or a fourth-generation language.

VGA (video graphics adapter) A common screen standard with 640 by 480 pixels.

Videoconferencing Computer conferencing combined with cameras and wall-size screens.

Virtual reality A system in which a user is immersed in a computer-created environment, so that the user physically interacts with the computer-produced three-dimensional scene.

Virus A set of illicit instructions that passes itself on to other programs in which it comes in contact.

Vision robot A robot that can recognize an object by its shape or color.

Voice input The process of presenting input data to the computer through the spoken word. Also called speech recognition.

Voice mail A system in which the user can dictate a message into the voice mail system, where it is digitized and stored in the recipient's voice mailbox. Later the recipient can dial the mailbox, and the system delivers the message in audio form.

Voice-output device See Voice synthesizer.

Voice synthesizer A device that converts data in main storage to sounds understandable as speech to humans. Also called an audio-response unit or a voice-output device.

Volatile Refers to the loss of data in semiconductor storage when the current is interrupted or turned off.

WAN See Wide area network.

Wand reader An input device that scans the special letters and numbers on price tags in retail stores.

Weight The variation in the heaviness of a typeface; for example, type is much heavier when printed in **boldface.**

"What-if" analysis An approach, using spreadsheets, to experiment with different figures to determine potential outcomes.

Wide area network (WAN) A network of geographically distant computers and terminals.

Winchester disk A sealed disk drive containing disks, access arms, and read/write heads. Also called a sealed module.

Wire pairs Wires twisted together in an insulated cable. Wire pairs are frequently used to transmit information over short distances. Also called twisted pairs.

Word processing Computer-based creation, editing, formatting, storing, and printing of text.

Word wrap A word processing feature that automatically starts a word at the left margin of the next line if there is not enough room for it on the previous line.

Workgroup computing Every aspect of a group of workers using computer technology to meet a common goal.

Worksheet A spreadsheet.

Workstation A personal computer attached to a LAN.

Worm A program that transfers itself from computer to computer over a network and then plants itself as a file on the target computer's disk.

WORM See Write once, read many.

Write once, read many (WORM) Describes media that can be written on only once; then it becomes read-only media.

x-axis The horizontal reference line of a graph; it usually represents units of time.

y-axis The vertical reference line of a graph; it usually represents values or amounts, such as dollars, staffing levels, or units sold.

Credits

6.6 Courtesy of International Business Machines.
6.7 ©HMS Images/The Image Bank.
6.8 Courtesy of AT&T.
6.9c Courtesy of America Online, Inc.
6.10 ©Louis Psihoyos/Matrix.
6.11 ©J. Barry O'Rourke/The Stock Market.

Part 3 opener
© Alain McLaughlin and The Monterey Bay Aquarium.

Chapter 7
CT Jim Folts/Benjamin/Cummings.
Margin Note:Department of the Navy.
PCA ©Chuck Savage/Uniphoto.

Chapter 8
CT © David Burnett/ Digital Originals™
Margin Note: Courtesy of ©IDG Books Worldwide, Inc.
8.4 Courtesy of Microsoft Corporation.
8.5a Lotus Development Corporation
8.5b Courtesy of Borland International.
8.5c Courtesy of Aldus Corporation.

Part 4 opener © Ted Soqui.

Chapter 9
CT © Bob Daemmrich/Stock Boston.
PCA © Greg Buchman/The Big Pixel.
9.1a ©Richard Gross/The Stock Market.
9.1b ©Gabe Palmer/Mugshots/The Stock Market.
9.1c Courtesy of Hewlett Packard Corporation.
9.1d Courtesy of Compaq Computer Corporation.
9.2 ©Howard Grey/TS Images.
9.3 Courtesy of Lotus Development Corporation.

Chapter 10
PCA Misco, Inc.
10.3 Courtesy of Eyedentify, Inc.

Chapter 11
Margin Note (2 photos)©Hank Morgan/Rainbow.
PCA ©Andy Freeberg/Discover Magazine.
11.2 ©Ed Kashi/Phototake.
11.3a,b Courtesy of Aion Development Corporation.
11.4a ©Andy Sacks/TS Images.
11.4b Courtesy of Japan Airlines.
11.5a-d ©Thinking Machines Corporation.
11.6 Courtesy of Control Data Corporation.
11.7a ©P. Howell/Gamma-Liaison.
11.7b Courtesy of VPL Research.
11.7c ©David Sutton.

Part 5 openers © Ted Soqui.

Chapter 12
MAC. ©Richard Tauber.
PCA.1 Courtesy of Mike Royko, Tribune Media Services.
PCA.2 Courtesy of Esther Dyson.
12.11, 12.12 ©Richard Tauber.
12.16 © Adam Zakin.

Chapter 13
MAC Courtesy of Aldus Corporation.
Margin Note: © Jon Riley/TS Images.
PCA.1 Courtesy of Cricket.
PCA.2 Courtesy of SAS Institute, Inc.
PCA.3 Courtesy of WordPerfect Corporation.
13.9.a Courtesy of Harvard Graphics.
13.9.b,c Courtesy of Micrografx.
13.9.d Courtesy of Computer Support Corporation.
13.9.e Courtesy of Claris Corporation.
13.9.f Courtsy of Software Publishing Corporation.
13.10 Courtesy of Aldus Corporation.

Chapter 14
CT © Fred Bodin.
Margin Note: © Fred Bodin.

Historical Appendix
H1 Reprinted from POPULAR ELECTRONICS, January 1975/ ©1975 Ziff-Davis Publishing. Company.
H2 IBM Archives.
H3 Culver Pictures.
H4 IBM Archives.
H5 Iowa State University of Science and Technology.
H6-7b IBM Archives.
H9 Courtesy of Inmac, Santa Clara, CA
Margin Note:1 ©Marjorie Nichols/The Computer Museum, Boston
Margin Note:.2 IBM Archives.
Margin Note:3 Courtesy of Intel.
Margin Note:4 Computer Museum, Boston.
PCA © Steve Jobs/Reportage Stock.
PCA.2 ©Matthew McVay/Stock Boston.
PCA.3 Courtey of EFF. Photo by Seth Resnick

Graphics Gallery
opener© Cynthia Satloff.
1 © Marc Yankus.
2-4 © Gregory MacNicol.
5 ©Bill Frymire.
6 © John Fitzgerald.
7 © Joseph Maas/Paragon 3.
8 ©Tom Cushwa.
9 © Greg Buchman/The Big Pixel.
10 ©Steve Lyons.
11 ©Joseph Maas/Paragon 3.

12 ©Lilla Rogers.
13,14 © Annie Higbee.
15-17 © Marc Yankus.
18 Created in Fractal Design Painter by John Taylor Dismukes at Capstone Studios, L.A.
19 © Marc Yankus.
20 © Peter McCormick, courtesy of CorelDraw.
21 ©Gary Preister/CorelDraw.
22 Courtesy of Pacific Data Images.
23 Intergraph.
24 HSC Software/KAI'S Powertools.
25 Chris Purcell/CorelDraw.
26 © Mark Yankus.
27-30 ©Katrin Eisman.
31 XAOS.

Multimedia gallery
opener: ©Rick Smolan/Against All Odds.
2 Courtesy of Microsoft Corporation.
2, btm: © Sigma Designs.
3, 1–3 Courtesy of Microsoft Corporation.
4, 5 & 17–19 Courtesy of Discovery Communications.
6, 7 Courtesy of Brøderbund Software, Inc.
23 Courtesy of E Book, Inc.
26–28 Courtesy of Bureau Development, Inc.
all others: Courtesy of Microsoft Corporation.

Buyer's Guide
1 ©Fredrik D. Bodin.
2 Courtesy of International Business Machines.
3 Courtesy of Apple Corporation.
4.1 Courtesy of International Business Machines.
4.2 Courtesy of NEC.
5 Courtesy of Microcomputer Accessories.
6 Courtesy of International Business Machines.
7 ©John Curtis.
8.1 Courtesy of BASF Corporation.
8.2 Microscience International Corporation.
9,10 Courtesy of Hewlett Packard.
11.1 Courtesy of QMS Corporation.
11.2,3 Courtesy of Eastman/Kodak.
12 Courtesy of Sparc.
13 Courtesy of Edstrom.
14 ©John Curtis.
15 Courtesy of Inmac.
16 ©Richard Tauber.

Index

D